Martyrdom a

MARTYRDOM AND TERRORISM

Pre-Modern to Contemporary Perspectives

Edited by

DOMINIC JANES

ALEX HOUEN

OXFORD
UNIVERSITY PRESS

OXFORD
UNIVERSITY PRESS

Oxford University Press is a department of the University of Oxford.
It furthers the University's objective of excellence in research, scholarship,
and education by publishing worldwide.

Oxford   New York
Auckland   Cape Town   Dar es Salaam   Hong Kong   Karachi
Kuala Lumpur   Madrid   Melbourne   Mexico City   Nairobi
New Delhi   Shanghai   Taipei   Toronto

With offices in
Argentina   Austria   Brazil   Chile   Czech Republic   France   Greece
Guatemala   Hungary   Italy   Japan   Poland   Portugal   Singapore
South Korea   Switzerland   Thailand   Turkey   Ukraine   Vietnam

Oxford is a registered trademark of Oxford University Press
in the UK and certain other countries.

Published in the United States of America by
Oxford University Press
198 Madison Avenue, New York, NY 10016

© Oxford University Press 2014

CIP data is on file at the Library of Congress

ISBN 978–0–19–995985–3 (hbk); 978–0–19–995987–7 (pbk)

1 3 5 7 9 8 6 4 2
Printed in the United States of America
on acid-free paper

Contents

List of Illustrations

Acknowledgments

THE EDITORS WISH to express their thanks to the staff of the University of Notre Dame London Center and Birkbeck College, University of London who arranged the hosting of the meeting of the contributors to this volume in April 2011. In particular, Prof. Greg Kucich, the director of the Notre Dame London Center, played a vital role in coordinating those proceedings. Funding towards meeting the costs of this event was provided by the University of Notre Dame. Dominic Janes was supported in his research for, and editing work on, this volume by the award of a Fellowship from the Arts and Humanities Research Council (UK) for the academic year 2011/12.

Contributors

ASMA AFSARUDDIN is Professor of Islamic Studies and Chairperson of the Department of Near Eastern Languages and Cultures at Indiana University, Bloomington. Her fields of specialization are the pre-modern and modern religious and political thought of Islam, Qur'an and hadith, Islamic intellectual history, and gender. She is the author of numerous articles and books including *Excellence and Precedence: Medieval Islamic Discourse on Legitimate Leadership* (2002) and *The First Muslims: History and Memory* (2008), which recently won the Dost award from the Turkish Women's Association. She is currently a senior editor for the *Oxford Encyclopedia of Islam and Women* and a book review editor for the *International Journal of Middle East Studies*. Her new book is *Striving in the Path of God: Jihad and Martyrdom in Islamic Thought*, research for which was funded by grants from the Harry Frank Guggenheim Foundation and the Carnegie Corporation of New York.

DAVID ANDRESS is Professor of Modern History at the University of Portsmouth. His work has focused on the French Revolution and on the complex ways in which succeeding generations of historians have sought to co-opt or condemn its relationship to European modernity. Key products of this research include *The Terror: Civil War in the French Revolution* (2005) and *1789: Threshold of the Modern World* (2008). The other focus of his research is an attempt to grapple with the complex resonances of cultural change in the decades before 1789 and their potential shaping influence, as "cultural forms," on the mental apparatus of people attempting to construct, and live through, the "political processes" of revolutionary modernity.

AKIL N. AWAN is Lecturer in History at Royal Holloway, University of London. His key research interests are focused on the root causes and antecedents of Islamic political radicalism and terrorism amongst global Muslim communities. In particular he has been exploring the International Mujahedeen movement during the Afghan-Soviet War (1979–89), Bosnian War (1992–95), and Chechen Wars (1994–96; 1999–); the history and evolution of al-Qaeda and the use of virtual media and the Internet by jihadist groups.

GUY BEINER is Senior Lecturer in History at Ben-Gurion University of the Negev in Israel. He was a Government of Ireland scholar at University College Dublin, Government of Ireland research fellow at Trinity College Dublin, National Endowment for the Humanities Fellow in Irish Studies at the University of Notre Dame and Gerda Henkel Marie Curie Fellow at the University of Oxford. His book, *Remembering the Year of the French: Irish Folk History and Social Memory* (2007), won several international awards.

KATE COOPER is Professor of Ancient History at the University of Manchester. Her main research interest is the construction of gender roles in religious communities in late antiquity and the early Middle Ages, and the role of gender ideals in religious conflict during that period. She has published extensively on these topics; notably *The Virgin and the Bride: Idealised Womanhood in Late Antiquity* (1996) and *The Fall of the Roman Household* (2007). She is currently working on a study of the theme of martyrdom as a device for spiritual self-understanding among lay women in late Antiquity and the early Middle Ages.

JULIA V. DOUTHWAITE is Professor of French at the University of Notre Dame. She is author of *Exotic Women* (1992), *The Wild Girl, Natural Man, and the Monster* (2002) and *The Frankenstein of 1790 and Other Lost Chapters from Revolutionary France* (2012). In 2011–12, she organized and curated the American début of *DIGNITY*, a photographic exhibit created by Amnesty International France, which ran at Notre Dame alongside a lecture series on Jean-Jacques Rousseau and the history of human rights. A companion volume, entitled *Art in the Service of Humanity: Rousseau and DIGNITY*, is in progress.

ALEX HOUEN is University Senior Lecturer in Modern English Literature and fellow of Pembroke College at the University of Cambridge. He is the author of *Terrorism and Modern Literature: From Joseph Conrad to Ciaran Carson* (2002) and *Powers of Possibility: Experimental American Writing since the 1960s* (2011), as well as of various articles and chapters on sacrifice and political violence.

DOMINIC JANES is Reader in Cultural History and Visual Studies at Birkbeck, University of London. In addition to a spell as a lecturer at Lancaster University, he has been a research fellow at London and Cambridge universities. His most recent books are *Victorian Reformation: The Fight over Idolatry in the Church of England, 1840–1860* (2009) and *Walsingham in Literature and Culture from the Middle Ages to Modernity*, co-edited with Gary Waller (2010). He has been awarded a fellowship from the Arts and Humanities Research Council (UK) during which time he has completed a *Visions of Queer Martyrdom from John Henry Newman to Derek Jarman*. This is a study of the role of notions of martyrdom and victimhood in artistic representations and cultural constructions of same-sex desire in Britain since the nineteenth century.

JOLYON MITCHELL is Professor of Communications, Arts and Religion; Director of the Centre for Theology and Public Issues (CTPI) and Acting Director of the Institute for Advanced Studies in the Humanities (IASH) at the University of Edinburgh. Prior to working at Edinburgh he was a producer and journalist with the BBC World Service. He is the author or editor of numerous books, articles and essays. His most recent publications include *Promoting Peace, Inciting Violence: The Role of Religion and Media* (2012) and *Martyrdom: A Very Short Introduction* (2012).

SUSANNAH MONTA is John Cardinal O'Hara, C.S.C. and Glynn Family Honors Associate Professor of English and editor of the journal *Religion and Literature* at the University of Notre Dame. Her book *Martyrdom and Literature in Early Modern England* (2005) won the Book of the Year award from the MLA-affiliated Conference on Christianity and Literature. With Margaret W. Ferguson, she edited *Teaching Early Modern English Prose* (2010), and is preparing an edition of Anthony Copley's *A Fig for Fortune* (1596), the first published response to Edmund Spenser's *Faerie Queene*. Her current project, "Sacred Echoes: Repetitive Prayer in Reformation-Era Poetics," examines the devotional and aesthetic uses of repetition in early modern prayer, poetry, and rhetoric.

RONALD SCHECHTER is Associate Professor of History at the College of *William and Mary*. His work has focused on eighteenth-century France, with a particular emphasis on Jewish–Gentile relations from the Enlightenment through the Napoleonic period. A key result of this research was *Obstinate Hebrews: Representations of Jews in France, 1715–1815* (2003). Projects underway include research on the image of "the Jewess" in modern European culture and an intellectual/cultural history of terror during the Age of the Enlightenment.

GARY WALLER is Professor of Literature, Cultural Studies and Theatre Studies at SUNY Purchase, where he was Vice President for Academic Affairs and Provost from 1995 to 2004. He was previously Donaldson Bye-Fellow at Magdalene College, Cambridge, and has taught and held administrative positions at the Universities of Auckland, Dalhousie, Wilfrid Laurier, Carnegie Mellon, and Hartford. His most recent books include *Walsingham from the Middle Ages to Modernity*, co-edited with Dominic Janes (2010), *Walsingham and the English Imagination* (2011), and *The Virgin Mary in Late Medieval and Early Modern English Literature and Popular Culture* (2011).

Martyrdom and Terrorism

Introduction

Dominic Janes and Alex Houen

MARTYRDOM AND TERRORISM have histories that are interlinked in fascinating and important ways, a fact that has been highlighted by the recent rise in suicide bombing. Yet, when considered as cultural constructions, the histories of martyrdom and terrorism have followed distinctive trajectories. This is immediately signaled by the fact that in the English language the first of these terms substantially pre-dates the other. While the English word "martyr" was derived from the classical Greek *marturos* and was adopted in the course of the Middle Ages, the term "terrorist" originated in the late eighteenth century. It was coined to refer to the allegedly illegitimate use of violence by the revolutionary government of France against its own people in the period of the "Terror" (1793–94).[1] By the early twentieth century the word had shifted to refer to the illegitimate use of violence *against* the state which could be seen as, in some sense, operating within the nation, but which was distinguished from criminality on the grounds that its explicit aim was to intimidate through the causation of terror. The terrorist, therefore, was viewed as someone whose core attribute was not possession of legitimate aspiration for political change but rather that of the perverse desire for destabilization and anarchy. In more contemporary discourses of terrorism (and following the events of 9/11), apart from the direct threat of being killed or injured, the horror that Western societies have experienced has involved the appearance of a new sense of the vulnerability of the body politic and, therefore, of the modern self with its direct dependency on security of property. The terrorist has, thus, been

---

1. Years refer to the "Christian era" unless otherwise noted.

constructed by national authorities as the epitome of transgression against economic resources and moral, physical, and political boundaries.

Many of those committing recent terrorist attacks have been intent, and have often succeeded, in killing themselves in the process. By so doing they have established themselves and/or been seen as martyrs to their cause. However, those dying in religious conflict may understand their action through reference to a concept of martyrdom as not simply a descriptive category, but as an act with spiritual force. Martyrdom is, in a certain sense, central to the Christian tradition, insofar as this is an appropriate description for Christ's Passion. Moreover, for many Christian denominations the acts of the early Church martyrs represent extraordinary examples of spiritual heroism. It is, however, the case that these people appeared to be criminals, and perhaps comparable (at least in cultural terms) to terrorists, from the viewpoint of the Roman authorities. This raises the important issue of the presence of what might be termed terrorist-like cultural formations before the arrival of that particular term. This volume of essays, looking back as it does over two thousand years of history, albeit with a focus on modernity, therefore aims to address the cultural origins and traditions of both terrorism and martyrdom.

Because the volume focuses on relations between Europe and the Middle East it is also concerned to explore the role of martyrdom and terrorism in relation to both Christian and Islamic traditions. As with Christian conceptions of martyrdom, Islamic notions link *shahadat* (martyrdom) to "bearing witness" to faith and God. In early Christianity, martyrdom was not necessarily limited to those who were persecuted to the point of death; a martyr could be one who led a good, charitable life. Martyrdom in Islamic thinking was similarly a complex phenomenon. In both instances, the association of religious martyrdom with political terror also has a complex legacy. Therefore, not only does this volume explore the repercussions of these legacies—following, for example, Christian martyrdom from Roman times through to the period of its interaction with secular perspectives of nationalism and imperialism during French Revolution and after—it also explores how Islamic and Christian martyrdom compare historically.

A number of useful introductions to the topics of martyrdom and terrorism have recently been published.[2] The purpose of this chapter is not,

---

2. Key works on martyrdom include G. W. Bowersock, *Martyrdom and Rome* (Cambridge: Cambridge University Press, 1995); Daniel Boyarin, *Dying for God: Martyrdom and the Making of Christianity and Judaism* (Stanford, Calif.: Stanford University Press,

therefore, to attempt to present a complete survey of these two topics, but to set out a set of key issues which underlie the studies of this subject by the contributors to this volume. To begin with martyrdom; most commonly this is associated with either exemplary death, or a degree of related suffering, or both. Nevertheless, its origins within the Christian tradition are highlighted by the sub-definition of the word as referring to "a person who chooses to suffer death rather than renounce faith in Christ or obedience to his teachings, a Christian way of life, or adherence to a law or tenet of the Church; (also) a person who chooses to suffer death rather than renounce the beliefs or tenets of a particular Christian denomination, sect, etc."[3] The word can also be used to refer to those who have suffered in similar ways, but in a non-Christian, or indeed a non-religious context. It might be used to refer hyperbolically to all manner of suffering, as when the prominent actress and writer Fanny Kemble wrote that "she is a martyr to dyspepsia and bad cooking."[4] This word has, thus, also been employed since the fourteenth century in a variety of variously humorous or ironic ways in reference to making "a real or pretended sacrifice of one's inclinations in order to gain credit."[5]

This range of more or less dignified meanings highlights that the religious associations of martyrdom are sometimes, but not always, treated with respect. An important reason for ambivalence within English over the use of the term "martyr" is that many of those who have been held to have

---

1999); Elizabeth A. Castelli, *Martyrdom and Memory: Early Christian Culture Making* (New York: Columbia University Press, 2004); Brian Wicker, ed., *Witnesses to Faith? Martyrdom in Christianity and Islam* (Ashgate: Aldershot, 2006); David Cook, *Martyrdom in Islam* (Cambridge: Cambridge University Press, 2007); Paul Middleton, *Martyrdom: A Guide for the Perplexed* (London: Continuum, 2011); and Jolyon Mitchell, *Martyrdom: A Very Short Introduction* (Oxford: Oxford University Press, 2013).

Key works on terrorism include David C. Rapoport and Yonah Alexander, eds., *The Morality of Terrorism: Religious and Secular Justifications* (New York: Pergamon Press, 1982); William Perdue, *Terrorism and the State: A Critique of Domination through Fear* (Westport, Conn.: Praeger, 1989); Walter Laqueur, *Terrorism* (Aldershot: Dartmouth, 1996); Bruce Hoffman, *Inside Terrorism* (London: Victor Gollancz, 1998); Charles Townshend, *Terrorism: A Very Short Introduction* (Oxford: Oxford University Press, 2002); Andrew Sinclair, *An Anatomy of Terror: A History of Terrorism* (London: Macmillan, 2003); and Richard Jackson, Jeroen Gunning, and Marie Breen Smyth, *Terrorism: A Critical Introduction* (Basingstoke: Palgrave Macmillan, 2011).

3. See the *Oxford English Dictionary*, http://dictionary.oed.com.

4. Frances Anne Kemble, *Records of Later Life* (London: Richard Bentley, 1882), vol. 3, p. 186.

5. See, for example, by J. W. Cross, ed., *George Eliot's Life as Told in her Letters and Journals* (Edinburgh: Blackwood, 1886), vol. 3, p. 159.

this status are venerated as saints within the Roman Catholic Church. The history of anti-Catholicism within much of the English-speaking world since the Reformation has led, on occasion, to hostility to the category of martyrdom as being something intimately associated with the cult of the saints and, thus, as being inimical to Protestantism. As Janes argues in the current volume, this did not stop many Protestants from admiring those who were willing to die for their beliefs, as under the persecutions of the Catholic Queen Mary of England (1553–58), and referring to them as martyrs, but it did mean that doctrinal correctness, rather than simply attestation of Christian faith, was required for the perceived attainment of this status of heroism. Awareness that people were willing to suffer or die for the sake of various forms of Christianity, and indeed for other faiths or even for non-religious beliefs, bred a tendency to regard martyrdom as being, in itself, a culturally contestable state that could, in due course, be claimed by pressure groups of all kinds including secular ones.

Thus when Emily Davidson died after stepping out in front of the King's horse at the Epsom Derby on June 4, 1913, she was hailed as a martyr by fellow members of the suffragette movement but could also be projected as mentally ill or insane by opponents of the movement for votes for women. It should be recalled that suicide was a criminal act under English law until 1961, a provision that had its origin in Christian understandings of self-murder as a sin. Thus it has been widely thought important in the context of British notions of martyrdom to establish whether the individual concerned was, or was not, seeking his or her own death—something that is often hard to prove for certain. It might seem likely that someone stepping in front of an oncoming horse would be killed, or at least injured, but how can we know if that was Dickinson's intention? Since admirers and denigrators would like to know the answers to such questions, it is important to understand the work of martyrdom as being a collective effort. Martyrs, especially those who die in the process, only take the first step in their ascription to this category. Martyrdom is a social formation and for a cult to spread requires the witness not just of the martyr but of others who will attest to them. Thus, a crucial place in the history of martyrdom is occupied by the mediated forms, traditionally texts such as hagiographies, which evidenced the acts of persecution and sacrifice. These can be studied in their own right as a literary form whose origins can be traced by comparing the biblical accounts of the Maccabean martyrs killed during the Jewish revolt against the Seleucids during the second century B.C. with the "martyr acts" of those who suffered and died at the hands of Roman magistrates for refusing to sacrifice to the pagan gods.

In classical Rome and Greece suicide was not regarded as taboo; it was, in fact, seen as laudable and as an honorable evidence of personal self-control. The Christian cult of martyrdom, therefore, can be seen as having developed in the context of a culture which afforded acclaim to those who were able to endure pain and death with equanimity. Sacrificing one's life for one's family or community was a matter of honor, whereas clinging onto life was contemptible. Carlin Barton has commented that "Romans rarely identified with or wanted to be seen as victims, even in the direst circumstances. And so their stories of the vindication of honor are designed not to elicit pity, nor to reveal a victim, but to reveal an un-conquered will."[6] Suicide was thus deemed honorable when it represented active control over one's fate. Early Christians were influenced by these attitudes, but they understood their social contract to be with the community of fellow believers as present in Heaven as well as on Earth. This reinforced the notion of the value of bodily self-sacrifice, through the concept of the immortality of the soul.[7] It is, therefore, ironic that it was an aspect of classical culture that enabled Christians to subvert the mechanism intended for their repression. The Roman arena, and its associated spectacles of death, was intended to deprive criminals of their honor through stripping them of agency.[8] However, Christians appeared to have chosen to die, and their deaths were widely seen as acts of self-sacrifice for the good of their community. Martyrs were, therefore, constructed as fully active citizens of the city of God. Moreover, the writing of martyr acts ensured that these performances were not only remembered but individualized as acts of personal self-expression.[9] Martyrdom was, in these accounts, an act of heroism ultimately legitimized by the example of the Passion of Jesus Christ. Prosecution was thereby turned into persecution.

---

6. Carlin Barton, "Honor and Sacredness in the Roman and Christian Worlds," in Margaret Cormack, ed., *Sacrificing the Self: Perspectives on Martyrdom and Religion* (Oxford: Oxford University Press, 2002), pp. 23–38, at p. 27.

7. Carole Straw, " 'A Very Special Death': Christian Martyrdom in its Classical Context," in Cormack, *Sacrificing the Self*, pp. 39–57 at p. 50.

8. L. Stephanie Cobb, *Dying to be Men: Gender and Language in Early Christian Martyr Texts* (New York: Columbia University Press, 2008) and Susanna Elm, "Roman Pain and the Rise of Christianity," in Susanna Elm and Stefan N. Willich, eds., *Quo Vadis: Medical Healing, Past Concepts and New Approaches,* International Library of Ethics, Law and the New Medicine 44 (Berlin: Springer, 2009), pp. 41–54.

9. Donald G. Kyle, *Spectacles of Death in Ancient Rome* (London: Routledge, 1998), p. 243.

Many martyr narratives—which today may be transmitted by a variety of media, often visual and digital—are deliberately and emphatically one-sided accounts of the triumph of good over evil, but modern academic study seeks to understand such accounts as forms of propaganda for a particular cause. The study of such acts, therefore, needs to establish a theoretical standpoint in relation to both the validity of martyrdom as an act of resistance, as well as the significance of the beliefs in question on a particular occasion. Contemporary power dynamics may reveal greater or lesser degrees of agency on the part of those involved. Thus, depending on one's viewpoint, a particular martyr may appear as a victim or as an aggressor, or indeed both. This puts the issue of personal volition under the spotlight. For instance, Paul Middleton has advanced the notion of what he calls "radical martyrdom" in early antiquity.[10] By this he seeks to differentiate between those who did or did not actively seek their own deaths at the hands of the Roman authorities. Those who actively sought their death can be understood to have done so as a way of inflicting some form of damage on their opponents. They exchanged, as it were, a physical attack on their body for an ideological attack on the moral position of their pagan adversaries. Their actions were ones of witnessing, but they achieved their effect by being witnessed. Thus, it was crucial that what they achieved was seen to have been done. The partisan martyr acts were essential to this process, since the circulation of truth claims in textual form had the potential to reach a substantial audience over time and space.

It is in this conceptual realm of the martyr as either active agent, or the active agent of subsequent propagandists, that we can begin to talk about the potential political power of martyrdom.[11] On that score, the connections with terrorism also become more apparent. While terrorists are often associated with those who kill and injure people indiscriminately, their underlying aim is most often an ideological one of changing power relations through spreading fear. The attempt to precipitate such change has frequently involved fighting over two things: who has the right to use violence and what kinds of violence are legitimate. In other words, terrorism has often been a matter of contesting its own illegitimate status as "terrorism." And both the definition and agency of terrorist violence have

---

10. Paul Middleton, *Radical Martyrdom and Cosmic Conflict in Early Christianity*, Library of New Testament Studies 307 (London: T. and T. Clark, 2006).

11. Sophia Moskalenko and Clark McCauley, "The Political Power of Martyrdom," *Terrorism and Political Violence* 24.3 (2012), pp. 504–10.

also been caught up in that contestation—a point that is encapsulated by the well-worn adage that "one person's terrorist is another person's freedom fighter." Such a conflict of views is symptomatic of the fact that there is still no internationally agreed definition of what constitutes terrorism. The main reason for this is that despite numerous international conventions and conferences on terrorism over the last three decades, nation-states have been wary of allowing certain kinds of violence to be defined as "terrorism" within international law because this would render states themselves vulnerable to charges of using terrorism and, therefore, susceptible to counterterrorist interventions. So although practices such as hijacking, hostage-taking, and assassination are outlawed in international law, they are not defined as acts of "terrorism," per se—if they were, it would certainly put recent practices of "extraordinary rendition" and "targeted killing" in the "war on terror" in a different light. Indeed, the war on terror is indicative of how war, as well as terrorism, has frequently involved contesting the boundaries of legitimacy in respect to modes and agents of violence. In detaining suspected terrorists as "unlawful combatants," for example, the United States conflated terrorism with the waging of war by illegitimate means. Yet the recent US campaign of "drone" strikes in designated "kill zones" in Pakistan, for example, was itself a mode of war that was of questionable legality, as the UN special rapporteur on extrajudicial killings has noted.[12] As Derek Gregory has argued, because the drones were operated remotely from the United States by CIA *civilians* who were not subject to the US Uniform Code of Justice, those operatives could themselves be seen as being akin to "unlawful combatants."[13]

Another reason for the definitional haze around terrorism is that individual nation-states have been invested in adopting a *broad* domestic definition of terrorism in order to ensure flexibility of counterterrorism. The United Kingdom, for example, defines terrorism as "the use or threat, for the purpose of advancing a political, religious, or ideological course of action, of serious violence" against "the public or a section of the public."[14] Terrorism here is thus limited to *instrumental* violence carried out as a

---

12. Owen Bowcott, "Drone Strikes Threaten 50 Years of International Law, Says UN Rapporteur," *Guardian*, June 21, 2012, http://www.guardian.co.uk/world/2012/jun/21/drone-strikes-international-law-un.

13. Derek Gregory, "The Everywhere War," *Geographical Journal* 177.3 (2011), pp. 238–50.

14. The UK Terrorism Act (2000), part I, section I, http://www.legislation.gov.uk/ukpga/2000/11/contents.

means of advancing a particular cause. Yet in extending the ambit of such violence to that which targets "a person" or "involves serious damage to property" the definition means that individuals engaged in ecological activism or hacking into corporate IT systems run the risk of their actions being categorized as "eco-terrorism," and "cyber-terrorism," respectively. That is to say, the definition is designed to enable flexibility in ascribing terrorism to criminal violence, while emphasizing that such violence does not need to be aimed at the state more generally. In contrast, the European Union's definition of terrorism (like that of the United States) is politically slanted towards offences that seek to intimidate or influence the state or a society in general, although that emphasis is tempered by including "international organizations" no less than "country," "population," and "government" as terrorism's intended target.[15] What the various contrasting definitions of terrorism show is that it has no fixed character or essence as a practice and strategy. Alex Schmid and Albert Jongman, in their 1988 study of terrorism, identified 109 definitions of it.[16] In contrast, recent work in "Critical Terrorism Studies" has eschewed the importance of settling on a universal definition of terrorism and has instead emphasized its contested and mediated nature.[17] Just as martyrdom has changed over the ages as a result of being subject to contestation, so, too, has terrorism.

Over recent years there has been a growth of academic interest in thinking about religious terrorism precisely because we have increasingly seen one person's martyr represented as another person's terrorist. From within critical terrorism studies, however, the category of "religious terrorism" has recently been declared to be "inaccurate and analytically unhelpful" because of the difficulty of defining any terrorist organization as purely religious when even avowedly religious organizations such as Hamas or Hezbollah, for example, have nationalist and secular aspirations and targets.[18] Being wary of categorizing terrorist violence makes sense insofar as the nature of terrorism has always been contested, but rejecting the usefulness of "religious terrorism" as a category can itself be analytically unhelpful if this discourages consideration of how religion

---

15. Council of the European Union, *Council Framework Decision 2002/475 on Combating Terrorism* (June 13, 2002), 2002/475/JHA, Article I, http://www.unhcr.org/refworld/docid/3f5342994.html.

16. Alex Schmid and Albert Jongman, *Political Terrorism: A New Guide to Actors, Authors, Concepts, Databases, Theories and Literature* (New Brunswick, N.J.: Transaction, 1988).

17. See, for example, Jackson et al., *Terrorism*.

18. Ibid., p. 169.

and terrorism have indeed been intertwined in various ways throughout history. This volume is intended to contribute to that debate by examining instances of how both martyrdom and terrorism have entailed fraught exchanges between matters of religion, politics, and culture. Thus, contributors to this volume have analyzed how religious martyrdom has taken on a political aspect when, for example, it has involved terrorist violence that has been used to defend a territory or community of faith against an enemy, or when it has involved fighting and dying for a secular ideal. Similarly, contributors have focused on militancy that has commonly been described as terroristic on account of it being deemed to be violence that is illegitimate and/or a threat to political order, when that very order (like the terrorism pitted against it) has itself often been imbricated with religion.

As we have already acknowledged, martyrdom has a longer history as a term than terrorism, but in order to consider how the two have overlapped we need to address the fact that religion and martyrdom have themselves been implicated in defending the bounds of legitimate militancy in periods pre-dating the "Terror" of the French Revolution when the term "terrorism" gained currency. Therefore, the current volume interrogates the way in which religious and secular practices and understandings of terrorism and martyrdom have interacted both prior to and since that time in the context of nationalism and imperialism. Discussions of modern terrorism have always revolved around its perceived lack of legitimacy as violence, yet debates about what constitutes legitimate and illegitimate militancy have a longer history in which religion and martyrdom have played a significant role. Taking a long view of that role back to antiquity, this volume's view of martyrdom thus enables analysis of the extent to which modern religious terrorism is comparable to earlier precedents of terroristic militancy. Before outlining how each chapter contributes to the volume's comparative approach, it will be useful here to examine the issues raised by some salient examples of how Christianity and Islam have played a part in both reinforcing and undermining distinctions between martyrdom, war, and terroristic militancy over the ages. In doing so, we will also make some reflections on secular terrorism and martyrdom.

Within the Christian tradition, it was St. Augustine who, before the collapse of the Roman Empire, set out rules for what justified going to war (*jus ad bellum*) as well as rules of legitimate combat in war (*jus in bello*). The main *ad bellum* conditions stated that war should only be declared by legitimate authorities, and for specific just causes, such as avenging grave injury, self-defense against external attack, and protection of citizens. Regarding rules of conduct within war, Augustine stipulated that noncombatants such as women, children, and the elderly should not be attacked.[19] Taken together, these criteria have formed the basis of a "just war tradition" that has also seen contributions from Thomas Aquinas and notable jurists such as Hugo Grotius, Francisco de Vitoria, and Francisco Suárez.[20] Just war theory underpins current international laws of armed conflict, as well as the Geneva Conventions and the articles on war in the UN Charter. To that extent, just war theory has also been important in establishing what kinds of militancy are illegitimate, and in recent times, that has meant that militants deemed to be "unlawful combatants" have been viewed as terrorists rather than soldiers.

While early just war theory was clearly intended to prevent rulers and armies from behaving in unregulated ways like pirates and outlaws, it also helped to consolidate a concept of Christian Holy War which, in practice, did not always adhere to the just war criteria that Augustine had formulated. Waging war to obey divine command was prescribed by Augustine as a just *ad bellum* cause, and between the seventh and ninth centuries there were a number of Christian Holy Wars waged against pagans by figures such as Charlemagne and the English kings St. Oswald and St. Edmund. As Paul Middleton has written, "Once killing in battle was theologically justified as participation in Christian Holy War, it was only a small step before the dead in such conflicts were viewed as martyrs."[21] By the eleventh century all those who fought in wars blessed by the Pope were deemed to be *militia Christi* insofar as they were seen to be imitating the trials of Christ.

Yet with the onset of the First Crusade (1096–99) the correlation of just war principles and Holy war was sometimes questionable. Those who went on the war-pilgrimage were by no means all legitimate soldiers, and neither was all of the militancy "just" on Augustine's terms, despite the fact that those Christians who fought and died in the Crusades were seen by many as martyrs. For example, along their way to Constantinople mixed groups of Crusading pilgrims, such as those led by Peter the Hermit, committed atrocities against Jewish communities and certainly did not pay

---

19. On Augustine's contribution to just war theory, see Jonathan Ebel, "Christianity and Violence," in Andrew R. Murphy, ed., *The Blackwell Companion to Religion and Violence* (Oxford: Wiley-Blackwell, 2011), pp. 149–62.

20. On just war theory more generally, see the various essays in Larry May, ed., *War: Essays in Political Philosophy* (Cambridge: Cambridge University Press, 2008).

21. Middleton, *Martyrdom*, p. 86.

heed to the just war stricture of noncombatant immunity.[22] That was also the case in the Crusaders' siege of Jerusalem (1099) when they set about indiscriminately annihilating the Muslim and Jewish inhabitants of the city. To the extent that such violence was systematic, terrifying, and did not adhere to the concept of just war, such "holy" campaigns can be likened to terrorism; and that comparison has already been made by various commentators within terrorism studies.[23] Those commentators also cite the use of torture in the Inquisition, and the violent excesses of the Spanish and Portuguese conquistadores in South America as other early examples of systematic terror and militancy being deployed in the name of Christianity.

While it is reasonable to compare certain instances of early Christian militancy and martyrdom to modern-day terrorism, it is important to bear in mind notable divergences of perspective. From the modern standpoint, while there has been considerable attention paid to the phenomenon of state terrorism, most scholarship has focused on terrorism deemed to be illegitimate for being carried out by nonstate groups. But the emphasis on pinning war's legitimacy to state authority was consolidated in Europe only with the signing of the Peace of Westphalia in 1648, which was intended to put an end to the religious wars between Catholicism and Protestantism that raged in Europe in the wake of the Protestant Reformation. These wars, most notably the Thirty Years War (1618–48), included sustained campaigns of terror and atrocity and involved groups of militants other than legitimate state forces.[24] That mixture of terror and militancy (including against noncombatants) waged by nonstate actors fits with modern conceptions of terrorism, but it is important to remember that nation-states did not have a complete monopoly on sovereignty and political legitimacy at this time, for some European countries were themselves broken up into rival mini-states, dukedoms, and principalities, the leaders of which often used mercenaries to fight their military campaigns. In other words, distinctions between state and nonstate militancy were frequently equivocal in these wars of religion which also involved

22. See Christopher Tyerman, *Chronicles of the First Crusade* (London: Penguin, 2011), chap. 2.

23. See, for example, Sinclair, *An Anatomy of Terror*, pp. 21–23; also Gérard Chaliand and Arnauld Blin, eds., *The History of Terrorism, from Antiquity to Al Qaeda*, trans. Edward Schneider, Kathryn Pulver, and Jesse Bowner (Berkeley: University of California Press, 2007).

24. See Peter Wilson, *Europe's Tragedy: A New History of the Thirty Years War* (London: Allen Lane, 2009).

contesting the legitimacy of the enemy's faith and political power. Modern criteria for judging terrorism are thus divergent from the criteria used at the time to determine the rectitude of militancy, for those involved in the religious wars measured the justness of their militancy and their martyrdom not so much in terms of state legitimacy, or distinctions of lawful and unlawful combatants, as primarily in terms of doing God's will by defending their faith and/or using the violent means necessary to rid the world of heresy. With the signing of the Peace of Westphalia, though, the major European countries of the time agreed to respect the territorial integrity of each other's countries, and this led to the legitimacy of war being tied to nation-state sovereignty. Conceptions of the justness of militancy thus shifted from being rooted in religion to being based in political sovereignty and statehood.

Ironically, that shift in the conception of just warfare is also evident in the French Revolution's reign of "Terror" (1793–94) that gave rise to the term "terrorism." The revolution had substituted the sovereignty of monarchy (seen as ruling by the grace of God) with the sovereign will of the people. Enforcing the revolution entailed instituting state secularism to the extent that devotion to Roman Catholicism was replaced by worship of a deist "Supreme Being" that was in accordance with revolutionary ideals. That development—as David Andress, Julia Douthwaite, and Ronald Schechter discuss in this volume—also led to conceptions of secular revolutionary martyrdom. For Chaliand and Blin, the secular turn of the French Revolution is a prelude to the development of the modern revolutionary terrorism of the nineteenth and early twentieth century which "essentially had no religious dimension."[25] That is a reasonable comment insofar as most Anarchists and Russian Nihilists were atheist. Yet just as the martyr acts of the French Revolution had a distinctly spiritual aspect to them so, too, did those of some of the more modern revolutionary terrorist movements. The Russian Nihilist, Sergei Kravchinsky, for example, wrote of the advent of the Nihilist figure of the "Terrorist" as being like a revolutionary, inverted Second Coming:

> Proud as Satan rebelling against God, [the Terrorist] opposed his own will to that of the man who alone, amid a nation of slaves, claimed the right of having a will [i.e., the Tsar]. But how different

25. Chaliand and Blin, *The History of Terrorism*, p. 96.

is this terrestrial god from the old Jehovah of Moses! How he hides
his trembling head under the daring blows of the Terrorist![26]

Since Kravchinsky's time there has, of course, been modern terrorism
that has had a straightforwardly religious dimension. Examples of revolutionary groups that have been deemed to be "terrorist" and that harbor
religion in their ideology to various degrees include the Irish Republican
and Irish Loyalist movements, as well as "Islamist" organizations ranging
from Hezbollah to al Qaeda. It is also true that the militancy and various kinds of martyrdom claimed by these terrorist movements have been
inflected with elements of secular politics and culture. With the recent
"war on terror[ism]" it is thus too reductive to claim that we have been
faced with a simple clash between secular war and religious terrorism. As
Alex Houen has argued elsewhere, the war on terror has, in part, been a
conflict over sacrifice; for while Islamist organizations have viewed martyrdom operations as acts of "self-sacrifice" in the name of Holy War, the
Bush administration repeatedly invoked "sacrifices" being made by US
armed personnel in fighting and dying for national ideals of "freedom"
and "democracy."[27] This does not mean that the sacrifices made on both
sides have essentially been the same: the Bush administration certainly
did not describe its fallen heroes as "martyrs." But it is wrong to see
Islamist sacrifices as purely religious when they have also been made with
political intentions, and it is equally wrong to see the US sacrifices as
purely secular when there has been a certain idealism of spirit associated
with fighting for freedom and democracy, just as there was for the French
revolutionaries who died opposing the power of Christian monarchy.

The recent spread of Islamist "suicide bombing" has drawn an attendant surge of interest in reconsidering religious terrorism and martyrdom.[28] That is all the more reason to take a long view of how Islam,

---

26. Sergei Kravchinsky, *Underground Russia* (London: Smith and Elder, 1883), p. 44.

27. Alex Houen, "Sacrificial Militancy and the Wars around Terror," in Elleke Boehmer and
Stephen Morton, eds., *Terror and the Postcolonial* (Oxford: Wiley-Blackwell, 2010), pp. 113–40.

28. See, for example, Talal Asad, *On Suicide Bombing* (New York: Columbia University Press,
2002); John L. Esposito, *Unholy War: Terror in the Name of Islam* (Oxford: Oxford University
Press, 2002); Mark Juergensmeyer, *Terror in the Mind of God: The Global Rise of Religious
Violence* (Berkeley: University of California Press, 2003); Mia Bloom, *Dying to Kill: The
Allure of Suicide Terror* (New York: Columbia University Press, 2005); Farhad Khosrokhavar,
Suicide Bombers: Allah's New Martyrs, trans. David Macey (London: Pluto, 2005); and Diego
Gambetta, ed., *Making Sense of Suicide Missions* (Oxford: Oxford University Press, 2005).

like Christianity, has been implicated in reinforcing and undermining distinctions of martyrdom, war, and terrorism throughout the ages. For Shi'a Islam the tradition of self-sacrificial militancy extends back to the Battle of Karbala in 680 when the Shi'ite leader Hussein Ibn Ali and his followers died fighting for their faith against more numerous Sunni forces. Hussein's death was clearly inspirational for the Ishmaelite sect of "Assassins" that is commonly described as being a precursor to modern Islamist terrorism. Between 1090 and 1272 the sect spread from Persia to Syria and stabbed to death a variety of princes, generals and governors, Sunni clerics and two caliphs in addition to a number of crusader lords. Because the Assassins were prepared to die in making their attacks, commentators have compared them to contemporary suicide bombers. As Christoph Reuter has pointed out, though, in making such comparisons we need to be mindful of the fact that the Assassins were Shi'ite whereas al Qaeda's self-sacrificial martyrs are mostly inspired by radical Sunni ideology.[29] Any similarity between the two needs to be measured with regard to the complex history of developments within Islam that have influenced the relation of militant martyrdom to *Jihad* (Holy War). And this means that, as when we compare early forms of Christian militant martyrdom to contemporary terrorism, we need to be wary of evaluating the terroristic nature of past Islamic precedents in terms of current political values pertaining to state sovereignty and the legitimation of militancy that were consolidated in Europe only after 1648.

Within the Islamic tradition, relations of martyrdom and Holy War were formulated in a range of theological and juristic writings between the eighth and ninth centuries. Taken together, these writings are comparable to the European just war theory that has its roots in Christian doctrine. In the Quran, martyrdom is predominantly associated with bearing witness to one's faith and the good of one's community. References to martyrdom in the sense of dying in battle for one's religion are rare. By the eighth century the Islamic concept of martyrdom was so broad that it could denote anyone who had led a faithful life and so died a worthy death. Major Islamic conquests such as those in Persia and Roman Byzantine territory, however, gave cause for prescribing relations of martyrdom and *Jihad* in detail. Various *hadiths* (reports on the sayings and actions of the Prophet Muhammad and his followers) were written on relations of martyrdom

---

29. Christoph Reuter, *My Life is a Weapon: A Modern History of Suicide Bombing*, trans. Helena Ragg-Kirby (Princeton: Princeton University Press, 2004), p. 27.

and *Jihad*, and this "Jihad literature" included guidance on the nature and conduct of martyrs as well as on rules of war.[30] This body of *Jihad* writings was also codified by Islamic jurists in the late eighth and ninth centuries into a set of laws that contributed to the larger body of Islamic *Shari'a* (Divine Law), and these laws prescribed rules of combat, which included not killing noncombatants such as women, children, and the elderly. In that respect the *Jihad* writings and laws are comparable to early just war theory, for both address questions of justification, authority, and conduct regarding combat.

As James Turner Johnson has pointed out, though, there is a particular divergence between just war theory and the Islamic legal literature on *Jihad*, as the latter states that *Jihad* can become an obligation not just for Islamic armed forces but also for individual male adults more generally.[31] The classical conception of *Jihad* by the sword entailed an Islamic community being called to arms by an Islamic leader (Caliph) to wage war in order to extend the rule of Islam or defend it against its enemy attacks. That is not to say that the entire community would necessarily turn into combatants; honoring the obligation to support *Jihad* could take the form of aiding the war effort in other ways. Yet it was also true that when there was an enemy invasion, prior to a Caliphal call to arms, any Muslim males near the invading troops had an individual duty to wage *Jihad* in defense even in the absence of a Caliphal army nearby. This concept of the individual duty (*fard 'ayn*) to wage *Jihad* has become particularly controversial recently; with the absence of an Islamic Caliphate, Osama bin Laden and other al Qaeda militants have contended that it is all the more important to honor the individual obligation of defending Islamic holy lands against enemy invasions. The majority of Muslims, however, have viewed the legitimacy of al Qaeda's militancy to be tendentious and thus more a matter of terrorism than of *Jihad*. Then again, we also need to remember there is a long history of disagreements about theological legitimacy in the Islamic tradition. Just as Christianity has had its own religious wars between Catholics and Protestants, so Islam has seen numerous conflicts between Sunnis and Shias over the legitimacy of their religious faith and militancy. The Assassins provide an early example and the Saudi Arabian

---

30. David Cook, *Understanding Jihad* (Berkeley: University of California Press, 2005), chap. 1.

31. James Turner Johnson, "Just War and Jihad of the Sword," in Murphy, *The Blackwell Companion*, pp. 277–78.

Wahhabis a later one; this time of a Sunni movement occupying and destroying holy Shi'a cities such as Karbala, Mecca, and Medina in the early nineteenth century.

Another similarity that the Islamic tradition bears to the Christian one is that the means, ends, and justifications of militant martyrdom have increasingly been infused with political and secular aims and ideologies. That is largely a result of fighting against European colonization since the decline of the Ottoman Empire—which had been described in 1603 by the English historian Richard Knolles as "the present terror of the world"— that began in the early seventeenth century.[32] In Malabar, Aceh, and the Philippines in the eighteenth century, militant Muslims sometimes employed suicidal attacks in their fight against European colonial rule. In the nineteenth century, there were various Jihadist uprisings against the French in Algeria, the British in Egypt, and the Russians in the Caucasus.[33] In the twentieth century, the revolutionary writings of Sunni figures such as Hasan al-Banna, Said Qutb, and Abd al-Salam Faraj were partly responding to the effects of European colonization and have subsequently influenced contemporary Islamist militants' reinterpretations of *Jihad* and martyrdom. Qutb and Faraj in particular were influential in emphasizing the individual duty of Muslims to wage *Jihad* against foreign occupation. Within Shi'a Islam, Ayatollah Khomeini and Ali Shariati in Iran played an important role in recasting the importance of self-sacrificial martyrdom in relation to combat in the Iran-Iraq war. The Lebanese Shi'ite organization Hezbollah subsequently pioneered suicide bombing as an Islamist tactic in an attack against US Marines in 1983.

That is not to say that suicide bombing is inherently Islamist; the first recorded suicide bomber was the Anarchist, Nisan Farber, in 1904, and there have been secular organizations such as the Tamil Tigers that have also used suicide bombers. Regarding Islamist suicide attacks in recent years, the main reason why so many people struggle to see them as anything other than terrorism is because of the fact that they have frequently been indiscriminate in targeting noncombatant civilians. On that score, al Qaeda's 9/11 attacks, for example, marked a deviation not only from classical juristic writings on *Jihad* but also from the twentieth-century writings of Sunni radicals such as Hassan al-Banna, Abul A'la Maududi,

---

32. Quoted in Daniel Goffman, *The Ottoman Empire and Early Modern Europe* (Cambridge: Cambridge University Press, 2002), p. 19.

33. See Cook, *Understanding Jihad*, chap. 4.

and Said Qutb who did not advocate attacking noncombatants. As was clear from his 1998 *fatwa*, bin Laden did not think there were any innocent civilians in the infidel countries he deemed to be opposed to Islam. Establishing the extent to which the justifications of militant martyrdom made by movements such as al Qaeda diverge from earlier precedents necessitates the kind of comparative historical approach that we are building in this volume.

It is, of course, impossible to address every aspect of such complex phenomena as these in the course of a single edited collection. The core methodologies of this volume, therefore, focus on comparative exploration of the historical study of cultural and social formations and of related literary and visual discourses. Alternative approaches might, for instance, explore these phenomena from the viewpoints of anthropology or moral philosophy.[34] The book's chapters are organized around specific geographical, chronological, and presentational foci in order to give the essays a tightly organized and interrelated formation. The geographical focus of the volume is on Europe, with particular interest paid to developments during the course of the French Revolution that saw the birth of the concept of terrorism. Key developments in the Middle East are viewed from the standpoint of Europe and its long-standing relations with the Islamic world. The chronological focus of the collection is on the development of ideas from antiquity to modernity.

The first section of this book, "Pre- and Early modern Violence and Martyrdom," first provides explorations of current understandings of the development of martyrdom in early Christianity and Islam and then, second, explores the discursive territories of crime, sedition, and treason which prefigured the emergence of the terrorist in political discourse. Cooper explains that, contrary to what is often thought, there was not, in fact, a concerted campaign by the Roman authorities against Christians until well into the third century A.D. Moreover, Christian witness to the faith could be achieved in many ways other than through an exemplary death. Those Christians who did, however, lose their lives at the hands of Roman judges set examples of principled dissent which morally questioned the use of terror within the

---

34. The work of René Girard is particularly pertinent to such enterprises. For examples of analyses influenced by his theorization of the role of violence and sacrifice in the maintenance of social group cohesion, see Carolyn Marvin and David W. Ingle, "Blood Sacrifice and the Nation: Revisiting Civil Religion," *Journal of the American Academy of Religion* 64.4 (1996), pp. 767–80 and Mark Juergensmeyer, "Martyrdom and Sacrifice in a Time of Terror," *Social Research* 75.2 (2008), pp. 417–34.

empire. Afsaruddin explains that Christian conceptions of martyrdom influenced the development of related concepts within early Islam which, in a
similar manner, only evolved over time to become increasingly focused on
the "red martyrdom" of death. She emphasizes that the harnessing together
of military forms of active martyrdom with *Jihad* took place in association
with political pressures within the Islamic world.

Monta explores the way in which Protestants and Catholics contested the
role of Church and State in early Modern England. Roman Catholics tended
to condemn their Protestant opponents as heretics, whereas Catholics were
condemned by the Protestant Tudor monarchs as traitors. As in the Roman
Empire, the use of terror by the state was understood to be legitimate if
it was necessary for the preservation of the moral and political order. The
effect of prosecution under the heading of treachery was to deny the condemned the status of martyr because they were projected as having acted
for worldly rather than spiritual reasons. But as Waller also shows, in this
period it was not possible neatly to separate this-worldly and other-worldly
duties and obligations. Waller's study highlights examples of texts taken
from the works of Milton and Shakespeare with the aim of exploring the
psychological interdependence of violence and sacrifice in the early modern
period. He argues, further, that study of the literature of the time can also
provide insights into irruptions of religious violence in later centuries.

The second part of this book, "The French Revolution and the Invention
of Terrorism," provides an in-depth examination of the pivotal events of
the early 1790s and the way in which religious modes of expression and
feeling influenced secular politics. Douthwaite looks at ways in which the
rhetoric of sacrifice could be used to define revolutionary leaders and their
victims as either terrorists, or martyrs, or both. She stresses the importance of the diversity of loyalties at this time—whether to God, the State,
or the family. Andress explores Robespierre's use of sentimental rhetoric
in his attempts to focus loyalties on the State through emotional appeals
to moral virtue. He argues that Robespierre's frequent invocation of a martyred and to-be-martyred "people," and his association of the prospect of
personal martyrdom with the collective fate of the people, is one of the
most consistent tropes of his speechmaking. It plays a key role in the establishment of his moral authority in a turbulent political context, while also
helping to create a culture of victimhood that could be turned against him
as the Terror he had helped to create threatened to engulf the entire political class. Schechter argues not simply for the moralizing nature of the
revolutionary enterprise but for its reinterpretation as comparable with

forms of religious faith. Actors did not leave the revolutionary stage at their deaths but, in the form of the "shades," participated as martyrs in calls for the escalation of terror. Janes explains that the French Revolution had a powerfully complicating effect upon previously starkly oppositional British images of Protestant virtue and Catholic vice. The fact that many of the victims of the Revolution were Roman Catholics, executed by men who were either deists or atheists, led to the reconsideration of key texts of Protestant witness, such as the sixteenth-century *Act[e]s and Monuments* of John Foxe.

The third part of this book, "Martyrdom, Terrorism, and the Modern West," explores some of the ways in which deep-seated patterns of religious thinking have influenced modern and contemporary understandings of heroism, sacrifice, and terror. It also includes discussions of how changing media and communications technologies have had an impact on the wider, and indeed global, reception of the "bearing witness" of those acclaimed by their admirers as martyrs. Beiner looks at the way in which deep-rooted traditions of Roman Catholic martyrdom were harnessed, despite opposition from the Church, to buttress the movement for an independent Ireland during the nineteenth and early twentieth centuries. He argues that it was not simply the actions of Fenian terrorist bombers, but also the response to their repression by the British, that resulted in a cult of political martyrdom that made a major contribution to the movement toward Irish independence.

In the wake of the July 7, 2005, London suicide bombings by British Islamists, various commentators compared the attacks to the Blitz on London in World War II. It is more accurate, however, to draw comparisons to the Fenian and Anarchist bombings of London in the late Victorian period, as Alex Houen argued at the time.[35] In the next chapter Awan moves the focus to the contemporary period through examining the rise of Jihadist terrorism in Britain and the underlying reasons behind the Jihadists' investments in notions of martyrdom and sacrifice. He also examines the life narratives, as well as political and religious motivations, of particular Jihadists such as Muhammad Siddique Khan (ringleader of the 7/7 London bombings), Shahzad Tanweer, and Richard Reid. Following this, Houen explores British and Irish responses to the kidnappings and deaths of Kenneth Bigley and Margaret Hassan at the hands of

---

35. See Graham Bowley, "Letter from Britain: British Literature Offers Few Answers to July 7," *New York Times*, August 10, 2005, http://www.nytimes.com/2005/08/09/world/europe/09iht-letter.html.

militant groups in the Iraq War. He looks at the way in which the kidnappers forced their captives to present themselves as abject rather than as heroic victims, and how in Hassan's case her Catholicism enabled her to be claimed by the Roman Catholic Church as having been a martyr on account of having borne witness to her faith. The final chapter in the book, by Mitchell, emphasizes the role that screen media can play in casting individuals as terrorists or martyrs. He focuses on how changing forms of visual media have affected how martyrdoms and terrorist acts have been presented and represented since the twentieth century. With reference to cinema, television, and the contemporary multiplication of images on the Internet, he explores the extent to which the contemporary intimacy of terrorism and martyrdom is figured in screen media in terms of "ends" that repeatedly link death and teleology.

The carefully contextualized studies presented by the scholars who have contributed to this collection are being published in the context of a media culture that is often suffused to the point of saturation with imagery of martyrdom and terrorism. It is to be hoped that this volume will contribute to informed contemporary public debate at the same time as advancing specialized historical research. This work is also presented with a modestly optimistic sense of what might be achieved by highlighting the importance of asking what opportunities for understanding and reconciliation might yet be facilitated through systematic examination of the comparative cultural constructions of martyrdom and terrorism in religious and secular cultures. Many related questions emerge from these essays: such as how the "bearing witness" of a contemporary martyr relates to that of his or her precursors and how such acts of witnessing have been directly influenced by the growth of the media and communications technologies which have provided many recent acts of terrorism with unprecedented public impact. Through multidisciplinary analyses this volume seeks to open up such questions to fresh contextual analysis and to advance the development of a comparative history of the practices and discourses of martyrdom and terrorism from antiquity to the twenty-first century.

ONE

*Pre- and Early Modern Violence
and Martyrdom*

I

Martyrdom, Memory, and the "Media Event"

VISIONARY WRITING AND CHRISTIAN APOLOGY IN SECOND-CENTURY CHRISTIANITY

Kate Cooper

IN HIS SECOND *Apology*, written at Rome in the 150s, the Christian philosopher Justin Martyr tells the story of an unusually nasty divorce. A wife had joined the fellowship of the Christians and her husband, who according to Justin should be gratified by her wish to adopt a life of modest virtue. Instead he was irritated by her attempt to reform his behaviour, in line with the stricter morals of her new community. As a way of separating herself from his dissolute life, she served him with a *repudium*, a bill of unilateral divorce. Perhaps unsurprisingly, the husband sought to revenge his honour, and denounced her—along with her Christian teacher—to the authorities.

The Christian wife in Justin's story remains nameless, perhaps as a gesture of respect for her modesty. In any case Justin's real interest is not in the troubled woman, nor her difficulties with her belligerent husband. Rather, it is with with the witness borne by the Christian men in her new circle: her teacher, Ptolemy, and a bystander, known to history as the martyr Lucius, who stands up for Ptolemy when he is denounced. Justin tells us that when Ptolemy is brought before Urbicus, the Urban Prefect, he is condemned and led away to punishment. Then Lucius steps forward:

> seeing the unreasonable judgment that had thus been given, he
> said to Urbicus: "What is the ground of this judgment? Why have

you punished this man, not as an adulterer, nor fornicator, nor mur-
derer, nor thief, nor robber, nor convicted of any crime at all, but
who has only confessed that he is called by the name of Christian?
This judgment of yours, O Urbicus, does not become the Emperor
Pius, nor the philosopher, the son of Cæsar, nor the sacred senate."[1]

The response of Urbicus is to suspect Lucius himself of being a Christian.
And when Lucius confesses that this is so, he too is led away to punishment.

The story of Ptolemy, Lucius, and the prefect Urbicus is the earliest
narrative account of a Christian brought to trial before the Roman authorities. It offers a powerful narrative capsule of the idea of the Christian
martyr as a moral hero, an idea that has become central to the Christian
tradition across the centuries. Yet Justin's apology can still surprise the
modern reader. It offers a useful starting point for dispelling a number of
misconceptions which undermine our understanding of early Christian
martyrdom.

To begin with, it is still a common misconception that a systematic
policy was aimed at Christians by Roman law or Roman governors, although scholarship over the last half-century has shown that there is
no non-Christian evidence to corroborate the idea—often suggested in
Christian sources—that the Christians were an explicit target of persecution. Indeed, a recent study by Candida Moss, *The Myth of Persecution*,
has suggested that the Christian "persecution complex" was the result of
internal Christian identity politics.[2]

Equally important is the common misconception that Christian
martyrdom—as the Christians themselves understood it—necessarily
involved violence and death. The title of a recent and valuable primary
source collection, *Martyrdom and Noble Death*, reflects the way the two
concepts are paired in the modern imagination, though ancient writers
were acutely aware of the difference.[3]

The Greek words *martyros* and *martyria* mean, quite straightforwardly,
"witness." The first term refers to an individual who offers evidence in the

1. Justin Martyr, *Second Apology*, 2, in *The Apostolic Fathers, Justin Martyr, Irenaeus, vol. 1
of The Ante-Nicene Fathers: Translations of the Writings of the Fathers down to* A.D. *325*, ed.
Alexander Roberts and James Donaldson (Edinburgh: T. and T. Clark, 1867–72).

2. Candida Moss, *The Myth of Persecution: How Early Christians Invented a Story of Martyrdom*
(San Francisco: Harper Collins, 2013).

3. Jan Willem van Henten and Friedrich Avemarie, *Martyrdom and Noble Death: Selected
Texts from Graeco-Roman, Jewish and Christian Antiquity* (London: Routledge, 2002).

context of a trial or investigation, and the latter denotes the act of giving that evidence. The terms crop up frequently in legal papyri of the early Christian period, and it is clear that early Christian writers understood them in this way. To be sure, some of the faithful maintained that to die for the cause was the quintessential act of witness—but this view was not universally accepted.

A further common misconception is that early Christian martyrdom involved a face-off between the Christian "Church" and the Roman "State." The point to recognize here is that neither "Church" nor "State" as presently understood existed in Mediterranean antiquity before the reign of Constantine the Great (d. 337), the first Roman Emperor to establish the Christian churches on a legitimate, legally recognized basis. Before Constantine, the churches were local organizations that were loosely bound—when they were bound at all—into a fluid and shifting network.

It is likely that the Roman authorities saw no unique or outstanding dangers in the religious dissent of early Christian communities. In the provinces, dissent of one kind or another was everywhere. The Romans armies had achieved their Mediterranean-wide empire through an inspired mix of business-friendly policy and routine brutality, and if the wealthiest landowners were on the whole satisfied with membership in the *pax Romana*—the "peace of Rome"—there were persistent disturbances in both cities and rural areas, anything from petty thieving to full-scale rioting by those who had no stake in the profit being made by the Roman overlords and the sycophantic regional elites who collaborated with them. In this context, violence was understood to be the prerogative of the conqueror, not of the conquered.[4]

The discourse of Christian martyrdom seems to have been a by-product of the routine imposition of terror on dissident groups by the Roman authorities. From sources like the *Judean Wars* of Flavius Josephus it is clear that when Roman governors felt that local populations were in any danger of establishing autonomy, they took swift, decisive, and brutal action. But the reaction of the inhabitants of Judaea to the imposition of Hellenic (and subsequently Roman) power would prove distinctive.[5] Taking its root in

---

4. Ramsay MacMullen, *Enemies of the Roman Order: Treason, Unrest, and Alienation in the Empire* (Cambridge, Mass.: Harvard University Press, 1967).

5. On Jewish resistance, see Shaye J. D. Cohen, *From the Maccabees to the Mishnah*, 2nd ed. (Louisville, Ky.: Westminster John Knox Press, [1987] 2006); and for the wider context, Lee I. Levine, *Judaism and Hellenism in Antiquity: Conflict or Confluence?* (Seattle: University of

the Jewish traditions of resistance to the Hellenic empire of the Seleucid descendents of Alexander the Great, the Christian discourse of principled resistance to Roman power would flower in the second and third centuries.[6] In the fourth century, when the Emperor Constantine assimilated Christian faith as a legitimate element of the Roman state religion, Christian writers began to invoke the heritage of principled resistance in dealing with the emperors and governors who now claimed their loyalty. Recently scholars have begun to chart how this legacy was used in the fourth and fifth centuries to justify acts of violent civil disobedience, such as the religious riots which seized the cities of the Eastern Mediterranean.[7] The connection between death and Christian witness was not intrinsic to the theology of martyrdom, but over time it would become a powerful and evocative element of Christian rhetoric.

Were the Christians "Persecuted"?

Scholars have puzzled since the time of Pliny over the precise nature of the charge against Christians in Roman law.[8] The only early Roman

Washington Press, 1998) and Seth Schwartz, *Imperialism and Jewish Society, 200 BCE to 640 CE* (Princeton: Princeton University Press, 2001).

6. Scholars disagree over the extent to which Christian writers developed an original approach to the issue of martyrdom and witness. W. H. C. Frend, *Martyrdom and Persecution in the Early Church: A Study of a Conflict from the Maccabees to Donatus* (Oxford: Blackwell, 1965) sees the Christian discourse as a largely unoriginal hybrid of Jewish, Greek, and Roman elements, while Glen Bowersock, *Martyrdom and Rome* (Cambridge: Cambridge University Press, 1995), argues that its development was distinctive and essentially without precedent. Daniel Boyarin, *Dying for God: Martyrdom and the Making of Christianity and Judaism* (Stanford, Calif.: Stanford University Press, 1999), suggests that "Christianity" and "Judaism" were overlapping spheres of identification for small-scale face-to-face communities during this period and sees the evolving debate over martyrdom and witness as one of the core issues according to which fixed boundaries began to be established.

7. On fourth-century violence and the rhetoric of martyrdom, see Michael Gaddis, *There Is No Crime for Those Who Have Christ: Religious Violence in the Christian Roman Empire*, (Berkeley: University of California Press, 2005). See also Dayna S. Kalleres "Imagining Martyrdom during Theodosian Peace: John Chrysostom and the Problem of the Judaizers," in Jakob Engberg, Uffe Holmsgaard Eriksen, and Anders Klostergaard Petersen, eds., *Contextualising Early Christian Martyrdom* (Frankfurt: Peter Lang, 2011), pp. 257–75; and Edward Watts, *Riot in Alexandria: Tradition and Group Dynamics in Late Antique Pagan and Christian Communities* (Berkeley: University of California Press, 2010).

8. T. D. Barnes, "Legislation against the Christians," *Journal of Roman Studies* 58 (1968), pp. 32–50, established that there was no specific legislation against the Christians. Still valuable are A. N. Sherwin-White, "The Early Persecutions and Roman Law Again," *Journal of Theological Studies* 3 (1952), pp. 199–213, along with an exchange between Sherwin-White and G. E. M. de Sainte Croix: G. E. M. de Sainte Croix, "Why were the Early Christians

administrative source for the Christians, the letter from Pliny the Younger, the second-century Roman governor of Bithynia and Pontus, to the Emperor Trajan asking for guidance on how to handle the Christians he had found in his province, is revealing on this point. In the letter, Pliny states that he has never encountered Christians before, and though he understands they are dangerous, he has not been able to discover why. He poses a number of questions to the Emperor: does the mere fact of being Christian constitute a crime, or should he expect to find Christians engaging in crimes of the kind with which he is already familiar?[9] Justin's story reflects a similar confusion about whether or how Christian thought and practice are proscribed by Roman law. When the bystander Lucius speaks up for Ptolemy at his hearing, he expresses indignation at the charge against him, which has no clear-cut basis.

The scarcity of the evidence on this point prompts a far-reaching question. Were the early Christians persecuted at all? W. H. C. Frend noted a half-century ago that the evidence is problematic. In the first two centuries there is very limited evidence for Christian encounters with the Roman authorities and none at all that they were actively sought out. Before the reign of Decius in the mid-third century (A.D. 249–51), the evidence for Christian deaths in the context of state-sponsored violence is limited to less than a dozen texts, many of them of uncertain date. More recently, it has been argued that even the persecution of Decius was not aimed especially at the Christians. Rather, Christians in a limited number of cities seem to have fallen foul of a policy aimed at deviance more generally.[10]

The procedures of Roman criminal law did not rest on a police force that could be mobilized to seek out deviants. Because it was a system of accusatory justice, depending on the private motivation of individuals to bring charges against those they believed to be criminals, the prosecution of crime was often patchy and inconsistent. Generally, it fell to the

---

Persecuted?" *Past and Present* 26 (1963), pp. 6–38; A. N. Sherwin-White, "Why were the Early Christians Persecuted? An Amendment," *Past and Present* 27 (1964), pp. 23–27; and G. E. M. de Sainte Croix, "Why Were the Early Christians Persecuted? A Rejoinder," *Past and Present* 27 (1964), pp. 28–33. More recently, see Jakob Engberg, "Martyrdom and Persecution: Pagan Perspectives on the Prosecution and Execution of Christians, c. 110–210 AD," in Engberg, Eriksen, and Petersen, *Contextualising Early Christian Martyrdom*, pp. 93–118.

9. For a well-informed reassessment of the difficulties encountered by Christians, see Jakob Engberg, *Impulsore Chresto: Opposition to Christianity in the Roman Empire, c.50–250 AD*, trans. Gregory Carter (Frankfurt: Peter Lang, 2007).

10. J. B. Rives, "The Decree of Decius and the Religion of Empire," *Journal of Roman Studies* 89 (1999), pp. 135–54.

victim of the crime to bring a charge, but in certain cases, it was possible for a third party who wanted to punish or sideline a rival or enemy to bring change. This point is illustrated by the angry husband in Justin's story: when his Christian wife divorces him, his way of getting back at her is to bring a charge of superstition against her. In this context, it is unlikely that the Christians were the target of systematic policy. To begin with, the majority of the Roman population seem to have become aware of the existence of the Christian minority only very slowly. As a rule, we do not know how they came to the attention of the authorities, even in the recorded instances of interrogation and punishment. In the first two centuries, the few Christians who are attested as having been interrogated may have found themselves on the wrong side of the Roman legal system for any number of reasons. This was not an uncommon experience for members of marginal groups in the empire's provincial cities.

In a number of second-century sources Christians are interrogated before a governor or magistrate, but only a very few attest the actual execution of Christians. For example, Justin's story does not record how Ptolemy and Lucius were punished, merely that they were "led away." Other sources refer to Christians being led away for unspecified punishment after a hearing, or to Christians exhibiting bravery in a context where they can expect to be executed. Since we have no firm evidence for the nature of the charge against the Christians, we should be aware that in those sources where death is not specified, punishments other than execution may have been imposed. Exile, loss of property, and loss of citizen rights were all possibilities. In Justin's story of Ptolemy and Lucius, the punishment is unspecified. Christians were sometimes executed as criminals in the first three centuries, but so rarely that if they were ever singled out for systematic treatment it can only have been during specific (and infrequent) episodes. In at least a few cases, Christians were executed, and sometimes publicly, after a judicial process. From the mid-second century, "acts" began to be written to commemorate the witness of the martyrs. In the *Acts of the Scillitan Martyrs*, who were interrogated in the governor's chambers at Carthage on July 17, 180, we are told that the martyrs were led away to be beheaded after sentencing, but whether the execution itself was public is not clear.[11]

---

11. The text can be found in Herbert Musurillo, *Acts of the Christian Martyrs* (Oxford: Clarendon Press, 1972).

The Spectacular Self: Suffering, Conflict, and Performance in the Early Christian Imagination

If the second century is remembered as an age when the Christians were thrown to the lions, the reason may be a development in Christian rhetoric as much as in Roman practice.[12] From the mid-second century, we begin to see the emergence of the Christian apologists, including Justin Martyr, whose account of Ptolemy and Lucius we encountered above. These second- and third-century writers argued that Christianity should be classed as a licit minority group rather than a criminal affiliation (hence the name "apologists," from the Greek ἀπολογία, "speaking in defense"). But they did more than this: in a context where each province was host to dozens or even hundreds of minority groups who were viewed with suspicion—and often repressed with brutality—by the imperial administration, the Christian writers of the second century created the impression in the imagination of their readers that Christianity had been singled out as a target for particularly unjust treatment. As the apologists began to spread the idea that Christians were being punished unjustly by the Roman authorities, they spread too the idea that the witness of the unjustly punished was one of the most effective means by which the faith was becoming known and admired.

A strand of visionary thinking about the unjust suffering of the righteous is one of the most distinctive legacies which early Christian communities inherited from the New Testament period. A cluster of sayings of Jesus and the apostle Paul had linked the Christian life to a contest with demonic powers, part of a larger conflict between the forces of good and evil. When the end of the world came—and these writers expected that it would come soon—the powers of this world would be brought low, and the meek would inherit the earth. These apocalyptic ideas carried a powerful ethical charge. But if the ideas were magnetic in themselves, it is also important that they were expressed in vivid and memorable thought-pictures. Paul had captured the suddenness and surprise of the coming end time by warning that "the day of the Lord will come like a thief in the night" (1 Thess. 5:2). In his first Letter to the Corinthians, Paul explicitly visualizes the Christian life as an athletic performance:

---

12. Judith Lieu, "The Audience of Apologetics: The Problem of the Martyr Acts," in Engberg, Eriksen, and Petersen, *Contextualizing Early Christian Martyrdom*, pp. 205-24.

Everyone who competes in the games goes into strict training. They do it to get a crown that will not last, but we do it to get a crown that will last forever. Therefore I do not run like someone running aimlessly; I do not fight like a boxer beating the air. No, I strike a blow to my body and make it my slave so that after I have preached to others, I myself will not be disqualified for the prize. (1 Cor. 9:25–27)

It was probably one of Paul's later followers who wrote the *Letter to the Ephesians*. This source recasts Paul's own musing on struggles and sufferings as a source of moral authority into the vivid imagery of the wrestling match, the *palē*.

Put on the full armour (*panoplia*) of God, so that you can take your stand against the devil's schemes. For our struggle (*palē*) is not against flesh and blood, but against the rulers, against the authorities, against the powers of this dark world and against the spiritual forces of evil in the heavenly realms. Therefore put on the full armour of God, so that when the day of evil comes, you may be able to stand your ground. (Eph. 6:11–13)

Here, the mere struggle with the flesh is seen as only the beginning of a contest against far greater powers. Putting on armor is a metaphor for living an ethical life according to Christian norms. It is significant that the encouragement is visualized as a battle. Visualizing virtue serves to fix it in memory. This is supported by modern cognitive research, which emphasizes the connection between visualization and the "stickiness" of memory elements.[13]

In an influential 1991 article, Maureen Tilley argued that early Christians who expected to be tortured or executed prepared themselves for the rigors of interrogation and execution through ascetic training.[14] In the ancient martyr narratives Tilley saw an echo of the psychological techniques adopted by modern dissidents facing torture at the hands of totalitarian regimes. Even if the martyr literature does not directly reflect historical reality, Tilley's point that the successful endurance of the

---

13. See, for example, the articles collected in Sven Ake Christianson, *The Handbook of Emotion and Memory: Research and Theory* (London: Routledge, 1992).

14. Maureen Tilley, "The Ascetic Body and the (Un)making of the World of the Martyr," *Journal of the American Academy of Religion* 59 (1991), pp. 467–79.

martyrs could serve to communicate the power of their faith is invaluable. Tertullian of Carthage emphasized precisely this idea (see below). Also valuable here is a 1996 study by Judith Perkins, who has accounted for the subversive power of the martyr discourse by seeing a new view of subjectivity in their distinctive way of speaking about human suffering: "The early martyr acts...work to create and project 'a new mental set towards the world,' a new mental system for understanding human existence at the same time as they work to challenge the surrounding ideology of the Roman Empire."[15] As we consider how the martyrs were seen by their contemporaries, we will bear in mind how narratives of suffering can change a reader or hearer's own mental landscape.

The mental state of martyrs themselves is perhaps beyond the reach of the surviving evidence, but the communicative value of writing about martyrdom is not in doubt. Two second-century writers illustrate this point. One, Ignatius of Antioch, is a martyr-in-waiting, while the other, Tertullian of Carthage, is a Christian apologist who argues that Christians should be allowed to worship their own God without fearing a criminal charge. Both writers draw on the bravery of the martyrs as a way of broadcasting the moral authority of the faith. Ignatius wrote at the beginning of the second century, at a time when Christianity was still finding itself, slowly emerging from its status as a minority group within Judaism into a Mediterranean world filled with numerous other societies, religious sects, and voluntary associations. Tertullian, by contrast, wrote at the end of the century, when Christianity had begun to establish itself as an independent voice in the thriving cosmopolitan culture of Roman North Africa. Both writers were able to give Christianity a magnetic and distinctive identity through the idea of the brave individual standing against the crowd.

Ignatius of Antioch: The Spectacle of Martyrdom

The visionary letters of Ignatius of Antioch look to the gladiatorial games in the arena as an imaginative framework for thinking about heroic Christian virtue. At around the same time, the author of the Book of Revelation was painting a visionary picture of his own, of the end of the world as a battle between the forces of good and evil. This connection is especially valuable

---

15. Judith Perkins, *The Suffering Self: Pain and Narrative Representation in the Early Christian Era* (London: Routledge, 1995), p. 104; and see also Judith Perkins, *Roman Imperial Identities in the Early Christian Era* (London: Routledge, 2009).

because very little is known about Ignatius. Later writers pieced together a story of how he must have died, but the only contemporary source for him is the group of letters which he wrote to the churches of Asia Minor as he traveled to Rome to stand trial.

In these letters, Ignatius stakes his claim as an imitator of the sufferings of Jesus. But unlike Jesus, Ignatius is a Roman citizen and thus has the right to be tried in Rome. Writing under the reign of Trajan (98–117), Ignatius has in all likelihood heard stories of the great amphitheatre recently constructed in Rome, under the Flavian emperors Vespasian (69–79) and Titus (79–81), known to later centuries as the Colosseum. He knows, too, that gladiatorial games and the execution of criminals take place there. Other sources confirm that in Rome itself criminals could indeed be condemned *ad bestias* at this period, so when Ignatius writes that his most fervent wish is to be cast into the arena to do battle with the beasts he may be indicating the expected punishment for the charge on which he has been taken into custody (we have no firm information about the charge itself). Still, what Ignatius says here is perhaps simply a reflection of how the power of Rome reverberates in the imagination of the eastern provinces.

Writing ahead to the Christian community in Rome, Ignatius anticipates that they will try to intercede on his behalf in order to keep him from being executed, but he wants to dissuade them.

> I write to the Churches, and impress on them all, that I shall willingly die for God, unless you hinder me. I beseech of you not to show an unseasonable good-will towards me. Allow me to become food for the wild beasts, through whose instrumentality it will be granted me to attain to God. I am the wheat of God, and let me be ground by the teeth of the wild beasts, that I may be found the pure bread of Christ. Rather entice the wild beasts, that they may become my tomb, and may leave nothing of my body.[16]

Yet we should not be misled into thinking that Ignatius necessarily expected to die in the games. Later in the letter, he makes it clear that he sees the beasts of the arena as a metaphor.

---

16. Ignatius, *Letter to the Romans*, 4, in Maxwell Staniforth, ed. and tr., *Early Christian Writings: The Apostolic Fathers*, rev. Andrew Louth (Harmondsworth: Penguin Books, 1987).

From Syria even unto Rome I fight with beasts, both by land and sea, both by night and day, being bound to ten leopards, I mean a band of soldiers, who, even when they receive benefits, show themselves all the worse. But I am the more instructed by their injuries [to act as a disciple of Christ]; yet am I not thereby justified? [1 Cor. 4:4] May I enjoy the wild beasts that are prepared for me; and I pray they may be found eager to rush upon me, which also I will entice to devour me speedily, and not deal with me as with some, whom, out of fear, they have not touched. But if they be unwilling to assail me, I will compel them to do so.[17]

And elsewhere in Ignatius's letters he makes it clear that "martyrdom," as he understands it, is not a matter of death but rather a way of living which might, under certain circumstances, lead to premature death. In his study, "If I Suffer... Epistolary Authority in Ignatius of Antioch," Robert Stoops puts the point in the following way:

The 'if I suffer' should not be construed too narrowly. It includes more than the moment of martyrdom. Ignatius's condemnation gave him a chance to demonstrate his faith in a clear and public manner. However, suffering had a much broader meaning for him. The issue was not dying, but enduring to the end and escaping the ruler of this world.[18]

In other words, it is Ignatius's willingness to live for the faith whatever the cost, not the fact of suffering and death, which forms the basis for his spiritual authority.

Tertullian of Carthage: The Narrative Magnetism of Suffering

The fact of suffering and death was magnetic in the Christian imagination. Within decades of the letters of Ignatius, Christian apologists were

---

17. Ibid., *Letter to the Romans*, 5.

18. Robert Stoops, Jr., "If I Suffer... Epistolary Authority in Ignatius of Antioch," *Harvard Theological Review* 80 (1987), pp. 161–78, at p. 172. Stoops refers to the following letters of Ignatius to support this point: *Ephesians* 3.1; *Magnesians*, 1.3 and 9.1; *Trallians*, 1.1; *Romans*, 10.3; *Smyrneans*, 4.2, 9.2, and 12.2; and *To Polycarp*, 3.1–2 and 7.1.

claiming the courage of the martyrs as an invincible weapon in the battle for hearts and minds. The late second-century *Apology* addressed to the "rulers (*antistites*) of the Roman Empire" by Tertullian of Carthage is a case in point. Tertullian argues that the execution of Christians in the Roman arena had become a widespread practice.[19] Tertullian presents violence against Christians as the result of popular scapegoating: "If the Tiber rises so high it floods the walls, or the Nile so low it doesn't flood the fields, if the earth opens, or the heavens don't, if there is famine, if there is plague, instantly the howl goes up, 'The Christians to the lion!' "[20]

Tertullian warns that such executions will only result in increased admiration for Christianity by pagan and Christian alike. His famous phrase, "The blood of the Christians is seed," encapsulates this point.[21] The mechanism here is like that of the bystander in Justin's own *Apology*: when a Christian is unjustly accused, those watching are moved by an impulse of protective indignation. Addressing a defense of Christianity to Scapula, the Roman Proconsul of Africa, Tertullian argued that the deaths of the martyrs had a magnetic effect on the non-Christians in the crowd:

> those whom you regard as masters are only men, and one day they themselves must die. Yet still *this* community will be undying, for be assured that just in the time of its seeming overthrow it is built up into greater power. For anyone who witnesses the noble endurance of its martyrs, is struck by a scruple, and is inflamed with desire to examine into the matter in question; as soon as he comes to know the truth, he straightway enrols himself among the disciples.[22]

It is a bold claim. In reality, men and women who were executed for the sake of deviant religious beliefs could not necessarily expect to be admired by the Roman crowd. Whether Tertullian expected his work to be read by the authorities is debated; it is possible that the main audience for the narrative is the Christian community itself. But the emotional logic of his

---

19. Jesper Carlsen, "Exemplary Deaths in the Arena: Gladiatorial Fights and the Execution of Criminals," in Engberg, Eriksen, and Petersen, *Contextualizing Early Christian Martyrdom*, pp. 75–92.

20. Tertullian, *Apology*, 40, in Allan Menzies, ed., *Latin Christianity: Its Founder, Tertullian*, vol. 3 of Roberts and Donaldson, eds., *Ante-Nicene Fathers*; see note 1.

21. Ibid., *Apology*, 50.

22. Tertullian, *To Scapula*, 5, in Menzies, *Latin Christianity*.

case is compelling. Whether or not the martyrdom of the arena had the effect Tertullian claims for it, his own way of making the case gave it a place of privilege in the landscape of memory.

Martyrdom and the "Media Event": Ethics, Communication, and the Willingness to Die

The willingness of individuals to die in order to draw attention to their cause evokes a comparison to modern suicide terrorism, but significant differences must be taken into account. Most important, in ethical terms, is the willingness of modern terrorists to cause the death of innocent persons in the quest to call attention to their own suffering. This aspect of suicide terrorism has understandably dominated interpretative approaches to the problem.

> Suicide terrorism is particularly effective against democracies, which are sensitive to high casualty rates. Terrorists may calculate that a wave of suicide attacks will raise the costs for the affected populace and force it to push its government to shift its policies to end the violence directed at them.[23]

The logic here is that casualties sustained by the dominant population will lead to irresistible pressure on policymakers. The violence of early Christian martyrdoms seems intentionally to have been contained by the martyrs to their own suffering: there is no evidence that Christians brought to trial or execution sought to involve others in their own suffering.[24] The difference is certainly of central importance. Yet the willingness of the witness to die lends moral power to a message, and this narrative power fascinated Christian writers.

We are left, then, with a question: did the martyrdom of the arena play an important role in the communication of Christian ideas in the

---

23. Mohammed M. Hafez, *Suicide Bombers in Iraq: The Strategy and Ideology of Martyrdom* (Washington, D.C.: United States Institute of Peace Press, 2007), p. 214, characterizing Robert A. Pape, *Dying to Win: The Strategic Logic of Suicide Terrorism* (New York: Random House, 2006).

24. In a later period, after the peace of the Church under Constantine, there is evidence of Christian-on-Christian mob violence, justified by claims of sympathy with the cause of the martyrs, but this is beyond the scope of the present study; see Gaddis, *There Is No Crime*.

second century, or was its real communicative power in its emergence as a theme in Christian writing? Did pagan onlookers indeed perceive those Christians who were executed publicly in the arena as witnesses to an alternative view of reality? Did they find themselves drawn, irresistibly, to the message of the martyrs? And if so, was this the result of sheer moral admiration for their courage? Or did the assault to the senses caused by seeing, hearing, and smelling the violent assaults on their bodies play a role?[25] Were the historical deaths of the martyrs truly spectacular, or was the spectacle of suffering a literary technique for fixing their witness in memory? Did the audience at games and public executions admire the Christians for unusual courage, as Tertullian suggests? Indeed, we may ask whether the crowd was even aware of the fact that these particular criminals were Christian. If Christian executions happened as infrequently as scholars believe, it is likely that only in very limited contexts did the crowd know enough about Christianity or Christian attitudes to death to react in the way Tertullian describes. We will consider below whether the communicative value of martyrdom was in the effect on real historical spectators of women and men who showed physical courage in the arena, or in the achievement of writers whose memorable narratives reached a wide readership. In order to address this question we need to know how ideas and values gained currency in the Roman world.

The Flavian amphitheater in Rome loomed large in the second-century imagination, the decades after its erection saw a massive increase in the construction of Roman amphitheatres in provincial cities. These buildings represented both Rome's power and the prosperity of the cities themselves. The games held there were an expression of civic pride and at the same time a means of co-opting a volatile population to the purposes of the regional elite. From a modern perspective, it may come as a surprise to learn that in the provinces, the games were privately financed by the elite regional families who made up the city councils. The games were not only a contest in the sense that athletes and gladiators struggled with one

---

25. A substantial literature has grown up on spectacle in the Roman provinces, much of which takes Christian martyrdom as an important case study; see, for example, David Potter, "Martyrdom as Spectacle," in Ruth Scodel, ed., *Theater and Society in the Classical World* (Ann Arbor: University of Michigan Press, 1993), pp. 53–88; Carlin Barton, "The Scandal of the Arena," *Representations* 27 (1989), pp. 1–36; and Brent D. Shaw, "Body/Power/Identity: Passions of the Martyrs," *Journal of Early Christian Studies* 4 (1996), pp. 269–312. See also Kate Cooper, "The Voice of the Victim: Gender, Representation and Early Christian Martyrdom," *Bulletin of the John Rylands Library of Manchester* 80.3 (1998), pp. 147–57.

another; they were also the instrument through which the games-givers competed with one another for prestige. Men of the great land-owning families strained their resources to give ever more lavish games as a claim to prestige both for themselves and for their city.

This practice fed an upward spiral of competitive display, and this in turn led to a change in practice in the late second century. During the reign of Marcus Aurelius, Roman procurators began to sell condemned criminals to senators and decurions who were organizing gladiatorial games in the provinces. By substituting criminals for trained gladiators, the producers of the games could cut their costs dramatically, all the while maintaining the facade of splendid prosperity in the provinces.[26]

Those who attended the games were not only complicit in the assertion of hegemony; they were active collaborators. The Israeli scholar Doron Mendels, who has studied ancient martyr narratives through the lens of twentieth-century literature on the media event, suggests that in ancient as in modern society the most effective media used to project a message of social control were those which had a dynamic and interactive component, such as games and sacrifices.[27] By requiring participants to express their conformity in a visible and kinetic way, large-scale public gatherings would both test and develop the hierarchy of power. To disrupt these choreographies successfully was a considerable achievement, and one that could have far-reaching communicative power. The classicists Kathleen M. Coleman and Judith Perkins have argued that what Coleman has called the "Fatal Charades" of the amphitheatre in the first and second centuries, first in Rome and then in the provinces, made it a key location for asserting the power of the established order, and exacerbated the division in Roman society between valued and dispensable persons.[28] Building on Giorgio Agamben's exploration of the relationship between violence, subjectivity, and the law in the thought of Carl Schmidt and Walter Benjamin, Perkins has suggested that the development of the culture of the arena

---

26. The *Senatusconsultum* of 176–77 C.E. survives only as an inscription: *Corpus Inscriptionum Latinarum* ii. 6278 = Dessau, *Inscriptiones Latinae Selectae* 5163, which is discussed in Frend, *Martyrdom and Persecution*, p. 5.

27. Doron Mendels, *The Media Revolution of Early Christianity: An Essay on Eusebius's "Ecclesiastical History"* (Grand Rapids, Mich.: Eerdmans, 1999), at p. 4.

28. Kathleen Coleman, "Fatal Charades: Roman Executions Staged as Mythological Enactments," *Journal of Roman Studies* 80 (1990), pp. 44–73.

reflected a change in the balance of provincial stake-holding in the project of empire.[29]

> This production of new categories of no-account persons and the judicial changes taking shape during the early imperial period that devalued the status of numerous free persons across the empire, opening them to new violent punishments, helped to shred the traditional civic ideal and sparked a resentment that was a contributing factor in the appeal of Christianity.[30]

In this context, writers like Tertullian and Justin offered the heroic deaths of Christians in the arena as an inspired response to the degradation experienced by the population of the provinces.

But this is only part of the story. The real power of the martyr's witness was only provisionally in their effect on those who were present in the arena. An equally important role is played by the writers who celebrate the martyrs as exemplary heroes, whose witness could only inspire those who came into contact with them. We see in the case of Ignatius a writer who is able and willing to convert his own routine trial and execution into an act of heroic witness. Yet however bold the martyr's act of resistance, she or he had only limited control over what would be understood and remembered by those who lived on. In the long run, it was in the retelling that a martyr's story could reach the widest possible audience and could be crafted as a vessel for communicating a compelling message of spiritual power. A writer like Tertullian had the opportunity to guide and amplify his audience's senses to ensure that the "right" moral was drawn from the martyr's suffering. In narrative, the heroic resistance of the martyr is multiplied in the retelling at the same time as the eye or ear is guided to recognize its real value. The writers were perhaps engaged in wishful imagining, but the imagining itself was to become a potent cultural force. By capturing the moment of the martyr's gesture in a frame of unjust

---

29. See Giorgio Agamben, *Homo Sacer: Sovereign Power and Bare Life*, trans. Daniel Heller-Roazen (Stanford, Calif.: Stanford University Press, 1998) and *State of Exception*, trans. Kevin Attell (Chicago: University of Chicago Press, 2005).

30. Judith Perkins, "The Spectacle of 'Bare Life' in Martial's *Liber Spectaculorum* and Martyr Discourse," in Donald Lateiner, Barbara K. Gold, and Judith Perkins, eds., *Roman Literature, Gender, and Reception: Domina Illustris, Essays in Honor of Judith Peller Hallett* (London: Routledge, 2013). I am grateful to the author for making an early version of this essay available to me.

suffering and moral heroism, Tertullian and his fellow apologists were able to generate a unique atmosphere of moral solidarity for the Christian movement. To be sure, the Christians were not the only provincials to experience the brutality of Roman imperial rule, or to face a potentially senseless death under a brutal regime. But by comparison to others who suffered under the same circumstances, what marked out the Christian communities of resistance was an improvisational collaboration between the living and the dead. Those who survived were able to draw a valuable lesson from what happened to those who died, and in memory the death of "no-account persons" became a bold act of faith, a heroic gesture placing an earthly empire under the power of a heavenly kingdom.

2

Martyrdom in Islamic Thought and Praxis

A HISTORICAL SURVEY

Asma Afsaruddin

THIS CHAPTER SURVEYS the treatment of martyrdom, broadly defined, in the major textual sources of classical Islam, followed by a brief discussion of selective modern and contemporary debates on the parameters of martyrdom and the boundaries between legitimate and illegitimate violence. It provides summaries of the major perspectives on this critical topic to be found in the Qur'an, Islam's foundational text, and in the *hadith* literature containing the sayings attributed to the Prophet Muhammad. Additionally, a chronological survey of relevant sections from the rich exegetical literature of the classical and medieval periods (roughly between the seventh and fifteenth centuries of the Common Era) is selectively presented, allowing us to chart a shifting trajectory of meanings associated with the concept of martyrdom and to trace the development of a cult of military martyrdom over time in spite of the lack of scriptural support for such a cult. Such a diachronic study challenges the understanding of martyrdom in the Islamic context as a static and monolithic concept, unconnected to specific socio-historical circumstances and authorial proclivities.

It should be noted that the emphasis is on Sunni sources which record majoritarian Muslims' views of martyrdom and its various inflections. Shiʿi perspectives are briefly dwelt upon to allow for some essential historical differences to emerge and to nuance our understanding of martyrdom in the variegated Islamic context. Significantly, the rise of the modern nation-state has blurred a number of these sectarian differences as martyrdom acquired a new connotation in the twentieth century—deliberate self-immolation for the redemption of national honor and glory.

Martyrdom in the Qur'an

The Arabic term *shahid* used almost exclusively in later literature to refer to a martyr, military or otherwise, does not occur in the Qur'an in this sense. *Shahīd*, and its cognate *shāhid*,[1] refer in the Qur'an only to a legal or eyewitness, used for both God and humans in appropriate contexts (for example, Qur'an 3:98; 6:19; 41:53). Similarly, *shahada* in its Qur'anic usage signifies "witness/witnessing" and has nothing to do with martyrdom in the later conventional sense. Qur'anic phrases commonly understood to refer to the military martyr include *man qutila fi sabil allah/ alladhina qutilu fi sabil allah* ("those who are slain in the path of God"; cf. Qur'an 2:154; 3:169) and variations thereof. Only in later extra-Qur'anic literature (biographies of the Prophet, exegeses of the Qur'an, and *hadith*) does *shahid*—and its plural *shuhada'*—acquire the specific meaning of "one who bears witness for the faith," particularly by laying down his or her life.[2] Extraneous, particularly Christian, influence may be suspected in the semantic transformation of these terms. The Syriac word for martyr-witness *sahda* is very likely responsible for the Arabic *shahid*'s subsequent acquisition of the secondary meaning of "martyr."[3] Another concept of selling or bartering (*yashra/yashrun*) one's self or the life of this world for the hereafter (Qur'an 4:74; cf. 9:111) has also been connected to the notion of martyrdom.

---

1. These Arabic terms are fully transliterated here in order to show the differences in the original lexemes.

2. Even when scholars agree that the singular term *shahid* does not explicitly refer to a martyr in the Qur'an, they nevertheless proceed to translate the plural *shuhada'* unambiguously as "martyrs"; without a convincing explanation as to why the plural should signify something dramatically different compared to the singular; see, for example, Michael Bonner, *Jihad in Islamic History* (Princeton: Princeton University Press, 2006), p. 74; and David Cook, *Martyrdom in Islam* (Cambridge: Cambridge University Press, 2007), p. 16.

3. See Arthur Jeffrey, *The Foreign Vocabulary of the Qur'an* (Baroda, 1938), p. 187; A. J. Wensinck, "The Oriental Doctrine of the Martyrs," in his *Semietische Studiën uit de nalatenschap* (Leiden, 1941), pp. 91–113; and my chapter "Competing Perspectives on Jihad and 'Martyrdom' in Early Islamic Sources," in Brian Wicker, ed., *Witnesses to Faith? Martyrdom in Christianity and Islam* (Aldershot: Ashgate, 2006), pp. 15–31.

Such Qur'anic locutions are, therefore, ambiguous and do not in themselves explicitly refer to military martyrdom. In the exegetical literature, these expressions however have often been understood as endorsing the concept of earning martyrdom by dying on the battlefield; but it must be noted that the terms *shahid* or *shuhada'* are not always used in these contexts, particularly in earlier exegetical works. For example in his commentary on Qur'an 3:157 (which states, "If you are slain in the path of God or die, then there is pardon and mercy from God better than what they amass [in this world]"), the celebrated exegete al-Tabari (d. 923)[4] says that, according to this verse, the faithful should strive in the path of God and fight the enemies of God, secure in the knowledge that if they should be slain in battle or die while traveling, God has promised them pardon and mercy in the next world.[5] Al-Tabari does not use the term *shahid* or its derivatives to gloss the phrase *la-in qutiltum fi sabil allah* ("if you are slain in the path of God"), as occurs in this verse.

In his commentary on a related verse (Qur'an 22:58, which states, "Those who emigrated in the path of God and then were slain or died, God will provide handsome provisions for them; indeed God is the best of providers"), al-Tabari remarks that this verse refers to those early Muslims from the first generation (known as the Companions of the Prophet) who had departed from their native lands and families to emigrate to Medina in order to please God, serve him, and undertake the military jihad against His enemies.[6] Whether they were subsequently killed or died, the verse promises that God will confer on them abundant reward in Paradise on the Day of Judgment. Significantly, al-Tabari indicates that there were differences of opinion among early Muslims concerning the status of the military martyr versus the pious individual who died of natural causes—which of the two was the more morally excellent? Some were of the opinion that

---

4. All dates in this chapter are Common Era.

5. Al-Tabari, *Jami' al-bayan fi tafsir al-Qur'an* (Beirut: Dar al-kutub al- 'ilmiyya, 1997), vol. 3, p. 193.

6. Here in this passage al-Tabari is clearly referring to the combative jihad. The Arabic term *jihad* broadly refers to "struggle" and "striving" for a good and noble cause, even as mundane a cause as earning a livelihood to support one's family. In Islamic ethics, the eternal human struggle on earth is for the purpose of commanding good and preventing wrong, which should be attempted through a variety of means ranging from spiritual to physical, and may include armed combat in the face of an intractable enemy and persistent wrongdoing. For an overview of this spectrum of meanings, see the diverse collection of articles in Qamar-ul Huda, ed., *Crescent and Dove: Peace and Conflict Resolution in Islam* (Washington, D.C.: United States Institute of Peace, 2010).

the one who was slain and the one who died of natural causes were of the same status while others maintained that the one who was slain, that is on the battlefield, had achieved greater merit (*afdal*). Al-Tabari comments that this verse was revealed to the Prophet Muhammad in order to settle this internal debate among the faithful and to inform them that the one who is slain and the one who dies of natural causes in the path of God attain the same reward in the hereafter.[7] In other words, the average pious Muslim who dies of old age in his or her bed and the heroic warrior who falls on the battlefield defending Muslims attain to the same level of moral excellence; this verse, therefore, serves as an important corrective to a potential cultic reverence for military martyrdom. It is also noteworthy that al-Tabari notably does not use *shahid* or its derivatives in his explication of this verse.

Other exegetes indicate that the debate concerning which was the more meritorious manner of dying—naturally or being slain in the path of God—was a robust and persistent one. Thus the late twelfth-century commentator Fakhr al-Din al-Razi (d. 1210) explains that the phrase "Then they were slain or they died," in Qur'an 22:58 means that God's promise of a handsome provision (*rizq*) encompasses both equally. At the basic linguistic level, he comments, the verse does not indicate either preference or equal status for these two groups and does not on its surface support those who say that the one slain in jihad and the one who dies in his bed are equal in moral status. This understanding of an equal status finds support, however, in a *hadith* related by Anas b. Malik in which the Prophet said, "The one who is slain in the path of God the Exalted (*al-maqtul fi sabil allah ta'ala*) and the one who dies [of natural causes] in the path of God (*al-mutawaffa' fi sabil allah bi-ghayr qatl*) are the equal of one other in regard to the blessings and reward [that they are entitled to]."[8]

A similar range of views is indicated by the Cordoban Qur'an commentator al-Qurtubi (d. 1273) in his exegesis of Qur'an 22:58. He notes that some scholars were of the opinion that one who is slain in the path of God is better (*afdal*) than the one who dies of natural causes, but the revelation of this verse affirmed that both were equal in status and God would accord both a handsome provision in the hereafter. In spite of that, he notes, the religious law (*Shari'a*) as interpreted by the jurists appears to

7. Al-Tabari, *Jami' al-bayan*, vol. 9, p. 182.

8. Al-Razi, *al-Tafsir al-kabir* (Beirut: Dar ihya al-turath al-'arabi, 1999), vol. 8, p. 244.

indicate the superior status of the slain (*anna 'l-maqtul afdal*). Some scholars maintained that the one who is slain in the path of God and the one
who dies in the path of God is a martyr (*shahid*), but the slain individual
enjoys a distinctive status on account of what he encountered for the sake
of God (*ma asabahu fi dhat allah*). But other scholars (not identified by
al-Qurtubi) stated that they were equal, adducing as a proof-text Qur'an
4:100 which states, "Whoever emerges from his home in order to emigrate to God and His apostle, and is then overtaken by death, his reward
is already assured of with God." This verse after all makes no reference
to fighting and promises certain divine reward for the pious Muslim who
died on his way to Medina. Al-Qurtubi further cites here the well-known
hadith concerning the female Companion Umm Haram who was thrown
from her riding mount and died and was not slain—the Prophet said
addressing her, "You are among the first [rank of believers] (*anti min
al-awwalin*)." Other *hadiths* affirming the equal status of both groups of
people are recorded by al-Qurtubi.[9] These proof-texts clearly establish that
martyrdom was assigned to those who died after having lived pious and
exemplary lives, especially after having faced hardship in the pursuit of
some noble objective, and that military exploits were not a *sine qua non* in
the construction of martyrdom in the Islamic context, as is often assumed.

Two verses: "Do not say regarding those who are slain in the path of
God that they are dead; rather they are alive but you are not aware" (Qur'an
2:154) and "Do not consider as dead those who are slain in the path of God;
rather they are alive and well-provided for in the presence of their Lord"
(Qur'an 3:169) are the most frequently quoted in regard to the military
martyr and to the bounteous reward he will reap in the next world. Even
though these verses use the ambiguous, polysemous phrase *man qutila fi
sabil allah* ("those who are slain in the path of God")—a locution that could
semantically refer to different ways of being killed—almost all our exegetes use the term *shahid* and its derivatives in their explication of these
verses. For example, the early exegete Muqatil b. Sulayman (d. c.767) says
that Qur'an 2:154 was revealed in regard to fourteen Muslims who were
slain during the early battle of Badr (in 624). The revelation of this verse
served to inform the believers that those who were slain in the path of God
were not dead but alive, reaping their reward in paradise in the presence
of God. In recognition of their high moral status, the souls of the martyrs

9. Al-Qurtubi, *al-Jami' li-ahkam al-Qur'an* (Beirut: Dar al-kitab al-'arabi, 2001), vol. 12,
pp. 82–83.

(*al-shuhada'*) reside near the lotus tree closest to the throne of God (*sidrat al-muntaha*).[10] Qur'an 3:169, according to Muqatil, was also revealed concerning those killed in the battle of Badr, who are similarly not to be regarded as dead but as alive, enjoying the fruits (*al-thimar*) of heaven. God renders the souls of the martyrs as green birds which flit about in heaven under candelabra suspended over the divine throne. When they alight on these candelabra, God appears before them and asks them if He can provide for anything more. He asks the same question of them three times. On the third occasion, they wish aloud that their souls could be returned to their bodies, so that "we may fight in your path again." On having experienced God's generosity towards them, they wish to go back and inform their brethren of the joys that await them and to counsel that if they should encounter fighting, "they should hasten themselves towards martyrdom" (*sari'u bi-anfusihim ila 'l-shahada*). At that God informed them that He was about to reveal Qur'an 3:169 to His prophet so that he may inform their brethren about their enviable situation in paradise.[11]

In al-Tabari's commentary on Qur'an 2:154, we find a much more detailed description of the type of heavenly rewards awaiting specific categories of believers, indicating the extent to which this issue had begun to exercise the minds of exegetes by the late ninth century. He begins by commenting that in this verse God addresses the believers and exhorts them to seek His help while patiently obeying Him in their striving against their enemies, forsaking all that constitutes disobedience to Him and in carrying out the rest of their religious obligations. They are also commanded not to say regarding those who are slain in the path of God that they are dead (*mayyit*), for the dead are lifeless and deprived of their senses, unable to enjoy pleasures and experience bliss. Rather, "those among you and from the rest of My creation who are killed in the path of God are alive in My presence, [immersed] in life and bliss, [enjoying] a blissful existence and glorious provisions, exulting in what I have bestowed on them of My bounty and conferred on them of My generosity."[12]

With regard to Qur'an 3:169, al-Tabari relates it specifically to those Companions killed at the second major battle of Uhud (in 625). This verse served to inform the Prophet that he should not regard these fallen

---

10. Muqatil b. Sulayman, *Tafsir*, ed. 'Abd Allah Mahmud Shihata (Beirut: Mu'assasat al-ta'rikh al-'arabi, 2002), vol. 1, p. 151.

11. Ibid., vol. 1, p. 314.

12. Al-Tabari, *Jami' al-bayan*, vol. 2, p. 42.

Companions as dead; that is to say that they are devoid of feeling and the ability to feel pleasure. Rather, "they are alive in My presence, delighting in My sustenance, exulting and rejoicing in what I grant them from my generosity and mercy, bestowing on them the abundance of My reward and provisions."[13] Al-Tabari then proceeds to relate several reports which detail the heavenly pleasures awaiting the souls of the martyrs. In one of these reports, on the authority of the famous Companion Ibn 'Abbas, Muhammad is quoted as saying that those who had been slain at Uhud would be transformed into souls residing in green birds who would frequent the rivers of paradise, eat of its fruits and alight on golden candelabra in the shadow of the Divine Throne. Al-Tabari's cause of revelation for this verse is similar to the one given by Muqatil: When these martyrs wished out loud that they could inform their brethren on earth about their blissful state, God revealed these verses (3:169–70).[14] This sampling of exegeses of Qur'ān 2:154 and 3:169 is highly revealing of how a cultic reverence for military martyrdom progressively came to be articulated and read back into these verses, despite the lack of overt reference to first, the military martyr; and second, to any assumption of their higher status vis-à-vis other believers who died, for example, while emigrating to Medina.[15] Many exegetes elaborate upon bounteous posthumous, pre-resurrection pleasures, not mentioned in the Qur'an, earmarked primarily for military martyrs to indicate their special status before God and, furthermore, to apparently exhort an otherwise reluctant population to enlist in the imperial armies of the first two dynasties in Islamic history—the Umayyads (reigned between 661–750) and the 'Abbasids (750–1258).[16]

Martyrdom in the Hadith Literature

A number of early *hadith* compilations in particular preserve multiple definitions of martyrdom, engendered by the polyvalent Qur'anic locution *man qutila fi sabil allah*, which increasingly becomes conflated with the term

---

13. Ibid., vol. 3, p. 513.

14. Ibid., vol. 3, pp. 513–16. For a fuller discussion of these verses, see my *Striving in the Path of God: Jihad and Martyrdom in Islamic Thought* (Oxford: Oxford University Press, 2013), chap. 4.

15. The emigration to Medina from Mecca by Muslims to escape the persecution of the pagan Arabs, known in Arabic as *hijra*, is dated to 622 c.e. and marks the commencement of the Islamic era. It was deemed to be a particularly meritorious act for the earliest Muslims.

16. See my *Striving in the Path of God*, pp. 95–290, for further discussion of this topic.

shahid. But even *shahid,* which in later literature, predominantly refers to the military martyr, is glossed in various ways in the early literature. Thus the *Musannaf* of 'Abd al-Razzaq b. Hammam al-San'ani (d. 827) contains a number of early Companion reports which relate competing definitions of *shahid.* One report attributed to the Companion Abu Hurayra states that the *shahid* is one who, were he to die in his bed, would enter heaven (the explanatory note that follows states that it refers to someone who dies in his bed and is without sin, *la dhanb lahu*).[17] Another report related by the early Muslim authority Masruq b. al-Ajda' (d. 683) declares that there are four types of *shahada* or martyrdom for Muslims: the plague, parturition or delivery of a child, drowning, and a stomach ailment.[18] Significantly, there is no mention of martyrdom being earned on account of dying on the battlefield in this early report. An expanded version of this report, how-ever, originating with the Companion Abu Hurayra, quotes the Prophet as adding to this list of those who achieve martyrdom "one who is killed in the way of God (*man qutila fi sabil Allah*)."[19] It is this expanded version containing the full, five definitions of a *shahid* that is recorded later in the famous *hadith* collection, known as the *Sahih* of al-Bukhari.[20]

The *Muwatta'* of the early Medinan jurist Malik b. Anas (d. 795) records that the Prophet identified seven kinds of martyrs, in addition to those who died from fighting in God's way. Thus, "he who dies as a victim of an epidemic is a martyr; he who dies from drowning is a martyr; he who dies from pleurisy is a martyr; he who dies from diarrhoea is a martyr; he who dies by [being burned in] fire is a martyr; he who dies by being struck by a dilapidated wall falling is a martyr; and the woman who dies in childbed is a martyr."[21] The *Muwatta'* also records the *hadith* that all the martyr's sins are forgiven except for his debt; here the martyr is assumed to be the military martyr who is singled out for this special distinction.[22]

---

17. 'Abd al-Razzaq, *al-Musannaf,* ed. Ayman Nasr al-Din al-Azhari (Beirut: Dar al-kutub al-'ilmiyya, 2000), vol. 5, p. 268. For a variant, see Muslim, *Sahih* (Beirut: Dar Ibn Hazm, 1995), vol. 3, pp. 1204–5.

18. 'Abd al-Razzaq, *Musannaf,* vol. 5, p. 271.

19. Ibid., vol. 5, pp. 270–71.

20. Al-Bukhari, *Sahih,* ed. Qasim al-Shamma'i al-Rifa'i (Beirut: Dar al-qalam, n.d.), vol. 2, pp. 420–21.

21. Malik b. Anas, *Al-Muwatta',* ed. Bashshar 'Awad Ma'ruf and Mahmud Muhammad Khalil (Beirut: Mu'assasat al-risala, 1993), vol. 1, pp. 366–67.

22. Ibid., vol. 1, p. 365.

The *Musannaf* of Ibn Abi Shayba (d. 849), another well-known early *hadith* work, also records a diversity of early and competing views on what constitutes martyrdom and who qualifies for it. A *hadith* which is *mursal* (that is, lacking the name of the Companion, that is to say a first generation Muslim who would have heard it directly from the Prophet) is narrated by the famous Successor (from the second generation of Muslims after the Companions) al-Hasan al-Basri (d. 728), in which the Prophet remarks that the average (pious) person after death is pleased with his or her reward in the hereafter and has no desire to return to this world. But when he becomes aware of the abundance of good things (*al-na'im*) which awaits the martyr (*al-shahid*), then he yearns to go back in order to be slain again.[23] Here the *shahid* is specifically identified as a military martyr, whose moral status in this report is higher than that of a pious noncombatant believer. Another report attributed to a Companion (not the Prophet) assigns specific, detailed rewards to the military martyr denied to any other. It is narrated by the early Syrian authority Makhul (d. 731) who was known for his hawkish views and who was an ardent supporter of the Umayyads and their battles against the Byzantines. He states, "The martyr has six distinctive features in the presence of God: God forgives his sins as soon as the first drop of his blood strikes the earth; he will enjoy the vestments of faith; he will marry a dark-eyed celestial damsel (*al-hur al-'ayn*); a door to paradise will open for him; he will be spared the torments of the grave; and, finally, he will be kept safe from the greatest fear, that of the Day of Resurrection."[24] The report is clearly meant to exhort reluctant young, impressionable men to enlist in the army of the otherwise unpopular Umayyad rulers, widely regarded as impious and illegitimate by the majority of Muslims, and to die for them.

But, as in 'Abd al-Razzaq's *Musannaf*, other *hadith*s and non-prophetic reports challenge a circumscribed understanding of martyrdom that was clearly gaining ground in the early eighth century. In one such significant *hadith*, the prominent Companion Abu Hurayra, relates, I heard the Messenger of God, peace and blessings be upon him, ask,

"Who do you regard as *shahid*?" Those present replied, "One who is slain in the path of God (*al-maqtul fi sabil allah*)." The Prophet

---

23. Ibn Abi Shayba, *al-Kitab al-Musannaf fi 'l-ahadith wa-'l-athar*, ed. Muhammad 'Abd al-Salam Shahin (Beirut: Dar al-kutub al- 'ilmiyya, 1995), vol. 4, p. 226.

24. Ibid.

exclaimed, "Then the martyrs of my community would be few indeed! The one who is slain (*al-qatil*) in the path of God is a martyr; the one who is felled to the ground from his mount in the path of God is a martyr; the one who drowns in the path of God is a martyr; and the one who is stricken by pleurisy in the path of God."[25]

In a variant *hadith* narrated by another Companion ʿUbada b. al-Samit, the Prophet asks a similar question of his Companions regarding those who are to be considered among the martyrs. When they identified as a martyr the one who fights in the path of God and is then slain, Muhammad exclaimed that the martyrs of his community would be too few in number. He consequently proceeded to include among martyrs, beside the one slain in the path of God, the one who dies from a stomach ailment and the woman who dies during pregnancy.[26] Other variants are given. A non-prophetic variant report states simply, "The plague is martyrdom; drowning is martyrdom, as is [dying from a] stomach [ailment] and [from] parturition."[27]

Two other variants recorded by Ibn Abi Shayba are worthy of note. According to one of them, the famous Companion ʿAbd Allah b. Masʿud is said to have included the one who drowns in the sea, or falls from the mountains, or is devoured by wild animals among "the martyrs in the presence of God on the Day of Resurrection." The other variant quotes Masruq as saying, "The plague, the stomach [ailment], parturition, drowning, and whatever afflicts a Muslim constitutes martyrdom (*shahada*) for him."[28] In these reports, martyrdom is expansively construed as death resulting from any kind of suffering and pain endured by the faithful during their earthly existence. These reports do not use the phrase *fi sabil allah* for non-military afflictions but the implication is nevertheless clear: earthly suffering of the righteous leading to death earns them martyrdom at least on a par with the military kind. The existence of these reports also makes clear that the definition of martyrdom and the status of the martyr, military and non-military, were highly contested issues in the formative period

---

25. Ibid., vol. 4, p. 227.

26. Ibid.

27. Ibid.

28. Ibid.

and are reflective of what we might term a robust politics of piety underway in this time.

*Hadith*s and reports which preserve the early expansive meanings of *shahid* and *shahada*, as encountered in the two *Musannaf* works and the *Muwatta'* of Malik, are also preserved in early treatises on jihad, such as the *Kitab al-jihad* of the Khurasanian merchant and religious scholar Ibn al-Mubarak (d. 797).[29] Thus according to a *hadith* recorded by Ibn al-Mubarak, the Prophet once asked some of his Companions what they regarded as martyrdom (*al-shahada*). They said that it was being killed in the way of God. The Prophet then responded with the seven categories of martyrs.[30] Another report goes back to the Companion 'Umar b. al-Khattab, the second caliph of Islam, who is said to have remarked, "Indeed there are some people who fight out of a desire for this world, while others fight for glory and renown, and yet others who fight only reactively. But there are those who fight 'desiring/seeking the face of God' (*ibtigha' wajh allah*), and they are the martyrs (*al-shuhada'*)."[31] This last report emphasizes correct intent (*niyya*)—fighting only for the sake of God—in determining genuine military martyrdom.

In comparison with the earlier *Musannaf* works, certain reports recorded in the *Sahih* of al-Bukhari clearly assign a more privileged status to military martyrs with special rewards in the hereafter earmarked for them alone. One such *hadith* states that there is an "abode of martyrs" (*dar al-shuhada'*), the best and most excellent of abodes in the hereafter, which was not mentioned in earlier collections.[32] Another *hadith* on the authority of the well-known Companion Abu Hurayra declares that whoever is wounded in the path of God (and God knows best who is truly wounded in His path) will be resurrected on the Day of Judgment with the color of blood and breath of musk.[33]

Some *hadith*s warn, however, that the exalted status of the warrior (*mujahid*) should not lead to the deliberate courting of martyrdom on

---

29. For an analysis of Ibn al-Mubarak's *Kitab al-jihad*, see Michael Bonner, "Some Observations Concerning the Early Development of Jihad on the Arab-Byzantine Frontier," *Studia Islamica* 75 (1992), pp. 19–31.

30. Ibn Abi Shayba, *al-Kitab al-Musannaf*, p. 40.

31. Ibid., p. 19.

32. Al-Bukhari, *Sahih*, vol. 4, p. 409.

33. Ibid., vol. 4, p. 412.

the part of the faithful by seeking to confront the enemy. As recorded by al-Bukhari, a *hadith* on the authority of 'Abd Allah b. Abi Awfa relates that the Prophet, during a military campaign, would customarily wait till the sun had tilted toward the West and then address his troops thus, "Do not wish to meet the enemy, O People, and ask forgiveness of God. When you meet them, be forbearing (*fa-'sbiru*) and know that paradise lies below the shade of the swords."[34]

The *Sunan* of al-Tirmidhi (d. 892), another authoritative *hadith* collection, includes a noteworthy *hadith* related by the second caliph 'Umar (d. 644) in which he states that he had heard the Prophet enumerate four types of martyrs (*al-shuhada'*): (1) a believing man of strong faith who meets the enemy with resolute and honest intent and is slain; he is the best kind; (2) a believing man of strong faith who on encountering the enemy falters due to a twinge of cowardice and is slain; he is in the second rank; (3) a believing man who mixes good deeds with bad but meets the enemy with honest intent and is slain; he is in the third rank; and (4) a believing man who sins against himself but meets the enemy with resolute intent and is slain; he is in the fourth rank.[35] Significantly, this *hadith* from 'Umar has replaced the five to seven categories of noncombative and combative martyrs (as enumerated in the earlier collections of Malik, al-Bukhari, and Muslim), with only combative ones. The progressively higher moral evaluation of the military martyr over the non-military one through the centuries is clearly signaled in this report.

Other Constructions of Martyrdom

This higher evaluation of military martyrdom becomes more blatant and pervasive in later popular *fada'il al-jihad* ("the excellences of the military jihad") works, especially those composed during the Mamluk period in the context of Crusader and Mongol attacks. One such work is the *Mashari' al-ashwaq ila masari' al-'ushshaq fi 'l-jihad wa-fada'ilihi* ("The Watering-Holes of Longing for the Battle-Grounds of Lovers") composed by the anti-Crusader warrior, Ahmad b. Ibrahim Ibn al-Nahhas (d. 1411). In the fraught circumstances in which Muslims found themselves at this historical juncture, Ibn al-Nahhas's tone in this treatise is urgent

---

34. Ibid., vol. 4, pp. 481–82.

35. Al-Tirmidhi, *Sunan*, ed. Muhammad Fu'ad 'Abd al-Baqi (Beirut: Dar al-kutub al-'ilmiyya, n.d.), vol. 4, p. 152.

and hortatory, attempting to rouse the faithful to repel the invaders by recording reports which extol the benefits of fighting and promise exaggerated rewards in the hereafter to the military martyr. Thus there is an extensive section on the merits of jihad and those who undertake it (fadl al-jihad wa-'l-mujahidin fi sabil allah). In some reports recorded by the author, jihad is declared to be more meritorious than giving the call to prayer; or more meritorious than offering water to pilgrims during the hajj and undertaking the lesser pilgrimage.[36] Yet other reports maintain that the combative jihad was the best of all actions without exception ('ala 'l-itlaq); that jihad was the most beloved of all actions to God; that the fighter (mujahid) was the best of all people, and that no one is able to carry out a deed that was the equivalent of al-jihad fi sabil allah.[37]

But noncombative significations of jihad and martyrdom continued to persist in the later period and their purview even expanded in certain kinds of literature. For example, in treatises on the excellences of knowledge, the status of martyr was extended to an individual who died while engaged in the pursuit and dissemination of knowledge. This is encoded in a report emanating from the two Companions Abu Hurayra and Abu Dharr, as recorded by the eleventh-century Andalusian scholar Ibn 'Abd al-Barr (d. 1071) which quotes the Prophet as saying, "When death overtakes the seeker of knowledge while he is so engaged, then he dies a martyr."[38] Another hadith related by the Companion Abu Hurayra, is recorded by Ibn 'Abd al-Barr, who states, "The prophets are two ranks higher in excellence than the scholars while the scholars are a rank above the martyrs in excellence," signifying a categorical diminution in the status of the warrior, both in this world and the next.[39] Seeking knowledge was deemed to be as meritorious as defending Islamic realms, as clearly indicated in a hadith recorded by al-Tirmidhi in which Muhammad states, "Whoever departs in the pursuit of knowledge is in the path of God (fi sabil

---

36. Mashari' 'l-ashwaq ila masari' al-'ushshaq fi 'l-jihad wa-fada'ilihi (Beirut: Dar al-basha'ir al-islamiyya, 2002), vol. 1, pp. 138–40. The Hajj refers to the annual pilgrimage to Mecca to be undertaken by Muslims at least once in their lifetime if their financial circumstances permit. The "lesser pilgrimage" ('umra in Arabic) may be undertaken at any time of the year, is shorter in duration compared to the Hajj, and is an act of supererogation.

37. Mashari' 'l-ashwaq, vol. 1, pp. 141–51.

38. Ibn 'Abd al-Barr, Jami' bayan al-'ilm wa-fadlihi, ed. 'Abd al-Hamid Muhammad al-Sa'dani (Beirut: Dar al-kutub al- 'ilmiyya, 2000), p. 49; also in Ibn Qayyim al-Jawziyya, Fadl al-'ilm wa-l-'ulama', ed. Salih Ahmad al-Shami (Beirut: al-Maktab al-islami, 2001), p. 100.

39. Ibn 'Abd al-Barr, Jami' bayan al-'ilm, p. 18.

Allah) until he returns."[40] Of note is the use of the phrase *fi sabil Allah* in conjunction with the pursuit of knowledge in this *hadith*, a phrase otherwise more commonly used in reference to armed combat.

The chaste individual who died of unrequited romantic love also came to be considered a martyr in certain circles.[41] Sufi mystical literature in general further emphasizes the greater internal jihad of the individual against his/her carnal self (*nafs*), famously advocated by Muhammad upon his return from a military campaign, "We have returned from the lesser *jihad* to the greater *jihad*."[42] A greater emphasis on the *jihad al-nafs,* that is to say "the struggle of the self/soul," implies that any pious believer who patiently endures life's trials and tribulations may attain to martyrdom upon death, a view already indicated by *hadiths* found in early compilations, as we noted earlier. The qualities of patience and forbearance, encompassed by the Arabic Qur'anic term *sabr* and its derivatives, in fact became the counterfoil to martial swashbuckling virtues and emphasized by many as the most important component of the overall human striving on earth, that is to say, of jihad in the broadest sense. In tandem with treatises written to extol the merits of the military jihad, we thus find fairly early treatises written in praise of *sabr* or patient forbearance.

One such early monograph available to us on the merits of patience and forbearance is the ninth-century work of Abu Bakr 'Abd Allah b. Muhammad ibn Abi 'l-Dunya (d. 894), called *al-Sabr wa-'l-thawab 'alayhi* ("Patience and the Rewards for It"). Renowned for his piety and abstemiousness, Ibn Abi 'l-Dunya was a popular teacher and was the author of over one hundred works. Most of Ibn Abi 'l-Dunya's works, like the current one under discussion, deal with ethics and the cultivation of exemplary virtues, such as patience, humility, trust in God, charity, and so on. *Al-Sabr wa-'l-thawab 'alayhi* is remarkable for having preserved from a relatively early period *hadiths*, Companion reports, and other kinds of anecdotes, which eulogize the attribute of *sabr* as superior to other qualities and give assurance of bounteous rewards in the hereafter for those who possess and manifest this attribute. In this work, patience above all is defined as an essential aspect of faith (*al-iman*). Thus according to 'Ali

---

40. Cited by Ibn Qayyim al-Jawziyya, *Fadl al-'ilm*, p. 99.

41. See, for example, Lois Giffen, *Theory of Profane Love among the Arabs: The Development of a Genre* (New York: University of London Press, 1971), esp. pp. 99–116.

42. See Jack Renard, "*Al-Jihad al-akbar:* Notes on a Theme in Islamic Spirituality," *Muslim World* 78 (1988), pp. 225–42.

b. Abi Talib, patience in relation to faith is in the position of the head to the body, with the implication that faith itself would be gravely impaired if patience were to be severed from it. Subsequently 'Ali went even further and proclaimed that whoever lacks patience, lacks faith.[43] *Sabr* is also non-aggressive and non-vindictive, according to some. Thus the early Basran pious scholar al-Hasan al-Basri is said to have declared, "O mankind, do not cause harm; if you are harmed, be patiently forbearing!"[44] According to the Kufan pietist Muhammad b. Suqa, patiently awaiting deliverance (*al-faraj*) from a trial is an act of worship.[45] Since trials and tribulations are a constant staple of life, "the believer is in need of patience as much as he is in need of food and drink."[46]

This perspective is affirmed in *hadiths* and other kinds of reports and anecdotes recorded by Ibn Abi 'l-Dunya which point to the greater moral excellence of those who possess *sabr*. In one such *hadith*, the Prophet is quoted as saying, "Whoever is patient (*yasbir*), God will grant him solace (*yusabbiruhu*), and no one has been granted anything better or more abundant than patience."[47] Other reports included by Ibn Abi 'l-Dunya explicitly proclaim that those practicing the virtues of veracity and patience are equivalent in moral status to the military martyr. In one such report, 'Abd al-'Aziz b. Abi Rawwad (d. 775), a pious scholar of Khurasanian descent, related that, "A statement affirming the truth (*al-qawl bi -'l-haqq*) and patience in abiding by it is equivalent to the deeds of the martyrs."[48] Another report goes further and establishes the moral superiority of the patient, forbearing individual over all others, including the military martyr. Ibn Abi 'l-Dunya quotes this report on the authority of 'Isma Abi Hukayma, who related,

> The Messenger of God, peace and blessings be upon him, wept and we asked him, "What has caused you to weep, O Messenger of God?" He replied, "I reflected on the last of my community and the

---

43. See Ibn Abi 'l-Dunya, *Al-Sabr wa-'l-thawab 'alayhi* (Beirut: Dar Ibn Hazm, 1997), p. 24.

44. Ibid., p. 26.

45. Ibn Hajar, *Tahdhib*, vol. 5, pp. 126–27; generally regarded as a reliable authority, and Ibn Abi 'l-Dunya, *Sabr*, p. 87.

46. Ibid., p. 61.

47. Ibid., p. 17.

48. Ibid., p. 116.

tribulations they will face. But the patient from among them who arrives will be given the reward of two martyrs (*shahidayn*)."[49]

This report is highly significant because it categorically challenges other, better known reports which assign the greatest merit to military martyrs and posits instead a different, non-martial and nonviolent understanding of virtuous self-sacrifice.

Because of the trajectory of Shi'i history, "redemptive suffering" and martyrdom loom large in the Shi'i consciousness and find ample reflection in Shi'i literature.[50] From the perspective of the Twelver Shi'a (Ithna 'Ashariyya/Imamiya), all twelve Imams, starting with 'Ali, were martyred. The events at Karbala' (680) created a cultic reverence for martyrdom among the Shi'a, especially in relation to the family of the Prophet (*ahl al-bayt*), and more broadly in relation to believers who are assumed to have been oppressed and wrongly killed (*mazlumun*). In the absence of their rightful Imam, the military jihad has fallen into abeyance for the large majority of the Shi'a, and martyrdom is more a consequence of dying on account of suffering and persecution, rather than of military exploits on the battlefield. However after the Islamic Revolution in Iran in 1979 and during the Iranian war with Iraq in the 1980s, the notion of military martyrdom appears to have been revived and used to mobilize the population against national enemies.

Modern and Contemporary Notions of Martyrdom

In the context of European colonization of a broad swath of the Muslim world starting in the eighteenth century, jihad as defensive war made a dramatic revival among Muslim scholars and jurists. During the colonial period, the emphasis was on jihad as a righteous and legitimate struggle against foreign aggressors; Qur'anic verses such as 9:38–40, 9:123, and 8:60 were often deployed to exhort Muslims to defend themselves against their occupiers. Death and the attainment of martyrdom were usually not glorified, however, in such anti-colonial discourses.[51] After the peremptory end to the caliphate at the hands of the republican Turks in 1924,

---

49. Ibid., pp. 84–85.

50. Cf. M. Ayoub, *Redemptive Suffering in Islam* (The Hague: Mouton, 1978).

51. See Rudolph Peters, *Islam and Colonialism: The Doctrine of Jihad in Modern History* (The Hague: Mouton, 1979).

the rise of the powerful secular nation-state in Muslim majority societies has given rise to a new phenomenon—political Islam or Islamism. Hasan al-Banna (d. 1949) in 1928 established the Muslim Brotherhood and wrote a treatise on jihad which contained an entreaty to fellow Muslims to not be afraid to die an honorable death in defense of their lands and religion; in return they will gain eternal life in the next world and perfect bliss. Although al-Banna clearly recognized that jihad broadly encompasses the ethical imperative of enjoining the good and forbidding the wrong, he emphasized that the greatest of martyrdoms and of rewards for the *muja-hidin* are reserved for the one who "kills or is killed in the way of God." Jihad in the way of God has now been redefined by al-Banna as fighting against the nation-state (because it is not the proper Islamic state) and martyrdom is earned by those who lay down their lives in such a cause, although, he maintained, such *mujahidun* must continue to observe the classical stipulations concerning humane conduct during war.[52]

The South Asian Islamist Abu al-A'la Mawdudi (d. 1979) and the fiery Egyptian activist Sayyid Qutb (d. 1966), influenced by the former, developed some of these positions further, both being strongly influenced by revolutionary, totalitarian, and socialist movements of various kinds of their time. According to Mawdudi, Muslims in the modern world, besieged by hostile non-Muslims, must strive earnestly to spread the word of God and Muslim rule. The vehicle for doing this is the "Islamic State" and the means for achieving this goal is jihad.[53] In his militant screed *Ma 'alim fi 'l-tariq* ("Milestones"), Qutb states that the unchanging objective of Islam is to win over all of humanity to the worship of the one God, and the Islamic revolutionary movement under the guidance of an enlightened vanguard must wage jihad to bring this about.[54] Neither Mawdudi nor Qutb, however, engage in exhortations to actively seek death through this kind of relentless military activity.

Contemporary suicide bombers in the Palestinian Occupied Territories, in Lebanon, Afghanistan, Iraq, and elsewhere, who consider their actions "martyrdom operations" (*al- 'amaliyyat al-istishhadiyya*) and who legitimize their targeting of noncombatants under the rubric of jihad have thus

---

52. Hasan al-Banna, "Risalat al-jihad," in *al-Jihad fi sabil allah* (Cairo: Dar al-i'tisam, 1977), pp. 63–90.

53. Mawdudi, *Jihad in Islam* (Damascus: The Holy Qur'an Publishing House, 1977), p. 5.

54. Qutb, *Ma'alim fi 'l-tariq* (Beirut, 1982), esp. pp. 62–91.

considerably deviated from pre-modern constructions of martyrdom.[55] Suicide is categorically forbidden in the Qur'an (2:195; 4:29) and the classical rules of jihad forbade the targeting of noncombatants, traditionally women, children, elderly men, monks, serfs, and others who do not fight. A new kind of "contingency ethics" predicated on the existence of extreme, anomalous circumstances is invoked to justify such contemporary radical interpretations. Perhaps the best-known exponent of such a view is the Qatar-based Egyptian cleric Yusuf al-Qaradawi, who issued a *fatwa* permitting suicide bombings as justified self-defense in the Palestinian context as an emergency measure, but not in other contexts.[56]

The "in extremis" argument is frequently invoked in contemporary militant literature—especially in the context of foreign military occupation—to justify acts of violence which violate noncombatant immunity, acts that were condemned in the classical juridical literature as constituting *hiraba*—"terrorism" in today's parlance.[57] Thus one such contemporary writer, Abu Muhammad ʿAsim al-Maqdisi, maintains that suicide attacks are to be subsumed under the duty of jihad, which "becomes confirmed and obligatory if it occurs in an occupied and extorted [*sic*] Muslim land as is the case in Palestine."[58] It is noteworthy that the political scientist Robert Pape concluded in a recent significant study that there existed a causal relationship between foreign occupation and instances of suicide terrorism, in which context such acts become reconfigured as the ultimate sacrifice to recoup the lost glory of the homeland.[59]

In contrast to al-Qaradawi, other jurists, such as the Syrian *hadith* scholar Nasir al-Din al-Albani and the Saudi jurist Ibn ʿUthaymin, have

---

55. See Nawwaf Takruri, *al-ʿAmaliyyat al-istishhadiyya fi mizan al-fiqhi* (Damascus: N
. al-Takruri, 1997).

56. See John Kelsay, "Suicide Bombers: The 'Just War' Debate, Islamic Style," *The Christian Century*, August 14–27, 2002, pp. 22–25; and *Arguing the Just War in Islam* (Cambridge, Mass.: Harvard University Press, 2007), pp. 141–42.

57. For a lucid discussion of the various juridical perspectives on *hirāba*, see Sherman Jackson, "Domestic Terrorism in the Islamic Legal Tradition," *The Muslim World* 91 (2001), pp. 293–310.

58. Al-Maqdisi, *This is our ʿAqidah*, http://www.archive.org/stream/ThisIsOuraqidah-AbiMuhammadAl-maqdisi/our_aqeedah_djvu.txt, p. 12.

59. Robert Pape, *Dying to Win: The Strategic Logic of Suicide Terrorism* (New York: Random House, 2005), p. 23, where he states, "The bottom line, then, is that suicide terrorism is mainly a response to foreign occupation....modern suicide terrorism is best understood as an extreme strategy for national liberation against democracies with troops that pose an imminent threat to control the territory the terrorists view as their homeland."

condemned these so-called martyrdom operations as morally and legally indefensible in any and every situation. More recently, the Pakistani cleric Muhammad Tahir-ul Qadri has stated unambiguously, "Terrorism, in its very essence, is an act that symbolises infidelity and rejection of what Islam stands for. When the forbidden element of suicide is added to it, its severity and gravity becomes even greater." According to Qadri, militants belonging to al-Qaeda are to be regarded as rebels rather than legitimate martyrs and beyond the pale of Islam.[60] While pre-modern jurists recognized that war was a messy and unpredictable affair and that Realpolitik sometimes necessitated pragmatic exceptions to standard codes of humane conduct, none went so far as to condone or exhort deliberate self-immolation. The classical jurists were usually careful to state that the true intent of the military martyr can be known only to God, as noted above. Militant ideologues today who declare suicide bombers to be authentic military martyrs in advance of the next world clearly lack the prudence and moral judgment of the classical jurists, to say the very least.

---

60. Muhammad Tahir-ul-Qadri, *Fatwa on Suicide Bombings and Terrorism*, 2010, http://www.minhajbooks.com/english/bookid/462/Introduction-to-the-Fatwa-on-Sui cide-Bombings-and-Terrorism-by-Shaykh-ul-Islam-Dr-Muhammad-Tahir-ul-Qadri.html, paras. 35–36.

3

Rendering unto Caesar

THE RHETORICS OF DIVIDED LOYALTIES IN TUDOR ENGLAND

Susannah Brietz Monta

ACCORDING TO THE Synoptic Gospels, Jesus worked a miracle that would seem almost unachievable in early modern England: he neatly balanced competing loyalties to state authorities and to religion. In Matthew 22, Jesus is confronted by Pharisees and Herodians (whom the 1560 Geneva Bible's gloss helpfully identifies as "certaine flatterers of the court, which ever maintemed that religion, which King Herode best approved"). Seeking to entrap Jesus into making either a treasonous or a blasphemous statement, they ask him whether it is lawful to pay tribute to Caesar. As the Geneva gloss to the parallel passage in Luke 20:22 explains, "They thoght it unlawful to pay to a prince being an infidel, that which thei were wont to pay to God in his Temple." Jesus asks them to show him the tribute money; he then holds up the coin and, in the Geneva translators' words, asks "Whose is this image and superscription?" Told that it is Caesar's, Jesus solves the dilemma: "Give therefore to Cesar, the things which are Cesars, and give unto God, those which are Gods."[1] The questioners walk away, marveling at this tidy resolution.

The problem of dual allegiances was not, of course, resolved nearly so well in the early modern period, when the extent to which the State should exert authority over the Church in England provoked divisions

---

1. I cite the Geneva Bible's 1560 printing.

both between and among reformers and Catholics. Reformation biblical translations evince the troublesome nature of the relationship between a state whose laws supported particular religious establishments
and the Reformation era's various forms of religious belief and practice.
The Geneva Bible's marginal notes link the Caesar tribute question in all
three Synoptic Gospels to Romans 13:7, a verse emphasizing obedience
to established governments. In this, the Geneva translators follow Miles
Coverdale, who similarly glossed the passage in his 1539 Great Bible. The
Geneva Bible's conservative rival, the Bishops' Bible, also includes the reference to Romans 13, a chapter the Bishops' Bible describes as concerned
with "obedience to the rulers, who beare not the swoorde in vayne."[2] The
relevant passage in Romans 13 is carefully glossed in the generally lightly
annotated Bishops' Bible to stress obedience to earthly authorities: "we are
bounde in conscience by the woorde of God, to obey the hygher powers."
The link between Romans 13 and the Synoptic Gospels' Caesar passage survives into the 1611 King James Bible. In these Protestant translations, the
orderly submission of the godly to the prince—who in post-Reformation
England also ruled over a Protestant national church—is the primary
lesson of Jesus's answer to the Pharisees.

Not surprisingly, the Catholic translator Gregory Martin has a different
view. In Martin's 1582 translation of the New Testament, the relevant verse
appears as "Render therefore the things that are Caesars, to Caesar: and
the things that are Gods, to God."[3] Romans 13 is not linked to the passage; instead, Martin's cross-references point simply to the other Synoptic
Gospels' treatments of the same incident. Martin includes a sidenote
to Matthew 22:21 stressing the limits of state power over religious matters: "Neither must temporal Princes exact, nor their Subjects give unto
them, Ecclesiastical jurisdiction." For the Catholic Martin, the proper limits of Caesar's authority needed firm reinforcing. Martin expands on this
sidenote in his lengthy endnote to the passage, warning readers that they
must not "geve to Caesar, that is, to their Prince, the things that are dewe
to God, that is, to his Ecclesiasticall ministers." Martin cites early Church
authorities such as Ambrose of Milan who rebuked Arian emperors for
meddling in ecclesiastical concerns; as from the Catholic point of view
both Arians and Elizabeth I were considered heretics, the warning to the

---

2. I cite the 1578 printing. The Bishops' Bible also refers readers to Matthew 17 (which urges
the devout to pay earthly tolls so as not to offend earthly kings).

3. I cite the Rheims New Testament, translated by Gregory Martin and published in 1582.

Elizabethan regime is clear. Similarly, in his notes on the Caesar passage in Mark (Mark 12:17), Martin insists that "God [is] first to be served, and then the Prince." Jesus's rhetorically neat solution to the problem of dual allegiances is slightly recast so as to emphasize the proper hierarchy of obedience.

In Reformation England, the dilemma of dual allegiances extracted a bloody cost at the stake or the gibbet, where hundreds of Protestant and Catholic martyrs bore witness to Caesar's power over religious dissidents. For Reformation England, the martyr's dark opposite is not necessarily or precisely the terrorist—the word is not yet available in English—but the heretic, whose dangerously wrong religious beliefs may infect and thus damn others, or the traitor, a political plotter who works for the overthrow of peaceful government under the false guise of religious belief. The "terrors" that Tudor regimes feared—if we may use that word somewhat loosely—were the spread of dangerously wrong religious belief (and with it the overthrow of proper political and spiritual order), or the use of religion to foment political rebellion. One might argue, conversely, that persecutory regimes in Tudor England practiced terror insofar as they explicitly sought to make bloody examples of religious and political dissidents.[4] In this essay, I first consider broadly the phenomenon of early modern martyrdom.[5] Representations of early modern martyrs typically insist that martyrs asserted their loyalty to their sovereigns, despite the fact that those sovereigns' religio-political regimes were largely responsible for the martyrs' deaths. One of the most powerful rhetorical weapons for polemicists who attacked martyrological accounts was the accusation that would-be martyrs were guilty of seditious or treasonous behavior. In the essay's second section, I focus on a polemical exchange between William Cecil (1520–1598), Elizabeth I's most important advisor and councilor, and William Cardinal Allen (1532–1594), leader of English Catholic exiles, over whether Catholic priests executed by the Elizabethan regime

---

4. Vincent Carey, "Elizabeth I and State Terror in Sixteenth-Century Ireland," in Donald Stump, Linda Shenk, and Carole Levin, eds., *Elizabeth I and the "Sovereign Arts"* (Tempe, Ariz.: Medieval and Renaissance Texts and Studies, 2011), pp. 201–16.

5. Early modern English martyrdom has attracted much scholarship; see, *inter alia*, Thomas S. Freeman and Thomas F. Mayer, eds., *Martyrs and Martyrdom in England, c.1400–1700* (Woodbridge: Boydell Press, 2007); Susannah Monta, *Martyrdom and Literature in Early Modern England* (Cambridge: Cambridge University Press, 2005); Anne Dillon, *The Construction of Martyrdom in the English Catholic Community, 1535–1603* (Aldershot: Ashgate, 2001); and Brad S. Gregory, *Salvation at Stake: Christian Martyrdom in Early Modern Europe* (Cambridge, Mass.: Harvard University Press, 1999).

died as traitors to their sovereign, as official legal proceedings proclaimed, or as martyrs to the Catholic faith, as their co-religionists insisted. In both Cecil's and Allen's treatises, the authors' own rhetoric betrays the impossibility of neatly resolving the dilemma of conflicting allegiances, as seems to happen in the Synoptic Gospels. But perhaps that resolution itself was not so crisp. The exchange over Caesar takes place, as a head-note in Martin's translation indicates, during Holy Week, or the last week of Jesus's life, at the end of which Jesus was executed by state authorities for what local religious leaders deemed the crime of blasphemy. Religious dissidents wishing to imitate Jesus's distribution of loyalties had, then, an example that proved the difficulty of the task, or at least the extreme un-likelihood that a carefully distributed rendering of loyalties would obviate the literal rending of bodies.

The Making of Martyrs

In the records of Reformation England's martyrs the strain of dual alle-giances to conflicting temporal and spiritual powers is starkly apparent. Under Henry VIII, numerous reformers suffered both before and after the break with Rome, either directly at the hand of Henry's regime (such as Thomas Bilney in 1531, Robert Barnes in 1540, and Anne Askew in 1546) or at its behest (William Tyndale, in Antwerp in 1536).[6] Catholics also suf-fered under Henry VIII, most famously John Fisher, Bishop of Rochester, and Sir Thomas More, both in 1535 for denying the royal supremacy. The Catholic Mary Tudor's regime (1553–58) revived medieval heresy legislation in an attempt to eliminate Protestant resistance to its religious policies. The most notorious of these statues, De haeretico comburendo (1401), autho-rized secular authorities to burn those found by church courts to "perpe-trate and commit...Subversion of the...Catholic Faith and Doctrine of the Holy Church" and who refused to abjure (or, having abjured, lapsed again).[7] Because religious dissidence was linked in popular understanding and in law with sedition (De Haeretico Comburendo worries that heretical

---

6. On Barnes's posthumous role in Protestant propaganda, see Alec Ryrie, "'A saynt in the devyls name': Heroes and Villains in the Martyrdom of Robert Barnes," in Freeman and Mayer, Martyrs and Martyrdom, pp. 144–65. On Askew's martyrdom and legacy, see Susannah Monta, "The Inheritance of Anne Askew, English Protestant Martyr," Archiv für Reformationsgeschichte 94 (2003), pp. 134–60. For a scholarly but partisan view of Tyndale, see David Daniell, William Tyndale: A Biography (New Haven: Yale University Press, 2001).

7. Statutes of the Realm (London: Dawsons, 1810–28), vol. 2, 125–8: 2 Henry IV.

teachings may "excite and stir" people to "Sedition and Insurrection"), Protestant martyrs and their admirers labored to separate reformed religion from suspicions of sedition and to affirm their loyalty to the English state. Accounts of the burnings of approximately 284 Protestants at the stake between 1555 and 1558, most prominently those shaped and presented by John Foxe in his martyrology and ecclesiastical history known as the *Actes and Monuments* (1563, 1570, 1576, 1583), insist that Protestants and their forebears had nothing to do with sedition, suffering only for true religion.[8]

Under Elizabeth I, Catholics faced increasing pressure to conform to the established form of Protestant religion. A series of events—including a 1579 landing in Ireland of troops flying the papal flag, the intrigues of Mary, Queen of Scots, and growing tensions with Spain—led to increasingly harsh treason legislation designed to drive Catholics into conformity, bankruptcy, exile, or the harsh death, by drawing and quartering, of the traitor. The Catholic community debated the merits of recusancy (from *recusare*, to refuse), or conformity to the Church of England, while the Elizabethan government insisted in its polemic that it pursued Catholics for political, not religious, transgressions. Under the Tudors, approximately 239 men and women died as martyrs, according to the Catholic Church, despite the official charges (usually of treason) leveled against them.[9]

The strain of dual allegiances to conflicting temporal and spiritual powers, literalized in martyrs' bodily suffering, is also manifested formally in the period's martyrological rhetoric. It may seem perverse, given the legacy of suffering, to assert that martyrs in early modern England were made as well as found. This is not to say that the sufferings of those executed were not painfully real, or that many or even most of the surviving martyrological accounts are fictional. In cases where material written by diametrically opposed authors about the same execution survives, martyrologists and their opponents differ primarily not about what was said or done but rather about how to interpret the events they record. This is true in differing accounts of the martyrdom of Edmund Campion, S.J., by the Catholic priest Thomas Alfield and by the government apologist Anthony

---

8. On the numbers of Marian martyrs, including those burned at the stake and those who died in prison, see Thomas S. Freeman, "Appendix: The Marian Martyrs," in Susan Doran and Thomas S. Freeman, eds., *Mary Tudor: Old and New Perspectives* (New York: Palgrave, 2011), pp. 225–71.

9. Dillon, *Construction of Martyrdom*, p. 3.

Munday, for example, or in accounts of Thomas Cranmer's recantations of his Protestant faith shortly before his spectacular reversal at the stake in both the anti-Protestant *Cranmers Recantacyons* and John Foxe's laudatory *Actes and Monuments*.[10] For the authors of these accounts, the making or unmaking of a martyr depends, at least partly, on rhetorical presentation and interpretive argument.

As befits the word's etymology (Gk. *martyria*), in early modern lexicons "martyr" is most frequently defined in terms of forensic (judicial) rhetoric: as a witness.[11] Martyrologists present martyrs as religious witnesses testifying not only to the depth of their own religious convictions but to those convictions' absolute truth. This is of course the traditional epistemic force of hagiography. Yet as the sixteenth century wore on, the understanding of martyrdom as witness was increasingly linked to physical suffering.[12] The Augustinian refrain that the cause, not the punishment, makes a martyr (*non poena sed causa*) recurs in early modern martyrological texts. Yet it is also clear that the punishment could be persuasive; a martyr's words and actions are carefully presented (by martyrologists and, evidently, by many martyrs themselves) to maximize testimonial and persuasive impact. In some cases, witnesses to martyrdom (Henry Walpole at the Catholic martyr Edmund Campion's death, for instance, or Joyce Lewes at the Protestant martyr Lawrence Saunders's execution) converted to the martyr's faith.[13] Further, martyrs studied the behavior of others and in some cases rehearsed how they would speak and act in their final moments; thus the Foxean martyr Joyce Lewes planned what she would say at the stake before her execution in December of 1557.[14] Between late 1582 and 1584, Niccoló Circignani painted on the walls of the chapel of the English College at Rome a cycle of thirty-four frescoes of English saints and martyrs. These images depicted a historical continuity of Catholic

---

10. See the introduction to Gregory, *Salvation at Stake*.

11. See LEME (Lexicon of Early Modern English) entries for "martyr." Thomas Elyot's *Dictionary* (London, 1538) defines martyr as "a wytnesse" as does Richard Huloet, *Abecedarium Anglico Latinum* (London, 1552); such definitions predominate through the later sixteenth century.

12. See LEME; by the early seventeenth century, the idea of the martyr as a *suffering* witness becomes increasingly dominant. John Florio's *A World of Words* (1598) defines the martyr as "one suffring in witnes of another," and Randall Cotgrave, *A Dictionary of the French and English Tongues* (London, 1611) states that a martyr "suffers death for the truth."

13. Monta, *Martyrdom*, 10.

14. John Foxe, *Actes and Monuments* (London, 1583), p. 2012.

witness in England; College students reflected on these images to prepare for their own missions as English Catholic witnesses and for their possible martyrdoms.[15] Evidence of preparation for martyrdom need not indicate pathology or insincerity but rather may reveal an awareness of martyrdom's rhetorics, of the ways in which a martyr's behavior might persuade and confirm to co-religionists, present and future, that the martyr died for truth.

Martyrologists used a shared inheritance of martyrological conventions to draw sharp lines of religious distinction in the complex post-Reformation religious landscape. Because of cross-confessional emphases on continuity with Christian tradition, and despite some emergent confessional differences, Protestant and Catholic characterizations of martyrs frequently overlapped.[16] Most sixteenth- and early seventeenth-century martyrologists represented martyrs as fairly passive (with allowances for occasional brief jeremiads) and patient in suffering; they neither shunned nor sought death; they typically claimed to act according to their consciences and in imitation of and in concert with Christian tradition.

The phenomenon of early modern English martyrdom is bookended by saints and martyrs whose representations and commemorations combined political with religious causes. The popular pre-Reformation cult of Henry VI, for instance, blended political critique with religious devotion. By the mid-seventeenth century, martyrological treatments both of Charles I (executed in 1649) and of his Puritan and revolutionary opponents such as Sir Henry Vane the Younger (executed in 1662) enacted the apotheosis of political rivals.[17] Thomas Freeman has argued that representations of martyrdom narrowed in the sixteenth and early seventeenth centuries from their medieval precedents; alternate medieval models of martyrdom—such as a virtual martyrdom through virginity, contemplation, or asceticism—receded in favor of the dominant model of *imitatio*

---

15. Dillon, *Construction*, chap. 4.

16. See Monta, *Martyrdom*, chaps. 1 through 3, and Gregory, *Salvation at Stake*.

17. On Charles I as martyr, see Andrew Lacey, " 'Charles the First and Christ the Second': The Creation of a Political Martyr," in Freeman and Mayer, *Martyrs and Martyrdom*, pp. 203–20; Lois Potter, "The Royal Martyr in the Restoration," in Thomas N. Corns, ed., *The Royal Image: Representations of Charles I* (Cambridge: Cambridge University Press, 1999), pp. 240–62; and Laura Lunger Knoppers, "Reviving the Martyr-King: Charles I as Jacobite Icon," in Corns, *The Royal Image*, pp. 263–87. On Sir Henry Vane the Younger, see John Coffey, "The Martyrdom of Sir Henry Vane the Younger: From Apocalyptic Witness to Heroic Whig," in Freeman and Mayer, *Martyrs and Martyrdom*, pp. 221–40.

Christi.[18] John Foxe clearly highlights the Christ-like qualities of martyrs such as Thomas Haukes, executed in June 1555. A woodcut included in the four editions of the *Actes and Monuments* published during Foxe's lifetime shows Haukes clapping his hands amid the flames and crying, "O Lord, Receive my spirite." These words, not recorded in the text, echo the protomartyr Stephen and Christ himself. The woodcut locates Haukes's death firmly in Christian tradition; Haukes is to represent not heretical aberrance but orthodox continuity.

If the martyr is to imitate Christ, then he/she must not be seen to threaten Caesar: when shortly before his death Jesus was accused of discouraging the payment of tribute to Caesar, Pilate himself easily dismissed the charge.[19] If Christ's kingdom was not of this world, neither should martyrs foment political resistance. Sixteenth-century English martyrologies almost without exception represent the martyr as a figure without political intent, one who neither procures the deaths of others nor acts seditiously. The period's martyrologists carefully separate martyrs from politics, even in cases where the separation is patently dubious. John Foxe labors to distance Protestant martyrs from any hint of seditious activity, precisely because of the common polemical charge that Protestantism was inherently seditious. Sir John Oldcastle, a Lollard knight executed in 1417 for leading a rebellion, is the most famous case in point. Medieval chronicle sources indicate that Oldcastle was convicted of and executed for treason. The fiery Protestant polemicist John Bale carefully read medieval Catholic records against the grain to argue, in his *Brefe Chronycle* (Antwerp, 1544), that Oldcastle died for religion, as a martyr. Foxe followed Bale's lead, developing and buttressing his arguments. In his *Dialogi Sex* (Antwerp, 1566), the Catholic Nicholas Harpsfield roundly attacked Foxe's lauding of Oldcastle in the 1563 (first) edition of his *Actes and Monuments*. Foxe expended a great deal of energy in his second, 1570 edition to refute Harpsfield. The Oldcastle case—and the denial of any connection between Protestantism and treason—mattered deeply to Foxe. Yet despite Foxe's

---

18. Thomas Freeman, "*Imitatio Christi* with a Vengeance: The Politicisation of Martyrdom in Early Modern England," in Freeman and Mayer, *Martyrs and Martyrdom*, pp. 35–69. See also Danna Piroyansky, " 'Thus may a man be a martyr': The Notion, Language, and Experiences of Martyrdom in Late Medieval England," in Freeman and Mayer, *Martyrs and Martyrdom*, pp. 70–87, on the many ways martyrdom was understood in late medieval England.

19. Luke 23:1–4.

best efforts, disagreements about the reasons Oldcastle died persisted, as for example in Holinshed's *Chronicles* (1577, 1587).[20]

While the vast majority of Marian martyrs were executed under heresy statutes, a few died convicted of treason. Foxe celebrates George Eagles, an itinerant, uneducated preacher who earned the nicknamed "Trudgeover," as a simple witness to the truth. Chased by Marian authorities, Eagles tried to hide but was caught and convicted of treason for violating a statute against gatherings of six or more people (an anti-conventicle measure). Foxe complains that this statute is devised to "cloke an honest matter," hiding religion beneath treason's guise. Eagles did his best to get himself executed for religion, clearly proclaiming beliefs the Marian church authorities decreed heretical, but to no avail: he faced the traitor's death of hanging, drawing, and quartering. Nevertheless Foxe carefully emphasizes that Eagles died in as Christ-like a manner as possible. His betrayer is called a "Judas," and Foxe reports that Eagles died between two thieves, one who believed Eagles's testimony and hoped to join him in heaven, one who mocked it, a clear imitation of the narrative of Christ's death between two thieves, one believing, one scoffing.[21] Foxe's final comment on Eagles both marks and attempts to close the gap between the way Eagles died ("a moste unworthy manner") and the cause for which he suffered: "Thus the godly and blessed man, more worthy of heauen then earth, suffered great extremitie after a moste vnworthy maner, being counted but as an outcast of the worlde, yet at the handes of Christe and his churche a moste worthy martyr."[22] At the other end of the social spectrum is one of Foxe's most prominent martyrs, Thomas Cranmer, sometime Archbishop of Canterbury and chief architect of the *Book of Common Prayer*, who had been convicted of treason (for supporting Lady Jane Grey's claim to the throne over Mary Tudor's) before he was condemned for heresy. It must have been some comfort to him—and, certainly, to his martyrologist— that he was finally executed for heresy, not treason.

Catholic martyrologists had an even more difficult task, as Catholics were executed not under heresy statutes but treason legislation. Under Henry VIII legal definitions of treason were considerably expanded to

20. See Thomas Freeman and Susannah Monta, "Foxe and Holinshed," in Ian Archer, Felicity Heale, and Paulina Kewes, eds., *The Oxford Handbook to Holinshed* (Oxford: Oxford University Press, 2013).

21. Luke 23:39–43.

22. John Foxe, *Actes and Monuments* (London, 1570), pp. 2202–3.

include treasonous speech, not simply treasonous action.[23] Elizabeth's government further expanded legal definitions of treason. In 1571, it became treason to import, publish, or put into effect any bull or writing from Rome or to "maliciously, advisedly, and directly publish, set forth, and affirm" in speech or writing "that the Queen our said sovereign lady Queen Elizabeth is an heretic, schismatic, infidel or an usurper of the crown."[24] In 1581, reconciling others to the Catholic Church or being reconciled oneself was declared treason, while in 1585 the Act against Jesuits and Seminarians declared English Catholic priests found on English soil *de facto* traitors.

Because Catholics were prosecuted under treason statutes, Catholic martyrologists had to present their deaths by drawing and quartering—a graphic unmaking of the traitor's body meant to parallel and invert the traitor's would-be unmaking of the body of the state—as a martyr's death, despite attempts to portray it otherwise.[25] Diego de Yepez, confessor to Philip II and Bishop of Taracona, wrote a defense of English Catholics, including lengthy descriptions of Catholic martyrs. Yepez emphasizes officials' attempts to silence priests' confessions of the religious reasons for which they die and insists upon their ability to be heard anyway by those willing to listen. For instance, the priest John Cornelius, executed on July 4, 1594, tries to speak to the gathered crowd but is three times interrupted; yet the little he speaks is sufficient, according to Yepez, to persuade onlookers that he is guilty of no other fault but seeking to bring souls into the Catholic faith.[26] Thomas Alfield makes a similar claim about Edmund Campion; Campion was silenced, Alfield writes, as he began to claim that he died a martyr, yet he did manage to acknowledge Elizabeth as his queen and to convince those Alfield deems reasonable people that he "suferred only for religion."[27] In the seventeenth century, Latin martyrologies memorializing Catholic priests who died at Parliament's hands during the civil wars insist on the priests' loyalty to the king and the

---

23. Rebecca Lemon, *Treason by Words: Literature, Law, and Rebellion in Shakespeare's England* (Ithaca, N.Y.: Cornell University Press, 2006), chap. 1.

24. 13 Elizabeth c. 1, in *Statues of the Realm* (London, 1819), vol. 4, p. 526.

25. On the semiotics of the traitor's execution, see Curtis Breight, "The Strange Case of William Hacket, Elizabethan Messiah," *Journal of Medieval and Renaissance Studies* 19.1 (1989), pp. 35–67.

26. Diego de Yepez, *Historia Particular de la Persecución de Inglaterra* (Madrid, 1599), p. 639.

27. Thomas Alfield, *A True Report* (London, 1582), B1r, C2v.

nation, as well as their passive willingness to be sacrifices for the nation's sake. Thus Ambrose Corbie writes that Fr. Thomas Holland prayed "by name for the king, for the queen, for the royal family, for the parliament, and for the whole nation" and proclaimed his willingness to die repeatedly for his nation's good.[28] These martyrologists insist that Catholic priests both follow Christian traditions of martyrdom and maintain their loyalty to the state, rendering political loyalty to Caesar even as their own bodies were torn.

To evacuate the power of the suffering martyr, the imitator of Christ, Protestant polemicists such as William Cecil represent the Catholic martyr as a traitor, a devious figure who hides behind religious causes an intent to overthrow the English state. In rejoinder, William Cardinal Allen argues that Protestants were the real traitors; Allen writes that the former Protestant bishop and Marian martyr Nicholas Ridley was "an high traitor" (115), that leading Protestants such as Edwin Sandys, Elizabeth's Archbishop of York, were involved in the plot to thwart Mary Tudor's accession, and that "all the pack of your Protestants" were "confederated or acquainted with Wyatt's conspiracy and open rebellion against their prince and country" (115, 116).[29]

Cecil and Allen's polemical exchange, the focus of the rest of this chapter, concerns the execution of Edmund Campion and other Catholic priests in the early 1580s on treason charges. Their treatises both characterize and attempt to shape the ideal relationship between spiritual and temporal powers. Both Cecil and Allen attempt to separate religion from politics. Cecil argues that religion has nothing to do with legal proceedings under which such ostensibly religious activities as reconciling others to the Catholic Church are decreed treason. Allen claims that religious figures who act against the laws of the land have nothing to do with political disobedience. The strain of these arguments becomes evident insofar as religion and politics are deeply imbricated in the early modern period and inseparable even at the level of polemical rhetoric. Despite the international significance of the exchange, Cecil's and Allen's treatises have

---

28. Ambrose Corbie, *Certamen Triplex* (Antwerp, 1645), 36–37 (my translation); see also Monta, *Martyrdom*, chap. 7.

29. Citations of Allen, *A True, Sincere, and Modest Defense of English Catholics* (1584) and Cecil, *The Execution of Justice* (1583) are to *The Execution of Justice in England by William Cecil and A True, Sincere, and Modest Defense of English Catholics by William Allen*, ed. Robert M. Kingdon (Cornell University Press for the Folger Shakespeare Library, 1965). I write in memory of Robert Kingdon: requiescat in pace.

received little attention from literary scholars. Yet their treatises demonstrate the centrality of basic rhetorical and literary tools—figures, analogies, exempla, philology, biblical hermeneutics, address of audiences—to the making of martyrs and traitors, and, more broadly, to the making of a culture in which satisfying dual allegiances to Caesar and God proved vexingly difficult.

The Making of Traitors

The Cecil/Allen exchange concerns the execution of English Catholics under treason legislation. It takes shape against a background of steadily worsening relationships between Elizabeth I's regime and the papacy and continental Catholic powers. The early Elizabethan years saw the deprivation and/or resignation of many Marian bishops and a number of controversies between English Catholics and Protestants. Bishop John Jewel, for instance, engaged in a lengthy polemic with the Catholic exile Thomas Harding about the Elizabethan Settlement; Thomas Stapleton and Nicholas Harpsfield denigrated the first edition of Foxe's *Actes and Monuments* as memorializing, in Stapleton's infamous phrase, a "dong-hell...of stinking Martyrs."[30] Nevertheless, the regime seemed relatively content to wait for English Catholics to reconcile themselves to the new religious settlement. The regime expanded its treason legislation partly in response to events such as the 1569–70 northern rebellion and, most importantly, a papal bull issued (belatedly, as events turned out) in its support, *Regnans in Excelsis* (1570), which excommunicated Elizabeth I and absolved her Catholic subjects of allegiance to her. In Cecil's treatise, the rebellion and the bull are presented as evidence that Catholicism represents a grave political threat to the nation.

As tensions grew between the regime and its Catholic subjects, English Catholic exile communities expanded. The Oxford exile William Allen established colleges on the continent for disaffected English Catholics and worked to train priests for service in England. The first missionary priest executed under treason legislation was Cuthbert Mayne (in 1577). In 1579, the regime's worst nightmare seemed about to come true, as Spanish and

---

30. Thomas Stapleton, *The History of the Church of Englande* (Antwerp, 1565), 8v–9r; John Jewel, *Apologie or Answere in Defence of the Church of Englande*, trans. Anne, Lady Bacon (London, 1564); Thomas Harding, *A Confutation of a Booke Entituled "An Apologie of the Church of England"* (Antwerp, 1565); Jewel, *A Defence of the "Apologie of the Churche of England"* (London, 1567); and Nicholas Harpsfield, *Dialogi Sex* (Antwerp, 1566).

Italian troops flying the papal flag landed in Ireland to join with Irish troops in rebellion against English rule; Cecil's treatise uses this landing, together with the northern rebellion and its aftermath, to demonstrate that the English nation is in a state of war, and that the papacy behaves as a hostile foreign power. These troops were cornered and slaughtered in November 1580 after their surrender to Arthur de Wilton, Lord Grey, Lord Deputy of Ireland, at Smerwyck. In a spectacular case of ill timing, the first Jesuit missionary priests—Robert Persons and Edmund Campion— had arrived in England in the summer of 1580 and were none too quiet about their arrival. Campion's treatise *Rationes Decem*, published in late Spring 1581 on Persons's secret press, repeatedly asserts that the Jesuit missionaries were not to meddle in nor discuss political affairs. In another treatise, Campion's so-called "Brag"—a short piece circulated shortly after Campion's arrival in England whose nickname suggests it was read as a direct challenge—Campion insists that he is forbidden to deal in any matter of state policy and requests, in good humanist fashion, an open disputation on religious questions.[31] The regime was unsympathetic to Campion's claims of political innocence, and he immediately became a marked man; he was arrested in July 1581, tortured extensively, subjected to a form of debate with Protestant ministers in the Tower in which he was significantly disadvantaged, and finally executed for treason on 1 December 1581.[32]

The regime's execution of such a learned, respected figure shocked Catholic communities in England and abroad. While a star scholar at Oxford, Campion delivered a speech for Queen Elizabeth I herself (in 1566); he had enjoyed the patronage of Sir Henry Sidney, Lord Deputy of Ireland, after leaving Oxford in 1570 and made a name for himself as a neo-Latin writer on the continent.[33] Numerous publications in Latin and English celebrated him as a martyr.[34] In response to the international

---

31. The "Brag" was widely circulated; a copy survives in Foxe's papers (BL Harleian 422). It is reprinted in Evelyn Waugh, *Edmund Campion: A Life* (San Francisco: Ignatius Press, 2005; reprint of 1935 edition), pp. 205–209.

32. For a contemporary Catholic account of the Tower debates, see James V. Holleran, *A Jesuit Challenge: Edmund Campion's Debates at the Tower of London, 1581* (New York: Fordham University Press, 1999).

33. On Campion's biography, see McCoog's introduction to *The Reckoned Expense: Edmund Campion and the Early English Jesuits* (Woodbridge: Boydell, 1996).

34. These include, in Latin, portions of the *Concertatio Ecclesiae Catholicae in Anglia* (Trier, 1583); Pietro Bombino, *Vita et Martyrium Edmundi Campiani Martyris Angli è Societate Jesu* (Mantua, 1620); and P. Alegambe, *Mortes Illustres et Gesta eorum de Societate Jesu* (Rome,

scandal provoked by the executions of Campion and other Catholic priests, William Cecil, Elizabeth's leading minister, undertook a defense of English policy.

His treatise, *The Execution of Justice in England*, enjoyed what Robert Kingdon has called a semi-official status. The title pages of the first and second editions (both in 1583) do not carry a printer's name, but they do evince "the mark and use the type of Christopher Barker, an official printer to the Queen."[35] A Latin translation was published in London in March 1584; translations into French and Dutch followed in 1584, and an Italian translation in 1589. In a letter, Robert Persons claims that there was an earlier Italian translation and also a German one. The tract's authorship is Cecil's, despite the title page's ambiguity. Strype in his *Annals* states that he saw a draft in Cecil's own hand, while modern historian Conyers Read found parts of a draft by Cecil "scattered through the Domestic State Papers in the Public Record Office."[36] Appended to the *Execution* is a treatise entitled *A Declaration of the Favorable Dealing of Her Majesty's Commissioners*; not Cecil's, it may have been written by one of his clients, the lawyer, playwright, and religious translator Thomas Norton.

Cecil's defense prompted a lengthy retort from William Cardinal Allen, *A True, Sincere, and Modest Defense of English Catholics* (1584).[37] As Kingdon describes it, it is "in style and erudition…quite an improvement" on Cecil's work, with a detailed command of examples from the Bible and ecclesiastical history. Yet "its real importance stems…from the fact that it was widely circulated and possessed an official character of a sort." The title page does not identify the printer, author, date, or place of publication; yet correspondence between Robert Persons and Allen makes Allen's authorship clear. Allen's tract was first published in English; a copy was smuggled to Mary Stuart, Queen of Scots, under house arrest in England, four years prior to

---

1657); and in English, Alfield, *A True Report*, and William Cardinal Allen, *A Briefe Historie of the Glorious Martyrdom of Twelve Reverend Priests, Father Campion and His Companions* (Rheims?, 1582).

35. Kingdon, *The Execution*, "Introduction," p. xvii.

36. Ibid., p. xix.

37. Other, angrier responses include Antonio Possevino's answer to Cecil; see John Patrick Donnelly, "Antonio Possevino's Tribute to Edmund Campion," *ASHI* 57 (1988), pp. 163–69.

her execution. A translation into Latin was ready by 1584, and copies were presented to prominent Church officials.[38]

It is no surprise that these men chose to enter the polemical fray. Both Cecil and Allen were closely tied to opposing martyrological projects. Cecil's patronage supported the printing of Foxe's *Actes and Monuments*, and his image appears alongside those of Foxe and John Day (the work's printer) in the woodcut initial which begins the 1563 edition.[39] Amid intensified persecution of English Catholics and in response to Catholic efforts to represent these men as martyrs, Foxe and/or Day found it necessary to change the title page of their 1583 edition to stress that it documented "*true* martyrs" (emphasis added). Cecil's *The Execution of Justice in England*, which favorably compares Marian martyrs to Elizabethan Catholic traitors, participates in a similar project of distinction, and Cecil's treatise is indebted to Foxe's historical arguments for his own brief adductions of English and continental religious history.[40] For his part, Allen published in 1582 a treatise entitled *A Briefe Historie*, which documents the sufferings of Campion and eleven other priests; its translation into Latin formed the basis for the fullest English Catholic answer to John Foxe, the monumental *Concertatio Ecclesiae Catholicae in Anglia*.[41] For Cecil and Allen, the making—or unmaking—of traitors formed an integral part of the polemical projects on which they labored.

Cecil's primary task is to redefine apparent religious persecution as prosecution for treason. "Prosecute" and "persecute" are, of course, formed on the same root; Cecil is nevertheless determined to separate their meanings at least so far as they apply to government policy. Cecil first uses "prosecute" to describe the wishes of wrongdoers who "prosecute their wicked attempts to the full satisfaction of their disordered and

---

38. Kingdon, *The Execution*, pp. xxii–xxiii. One of Mary's letters thanks Allen for the book; see *The Letters and Memorials of William Cardinal Allen (1532–1594)*, ed. Thomas Francis Knox et al. (London, 1882), pp. 243–44.

39. Elizabeth Evenden and Thomas Freeman, "John Foxe, John Day, and the Printing of the Book of Martyrs," in Robin Myers, Michael Harris, and Giles Mandelbrote, eds., *Lives in Print* (New Castle: Oak Knoll Press, 2003), p. 27.

40. See Cecil, *The Execution*, pp. 20–21, where he discusses Marian martyrs and pp. 23–24, where he follows Foxe's argument that the papacy exerted corrupt illegitimate authority over political rulers such as the emperor Henry IV; Cecil's brief version of Henry IV's history (p. 24) roughly follows Foxe.

41. This work was published in multiple, expanded editions; the first was printed in Trier in 1583.

malicious appetites" (3). The Elizabethan government's prosecution of those who prosecute "wicked attempts" is simply the fitting response to what has already been initiated; state policy looks like rhetorical decorum. Cecil insists on Elizabeth's great "unwillingness...to have any blood spilled without this very urgent, just, and necessary cause, proceeding from themselves" (8). Punishment not only fits the crime but its triggering cause also emerges directly from the criminal himself.

Cecil attempts to argue that the English government does not persecute religious dissidents. But of course the treasonous crimes Catholic priests committed look a lot like religious ones. Both the fear of international retribution and a deep awareness of English antipathy for an overtly religious persecution—memories of Marian fires were still sharp—concern Cecil. He thus deploys a rhetoric of disclosure: what appears to be religious activity may be read politically, as treason. Cecil repeatedly invokes English Catholic involvement in hostile military action—the 1569–70 northern rebellion, the presence of English exile and priest Nicholas Sander alongside the papal troops who landed in Ireland in 1579—so that he may argue from the easily seen to the sinisterly hidden. Insisting that the executed priests, like all wrongdoers, hide their true intentions, he reads Catholic religion suspiciously, as a mask for political action. When captured, the priests

> like hypocrites...color and counterfeit...with profession of devotion in religion...in very truth, the whole scope of their secret labors is manifestly proved to be secretly to win all people with whom they dare deal so to allow of the Pope's said bulls and of his authority without exception as, in obeying thereof, they take themselves fully discharged of their allegiance and obedience to their lawful prince and country. (8–9)

Their "secret labors" are actions conducted "secretly," the near tautology reinforcing an unstated opposition: traitors operate in stealth, martyrs in open witness.[42]

---

42. Cecil's language reflects that in the treason statutes. 35 Eliz. c. 2 (1593) provides "for the better discovering" of those who "terming themselves Catholics, and being indeed spies and intelligencers...and hiding their most detestable and devilish purposes under a false pretext of religion and conscience, do secretly wander and shift from place to place within this realm, to corrupt and seduce her majesty's subjects, and to stir them to sedition and rebellion"; reprinted in *Documents of the Christian Church*, 2nd ed., ed. Henry Bettenson (Oxford: Oxford University Press, 1963), p. 243.

The labor of disclosure also took place in interrogations and in the torture chamber. The fear that priests might prepare English Catholics to aid, as a fifth column, a Catholic invasion drove the government's use of the so-called "bloody questions," which Cecil lists as "these few questions, very apt to try the truth or falsehood of any such seditious persons" ("few" was added in Cecil's second edition). Often administered under torture, the questions were designed to determine what a Catholic would do in the event of a papally sponsored invasion. In the torture chamber, the rhetoric of secrecy had agonizingly real consequences. For the torturers, truth is buried within the traitor; pain will force its exposure. For the priests, determined to withhold sensitive information—such as information received under the sacramental seal of confession, or concerning householders who sheltered priests—that inward space is sacrosanct, to be protected despite the body's ravages. Cecil imagines that priests themselves violate that inward realm and work to expose the political truths lying within the queen's subjects: "they search and sound the depths and secrets of all men's inward intentions...either against Her Majesty or for her" (39). Cecil translates an ostensibly religious inwardness into a political one ("either against Her Majesty or for her"). In Cecil's rhetoric, what Elizabeth Hanson has called the "hideous intimacy of torture"—the struggle it stages between those who would expose and those who would protect—is inverted: priests probe inward intentions, searching as they would later be searched by tormentors.[43] To defend torture Cecil again turns to decorum: those who would violate the "secrets of all men's inward intentions" are subjected to violation. This is only slightly more subtle than the appended *Declaration*, whose author claims that priests are tortured "in as charitable manner as such a thing might be." A more chilling example of what Alexandra Walsham calls "charitable hatred" would be hard to find.[44]

Cecil's decorous torture and rhetoric of political discovery adapt a common feature of anti-Catholic polemic: its claim to unmask the hypocrisy (I use the word in its etymological sense) of the Roman Church with its histrionic, seductive performances concealing the Antichrist within. Foxe's mocking of the "gauds and pageants" (such as the anointing of a rood) celebrating Mary Tudor and Philip II's wedding is but one case in point.[45]

---

43. Elizabeth Hanson, *Discovering the Subject in Renaissance England* (Cambridge: Cambridge University Press, 1998), chap. 2.

44. Alexandra Walsham, *Charitable Hatred: Tolerance and Intolerance in England, 1500–1700* (Manchester: Manchester University Press, 2006).

45. *Actes and Monuments* (London, 1583), 1472.

What Cecil proposes is an Elizabethan hermeneutics of suspicion, whereby Catholic religion's true signification is political. Such hermeneutics were not lost on Catholic writers. In a poem about Campion's execution, the author insists that Campion was no military threat but sought spiritual battle only: "He came by vow, the cause to conquer sinne, / his armor prayer, the word his targe & shield."[46] This poem circulated widely; it was appended to the end of Alfield's martyrology and set to music by William Byrd. It was also refuted by Anthony Munday, a government apologist: "he came by vowe, the cause, his Princesse foyle, / his armor, Treason, to his Countryes woe."[47] Cecil seems to respond to the common claim that the first poem elucidates: that priests could not be traitors as they are unarmed, their only weapons those of spiritual warfare. Thus Cecil terms the Pope "a foreign potentate and open enemy" who has "already declared the Queen to be no lawful queen, to have maintained the known rebels and traitors, to have invaded Her Majesty's dominions with open war" (37). Knowing the Pope's actions, priests therefore become "accessories and adherents proper to further and continue all rebellions and wars…if they will deny that none are traitors that are not armed, they will make Judas no traitor that came to Christ without armor, coloring his treason with a kiss" (37). If Catholic priests are like Judas, then Elizabeth I becomes the potential martyr, the one whose physical *imitatio Christi* Cecil's vigilant efforts are to prevent.

Cecil's argument may again be framed in terms of decorum: the government merely recognizes what the papacy has already done in turning religion into political hostility. In a passage that Cecil expanded in his second edition, he insists that upon promulgating *Regnans in Excelsis* the Pope

> left *verbum* and took *ferrum*, that is, left to feed by the word, **which was his office**, and began to strike with the sword, **which was forbidden him**, and stirred her noblemen and people directly to disobedience and to open rebellion, **which was the office of Dathan and Abiram**, and that her lewd subjects by his commandment had executed the same with all the forces which they could make or bring into the field; who with common reason can disallow that

---

46. In Alfield, *A True Report*, E1r.

47. *A breefe Aunswer made unto two seditious Pamphlets* (London, 1582), Dviir.

Her Majesty used her royal lawful authority and by her forces lawful
subdued rebels' forces unlawful, and punished the authors thereof
no otherwise than the Pope himself useth to do with his own rebellious subjects in the patrimony of his Church. (33; italics in original;
boldface marks the second edition's additions)

Cecil writes in neat parallels: lawful forces subdue unlawful, the Queen
punishes rebellious subjects as does the Pope. By exercising word and
sword, the Pope violates scriptural warrant for St. Peter's supposed
successors: "St. Peter was charged thrice at one time by his Lord and
Master: Pasce oves meas, 'Feed my sheep,' and peremptorily forbidden to
use a sword, in saying to him: Converte gladium tuum in locum suum, or,
Mitte gladium tuum in vaginam, that is, 'Turn thy sword into his place,'
or, 'Put thy sword into the scabbard' " (23). The regime's reading of priestly
words as militant actions is predicated upon the papacy's failure to distinguish *verbum* from *ferrum* in its attempted usurpation of Caesar's power.

Cecil insists, then, that the Elizabethan regime merely responds in
kind to the priests' own structures of treason. But his treatise also, perhaps
unwittingly, manifests skepticism about its own decorous methods of proceeding. If the bloody (or "few" and "very apt") questions are designed
to elicit an inward truth, they seem destined to fail insofar as Cecil constructs priests' inwardness itself as false: they have only "so-called conscience" within (47) and even their answers to their interrogators proceed
"colorably" (14). In addition to a model of treason as something which
lurks beneath the mask of rhetorical finesse, whereby treason may in turn
be disclosed by a superior rhetorical interpreter, Cecil posits an organic
model: that Catholicism may itself be seditious by nature. Playing on the
etymology of "seminary," Cecil suggests that Catholic seminaries' leaders
are "seditious seedmen and sowers of rebellion" (7). The sedition they
bring forth seems the natural result of the Catholicism they sow. Cecil's
claim that the government would cease its prosecution if Catholics would
only be open about their religious "travails" (40) thus seems suspect given
his figurative terms; if Catholic priests are by nature treasonous "seedmen
of sedition" (37), such a cessation would prove impossible. Cecil writes
that if Catholic priests would be open in their movements and religious
practices, "all color and occasion of shedding the blood of any more of [the
Queen's] natural subjects of this land, yea, all further bodily punishments,
should utterly cease" (40). Cecil distinguishes those sown in foreign soil
from England's natural subjects, and strikingly the government—not

the traitor—deploys "color and occasion." "Color" may mark a slip of the statesman's mask, as prosecution slides into persecution: does the English government color, or does it not? Must the "coloring" of treasons with religion be decorously countered by "coloring" religious persecution as legitimate prosecution?

Perhaps inevitably, the treatise ultimately bears witness to the limits of persuasion.[48] Cecil's treatise enacts a gradual reduction of audience, from its wide opening gambit to a final act of enclosure. In his first sentence, Cecil follows standard rhetorical practice by beginning with a point of broad agreement:

> It hath been in all ages and in all countries a common usage of all offenders for the most part, both great and small, to make defense of their lewd and unlawful facts by untruths and by coloring and covering their deeds (were they never so vile) with pretenses of some other causes of contrary operations or effects, to the intent not only to avoid punishment or shame but to continue, uphold, and prosecute their wicked attempts to the full satisfaction of their disordered and malicious appetites. (3)

Allen mocks this opening precisely as bad schoolboy rhetoric: labeling it an "exordium" (the opening of a speech in classical rhetoric), he complains that Cecil begins "with a common sentence, as meet for us and our matter as for him and his cause" (58). Allen's complaint targets Cecil's gambit for broad agreement, yet Cecil himself punctures the possibilities for broad persuasion as the treatise wears on, his audience seemingly contracting as he writes. Early in the treatise, Cecil remarks that despite "all manner gentle ways of persuasions" used with Catholic priests, the "canker of their rebellious humors" was "so deeply entered and graven into the hearts of many of them as they would not be removed from their traitorous determinations" (7). Treason is again a matter of either deep organicism or permanent marking, a natural trait or ingrained defect unsusceptible to "gentle," rhetorical proceedings. In the tract's final third, Cecil acknowledges that the identification of traitors is subjective,

---

48. Lander argues that polemic does not seek to persuade its addressee but to divide its audience into friends and enemies; it does not hope to convince the object of its attack but to sway a wider audience; see Jesse M. Lander, *Inventing Polemic: Religion, Print, and Literary Culture in Early Modern England* (Cambridge: Cambridge University Press, 2006).

or at least determined by categories of interpretation established prior to reading:

> Although these former reasons are sufficient to persuade all kind of reasonable persons to allow of her Majesty's actions to be good, reasonable, lawful, and necessary; yet because it may be that such as have by frequent reading of false artificial libels and by giving credit to them upon a prejudice or forejudgment afore grounded by their rooted opinions in favor of the Pope, will rest unsatisfied...it shall suffice briefly, in a manner of a repetition of the former reasons, to remember these things following. (32)

Again the organic metaphor ("rooted") delimits persuasion. By the treatise's end, that delimiting is complete:

> Now if this latter repetition, as it were, of all the former causes and reasons afore recited, may not serve to stop the boisterous mouths and the pestiferous tongues and venomous breaths of these that are infected with so gross errors as to defend seditious subjects, stirrers of rebellion against their natural prince and country, then are they to be left without any further argument to the judgment of the Almighty God, as persons that have covered their eyes against the sun's light, stopped their ears against the sound of justice, and oppressed their hearts against the force of reason; and, as the psalmist saith, "They speak lies, they are as venomous as the poison of a serpent, even like the deaf adder that stoppeth his ears." (39–40)

The sentence begins with the images drawn from Psalm 58 (lying mouths, poison, and venom) toward which it purportedly drives. The sentence reflects, in other words, the gradual tightening of the treatise's imagined audience to a closed interpretive circle. The Geneva Bible's translators explain the verses Cecil quotes thus: the wicked "passe in malice, and subtiltie the craftie serpent, which coulde preserve him selfe by stopping his eare from the inchanter." An impenetrable closing of the ears to Cecil's arguments—or to Cecil's rhetorical enchantments?—is here the sure sign of wicked intransigence. The appended *Declaration*—whose claim that the regime tortured people gently surely spoke only to those already supportive of the government's actions—looks like a logical extension of the gradual narrowing of persuasion that Cecil's treatise itself enacts.

Rendering unto Caesar?

Modern scholars have found in Cecil a persistent, determined use of rhetoric's resources for the good of the English Protestant state.[49] From Allen's perspective, Cecil's careful rhetoric conceals falsehood: "the libel maketh a solemn rhetorical tale" (88). But in Allen's treatise too rhetorical concerns are central—if anything, more self-consciously than in Cecil's. If Cecil uses a rhetoric of exposure, Allen attempts one of enclosure. In the process, Allen makes an accidental argument for freedom of conscience, though not in modern terms. For example, Allen shares Cecil's typically early modern suspicion of "privacy," as he usually distinguishes between that which is private—and therefore subjectively unstable—and that which is inward and thus presumed to be genuinely true.[50] Further, for Allen religion is not simply or only inward but also a public matter (70). This view is shared by Catholics who, like Allen, advocated strict recusancy and those (like the priest Alban Langdale) who argued that Catholics could attend services as dutiful citizens of the state provided they also gave public signs of their Catholicism.[51] Yet the circumstances facing Catholics in England mean that Allen is pressed to defend the right of priests to keep their innermost thoughts to themselves. Quoting the priest Thomas Cottam (ex. May 30, 1582), Allen argues that priests tortured for matters of religion withhold that which is most sacred from their tormentors:

> Indeed [quoth he] you are searchers of secrets, for you would needs know of me what penance I was enjoined by my ghostly father for my sins committed. And I acknowledge my frailty that to avoid the intolerable torment of the rack I confessed (God forgive me) what they demanded therein. But when they further urged me to utter also what my sins were for which that penance was enjoined

---

49. Stephen Alford, *Burghley: William Cecil at the Court of Elizabeth I* (New Haven: Yale University Press, 2008).

50. On meanings of "private," see Erica Longfellow, "Public, Private, and the Household in Early Seventeenth-Century England," *Journal of British Studies* 45.2 (2006), pp. 313–34.

51. See Alban Langdale's manuscript treatise, *Why Catholics may go to Church*, of 1580, of which selections appear in Robert Miola, ed., *Early Modern Catholicism: An Anthology of Primary Sources* (Oxford: Oxford University Press, 2007). On the increasing untenability of arguments for Catholic conformity in the wake of high-profile executions (such as that of Margaret Clitherow in 1586) and high-profile Catholic defections (such as that of Thomas Bell in 1592), see Peter Lake and Michael Questier, *The Trials of Margaret Clitherow: Persecution, Martyrdom, and the Politics of Sanctity in Elizabethan England* (London: Continuum, 2011).

me (a loathsome and unchristian question), I then answered that
I would not disclose my offenses saving to God and to my ghostly
father alone. (72)

Defending himself against the "searchers of secrets," Cottam defines the
words he spoke in the confessional as sacrosanct. Cottam's public confession of his inward secret both proclaims his religion clearly—he refutes
claims that he was questioned only on matters of treason and not of "mere
conscience, faith, and religion"—and yet does so in such a way as to protect the confessional's secrecy.

If Allen values a realm of conscience free from government scrutiny,
he shares with Cecil a suspicion of the private. In early modern English,
private can mean simply "not pertaining to the public good," or it can
refer to that which is particular or singular to an individual. For Cecil,
what is private or secret is almost always threatening. For Allen, what
is private is usually sectarian and (merely) subjective. For example, he
argues that it would be better for commonwealths if religious differences
between sovereign and people were resolved by the supreme pastor instead of "popular mutiny and fantasy of *private* men" (emphasis added).
The distinction between (Catholic) inwardness and (Protestant) privacy
grounds his statement that "most" of the regime's leaders are "untroubled
by conscience" (74). In late sixteenth-century martyrological discourse,
conscience does not refer primarily to personal ethical judgment or individual religious belief; instead, conscience is understood as a repository
for ultimate truth, a sort of interface with the divine. Neither Foxe nor
Allen can imagine that people truly adhering to their consciences would
differ in matters of religion. Because true consciences should align with
each other, Allen assumes that the regime's leaders must either lack or
fail to heed conscience, following instead mere private opinion.[52] Insofar
as Allen argues that Catholic priests should be able to preserve an inward
realm free of government intrusion, he makes a backdoor argument for
freedom of conscience. But he does not make a broader argument for
toleration, largely because, as Kingdon argues, he does not believe in it.[53]
His treatise elevates inward religious conviction, in alignment with papal
teaching and authority, over the claims of temporal powers but does not

52. See Monta, *Martyrdom and Literature*, chap. 1.

53. Kingdon, "Introduction," p. xxvi.

countenance conceptions of conscience upon which a theory of broader toleration might be based.

Because the state should hold its people's religious well-being as its highest good, Allen criticizes "Protestants and politiques" who through a perverse "analogy of faith" measure Christian religion only "so far forth as it serveth for policy and the advancement of the prince or temporal state" (203). Like Cecil, Allen reduces his adversaries' religion to political strategizing. Despite his criticism of Protestants' "analogy of faith," Allen makes extended use of analogy himself, likening, for example, English persecutors to Roman imperial ones and suffering Catholics to their victims. If Cecil employs decorum to argue for the regime's proportionate responses to treasonous threats, then Allen employs *analogia* (a figure of proportion which invites inference, expansion, and application beyond the structures of the text itself) to gesture lightly at some of his most militant arguments.

For example, Allen uses an analogy of the relationship between body and soul to suggest the differing responsibilities of spiritual and temporal powers:

> The condition of these two powers...is like unto the distinct state of the same spirit and body or flesh in a man, where either of them having their proper and peculiar operations, ends, and objects, which in other natures may be severed (as in brutes, where flesh is and not spirit; in angels, where spirit is but not flesh), are yet in man cojoined in person; and nevertheless so distinct in faculties and operations that the flesh hath her actions peculiar and the soul hers; but not without subalternation or dependence. (155)

Allen develops an analogy in which the body and soul, though dependent on each other, have separate and implicitly ordered spheres (it is clear which is brutish, which angelic). Later in the treatise, Allen's body-and-soul analogy becomes Pauline and more explicitly hierarchical. Allen draws upon Galatians 5:17 to suggest that "in a man's own person...the flesh resisteth the spirit and contrariwise the spirit the flesh, each one of them seeking after a sort to enlarge his own limits and commodities by some hindrance of the other." This strife is "either tolerable or not damnable so long as the inferior, which is the flesh, by over-greedy appetite of her own advancement destroyeth not the superior, which is the soul" (207). But when "the body politic" commits "evident rape and violence" against the

Catholic Church's sovereignty the result is state tyranny and "abominable apostasy, schism, and desolation" (208). The shift to Pauline contexts saddles the temporal power's analogical partner—the flesh—with sinful freight, as for Paul flesh is often concupiscence or persistent sinfulness. For Allen, as for Paul, some "moderate strife" may be inevitable so long as this life lingers. But in Allen's analogy it is clear which power should prevail.

Allen also uses biblical and historical exempla to defend the pope's right to depose heretics. Allen insists that he discusses general principles, not any person in particular: "affirming that [the Queen] may be deposed for heresy doth not at all avouch her to be [a heretic]" (131). Yet he effectively asks readers trained in humanist schoolrooms to arrest their most basic interpretive habits, whereby historical examples and general precepts are applied to contemporary circumstances. Thus Allen's references to St. Peter's power to strike dead the likes of Ananias and Sapphira could not have reassured the Queen that she was in no danger from those who upheld the power of Peter's successors (197), nor could Allen's repeated discussions of the emperor Theodosius's humble submission to the rebuke of St. Ambrose, Bishop of Milan (158, 249), have much assuaged her.[54]

Critical to Allen's argument are the Synoptic Gospel passages in which Jesus defeats potentially entrapping questions by urging listeners to "Render therfore the things that are Caesars, to Caesar: and the things that are Gods, to God" (trans. Martin). Interpreting this passage, Allen follows the 1582 Rheims annotations (Allen was closely involved with the translation). Those annotations interpret the passage so as to promote ecclesiastical over temporal authorities, as in these notes on Mark 12:

> Heretikes, to flatter temporal Princes, and by them to uphold their Heresies, doe not only inculcate mens dutie to the Prince, dissembling that which is dewe to God: but also give to the Prince more then dew, and take from God his right and dutie. But Christ allowing Caesar his right, warneth them also of their dutie toward God.[55]

---

54. Repeated allusions to Ambrose may be a subtle tribute to Campion, who wrote a neo-Latin play (*Ambrosia*, probably 1578) on Ambrose's confrontation with Theodosius.

55. The Geneva Bible also delimits how much should be ceded to Caesar: "Christians must obey their Magistrates, although they be wicked and extortioners, but so far as the authority that God hath over us may remain safe unto him, and his honor is not diminished." Notes like this are one reason conservative Protestants (such as Richard Bancroft) distrusted the Geneva translation.

Similarly, Allen likens Christ's situation to that of English Catholics. Considering the bloody questions, he writes,

> Some such demands the Scribes and Pharisees and other of the Jews' sectaries proposed in times past to our Savior, to entrap Him in speech and to drive Him to utter some treasonable words or conceit against the Emperor's regality....Of which tempting questions, though Christ by His divine wisdom easily discharged Himself, nevertheless they ceased not still to exclaim: *Hunc invenimus prohibentem tributa dare Caesari* [we have found this man forbidding the payment of tribute to Caesar] as others did afterward the like of St. Stephen and St. Paul; and even so now our English Sadducees are not satisfied but by blood, never resting till they have pressed or sucked out something, at least for men's intentions or other casual events to come, that may sound against their duties to the Queen. (128–29)

Allen alludes to the Caesar passage as well as to the charge articulated before Pontius Pilate that Jesus prohibited the giving of tribute to Caesar. Allen's argument places the Caesar passage within the context of Holy Week, during which the liturgy reenacts the last events of Jesus's life, and likens persecuting English authorities to persecuting Jewish authorities ("our English Sadducees"). He then issues a warning: "whosoever do give to Caesar that which is due to God...shall at length prove (with what human prowess, power, or prudence soever they sustain their factions) that they have unevenly and unadvisedly matched their combat." It is hard to take "combat" in purely metaphorical ways. Kingdon has charged Allen with a lack of "frankness." Allen was engaged in plots to invade England and overthrow its Protestant regime before, during, and after writing this treatise; further, the treatise in which he argues that missionary priests do not engage in political activities itself makes a lengthy case for the Pope's right to depose heretical rulers.[56] What Kingdon calls a lack of frankness may also be a by-product of the shifting audiences Allen imagines for himself. Initially, Allen (like Cecil) claims to address all reasonable people: "we trust in the reader's equity, be he Catholic or Protestant" (55). Allen shifts his mode of address, however, repeatedly. As often in lyric poetry, both directly addressed and slant audiences are invoked, including beleaguered English Catholics wondering whether to stay the course and foreign

---

56. Kingdon, *The Execution*, "Introduction," pp. xxxiii–xxxvi.

leaders meant to overhear and, presumably, convert ploughshares into swords.[57] Among Allen's stated reasons for making this treatise public is the desire to communicate "with our brethren in faith and the Churches of other provinces... both for their warning and our comfort and to excite in them Christian compassion toward us." Allen claims as his model for this language two of St. Basil's letters (letters 92 and 243).[58] What Allen does not state explicitly is that these letters, written at moments when Arians threatened to overpower Basil's orthodox Christians, asked for Western assistance both spiritual and imperial. Allen tells the truth but tells it slant: sympathetic readers who are or have access to foreign princes should infer the context for Basil's letters, overhear justifications for action, and be persuaded to act.

In his closing words Allen follows rhetorical advice by repeating his treatise's main points—that the regime produces, not uncovers, traitors; that Catholics will practice their religion openly if given "liberty of conscience"; that English Catholics' situation mirrors that of the persecuted early Church; and that persecution cannot eradicate Catholicism in England. He then invokes a piece of writing that made Campion a target and, in a sense, launched the entire controversy: Campion's apology or "Brag." On his arrival in England, Campion wrote an apology in anticipation of his capture:

> We have made a league—all the Jesuits in the world, whose succession and multitude must overreach all the practices of England—cheerfully to carry the cross you shall lay upon us, and never to despair your recovery, while we have a man left to enjoy your Tyburn, or to be racked with your torments, or consumed with your prisons. The expense is reckoned, the enterprise is begun; it is of God; it cannot be withstood. So the faith was planted: so it must be restored.[59]

Allen writes, "We are no better than our forefathers. We less fear death and set less by our lives than ever before. Our counts are cast and allowed"

---

57. Allen's claim that two-thirds of the English incline to Catholicism (see Allen, *Modest Defence*, p. 224) is both his own mistaken opinion and seemingly designed to appeal to would-be interventionist Catholic monarchs.

58. Allen may take up a suggestion in the 1582 Rheims New Testament endnote to Matthew 22 which cites Ambrose's funeral oration for Basil to support the statement that "a good emperour is within the Church, not above the Church."

59. In Evelyn Waugh, *Edmund Campion: A Life* (San Francisco: Ignatius Press, 2005; reprint of 1935 edition), p. 208.

(268). Enjoying Tyburn indeed: in Allen's echo Campion still haunts the regime. In letting Augustine have the last words—"Nemo delet de coelo constitutionem Dei; Nemo delet de terra Ecclesiam Dei" (268) (nobody destroys in heaven the order of God; nobody destroys on earth the Church of God)—Allen is concerned with God and the Church. He does not, finally, much worry about the preservation of Caesar's reign. Given Allen's consistent arguments for the elevation of spiritual over temporal powers and for the papacy's right to exercise temporal power in rebuking heresy, the "apostolical fight and combat" for which Allen and other Catholics are prepared may not be entirely spiritual. Allen has rendered unto Caesar less than the English government would require.

How, then, are distinctions drawn between martyrs and traitors in early modern England? Both Allen and Cecil enlist traditional resources of literary studies—philology, rhetoric, biblical hermeneutics, figurae—for the making of martyrs and traitors. Their treatises also mark the horizons of rhetorical effectiveness, often evincing a hermeneutic circle with particularly vicious consequences, through the 1580s and beyond. As the early modern period wears on, arguments for toleration emerge. Roger Williams's *The Bloudy Tenent, of Persecution* (1644) forcefully claims that "the blood of so many hundred thousand souls of *Protestants* and *Papists*, spilt in the *Wars* of *present* and *former Ages*, for their respective *Consciences*, is not *required* nor *accepted* by *Jesus Christ* the *Prince of Peace*" [original emphases].[60] And there are many instance of *de facto* toleration, of Catholics and Calvinists getting along in daily life, both in areas of England and the continent.[61] But in the 1580s, neither Allen nor Cecil was willing to relinquish his model of theocracy—Erastian, for Cecil, or the spiritual subjection of temporal powers to the papacy's religious government, for Allen. Neither could imagine a stable religiously plural state. Christ's aphoristic solution dividing duties neatly between temporal and spiritual authorities stumped not only the Pharisees: the enactment of its balanced solution in the early modern period, the rendering unto Caesar what is Caesar's and to God what is God's, would continue to elude.

---

60. "Williams, *The Bloudy Tenent* (London, 1644), a2.

61. Anthony Milton, *Catholic and Reformed: The Roman and Protestant Churches in English Protestant Thought, 1600–1640* (Cambridge: Cambridge University Press, 1995); Christine Kooi, *Calvinists and Catholics during Holland's Golden Age: Heretics and Idolaters* (Cambridge: Cambridge University Press, 2012); and Howard Louthan, ed., *Diversity and Dissent: Negotiating Religious Difference in Central Europe* (New York: Berghahn, 2011).

4

Kristeva's "New Knowledge"

TERRORISM, MARTYRDOM, AND PSYCHOANALYTIC HUMANISM: INSIGHTS FROM TWO EARLY MODERN INSTANCES

Gary Waller

The intellectual today faces a difficult, historical task worthy of the crisis of civilization: The task is neither more nor less than to help this new type of knowledge to gradually emerge.
JULIA KRISTEVA, *This Incredible Need to Believe* (2009)

IN CONSIDERING TERRORISM and martyrdom—terms that may often describe the same commitment or action—can we outline a psychological profile of those for whom these acts seem natural, even acceptable or praiseworthy, human responses? Are we looking at deep-seated psychological and genetic conditioning or at socially produced patterns of behavior? What historically produced patterns does belief in a supernatural justification for such responses produce, even at the elementary level of the "oceanic feeling" of religion about which Freud expressed such puzzlement?[1] Or are we trapped into supernatural explanations? Could modernity, as partially and incompletely as it has been absorbed by many societies, substantially change the seemingly universal connections between religious

---

1. Sigmund Freud, *Civilization and its Discontents*, trans. James Strachey (New York: W. W. Norton, 2005), pp. 35–36.

commitments and potential violence? And, further, might there be a gendered dimension to terrorism and martyrdom?

In this chapter I make only a gesture toward answering such questions, focusing on the "new knowledge" of psychoanalysis of which Kristeva writes in my epigraph. "Does psychoanalysis," she asks further, have anything to offer to an "understanding" or "reading" of terrorism?[2] Can psychoanalysis, which claims to occupy much of the same story-making space in the unconscious as religion, now open up a less invasive and ideologically confrontational space for discussion of the multiple interconnections between religion and violence than the religions themselves so often seem able to do? Kristeva's argument is that the crisis of the early twenty-first century poses the urgent challenge of constructing alternative ways of describing and educating human societies, and doing so—as she so movingly proclaimed to Pope Benedict XVI's 2011 multi-faith conference in Assisi—in terms of a renewed humanism. Can post-religious, humanist philosophies offer us a new degree of hope? Are there ways of detaching what Kristeva terms the human being's "incredible need to believe" from its derivative, "religion"? In her Assisi address, Kristeva explicitly aligned her psychoanalytic secular humanism—what elsewhere she has termed her stance as a "Christian Atheist"—with Christian, Renaissance, and Enlightenment humanism and challenged "religion" to take up its humanist vocation and oppose terrorism by means other than reactive violence.[3]

So the question arises: is there a necessary connection between religion and violence? The immensely rich metaphorical hinterland of religious discourses is ominously permeated with projections of violence, struggle, aggressiveness, war, and sacrifice of self and others. The history of religions shows that most have overwhelmingly been preoccupied with what is presented as a primordial and never-ending cosmic war between Good and Evil, and these metaphors and the inner struggles they represent are seemingly inevitably externalized into material realities. The analyst Ruth Stein observes that religiously committed clients characteristically depict their truths, struggles, and hopes through the symbolics of war, victory,

---

2. Julia Kristeva, *This Incredible Need to Believe*, trans. Beverley Bie Brahic (New York: Columbia University Press, 2009), p. xv.

3. For "Christian Atheist," see Julia Kristeva and Catherine Clément, *The Feminine and the Sacred* (New York: Columbia University Press, 2002), p. 175. For Kristeva's contribution to the Assisi conference, see http://www.kristeva.fr/assisi2011_en.html.

defeat; it is as if "a certain [in multiple senses] God has taken over and is monopolizing the psyche, and he now commands the would-be terrorist to kill the 'infidel' part of the psyche so that 'He, God, will be content'." The inner struggles of religion become concretized, with the evil split off, projected, and tagged onto what are cast out as infidels and heretics, in what Stein terms a "degenerative process of literalization." In that way, a communal psychological need is fulfilled: sanctioned and thereby "holy" violence, including self-directed as well as "other"-directed violence, justified as sacrifice or martyrdom, may be valorized as the ultimate religious act, not as a death-directed aberration. The historian-psychoanalyst Naomi Janowitz, whose research combines psychoanalysis with investigations of Judaism, Christianity, and Graeco-Roman religions in late antiquity, argues that the overwhelming bulk of martyrdom stories are associated with a firm belief in the afterlife and with a dual psychological motivation: to obey the father and be reunited with the mother. Commenting on the earliest chronicle of Jewish martyrs in the Hebrew Bible, in II Maccabees—which she sees as the prototype of all subsequent Jewish, Christian, and Muslim martyrdom—Janowitz argues that "martyrdom would never have emerged without the promise of an afterlife" and the fantasy of "lusting for death" in the words of the early Christian theologian Ignatius which, it is believed, will free the martyr from the "helpless dependence on the maternal imago" and satisfy the divine father who will "birth him into an eternal life better than the birth given him by his mother." It is a pattern, Janowitz ruefully comments, that we can expect "until such time as the myths themselves change."[4]

The commonplace thinking of political authorities has historically been to fight violence with more and to use such seemingly deep-seated religious urges as justification for such actions as if what a recent collection of essays terms "hating in the first person plural" is thereby sanctioned by the deepest reaches of the collective and individual unconscious.[5] The culture of the death drive was all too blatantly expressed in the Bush doctrine of "shock and awe" and the massive ideological incoherence and material

4. Naomi Janowitz, "Lusting for Death: Some Unconscious Fantasies in an Ancient Jewish Martyrdom Text," *Psychoanalytic Psychology* 23 (2006), p. 652. But note also the ways in Cooper's and Afsaruddin's chapters in this volume question the extent to which martyrdom (particularly ancient) has always fundamentally been linked to such "death lust."

5. Ruth Stein, "Evil as Love and as Liberation: The Mind of a Suicidal Religious Terrorist," *Psychoanalytical Dialogue* 12 (2002), pp. 393–420, at pp. 411 and 417.

destructiveness of state-sponsored terrorist invasion continued by his supposedly different presidential successor in Afghanistan and Pakistan, to mention only the most obvious current "theaters" of violence, a metaphor to which I will return. There is unquestionably a religious dimension projected by both sides of these conflicts: as Terry Eagleton commented on the Bush policies, the dangerous links between religion and politics are uncannily similar in Texas and among the Taliban. They represent, as Kristeva phrases it, different but ominously alike, "fundamentalism" and "obscurantism."[6]

Can psychoanalysis help in such circumstances? At best, it might be argued, the challenge of terrorism requires sober rationality, surely, not theoretical speculation or therapeutic processes open only to the affluent. We are, after all, dealing with a proliferation of specific and concrete actions and intentions, not just arguments and speculations. On one day a young woman professing an outlawed variation of a dominant religious creed was executed; here, a terrorist (or heroic martyr) strapped a bomb to him- or herself and its explosion killed forty people; and here, as we look back, perhaps indeed for guidance or justification, to the stories of our cultural past, a blinded captive killed himself along with many of his enemies by pulling down the pillars of a building to which he was tied, and felt (perhaps correctly, perhaps wrongly) that his actions were justified by (at least his own) god. Yet, however located in the material details of history such incidents described as "terrorism" or "martyrdom" may be, the very concepts of "event" or "material details" themselves are always already under dispute. In addition to political or historical dimensions, they may involve spiritual, psychological, or delusional projections to which psychoanalysis and related branches of cultural criticism may be able to speak and help us read.

How, then, might we depict and engage with that problematic dimension of such "events"? Traditionally, a variety of religious stories would have been immediately recognizable as applicable, and indeed many (or parodies of them) were all too apparent in post-9/11 rhetorics, most notably in such apocalyptic metaphors as "crusade" used by the Bush/Blair regimes or Bush's claim that "this confrontation is willed by God, who wants to use this conflict to erase his people's enemies before

---

6. Julia Kristeva, *The Sense and Nonsense of Revolt the Powers and Limits of Psychoanalysis*, trans. Jeanine Herman (New York: Columbia University Press, 2001), p. 21; Terry Eagleton, *Holy Terror* (Oxford: Oxford University Press, 2005), p. 2; and Kristeva, *Incredible Need*, p. 2.

a New Age begins."[7] For centuries, such metaphors and the worldviews from which they grew seemed to offer acceptable explanations and justifications. They are stories that seem to connect ominously with some of the deepest realities in what Freud named or invented as the unconscious, and to evoke further stories and behaviors that may lead to reactive and random destruction (terrorism) or altruistic self-immolation (martyrdom) and so serve to justify rather than remediate human destruction. Can, therefore, we find ways to avoid the emergence of the death-directedness of traditional explanations of such events? Must they always be death-directed? And can Kristeva's "new" or "risky" knowledge be of service here?

My earlier mention of the pre-Enlightenment (or the Early Modern period, as some literary and cultural historians have somewhat ambiguously termed it) was an era which the West rehearsed, as it were, the fears of modernization and ultimately the postmodern crisis of the death of God, and it leads me to this chapter's two brief case studies from the early modern period, in which the issues of violence, terrorism, and martyrdom surfaced with a ferocity that anticipates the period of European revolution of the late eighteenth and the holocausts of the twentieth centuries. I look, however, not to confessional documents or epochal historical events like the Thirty Years Wars of religion, the contrasting yet echoing Marian and Elizabethan persecutions in England, or the 1582 massacre of Huguenots, but more to what we conventionally regard as the cultural margins, to examples from poetry and drama where (as so often happens) pre-emergent alternatives within a culture are explored and given voice. In England, for instance, Shakespeare's plays register the mixture of boldness and nostalgia associated with losing the magical Catholic world of the Middle Ages, not quite knowing what it will be replaced by, and the self- and other-directed violence that impasse may generate. What is the status of the artistic imagination in the symbolization of violence? "The sleeping and the dead," pronounces Lady Macbeth, "are but as pictures"; and "'tis the eye of childhood / That fears a painted devil" (II. ii. 36–38). Yet, as Kristeva affirms, in a post-magical world, it is what is "painted," the "pictures," that provide us with perhaps our last access to the sacred.[8] We need to ask, I believe, what can the arts, even though they are seemingly

---

7. Quoted in http://www.alternet.org/news/140221, 19785.

8. S. K. Keitner, "Politics from 'a bit of a distance'," in Kelly Oliver, ed., *Psychoanalysis, Aesthetics, and Politics in the Work of Kristeva* (Albany: SUNY Press, 2009), p. 6.

at the cultural margins, tell us about the human self? Drama is especially subversive of monolithic assertions and inherently encouraging to alternative, even oppositional, experiences. In the theater, Peter Lake notes, "we are confronted with a sort of playpen in which participants could adapt and lay aside, ventriloquize and caricature, try on for size and discard a whole variety of subject positions, claims to authority, arguments and counter-arguments."[9] Theater thus poses a liminal space in which multiple perspectives can interact, allowing the drama to stage not only orthodoxy but its underlying ideological contradictions and the deep-seated often pre-discursive feelings that word, image, sound all try to capture.

I have therefore chosen two early modern dramatic texts to open some of these issues affecting the relationships between religion, terror, and martyrdom. I will first look at John Milton's *Samson Agonistes* (1671). This was a text written late in Milton's life, a decade after of the defeat of the Puritan revolution and the return of the monarchy, in which the terrorist/martyrdom paradox is foregrounded explicitly—some would say brutally and embarrassingly—and with poignant connections to what Milton saw as a contemporary attack on the institutions and expression of true religion. Then I bring my argument on the insights offered by a psychoanalytical reading of culture to its conclusion by looking at Shakespeare's *Macbeth*, a text constructed in the shadow of a particular terrorist attack that produced a number of victims who have been labeled as martyrs by those espousing their cause. Both works open up aspects of the archaic origins of religious violence: Milton's work focuses on religion and martyrdom, Shakespeare's on religion and terrorism. Both suggest ways we might think of how Kristeva's "new knowledge" might emerge and become part of cultural discourse.[10]

Gods (and goddesses) may disappear (just as in certain ages, Regina Schwartz argues, they may reappear), but early modern authorities, of whatever confessional allegiance, like most of their modern descendants, insisted that their God did not.[11] Traditionally, the Samson story in Judges

---

9. Peter Lake, with Michael Questier, *The Antichrist's Lewd Hat: Protestants, Papists and Players in Post-Reformation England* (New Haven: Yale University Press, 2002), p. 379.

10. Quotations from Milton's poem are taken from *Poems*, ed. John Cary with Alastair Fowler (London: Longman, 1968), and from Shakespeare's play, *Works*, ed. J. Blakemore Evans et al. (Boston: Houghton Mifflin, 1974). Specific references are incorporated into the text.

11. Regina Mara Schwartz, *Sacramental Poetics at the Dawn of Secularism: When God left the World* (Stanford, Calif.: Stanford University Press, 2008), p. 140.

was seen as reinforcing that belief. Samson's self-sacrificing destruction of the Philistines' temple, along with three thousand worshippers of their particular god, was regarded as an act of heroism, embodying a religious faith that, even though involving dramatic self-destruction, would bring about a just massacre and so constitute a valid expression of holy martyrdom authenticated by the deity the perpetrator served. By this reading, Samson conceives his role as that of revenger for his people's humiliation, using whatever means were deemed necessary. Until the Reformation, and beyond, that has been the dominant reading of the Samson story. But in the century following the Reformation, at least in Protestant Europe, the story becomes "split," to adapt a psychological term, with a range of readings of Samson, from patriotic hero to tragic self-delusive suicide—or as we would now say, from martyr to terrorist.

The somewhat rarified arena of modern Anglo-American Milton studies has in recent years been startled by *Samson Agonistes* being described, notably by John Carey, as the celebration of a xenophobic suicide-hero. In 2002, Carey proposed that Milton's version of Samson exemplified the motives, planning and behavior of a suicide bomber. The result was a storm, back and forth, between supporters of his argument and opponents of such blasphemies. The debate was in effect about what had hitherto been assumed to be an unchallenged commonsensical reading of the biblical story. The scandal, at least in 2002, so close to the tragedy of the previous year, was that a figure in the literary canon, the embodiment not just of English but Western and "civilized" Christian values, should be accused of having advocated an act of violence uncomfortably akin to the outrages against Western values perpetrated by modern terrorists. Carey in fact was raising the rather more sophisticated question of whether Milton approved of Samson's act, arguing that Samson may think he is carrying out God's will but might be mistaken, in which case (according to Milton's own soteriology) he would be damned. Milton's ambivalence, about which the text suggests he is not entirely conscious, comes through as something more broadly relevant than just *Samson Agonistes* or even Milton's own historical situatedness.

Why did the traditional (and still, among believers) dominant reading not see Samson's act as criminal and sinful? That very question, as Joseph Wittreich documents in detail, did in fact disturb increasing numbers of post-Reformation Protestant theologians.[12] The answer was, of course

---

12. John Carey, "A Work in Praise of Terrorism? September 11 and *Samson Agonistes*," *Times Literary Supplement*, no. 51886 (September 2002), pp. 15–16. See also Joseph Wittreich, *Why*

(often drawing on Hebrews 11:32 for further justification), that Samson's suicidal act was commanded by his religion, by God, and was therefore justifiable. Samson has carried out God's will, is his faithful servant, and his death is used to express Milton's encouragement to the defeated saints of the revolution to be patient and wait for the revival of the godly commonwealth. So, according to this reading, Milton tries to see Samson's suicide as a secondary accident, as "collateral damage" (as the modern obfuscation has it), with the death of the Philistines as God's judgment upon them. This hostility is justified by Samson's worshipping the true deity, "God, / Besides whom is no God, compar'd with Idols, / Disglorified, blasphem'd" and as Manoa, Samson's father, proclaims: "For God, / Nothing more certain, will not long defer / To vindicate the glory of his name." The Philistines, after all, worship superstitious, idolatrous gods— like Dagon the sea-idol—while Samson himself, as a Nazarite, is someone especially selected by and dedicated to the true God, and "design'd for great exploits" (162, 423, 440–442, 473–513). As Milton himself thundered, attacking those who saw Charles I as a royal martyr: "If to die for the testimony of his own conscience be enough to make him Martyr, what Heretic dying for direct blasphemie, as som have don, constantly, may not boast a Martyrdom?."[13] The question of whose god (or way of life) is the true one, and whose "blasphemie" unfortunately needs no obvious modern parallels.

For the Philistines, Samson is "A Murtherer, a Revolter, and a Robber." His wife Dalilah, whose tribe the biblical story intriguingly leaves ambiguous, finds herself in "long debate" and "hard contest" torn between desire and patriotic duty. For her, religion can also be seen as a motive: Samson is, after all, an "irreligious Dishonoror of dagon." Milton tells us that her religion is "superstition," but what slips through from the long treatment of Dalilah—the text, as it were, speaking against its author and indeed against the dominant interpretation of her as a scheming, alien whore— is that she, like Samson himself, is determined to uphold the righteousness of her own tribe's god (1180, 863–64, 15). As Cheryl Exum notes,

Milton Matters: A New Preface to his Writings (New York: Palgrave, 2006), pp. 141–94, and Alan Rudrum, "Review: Milton Scholarship and the 'Agon' over 'Samson Agonistes'," *Huntington Library Quarterly* 65 (2002), pp. 465–88. I am grateful to Professor Alison Chapman for her sharp observations on matters Miltonic in an early draft of this paper as well as elsewhere.

13. John Milton, *Eikonoklastes*, in *Complete Works*, ed. Merritt Y. Hughes (New Haven: Yale University Press, 1962), vol. 3, p. 376.

"patriotism is a believable motive" for Dalilah just as it is for Samson. Samson therefore can be read as starting as a patriot, propelled by providential guidance and perhaps ending as a deluded suicide—or as we would perhaps say, as a terrorist—who carries out his determination "both to destroy and be destroy'd," resulting in a state, Milton tells us in the final lines, "calm of mind all passion spent" (1587, 1758). And the poem, and arguably at some level the poet himself, disturbingly asks, at what cost? Milton's work is a clear example of how a text speaks despite its author, exceeding the authorial viewpoint even when that author is himself skeptical of the orthodoxies he has inherited. The unconscious of the text speaks out, revealing more of its author and its time than each would have wanted, and opening questions that are before us today.

Now I turn to an example from Shakespeare. On a topical level, we might note that there have been a number of recent productions and interpretations of *Macbeth* (1606) that highlight what are felt to be striking comparisons with terrorists in our own time, for instance, as paralleling the rise of Saddam Hussein or Slobodan Milošević (with his wife Mirjana Marković as the "Lady MacBeth of the Balkans"!) or as revealing the power politics of the American Revolution, the American Civil War, or post-Apartheid South Africa.[14] But there is more to *Macbeth* than such local applications, however pertinent they may be. Their variety does, of course, demonstrate that there is no "text in itself," an observation that, I suggest, also applies to seemingly sober documents like court records, Acts of Parliament, as well as to obviously open-ended literary and artistic texts. But more: the play offers us a different level of insight, a vision that shows Kristeva's "new knowledge" bubbling up from the unconscious and giving us horrific insights into the connection not just between violence, terrorism, and religion, but between violence, terrorism, and the sacred. *Macbeth* potentially takes us, in relentless and disturbing detail, into a collective *un*conscious of terrorism, a primordial level that appears to link unpredictable violence to the most primitive levels of the pre-conscious including what Kristeva describes as the "need to believe."[15]

---

14. John Wilders, ed., *Shakespeare in Production: Macbeth* (Cambridge: Cambridge University Press, 2004), p. 87.

15. Psychoanalytic[al] approaches to Shakespeare date back to Freud and Jung, and since the work of Norman Holland, Murray N. Schwartz, Janet Adelman, and many others in the 1980s, has been a major force in Shakespearean criticism, often interacting suggestively with cultural and feminist criticism. For a recent survey, see David Mikics, "Psychoanalytic Criticism of Shakespeare," *Literature Compass* 3 (2006), pp. 529–46.

Macbeth lies uneasily between a world in which the supernatural plays a part in supposedly influencing human affairs and one in which events are rather influenced by drives and reactions that "bubble" (I. iii. 77) up out of the human unconscious. Shakespeare layers his script with both kinds of explanation. Macbeth's "air-drawn dagger" is "of the mind" (III. iv. 62, II. i. 33); his wife's dreams arise from a "mind diseased" (V. v. 41); he tries to escape the "torture of the mind" that springs from "restless ecstasy" and continually threaten to "rise again" (III. ii. 21–22, III. iv. 80). These perturbations and horrors emerge from "a rooted sorrow" in humanity (V. v. 42), and throughout the play Shakespeare stretches to find metaphors for this level of what we would now term the unconscious. In the play's residual worldview it is the supernatural, and we can read the cosmic signs, the "great perturbation in nature" (V. i. 8) that is continually referenced as a series of metaphors probing to express the inexpressible, the "new knowledge" that had to wait until Freud's discoveries nearly four hundred years later.

As we think about Shakespeare's witches embodying the eruptions of the irrational into the play's actions, we may have to fight against the Aristotelian aestheticization of the unconscious that inevitably accompanies its emergence into discourse. We sit in our seats and tell ourselves: it is only a play. But theater, I suggest, has inherent access to a level of emotion that lies beneath the conscious surface. Aristotle's classic formula for the effects of tragedy, the stimulation of pity and fear, needs to be supplemented by his often neglected (though in the *Poetics*, disconnected) emphasis on the production of "wonder." Yet as we experience the tragic effect of *Macbeth*, probably more with than any other Shakespeare play, except perhaps at the ending of *King Lear* (1603–6) or *The Winter's Tale* (c.1611), we may ponder and indeed hope that the terror the play opens up becomes manageable and that the thing itself does not manifest in our experiences but remains only as that to which we struggle to make an aesthetic response. The witches embody the emergence of anarchy and magical thinking of both random terrorist acts and the terrorist state, the "abyss of meaninglessness" that Gordon Lawrence sees but not, the play suggests, only in late capitalism or any other period of history but in the very construction of the human.[16] On the surface we see a coup, a planned assault on authority, but articulated so that we see revealed the underlying

---

16. W. Gordon Lawrence, *Experiences in Social Dreaming* (London: Karnac Books, 2003), p. 56.

irrationality that expresses itself not just in calculated violence but in darker, more primitive surges.

There was, of course, a particular historical occasion for Shakespeare's staging of the witches in the play: the Gunpowder Plot. Those of us who grew up in Britain or the remnants of its empire and became some variety of Early Modern scholars no doubt look back with irony at the seemingly unselfconscious enjoyment we took every November 5 at exploding fireworks (like the conspirators), watching (like the early seventeenth-century spectators) as our parents (like the Jacobean government) oversaw the burning to ashes of a forlorn figure which we had ourselves constructed and to which the whole of the neighborhood had contributed, financially or morally. Such an event no doubt recalled the fates of various earlier heretics like the Lollards, as well as more recent martyrs (or terrorists), Protestant or Catholic.

Macbeth was likely staged before the king at Whitehall in August 1606, a year after the Gunpowder Plot. James I and VI was a firm believer in (and persecutor of) witches. He published a book, *Daemonologie*, in 1597— only six years before he became king of England and nine years before Shakespeare's play—which was reprinted in 1603, 1604, 1607, and 1616. James emphatically affirmed the existence of witches and their intimate connection with the devil, and therefore his official belief in the whole supernatural paraphernalia upon which the pre-enlightenment magical universe was constructed.[17] As Richard Wilson points out, with just a little glee, Macbeth's "secret, black, and midnight hags" (IV. i. 46) became the first witches in English literature or any published text to pervert the words of the Book of Common Prayer: that prayers will be heard and requests granted "when two or three are gathered together." Wilson instances trials in Catholic-friendly Lancashire following the 1604 Witchcraft Act, which decreed death for any who unlawfully "take up" any dead bodies or body parts. He links the paranoia on all sides of the conflict within a "Catholic gentry divided against itself," with some accusing others of encouraging witchcraft.[18]

In a further reassurance to empirical historians, the Play's Porter scene alludes to the plots and trials of Catholic terrorists (or martyrs). Ian Ward points out that Shakespeare aligns the terrorist with the figure

---

17. Richard Wilson, *Secret Shakespeare: Studies in Theatre, Religion and Resistance* (Manchester: Manchester University Press, 2004), pp. 187 and 201–2.

18. Wilson, *Secret Shakespeare*, pp. 188–89.

of the "equivocator" in the Porter's jokes, a term applied to Jesuits and their leader at the time, the notorious terrorist (or martyr), Fr. Garnet, a reference likely to be recognized by most of Shakespeare's London audience. "Equivocator" evoked repulsion and fear in the popular Protestant consciousness equivalent to early modern terms like "Machiavel," "dissimulation," or *King John*'s "commodity," all of which refer to activities and attitudes that manipulate or subvert what is taken as truth and patriotic loyalty. Ward's argument is that today, when terrorism and counterterrorism seem to be as much a struggle between equivocator and counter-equivocator, the parallel with *Macbeth* is instructive, and sobering.

Shakespeare, then, brings us into the contradictions and multiple anxieties of Jacobean England. But there is more: the witches open up what Souter and Wiltshire call "the unconscious fantasy that underpins being-in-the-body" and not least because of their gender, and their interactions not just with Macbeth but indirectly with his wife.[19] The murky world of the witches is Shakespeare's uncanny central embodiment of the bubbling unconscious and it is identified in this masculinist universe with the force of the female, with its perpetual threat to the insecure world of the hero, uncannily like the not-fully-born soldier-male of Klaus Theweleit's analysis of modern fascist subjectivity but which, as Theweleit himself argued, has uncanny reference back to the history of Western masculinity.[20] Drawing on nursery and folk rhymes, incantations, spells, the ritualistic non-naturalism of the witches' 4-beat lines have drawn comparison with the opening of Beethoven's Fifth Symphony, and Artaud's Theatre of Cruelty.[21] They are designed to open up a level of the primitive by which Lady Macbeth is brought face to face with her own participation in terrorism. They evoke the anarchy and destruction that lurks in the fatal combination of the archaic origins of religion and what will emerge throughout the play of the pairing of terrorism and martyrdom. Psychologists speak of "borderline" or fragmented patients who, Jeffrey Stern explains, have had their mirroring self-object ruptured, with their "archaic self-grandiosity" transformed not into "pleasure in self-functioning" but rather "trapped

---

19. Kat Torney Souter and John Wiltshire, "What Bloody Man Is That: Corporality and the Open Bodies of *Macbeth*," *Psychoanalysis Downunder* 2 (2002), http://apas.datalinkstaging.com/downunder/backissues/issue2.

20. Klaus Theweleit, *Male Fantasies*, 2 vols., trans. Stephen Conway, Chris Turner, and Erica Carter (Minneapolis: University of Minnesota Press, 1987).

21. Wilson, *Secret Shakespeare*, p. 186.

in an infantile conviction of their own omnipotence." The developmental arrest results in the lack of "such qualities of mature selfhood as empathy, humor, and wisdom" and a consequent intolerance of any "denial of their own perfection and omnipotence or...that of their god." "God" becomes, the psychoanalyst Ruth Stein explains, that part of the self "that sanctifies and assists in the killing of the impure, disturbing, 'infidel' section of the psyche." Borderline patients, she observes, characteristically display a deficient capacity for empathy or guilt about the effects of their actions on others.[22]

But the witches do not just embody the fear engendered in a moment like Macbeth and Banquo's confrontation with them—"What are these, / So withered and so wild in their attire, / That look not like th'inhabitants o'th'earth" (I. iii. 37–39)—but also in the fear that the unassimilable primitive urges of the destructive unconscious might hold over the future, and indeed retrospectively, over history. I mean here not only Brockbank's emphasis on the "destructive constraints that the past imposes on the present," illustrated by the pattern of rebellion, revenge, and counter-revenge of the Scottish thanes, including the saintly Duncan himself, but also the way such patterns determine the future.[23] The revelation of the "supernatural solicitings" to Macbeth lead inexorably to further and accelerating terror. That they "cannot be ill, cannot be good" (I. iii. 129–30) at least seems to stress the open-endedness of the future, but the drive toward terror tries to cut off options, tries to determine the future, and in a horrific sense, control time itself. What is at stake (and here we connect with the relationship of "religion" and the unconscious and what Kristeva describes as Christianity's positive legacy in an enhanced "new humanism") is the powerfully loaded word "man," in his exclamation that he who "dare do all may become a man," and his wife's response, "what beast was't that made you break this enterprise to me?" (I. vii. 46–49). There is, at a deep-rooted level, a potential for the "beast," for the violence and destruction and which can be justified all too easily as it bubbles to the surface in human institutions and rituals, including in a *realpolitik* bolstered by religion (again, the afore-mentioned US presidents).[24]

---

22. Jeffrey Stern, "Psychoanalysis, Terror and the Theater of Cruelty," *International Journal of Psychoanalytic Self Psychology* 4 (2009), p. 189; and Stein, "Evil as Love."

23. J. P. Brockbank, "Shakespeare's Language of the Unconscious," *Journal of the Royal Society of Medicine* 81 (1988), p. 196.

24. Kristeva, *Incredible Need*, p. 25; and Julia Kristeva, *Hatred and Forgiveness*, trans. Jeanine Herman (New York: Columbia University Press, 2010), p. 34.

Macbeth's soliloquies imply an attribution of obsessive addiction to the psychopathology of terrorism. It is as if he takes his cue from the witches and then has to feel his way through the consequences. These are speeches that get poetry close to the pre-social; to Kristeva's *chora*, where what she terms the "semiotic," the bodily drive of rhythms, tones, and movement, forces its way through into the "symbolic," the realm of conscious discourse.[25] In this preconscious world that is bubbling to the surface, fair is foul and foul is fair. We are living on this "bank and shoal of time" (I. vii. 6), a patch of consciousness, unstable shifting ground, surrounded by and always potentially overrun by the vastness of the sea of the unconscious. The ceremonies of kingship, both of Duncan and Macbeth himself are flimsy structures trying to "stride the blast" (I. vii. 28) of the death drive. Eli Sagan argues that Macbeth is a study of the regression to a borderline pathology; a man imagining that he will feel no guilt, and when he does, emerging as one "restored to a normal neurotic existence after a descent into a borderline hell."[26]

As with *Samson Agonistes*, *Macbeth* draws on deep-seated gender stereotypes to open up the insecurity of male apprehensions of the feminine. It depicts the emergence of the unconscious represented by the witches into the human or symbolic level of discourse in specifically gendered terms. Lady Macbeth wishes her maternal functions to be transformed from "milk" to "gall," her blood to be thickened as if aspiring to arousal by contrast with the "spongy" (i.e., soft or yielding) officers killed by her husband (I. vii. 71). The body is evoked as a series of gaping wounds, as if something horrendous is struggling to come to the surface: Duncan's blood, the bleeding soldier, the blood that gilds the grooms' faces, the witches' open caldron itself which symbolizes the seething underworld. It is "a paradoxically gestating womb," Souter and Wiltshire suggest, from which emerges a "bloody child." We are being enticed into a pre-linguistic space, a place where fantasies of violence, dismemberment, seaming from the nave to the chops, beheading, and massacre arise. Just as Freud saw Oedipus opening primitive unconscious fantasies, so the ghoulish interiors of Macbeth opened by the witches point to fluid, uncontrollable forces which can be staunched only by the imposition of violence: a "natural

---

25. Julia Kristeva, *Desire in Language: A Semiotic Approach to Literature and Art*, trans. Thomas Gora et al. (New York: Columbia University Press, 1980), pp. 132–39.

26. Eli Sagan, *Citizens and Cannibals: The French Revolution, the Struggle for Modernity, and the Origins of Ideological Terror* (New York: Rowman and Littlefield, 2001), p. 447.

maternal order" is being distorted by an "untrammelled masculinity." The maternal is beaten into a pulp of severed limbs and body parts. Children, who should be an image of fulfilment, creativity, and delight, are ripped from the womb, murdered, and fed gall rather than milk. The open body reveals the horror beneath: "a past, present, future, blood-bath, bodily orifices, from vaginas to gashes, cast a terrifying fantasy over the play."[27] Is the multiplication of the savagery and mess of male violence provoked by fear of the mess and monstrosity of the female? Is Shakespeare's vision here an early modern exemplification of Theweleit's observations on his modern fascists that "their goal is the ultimate form of discharge, namely self-extinction" and when confronted by women, including the woman-in-themselves, they desire to "display the whole morass of blood and excrement into which they perceive the female womb to be transformed in sexual intercourse, menstruation, or childbirth."[28]

Consistent with Theweleit's cultural analysis, in her clinical observations Stein argues that fantasy structures behind certain acts of terrorism "have aspects of a regressive return to the father and the banishment of the mother," replacing the plenitude and nourishment by destruction, suicide, renunciation of sexual pleasure, a process which eventually, she argues, eventually leads either to "serene resigned martyrdom"—we might think of Macbeth's resignation in the final Act as a parody of martyrdom—or to "explosive self-destruction" which is how the rebels against Macbeth see his reign. The destruction of the feminine marks, she comments, "a specific regressive-transcendent trajectory that is altogether different from falling into an all-engulfing maternal womb." The short, horrific scene of Lady Macduff and her children being slaughtered is more than a piece of ruthless political calculation. In terms ironically shared by Freud and patriarchal religions, the primitive father-God is pacified only if the feminine principle can be marginalized and, if necessary, destroyed.[29] At this point, we can link Macbeth's exploration of gendered unconscious with Milton's. Both Dalilah and Lady Macbeth are conventionally read as femmes fatales, each seducing a vulnerable male. Dalilah cuts Samson's hair: she is the castrating female; Lady Macbeth likewise taunts her husband into action,

27. Harald William Fawkner, *Deconstructing Macbeth: The Hyperontological View* (Rutherford, N.J.: Fairleigh Dickinson University Press, 1990), p. 129 and Wilson, *Secret Shakespeare*, p. 189.

28. Theweleit, *Male Fantasies*, vol. 2, pp. 278–79.

29. Stein, "Evil as Love."

threatening him with the loss of the archaic mother and, therefore, aban-
donment in a universe where his identity must be constructed by the external world, moment by moment, tomorrow by tomorrow.

Recuperative readings and stagings of *Macbeth* see a growing revulsion
in the play's world from violence, even within the Macbeths themselves.
We have encountered some of our most destructive fantasies, and slowly
in Macbeth's disintegration, and his wife's madness and suicide, we see a
renewed humanity reassert itself: "The time is free," pronounces MacDuff
at the play's end, as if the whole of human history has been redeemed
in the restoration of the legitimate Duncan line and the hierarchy centered on the "Lord's anointed temple" (V. ix. 22, II. iii. 60) of providential
monarchy. The most extreme recuperative reading may be Orson Welles's
1948 film, which saw the work as a Morality Play, a struggle between un-
ambiguous forces of good and evil, emphasized by the creation of a whole
new portmanteau character, the Holy Father, who combined the patriotic
pieties of a number of Scottish lords and who presided over the English
scenes where Malcolm intones the virtues of a perfect king (a scene originally probably designed to appeal to James). Less extreme in its desire
to reassure us with a restored status quo is the common humanist reading that stresses the witches' inability to ultimately control events, and
the triumph of the underlying power of the "milk of human kindness"
(I. v. 15) that the Macbeths reject but which reasserts itself by the end.
"Unnatural" (II. iv. 10) events call for some dimension of "human nature"
to revolt against violence and tyranny. Would it were so. But perhaps it
is an understandable fantasy reading, one born of the need we have to
believe that all will come right, whether we explain that providentially or
as a reflection of something inherent in the human. At the end the war-
lords continue to play out the old masculinist rituals. Who will be the next
victim? How, for example, will we get from Duncan's line to Banquo's?
Significantly, Donalbain withdraws from the campaign to seat his brother
Malcolm on the throne, and in Polanski's movie version, secretly goes off
to consult the witches: "there is no sense of redemption; the cycle of ambi-
tion and murder is about to begin again."[30] By such a reading, the destroy-
ers of Macbeth have only evolved to vengeance, not yet to forgiveness. As
with *Samson Agonistes*, at the end of *Macbeth*, the "crazy truth" of hatred
has not been untangled.[31]

---

30. Wilders, *Macbeth*, p. 60.

31. Kristeva, *Hatred and Forgiveness*, pp. 192–93.

Macbeth, then, becomes a model of how we might experience what Kristeva terms abjection, an enacted defilement rite in which terror ultimately functions to preserve the symbolic order and patriarchal society by bringing about a confrontation with the abject in order to finally eject it and redraw the boundaries that separate the human from the nonhuman, the subject from the "other," life from death.[32] Contemplating *Macbeth* acknowledges our desire to participate in what we recognize as inhuman and forbidden pleasure and our subsequent moral revulsion and desire to subsequently eject the abject which has given us this pleasure. We acknowledge the experience as having threatened our moral boundaries. It may also, depending on how the ending is presented to us, act as a way of turning back to the protection of the status quo. *Macbeth* also raises for us—as Angela Connolly does in relation to the modern horror film—the representation of the feminine and maternal as monstrous, and the idea that such "encounters with the abject 'Other'" may enable us to move toward "an increase in consciousness and a capacity to accept ethical guilt about our abject desires."[33]

Both *Samson Agonistes* and *Macbeth* are "literary" texts, not historical records, philosophical or political treatises, let alone contemporary opinion pieces or journalistic blogs. They take us, as all art does, into the world of the imaginary and dimensions of our humanity that in the past century have become increasingly subject to psychoanalytical exploration. *Macbeth* and *Samson Agonistes*, like the arts in our society, perhaps like humanistic learning itself, are seemingly marginalized by the dominant struggles of our time. What can we learn, then, from a psychoanalytic reading of these two "literary" texts as I have proposed? Does it help us locate examples of Kristeva's "new knowledge"? In an address to the Modern Language Association in 2005, she argued that "in taking over from theology and philosophy," the humanities replaced the old dualism of "divine" and "human" by the investigation of social bonds, structures of kinship, and "rites and myths, the psychic life, and the genesis of languages and written works." A new conception of the human is "thus being

---

32. Here my analysis draws on Barbara Creed, "Horror and the Monstrous-Feminine: An Imaginary Abjection," in Barry Keith Grant, ed., *The Dread of Difference: Gender and the Horror Film* (Austin: University of Texas Press, 1996). See also Angela Connolly, "Psychoanalytic Theory in Times of Terror," *Journal of Analytical Psychology* 48 (2003), pp. 407–31.

33. Connolly, "Psychoanalytic Theory," p. 418.

constituted" inviting us to construct a "reconstruction of the humanism we need" in our "dark times."[34]

Is such a search utopian in the light of the seemingly unavoidable coupling of violence and religion and the justifications, however contradictory, of what appears to some as terrorism and others as martyrdom? What insight might psychoanalysis have for our spiritual health, to what religions still call our "salvation"? I return to my starting point. How shall we deal with, even just describe, what Habermas and Derrida define as a historically unprecedented danger, given the combination of current fundamentalisms and technological grandiosity that dominate so much of our world? Will we perhaps, as they both suggest, even look back to 9/11 as the last example of a link between terror and territory, the last eruption of an archaic pattern? Are we in some sense, as Slavoj Žižek pronounces, echoing thousands of years of apocalyptic catastrophizing, "living in the end times"? If so, all the more reason to pay attention when Kristeva speaks of the urgent need to bring her concept of "new knowledge" to help us in this ancient and increasing dangerous situation. Will the competing fundamentalisms not merely "encourage" but eventually bring about "an explosion of the death drive"?[35] The old myths continue to live within us and provide a comforting "illusion that human beings have a great deal of trouble ridding themselves of," she comments, and they will no doubt continue to "lure" our psychological and intellectual life and provide a narcotic that makes living easier for generations to come. Elsewhere, more, if still guardedly, optimistic, she asks can we—especially those of us who are teachers, therapists, humanist scholars—take up the vital role of mediation and education, which is "neither more nor less than to help this new type of knowledge gradually emerge" through the "immanentism of transcendence" which, as she affirmed at Assisi, is Christianity's most hopeful legacy and humankind's best hope.

If we live in a dark time, we need not only to probe the sources and manifestations of that darkness, but take it as our human vocation to preserve and advocate its transformation. Like the great Renaissance artists, like Erasmus, Shakespeare, or Leonardo, we are in a time of "losing God," and we must learn "to displace transcendence towards the best" amongst us, finding relationships and insights not beyond but in the human,

---

34. Julia Kristeva, "Thinking in Dark Times," *Profession* (2006), pp. 13–21, at pp. 13, 15, and 17.

35. Slavoj Žižek, *Living in the End Times* (London: Verso, 2010); Kristeva, *Incredible Need*, p. 4.

promoting the paradoxical "unsustainable infinity" of desire, not its fulfilment in divine love, but in the "other of the other."[36] Just as for Derrida deconstruction is not just a way of playing with texts but a necessary vocation for philosophers, intellectuals, and educators, so psychoanalysis and its "new knowledge" is for Kristeva not just the talking cure, nor a therapeutic exercise; rather, it models for us a philosophy and a vital praxis that may start in a scholarly or therapeutic situation but could and should enter the world of religion, politics, terrorists, and/or martyrs.

36. Kristeva, *Incredible Need*, pp. 31, 25, 64, ix, vii, 4.

PART TWO

The French Revolution and the Invention of Terrorism

5

Martyrdom, Terrorism, and the Rhetoric of Sacrifice

THE CASES OF MARAT, ROBESPIERRE, AND LOISEROLLES

Julia V. Douthwaite

HOW DOES A self-sacrificing "martyr" become an evil-doing "terrorist"? The answer is through politics. Judging from today's press and TV, martyrdom is generally undertaken by natives of the Middle East, North Africa, or South-East Asia, and media reportage implies that they are animated by a fanaticism and a willingness to abnegate the self that is extremely foreign if not downright medieval. Misguided victims of cultish or irrational thinking, their devotion comes across as a kind of madness, made strange by its distance from us in space and time. As Akil N. Awan points out elsewhere in this book, such mythical sacrifices confound and perplex our sensibilities. And yet the phenomenon of political martyrdom is not of recent origin. It was originally linked to a secular cause that should be close to our hearts; it took shape in Western Europe at the moment when the modern notion of democratic governance first entered the world scene, that is, in the years of the French Revolution (1789–94).

Like the martyrs of *jihad* and other conflicts, Marat and Robespierre, the two most famous proponents of radical revolution in the 1790s, embraced the notion of heroic sacrifice. In their writings and speeches they saw themselves as men of virtue, consumed by patriotism, defying danger and even death itself in the name of a higher cause. Indeed their devotion led both to untimely death. Marat was assassinated at age 50 by the royalist Charlotte Corday, on July 13, 1793, and Robespierre was executed at age 36 on orders of the Revolutionary Tribunal on July 28, 1794 (10 Thermidor Year 2). Although their partisans were stunned by the news and a certain hagiography arose to celebrate the memory of Marat, especially, within months both men's reputations had slipped precipitously from martyr to terrorist and they remain notorious still. So potent is Robespierre's hold on the French imagination that his execution, on the day called "Thermidor," is synonymous with the Terror's end. This chapter shows how the two men crafted heroic identities for themselves, first as eulogists of famous Frenchmen of the recent past, and second as martyrs of the revolutionary cause. The analysis contrasts their efforts at self-promotion with some stories that circulated about them in the years following Thermidor, and shows how their names were harnessed to black legendry and reactionary politics in ways that they may never have imagined. In order to bring out the relevance of this material for the present, a final section examines the most respected martyr of the 1790s, a former navy general named Jean-Simon Loiserolles (1732–94), and suggests how problematic his reputation might become if it were revisited by today's policymakers in France. My point is that the terms "martyr" and "terrorist" are rhetorical constructs: generated by individual egos, popular opinion, and partisan warfare more than actual deeds and constantly subject to reinterpretation with the vagaries of political change.

Rhetorical confusion over the concept of martyrdom has long haunted studies of the French Revolution. The latest expert on the field, Ivan Gobry, admits as much in the preface to his *Dictionnaire des martyrs de la révolution* (2002). The martyrs listed in the *Dictionnaire*, Gobry claims, are all *confesseurs de la foi*: men and women who were killed because of their refusal to abjure the Catholic faith.[1] Interestingly, the publication of this *Dictionnaire* followed on the heels of Gobry's *Martyrs de la révolution française* (1989), which operates on a broader definition of martyrdom and thus contains "all kinds of innocent victims" (the martyrdom of Marat and Robespierre is mentioned in neither book, nor is Loiserolles).[2] Even

---

1. Ivan Gobry, "Avertissement," in *Dictionnaire des martyrs de la révolution* (Paris: Éditions Dualpha, 2002), pp. 11–12.

2. However Gobry excludes political actors—on both sides of the conflict—noting that even the leaders of the counterrevolution in the Vendée, Charette and La Rochejaquelein, cannot be considered "des victimes innocentes, bien que dignes d'admiration"; see Ivan Gobry, "Avertissement," in *Les Martyrs de la révolution française* (Paris: Librairie Académique Perrin, 1989), p. 9.

FIGURE 5.1. Charles-Louis Muller, *Roll Call of the Last Victims of the Reign of Terror* (1850)

Reproduced with courtesy of the Snite Museum of Art, University of Notre Dame.

though Gobry provides a detailed ranking system in the *Dictionnaire* that aims to separate the wheat from the chaff, so to speak, and indicates the extent of each person's loyalty to the Church through the use of capital letters, italics, and other typographical hints, there remains a great deal of imprecision. Hence King Louis XVI and Queen Marie-Antoinette are both listed in italics (the designation for those people whose status is troubled by doubts over the motivation behind their murders), while Louis's sister Élisabeth de France suffers no such opprobrium, nor does Jeanne Bériau (age 3) and her infant cousin Étienne (15 days old), both of whom succumbed during the reprisals against the Vendée in spring 1794. It is hard to square the ages of these children with the character attributed to them ("presenting all the signs of authentic martyrdom": refusing to betray the faith in word or in deed).[3]

Imprecision clouds the designation "terrorist" in revolutionary studies as well. The "reign of Terror" has long conjured up attacks against tearful holy men and sad-eyed aristocrats, thanks to sentimental novels like Charles Dickens's *A Tale of Two Cities* (1859) and pseudo-history paintings such as Charles-Louis Muller's *Roll Call of the Last Victims of the Reign of Terror* (1850) (fig. 5.1). But as historian Richard Cobb pointed out almost forty years ago and more recent researchers such as Alan Forrest have

---

3. Gobry, *Dictionnaire*, pp. 264, 271–72, 151, and 389.

reminded us since, the ten-month-long period of repression also punished prostitutes, peasants, the urban working class, and soldiers—career
military men and those who were mobilized by the draft of 1793. And it left
many people untouched.[4] Indeed, the most thought-provoking recent discussions of the topic build on Cobbesian doubts about its political coher-
ence and question the very concept of "a reign of Terror." In his 2006 book
Violence et révolution and follow-up article in *Les Politiques de la Terreur*
(2008), Jean-Clément Martin argues that it is ridiculous to assign even
a date to the event because there never was any actual system of Terror
adopted by the representative government in 1793–94.[5] Rather, he contends that at its founding moment in fall 1793 there were a variety of militant demonstrations, populist demands, and spectacles of demagoguery
which, for all their clamoring for a system of Terror, fell on deaf ears in the
Convention.[6] Fulminating against critics who irresponsibly employ the
term "Terror" to vilify the left-wing Jacobin-majority legislature, Martin
demands that scholars instead define exactly what they mean in studying the particular institutions, popular demands, repressive measures,
and the more or less contradictory laws passed in 1793–94. The existence
of a judicial system that resorted to violence does not necessarily justify
the adjective. Just as Howard Brown demonstrated that repressive practices were no stranger to the French judiciary well into the 1830s, Martin
reminds us that the ancien régime and early constitutional phase of the
Revolution were rife with incidents of ghastly torture (used to get confessions from prisoners), and drawn-out, bloody scenes of public execution.[7]
A glance at the court reportage in major Parisian newspapers during the
"happy year" of 1790, for instance, brings up a gory cluster of results: one
thief was sentenced to be whipped and branded, and three other felons

---

4. Richard Cobb, *The French and their Revolution*, ed. David Gilmour (New York: New Press,
1998), pp. 350–51; and Alan Forrest, "L'Armée, la guerre et les politiques de la Terreur," in
Michel Biard, ed., *Les Politiques de la Terreur, 1793–1794* (Rennes: Presses Universitaires de
Rennes, 2008), pp. 53–67. Executions of peasants and the working class comprised 89 percent of the deaths in the Vendée, according to Donald Greer, *Incidence of the Terror during the
French Revolution: A Statistical Interpretation* (Cambridge, Mass.: Harvard University Press,
1935), p. 164.

5. Jean-Clément Martin, *Violence et révolution: Essai sur la naissance d'un mythe national*
(Paris: Seuil, 2006), pp. 186–93; Jean-Clément Martin, "Violences et justice," in Biard, *Les
Politiques de la Terreur*, pp. 129–40.

6. Martin, "Violences," pp. 132–33.

7. Howard G. Brown, *Ending the French Revolution: Violence, Justice, and Repression from the
Terror to Napoleon* (Charlottesville: University of Virginia Press, 2006), p. 3.

were sentenced to be broken publicly on the wheel (*rompu vif en place de Grève*).[8] So offensive were these practices that they generated resistance and even popular violence on occasion by a citizenry that was increasingly revolted by cruelties used against petty criminals. Modern readers may have forgotten that the adjective terrorist (*terroriste*) did not gain wide acceptance until after Robespierre's execution in July 1794 and that the label was applied most energetically by his colleagues in the Convention who were anxious to disassociate themselves from Robespierre and other deceased of the purge.[9] By August 1794 journalists started propagating "terrorist" stereotypes and pinned the worst abuses on identifiable scapegoats, notably Maximilien Robespierre (1758–1794), his comrades-in-arms among the Jacobins, and militants in the working class (or sans-culottes) broadly writ. Although his assassination a year earlier had cleansed most of the crimes from the name of journalist Jean-Paul Marat (1743–1793), his name too was relaunched into villainy after Thermidor.

Like many would-be members of the Enlightenment Republic of Letters, Marat and Robespierre in their early years had tried to ingratiate themselves into the ruling class by penning panegyrics, that is, the genre of the academic *éloge* (homage or eulogy). In the 1750s to 1780s, such competitions abounded in France; from the mighty Académie française to minor provincial academies, the eulogy occupied a central role in French cultural life. David Bell and Jean-Claude Bonnet have traced the influence of the genre on the nascent nationalism of Bourbon France, showing how the subject for these eloquence competitions shifted during this period from devotional religious topics to honorees of recent memory.[10] Marat wrote the *Éloge de Montesquieu* (1785) in response to a prize competition launched by the Academy of Bordeaux, long-time home of the Enlightenment philosopher Charles-Louis de Secondat, baron de Montesquieu (1689–1755). Robespierre's *Éloge de Gresset* (1784) was written in response to a similar contest sponsored by the provincial academy of Amiens and was worth 1,200 livres (approximately £455 GBP or $700

---

8. *Chronique de Paris*, multiple numbers, October–November 1790. François Furet and Denis Richet baptized 1790, year of the much-touted Festival of the Federation, as the "happy year" in *La Révolution française* (Paris: Fayard, 1973), chap. 4.

9. The first usage of *terroriste* (adj.) in French is attributed to Gracchus Babeuf, *Journal de la liberté de la presse* 4, 25 fructidor An. 2 (c. September 11, 1794), pp. 3 and 5.

10. David A. Bell, *The Cult of the Nation in France: Inventing Nationalism, 1680–1800* (Cambridge, Mass.: Harvard University Press, 2001), pp. 108–11, and Jean-Claude Bonnet, *Naissance du Panthéon: Essai sur le culte des grands hommes* (Paris: Fayard, 1998), pp. 83–111.

USD). Although neither won the prize, these texts are interesting in that they reveal men who were indebted to the rhetoric, values, and mores of society under King Louis XVI.

Robespierre's *Éloge* celebrated the life and work of one-time Jesuit Jean-Baptiste-Louis Gresset (1709–1777; a native of Amiens), who was best known for his mock-heroic poem *Ver-vert*, published in 1734 when the author was 25 years old. Translated as *Ver-vert, or the Nunnery Parrot*, this work describes with malicious humor the adventures of a convent parrot whose saucy comments get him into trouble. The poem itself, with its off-hand comments on the nuns' vanity and petty jealousies, got Gresset into trouble. Soon after its appearance, the poem was translated into German, Portuguese, and Italian. And soon after that, Gresset was expelled from the Jesuits. A favorite of Madame de Pompadour and a habitué of stylish Parisian salons, Gresset nevertheless thrived for some years in the capital and produced more light poetry and a few successful plays before retiring to Amiens where he reportedly tried to atone for the irreverence of his writing and his ill-spent youth. This compunction was regarded as excessive by Voltaire, who quipped: "Gresset se trompe, il n'est pas si coupable" (Gresset is wrong; he is not that guilty).[11] At death all his works were burned by the family.

In his *Éloge*, Robespierre sympathetically portrays both sides of Gresset: the naughty wit and the penitent soul. Then an up-and-coming lawyer aged 27, working in the nearby town of Arras, Robespierre praises his countryman for the light-hearted humor that seemed to emanate effortlessly from his pen. "Read *Ver-vert*, you who aspire to master badinage and graceful writing, read Ver-vert, you who only seek amusement; and, you who nature has deprived the gift of laughter, read it and you will know a new source of pleasure."[12] He defends the author against those "austere and melancholy censors" who brought about his misfortune and expresses regret that Gresset's *badinage* is no longer in style.[13] This defense of frivolity may seem surprising, coming from the man who would later be known as "The Incorruptible." But if one separates the man from

---

11. Voltaire, cited in J. Wogue, *J.-B.-L. Gresset: Sa vie, ses œuvres* (Paris: Lecène, Oudin et cie, 1894), p. 267.

12. Maximilien Robespierre, *Éloge de Gresset par Robespierre*, ed. D. Jouaust (Paris: Académie des Bibliophiles, 1868), p. 10.

13. Ibid., pp. 11–12, "Le badinage n'est plus de saison; l'intrigue et le crédit ont secondé le courroux de ses ennemis."

the teleological logic that explains the 1780s as leading inexorably to revolution, Robespierre's embrace of Gresset makes more sense.

As Elena Russo has reminded us, style was a highly political matter in the 1780s; each had its own particular inflection and significance. Most popular during the early to mid-1700s was the sensuous rococo style made fashionable by King Louis XV's mistress Madame de Pompadour, the painters Boucher and Watteau, and the dramaturge Marivaux. It was also known as the modern or, pejoratively, the "little style" (*le goût moderne* or *le petit goût*).[14] To understand the politics of the "modern style" and its challenge to reigning hierarchies, one need only conjure up the frothy fun of a fantasy landscape by Watteau or a flirty comedy of wits by Marivaux, and contrast it to the serious-minded civic virtue emanating from Jacques-Louis David's neoclassical paintings, which exemplify the so-called "ancient style" (*le grand goût* or *le goût à l'antique*). However, one must recall that eighteenth-century writers, artists, and their patrons operated in a mindset far removed from the romantic notion of authenticity that would emerge in the nineteenth century and which remains current to a certain extent today. Although the lyrical sincerity of Jean-Jacques Rousseau was highly popular among readers of his novel, *La Nouvelle Héloïse* (1762), and would eventually usher in the earnest rhetoric of transparency that characterized Jacobin discourse of 1792–94, the Robespierre of 1784 was likely operating under different expectations. He did not necessarily conceive of his work primarily as a means to express his personal voice or attain transcendence, it was also a strategic means of self-promotion.

Robespierre's public persona was less clear-cut than one might think. As times changed and other members of his class and political party adopted the style of the sans-culottes (unpowdered hair and long pants, such as sailors or peasants wore), Robespierre rarely appeared without a powdered wig, silk stockings, and tight breeches. Furthermore, his writing style remained anchored in a certain kind of Bourbon aesthetics. As late as February 13, 1791, we find Robespierre employing the *petit goût* of flattery and *badinage* in his correspondence. Witness the letter he wrote to the painter Adélaide Labille-Guiard replying to her request to paint his portrait in her series of deputies to the National Assembly.[15] The fawning

---

14. Elena Russo, *Styles of Enlightenment: Taste, Politics, and Authorship in Eighteenth-Century France* (Baltimore: Johns Hopkins University Press, 2007), pp. 3–15.

15. Letter from Robespierre, February 13, 1791, cited in Anne Marie Passez, *Adélaide Labille-Guiard, 1749–1803: Biographie et catalogue raisonné de son œuvre* (Paris: Arts et Métiers

and somewhat pompous language of this letter, in which he calls his lady correspondent "The Graces" and suggests that a "jealous God" has kept him from replying to her as he ought, may strike modern readers as preposterous, but it was standard fare among the opinion-makers of his time and that is precisely the point.

Nevertheless a signature severity can be noted in Robespierre's support of the spiritual loner that Gresset became later in life.[16] As a defender of the man's virtue under fire, Robespierre justifies Gresset's withdrawal from society in a section that takes up almost one-third of the 50-page, 22 cm, *Éloge*. He claims to do so because he "loves virtue more than letters" and that all the genius in the world cannot equal "a glorious action" (*une belle action*).[17] In a veiled rebuke at Voltaire's irreverent epigraph, Robespierre declares that it matters little whether Gresset's principles were too severe or not, because they were his own and he had the courage to live up to them.[18] Consonant with the profile that he would adopt among the Jacobins, Robespierre depicts himself as the embattled champion of a solitary underdog and argues that there exist timeless values that are more important than celebrity: namely the esteem and veneration of the public, love of country, and one's own conscience.

A similar effort at rhetorical self-fashioning can be found in *L'Éloge de Montesquieu*, penned when Dr. Marat was a mature and rather successful man of 42 years. Although his writings had yet to receive the laurels of the Académie des sciences (and never would), he had achieved a certain esteem at court and in the capital. At age 34, he had been named physician to the household troops of the king's brother le comte d'Artois (future King Charles X). His popularity among certain society ladies who partook of his medical services was well known; the beautiful marquise de

Graphiques, 1973), p. 247, "On m'a dit que les Grâces voulaient faire mon portrait. Je serais trop indigne d'une telle faveur si je n'en avais senti tout le prix. Cependant, puisqu'un surcroît d'embarras et d'affaires ou puisqu'un Dieu jaloux ne m'a pas permis de leur témoigner jusqu'ici tout mon empressement, il faut que mes excuses précèdent les hommages que je leur dois. Je les prie donc de vouloir bien agréer les unes et de m'indiquer où je pourrais leur présenter les autres."

16. Ruth Scurr, *Fatal Purity: Robespierre and the French Revolution* (New York: Henry Holt and Co., 2006), pp. 49–51, esp. p. 50.

17. Robespierre, *Éloge*, pp. 30–31. For similarities between the *Éloge* and Robespierre's political writings, see Mircea Platon, "Robespierre's *Éloge de Gresset*: Sources of Robespierre's Anti-philosophe Discourse," *Intellectual History Review* 20.4 (2010), pp. 479–502.

18. Robespierre, *Éloge*, p. 31.

Laubespine would later be linked to the outpouring of grief occasioned by his murder. Word has it that he was lover of at least one aristocrat.[19] He had already ventured into political writing with the 1774 *Chains of Slavery,* and his discourse on "medical electricity" won the prize of the Académie de Rouen in 1783. In the *Éloge de Montesquieu,* Marat adopts the obsequious rhetoric of a humble supplicant at the foot of an altar to the "illustrious citizen who honored France," yet he also suggests how he would emulate this hero.[20] The virtues that Marat praises in Montesquieu were the same ones he aspired to: he praises the subject's "discernment," his "firm vision," and the civic mindedness that made him destined to "direct public opinion."[21] In a clever sleight of hand, Marat the eulogist divorces the baron de Montesquieu from his wealth and inheritance, and insists that he was a self-made man (*qui fut tout pour lui-même*).[22] Furthermore, in order to exonerate Montesquieu from charges of insensitivity, Marat stresses the importance of the stylistic *bienséances* or social conventions that governed intellectual discourse during the 1720s to 1750s.

Despite what readers of Montesquieu might think, Marat claims that the philosopher did not approve of the despotic practices of Oriental tyrants any more than he condoned the practice of slave trade among Occidental merchants. His experience at court and in the parliament of Bordeaux had taught the man to temper his language however; he knew that heavy-handed outrage or strident polemics would displease his noble readers, and so he opted for an indirect method instead—whence Montesquieu's delectable irony. To prove this point, Marat cites a number of seemingly callous comments on the lascivious proclivities of Oriental women and the brutish nature of Africans lifted from Montesquieu's *De l'esprit des lois (Spirit of the Laws,* 1748) and then debunks the text's linkage to the author's character by citing little-known (and apocryphal) anecdotes about his humanitarianism and warm heart. The writer was merely brandishing stereotypes that were in the air, he claims; Montesquieu's wit and irony (*le goût moderne*) allowed him to cast ridicule on other people's ideas all the while getting his important philosophical messages across.[23] Where earlier readers may have been led astray

---

19. Michel Vovelle, "Marat (1743–1793)," in Jean-Paul Marat, *Textes choisis,* ed. Michel Vovelle (Paris: Éditions Sociales, 1963), p. 10.

20. Jean-Paul Marat, *Éloge de Montesquieu, présenté à l'Académie de Bordeaux le 28 mars 1785,* ed. Arthur de Brézetz (Libourne: G. Maleville, 1883), p. 2.

21. Cited in Bonnet, *Naissance du Panthéon,* p. 275.

22. Marat, *Éloge,* p. 2.

23. Ibid., p. 67; and Russo, *Styles,* pp. 194–95.

by this cunning, Marat sets the record straight: a strategy he would pursue as a journalist. Readers of *L'Ami du peuple* would find similarly shocking comments about the Catholic clergy and the nobility in its pages, delivered in a bitter irony all his own (and slightly less subtle).

More than any other writer of the time, Marat constructed a myth of his own regeneration—and later of his martyrdom—that coincided with the nation's rebirth. At the beginning of 1789 his scientific career was going nowhere, his professional profile had plummeted after the sinecure with the Comte d'Artois had come to an end in 1784, his chronic skin disease was by now confining him to bed and bathtub, and he was reportedly at death's door when suddenly he heard about the convocation of the Estates General. "This news had a powerful effect on me," he wrote, "I underwent a salutary crisis, my courage was re-ignited, and the first thing I did was to give my fellow citizens a testament of my devotion."[24] Soon thereafter he set up a print shop and began publishing *L'Ami du peuple*, a virtually one-man editorial enlivened with letters from enthusiastic readers. In an era abounding with dramatic events and blood-curdling violence, Marat's role as the embattled editor of *L'Ami du peuple* and the frequent calls to action it contained brought him often under attack. Between 1789 and 1793, a police warrant was issued for his arrest at least seven times and he had to spend long periods in hiding. More than 650 issues were published from 1789 to September 1792.[25] His style became darker and more vehement as time went by; the head count he demanded mushroomed from a few hundred to several thousands, and the specters of impending doom and his own martyrdom also grew. Why did he take these risks, one might ask? Because the people "needed light," he claimed, "and they cared little to be enlightened."[26] Finally, in an act of astounding bravura, he allowed himself to be arrested and tried by the Revolutionary Tribunal... only to be acquitted days later to the mass rejoicing of his followers. Although his incendiary rhetoric and incitement to violence are suspected to have motivated some of the most hideous scenes of mass murder, such as the

24. Marat, cited in Olivier Coquard, *Jean-Paul Marat* (Paris: Fayard, 1993), p. 210. Coquard, *Marat*, 219, notes that the attachment to a patrie (i.e., patriotism) was basically a means of social promotion.

25. For more on the publication history of *L'Ami du peuple*, see Eugène Hatin, *Histoire politique et littéraire de la presse en France* (Paris: Poulet-Malassis et de Broise, 1860), vol. 6, pp. 160 and 190–99.

26. On his use of irony, see Louis R. Gottschalk, *Jean-Paul Marat, l'ami du peuple*, trans. G. Léon (Paris: Payot, 1929), p. 59.

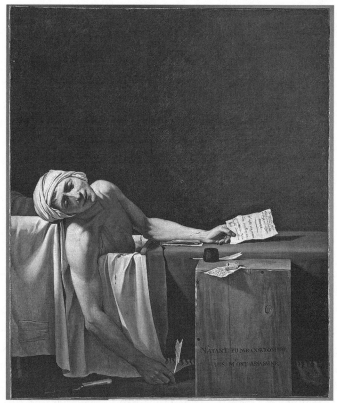

FIGURE 5.2. Jacques-Louis David, *La Mort de Marat* (1793)

Musee d'Art Ancien, Musees Royaux des Beaux-Arts, Brussels, Belgium, inv. 3261. Erich Lessing/Art Resource, New York.

September prison massacres of 1792, Marat's stance throughout was that of the honest underdog, the feisty and necessary spy who reveals the traitors in the people's midst. His untimely death at the hands of a rival political faction was a logical end, and ensured him the right to a martyr's halo.

Marat's fame would doubtless have waned years ago, if not for the gorgeous portrait by the prominent French painter, politician, and fellow Jacobin Jacques-Louis David, *La Mort de Marat* (*The Death of Marat*, or *Marat assassiné*, 1793) (fig. 5.2). Produced by order of the Convention in response to the groundswell of anger after Marat's murder, David's oil painting symbolizes the people's triumph over adversity. That is why the assassin, Charlotte Corday, is erased from the scene and why the dying man—who appears much younger than his 50 years—appears to be smiling through the pain. Resting in his bathtub, his head swaddled in a towel, wounded in the chest, Marat looks like a Christ-figure freshly released from the cross. He will never write again, but the pen, paper, and the unfinished correspondence on his make-shift desk are meant to inspire others—his readers and perhaps even the spectators before the canvas—to carry on the fight. David wanted his portrait to avenge the Left, and indeed thousands of engravings and copies were made of this portrait and blanketed the market in 1793–94; the portrait was prominently displayed in the French government chambers for fifteen months.[27]

Thanks to this painting, the history of Marat's assassination and funeral are well known still today, as is the bizarre cult created in his honor among the Parisian sans-culottes, washer-women and other poor folks who worshiped him.[28] But in order to capture the equivocal nuances that surrounded the "People's Friend" in the wake of the Terror, we must remember that his populism was somewhat tinged by the prejudices of his earlier life, and his actual involvement in the *grandes journées* of the Revolution was minimal. As Louis Gottschalk and other biographers have noted, Marat was no democrat. He had little faith in the people's intelligence or ability, or the efficacy of mass politics. Despite his newspaper's persona, a woeful entry in his diary dated 1792 notes, "It is not of old slaves that free citizens are made....these people are not educated, and nothing is so difficult as to educate them."[29] He generally kept such comments under wraps and instead invented himself a grand role, as the truth-telling journalist who rights wrongs in the service of the little people.[30] In *L'Ami du peuple*, he wrote at length on the sufferings he endured for their sake: he claimed to lose all his wealth, and to live for nine months on bread and water, to watch day and night over their safety, and to not have taken fifteen minutes of recreation for more than three years. Apart from a short stint as deputy, he held no elected office but affected a stalwart

27. For an excellent summary of the scholarship on David and *Marat*, see Guillaume Mazeau, *Le Bain de l'histoire: Charlotte Corday et l'attentat contre Marat, 1793–2009* (Seyssel: Champ Vallon, 2009).

28. Joseph Clarke, *Commemorating the Dead in Revolutionary France: Revolution and Remembrance, 1789–1799* (New York: Cambridge University Press, 2007), pp. 180–95.

29. Louis R. Gottschalk, *Jean-Paul Marat: A Study in Radicalism* (1927; repr. Chicago: University of Chicago Press, 1967), p. 105. Marat wrote: "Ce peuple n'est pas instruit; rien n'est même si difficile que de l'instruire; la chose est même impossible," cited in Gottschalk, *Jean-Paul Marat*, 107.

30. Mona Ozouf, "Marat," in *Dictionnaire critique de la Révolution française*, ed. François Furet and Mona Ozouf (Paris: Flammarion, 1988), pp. 280 and 282.

independence from the halls of power. He donned the style of a workman or sans-culotte, wearing unkempt clothing and harboring an uncouth manner in public. All of this was a public act, created and sustained in the name of his assumed persona. And by most accounts it worked; still today Marat has many admirers and his likeness is one of the most recognizable icons in modern art. His murder was the best thing that could happen to canonize Saint Marat.[31]

For Robespierre, on the other hand, the historical record would suggest that things did not work out as well. The most important difference in their fates is the attention to publicity that Marat pursued with a sure hand, a certain dose of cynicism, and extraordinary good luck, on the one hand, and the social awkwardness and the enormous pressures that hindered Robespierre's impact, on the other hand, especially in the build-up to Thermidor. Of course, the timing of his career doomed it also: the virtues of hard-line Jacobinism looked much more attractive to the populace in July 1793 than in July 1794. Robespierre's reputation fell in a dizzyingly rapid series of events and his indubitable involvement with the Terror made him a prime target of hatred after death. Whereas some argue that the man successfully transmitted the virtues of Jacobinism and even lived his own life accordingly, one must use caution in conflating language with belief. As Russo reminds us, political posturing and adroit self-fashioning were inherent to eighteenth-century style, whether it was the *petit goût* of upper-class sociability, or the *grand goût* of philosophically minded reform. We will never know whether Robespierre's sentimentalism really was part of his identity or not. The contrast in rhetoric outlined above suggests that he likely built the Incorruptible image willfully; just as he once used clever *badinage* to win over a society portraitist, he later adopted a language of virtuous perseverance and martyrdom to win over the people, who he portrayed as being just as long-suffering as himself. Given the extraordinary moral rigor of this language, it is unsurprising that his actions were eventually held up to judgment by his own words.[32] Or that they fell short.

31. Frank Paul Bowman, "Le Culte de Marat, figure de Jésus," in Bowman, *Le Christ romantique* (Geneva: Droz, 1973), p. 62 ff.; and on Marat's following in the 2000s, see Julia V. Douthwaite, "Les Martyres de Marat et de Sebastião: Une légende révolutionnaire mise à jour," in Martial Poirson, ed., *La Révolution française et le monde d'aujourd'hui* (Paris: Classiques Garnier, 2014), pp. 451–63.

32. Patrice Higonnet, *Goodness beyond Virtue: Jacobins during the French Revolution* (Cambridge, Mass.: Harvard University Press, 1998), pp. 249–50.

Religious tensions worked against Robespierre too. Although the Festival of the Supreme Being on June 8, 1794, initially seemed like a rousing success, it ended up generating a hostile backlash against its founder by Catholics resentful of its deist (some said atheist) aesthetic.[33] Some even claimed that Robespierre had cast himself as the Supreme Being. Fears spread about a dictatorship. And yet he clung to the rhetoric of self-sacrifice to the end. In his last speech to the Convention in July 1794, Robespierre seemed to sense that the tides were turning against him, but instead of admitting any personal responsibility or proposing a new course to release the country from martial law, he resorted to the same language that had sustained the repression, and warned colleagues of enemies lurking in their midst. He pegged his hopes on the listeners' fear of each other and their pity of him; exclaiming, "Who am I that I should be accused? A slave of liberty, a living martyr of the Republic...if you take away my [good] conscience, I am the most unfortunate of citizens, I do not even have any rights."[34] This self-portrait of the helpless citizen caught in enemy snares was hard to reconcile with other information that was circulating in the air, including the very visible positions of power he held since 1792, his rumored control of the Tribunal that had already condemned more than 2,000 people in Paris alone, his callous attitude toward Paris prisoners, and the supposed condemnation of his own sister Charlotte.[35] Perhaps that is why his proxy has come in for such rough treatment in fiction, art, and film: the public wants to see him punished.

While both men incited the nation to violence and harbored doubts over the people's capacity to govern themselves, Marat was more successful at projecting a believable persona of victim-under-siege during his life and, thanks to his murder and David's commemorative painting, he enjoyed an aura of sanctity for years after death.[36] Robespierre's old-fashioned sartorial choices and *honnêteté*, on the other hand, combined with a courtly respect for tradition and a Rousseauian sort of *sensibilité* or earnestness,

---

33. Jonathan Smyth, "Public Experience of the Revolution: The National Reaction to the Proclamation of the *Fête de l'Être Suprême*," in David Andress, ed., *Experiencing the French Revolution* (Oxford: Studies on Voltaire and the Eighteenth Century, 2013), pp. 155–76.

34. Maximilien Robespierre, *Œuvres de Maximilien Robespierre*, ed. Marc Bouloiseau and Albert Soboul (Paris: Presses Universitaires de France, 1967), vol. 10, p. 556.

35. Pierre Joseph Alexis Roussel (pseud. M. de Proussinalle), *Histoire secrète du Tribunal révolutionnaire* (Paris: Lerouge, 1815), vol. 2, p. 323.

36. Marie-Hélène Huet, *Rehearsing the Revolution: The Staging of Marat's Death, 1793–1797*, trans. Robert Hurley (Berkeley and Los Angeles: University of California Press, 1982), p. 63.

worked to incite fellow-feeling rather than the awful fury of *L'Ami du peuple*. This melodramatic language helps explain his meteoric rise to popularity from 1790 onward, but it also opened him to charges of hypocrisy when contrasted with the supposed atheism and power-mongering behind his prize works of revolutionary legislation, such as the Festival of the Supreme Being and the draconian Law of Prairial.[37] Despite the efforts of various biographers over the years, Robespierre's popularity has never been resurrected, nor quite understood.

The dizzying array of imagery and story associated with Robespierre and Marat after death makes it difficult to ascertain exactly how they were perceived by contemporaries, and it is uncertain that there is any one "true" perception at any rate. Consider a few examples of the art created to memorialize the two men: for the better, as in the worshipful poster of *Les Républicains montagnards de 1793*, or for the worse, as in the frontispiece from a 1794 biography of Robespierre, where his decapitated head serves a warning against other would-be dictators.[38] The two men's names are frequently cloaked in villainy, as following the news of the 1791–1804 slave uprisings in the French colony of Saint-Domingue, when colonial sympathizers depicted the slave leader Toussaint Louverture as a student of Robespierre, or when they dubbed a notoriously cruel representative-on-mission as "the Marat of the Antilles."[39]

Marat was lampooned with familiar sounding rhetoric and a similarly awful frontispiece in the memoirs of Pierre-Anne-Louis Maton de La Varenne (1761–1813) (fig. 5.3). A well-respected lawyer and member of the Paris parliament before 1789, Maton de La Varenne was arrested during a purge of suspected royalists and imprisoned in La Force right before the massacres of September 2–3, 1792. His memoirs focus primarily on Marat's responsibility for the slaughter: minute by minute and

---

37. On the sentimental style of Robespierre, see William Reddy, *The Navigation of Feeling: A Framework for the History of Emotions* (New York: Cambridge University Press, 2001), pp. 177–79, and Andress's contribution to this volume. On the Law of Suspects of 22 Prairial (June 10, 1794), see Ernest Hamel, *Histoire de Robespierre* (Paris: Chez l'auteur, 1867), vol. 3, p. 547; and Michel Eude, "La Loi de prairial," *Annales historiques de la Révolution française* 254 (October–December 1983), pp. 543–59.

38. On *Les Républicains montagnards de 1793*, see Pierre Gascar, *Album, Les Écrivains de la Révolution* (Paris: Gallimard, 1989), p. 244. For the Medusa-like image of Robespierre's head, see Julia V. Douthwaite, *The Frankenstein of 1790 and Other Lost Chapters from Revolutionary France* (Chicago: University of Chicago Press, 2012), p. 197.

39. Ibid., chap. 4, for the parallels between Toussaint-Louverture, Marat, and Robespierre made by colonial writers.

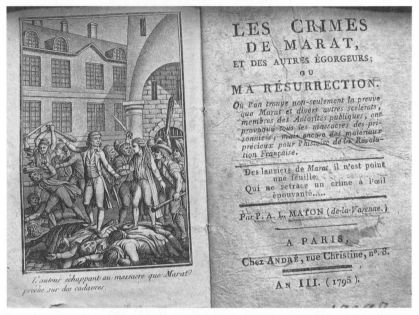

FIGURE 5.3. P. A. L. Maton (de-la-Varenne), *Les Crimes de Marat et des autres égorgeurs, ou Ma Résurrection* (Paris: Chez André, An 3 [1795])

Reproduced with courtesy of the Bibliothèque Nationale de France, Paris.

paragraph by paragraph, the reader relives the prisoner's anguish as he hears the shrieks of the dying amid the metallic thunk of axes falling and cringes at the heavy tread of the guards outside his cell. When his own turn arrives, the author dexterously shields his politics from sight, citing the personal integrity he had developed through years in the legal profession as proof of his innocence to a dumbfounded judge and awe-struck crowd of murderers. His narration of leaving the make-shift tribunal stages a melodramatic confrontation of Good versus Evil that is mirrored in the gory frontispiece to the book. As he tiptoes behind the blood-thirsty Marat waving a sword, he thinks: "I cringed in horror at the sight of an enormous pile of naked cadavers lying in the gutter, filthy with blood and mud, upon which I had to take an oath....I was saying the words they demanded from me, when one of my former clients fortuitously passed by. He recognized me, swore for me, embraced me a thousand times, and even brought the killers to my side."[40] Note how the good lawyer avoids

---

40. P. A. L. Maton (de-la-Varenne), *Les Crimes de Marat et des autres égorgeurs, ou Ma résurrection* (Paris: Chez André, An 3 [1795]), pp. 87–88.

sullying his honor by sidestepping the oath, and how he is saved by a symbol of his former power (a satisfied client of the royal court). Right and Wrong are clearly legible in this text and reveal its debt to the genre of *mémoires judiciaires* or court reportage.[41] Moreover, Maton de la Varenne indicts "atrocious Marat" not only for this incident but for numerous other horrors as well. He cites a pamphlet written by Marat which provoked the murder of prisoners in Lyons, Orléans, and Versailles, and in which the "People's Friend" describes the killing as "an indispensable act of justice for retaining, by terror, those legions of traitors hidden in the walls at the very moment when the people was preparing to march on its enemies."[42]

Finally, the author turns the tables completely against his enemy by employing a technique that Marat had made famous in *L'Ami du peuple*: he prophesizes his own murder. Claiming that one reader was so enraged on finding the name of her friend vilified in an earlier edition of *Les Crimes de Marat*, Maton de la Varenne informs readers that she has warned him: "I will be for the author another CHARLOTTE CORDAY" (138). Although he pooh-poohs the would-be assassin's "pretty project," this admission necessarily enlists the reader on Maton's side. Dire threats raise book sales and political emotions, as we know. The death threat against the author may very well have revved up sales of his other two books advertised on the inside cover of *Les Crimes*.

As one would expect, a figure named or resembling Robespierre appears in numerous novels published during the regimes of the Directory (1795–1799) and the Consulate (1799–1804) following Thermidor. He is a shadowy presence forcing others into peril in C. A. G. Pigault-Lebrun's burlesque *L'Enfant du carnaval* (1796) and he masterminds a long-distance campaign of repression through a diabolical representative-on-mission in Joseph de Rosny's somber memoirs-novel, *Les Infortunes de La Galetierre sous le régime de Robespierre* (Year 5, 1796–97). The events of Thermidor provide the dramatic dénouement to many a melodrama of émigré suffering, such as *Lioncel, ou l'émigré* (1800, by Louis de Bruno) and C. B. LeBastier, *Dorbeuil et Céliane de Valran: Leurs amours et leurs malheurs pendant la tyrannie de Robespierre* (Year 3, 1794–95). So-called "secret histories" of the Terror, such as Pierre Roussel's *Histoire secrète du Tribunal révolutionnaire* (written 1800; pub. 1815) depict Robespierre and his colleagues

---

41. Sarah Maza, *Private Lives and Public Affairs: The Causes Célèbres of Prerevolutionary France* (Berkeley and Los Angeles: University of California Press, 1993), p. 220.

42. Marat, cited in Maton (de-la-Varenne), *Les Crimes de Marat*, p. 96.

as a type that would dominate a certain vein in nineteenth-century letters, that is, the misanthropist whose low opinion of mankind or disgust with certain sectors of society justifies any number of crimes. In a leitmotif that would be exploited in tales from the nineteenth century up to the present, Robespierre and Marat dole out injustice with steely calm at meetings of the Committee of Public Safety, the Tribunal, and other sites of awful memory.[43]

But the names Marat and Robespierre have also been appropriated in more sympathetic ways. In Leo Tolstoy's *War and Peace* (1869) the political enthusiasms of a newcomer to Moscow society make him into "a sort of Marat" in the eyes of his aristocratic hosts. They may mock his radical ideas, but they ultimately forgive him and embrace this loveable character because of his callow youth and earnestness.[44] The dialogue between Catherine de Médici and Robespierre in Balzac's study of 1828 (*Sur Catherine de Médicis*) is even more interesting because it equates the assassination of political leaders with the execution of holy martyrs, and holds the people accountable for both. In a dream sequence set in 1786, the Renaissance queen awakens Robespierre one night to justify her long-ago actions. Although people abhor the massacre she ordered on Saint Bartholomew's Day 1572, during which anywhere from 2,000 to 20,000 Huguenots were exterminated by royal troops and mob violence, she claims that naysayers underestimated the Protestant threat to the French state. In chillingly direct terms, she propounds a doctrine that sounds very much like Robespierre's words during 1793–94, and explains that more people, not fewer, should have been killed to snuff out the enemies in their midst. The tranquility of a great nation exacts a blood tax now and then, she remarks: "Truths only emerge from hiding to take blood baths.... Christianity itself, essence of all truth because it came from God, was it founded without martyrs? Did blood not flow like water? Will it not flow in all times? You yourself will see what I mean, because you will be one of the masons of the new city promised by the apostles. When you wave a level over their heads, the people will applaud you, but when you want to start putting mortar between the bricks, they will

---

43. Malcolm Cook discusses some of this material in "Robespierre in French Fiction," in Colin Haydon and William Doyle, eds., *Robespierre* (Cambridge: Cambridge University Press, 1999), pp. 224–36.

44. Leo Tolstoy, *War and Peace*, trans. Louise and Aylmer Maude, ed. Amy Mandelker (New York: Oxford University Press, 2010), pp. 21 and 389.

kill you."[45] It is interesting to see how Balzac, spokesman of a staunchly antidemocratic politics, equates the revolution's overthrow of the weak Bourbon court with the Valois's suppression of an unruly Protestant faction. Although just and necessary, both events backfired. Instead of blaming strong leaders, Balzac suggests that one should condemn the ignorant masses for their ill-conceived actions, and the spineless rulers who fail to thwart them.[46]

Bearing all this in mind, we have seen how the vagaries of self-fashioning and politics were not the only forces impacting the reputations of Marat and Robespierre: their names also carry different religious connotations. Despite David's hagiography of *Marat*, the man is best known as the mastermind of the September massacres. Despite his embrace of religion (under the aegis of the Supreme Being), Robespierre is tarred with atheism. Neither attained the "martyrdom" he expected. Neither figures in Gobry's martyrologies, nor does Loiserolles, a layman who really did bear witness to a higher truth and whose death by guillotine still casts shame on the Republic. Loiserolles was the former military man who volunteered to go to the guillotine on 8 Thermidor Year 2 (July 26, 1794) in the place of his son (the timing could not have been worse: if Loiserolles's son had been condemned only one or two days later, they would have both survived). The son published a testimonial to his father in Parisian newspapers shortly after Thermidor; the incident circulated in popular poetry and song and left an indelible trace in the famous *Tableaux historiques de la Révolution française* (1804) (fig. 5.4).[47] Thomas Carlyle cited Loiserolles with admiration, and Dickens was inspired by his example to imagine the

---

45. Honoré de Balzac, *Sur Catherine de Médicis* in *La Comédie humaine*, ed. Marcel Bouteron (Paris: Gallimard, 1962), vol. 10, pp. 290–95, esp. p. 294, "Les vérités ne sortent de leurs puits que pour prendre des bains de sang.... Le christianisme lui-même, essence de toute vérité, puisqu'il vient de Dieu, s'est-il établi sans martyrs? le sang n'a-t-il pas coulé à flots? ne coulera-t-il pas toujours? Tu le sauras, toi qui dois être un des maçons de l'édifice social commencé par les apôtres. Tant que tu promèneras ton niveau sur les têtes, tu seras applaudi; puis quand tu voudras prendre la truelle, on te tuera."

46. As Balzac declared in *Du Gouvernement moderne* (1832), the lower classes (*la masse pauvre et ignorante*) should have no hand in elections, no access to arms, and no sovereignty. Legitimacy, as he saw it, was manifest in the exercise of power: it belongs to him who, in the historical circumstances in which he finds himself, is most able to protect the state and combat the forces that threaten it; see Honoré de Balzac, *Du Gouvernement moderne*, in *Œuvres diverses*, ed. Pierre-Georges Castex et al. (Paris: Gallimard, 1996), vol. 2, pp. 1075–76.

47. See the letter to the editor from Loiserolles fils and Louis-François Jauffret's poem, "Loiserolles, ou le triomphe de l'amour paternel," in *Le Journal de Paris national* (25 nivôse An 3 [January 14, 1795]), pp. 465–66.

FIGURE 5.4. "Cent-Quatrième Tableau de la Révolution: Loiserolles se dévoue à la mort pour son fils, le 26 juillet 1794; le 8 thermidor An deuxième de la République"

In *Collection complète des Tableaux historiques de la Révolution française composée de cent treize numéros en trois volumes* (Paris: Chez Auber, An 13 [1804]), vol. 2, p. 420, reproduced from the original held by the Department of Special Collections of the University Libraries of Notre Dame.

surprise ending of *A Tale of Two Cities,* in which the ne'er-do-well Sydney Carton sacrifices his life to save his erstwhile rival Charles Darnay and thus assures the survival of the Manette-Darnay clan for posterity.[48]

But being a martyr implies witnessing and self-sacrifice to a higher truth; what does Loiserolles symbolize? He was not a politically motivated martyr, such as the figures in David's *Oath of the Horatii* (1784) who cast off the love of mothers and wives to better serve *la patrie.* Nor was he a religiously motivated martyr; he did not abnegate himself to the Catholic Church or to any other entity of that kind. Rather, Loiserolles died because of his belief in a paternal ideal; his was a nonpartisan, areligious, private

---

48. Thomas Carlyle, *The French Revolution: A History* (New York: Thomas Y. Crowell, 1893), vol. 2, p. 368.

act of sacrifice.[49] It was also a rebellious act of *lèse-république*; by thwarting the Tribunal's judgment, he refuted its pre-eminence over his life. In the famous scene depicted in the *Tableaux*, Loiserolles holds up his right hand in what may be a mockery of the civic oath, revealing a loyalty to blood relations that runs deeper than his debt to *concitoyens*. This death should thus remind us of the kinds of allegiance that long preceded the First Republic—the ties of family and kinship that the Catholic Church had once sanctified, and that village life had fostered—and which are still perplexing the Fifth Republic today.

Were it to be re-evaluated in present-day terms, Loiserolles's sacrifice might well evoke a more ambivalent response than before; it might be suspected of *communautarisme*. The neologism, which is said to be "so unfamiliar to French mores that it was not until the 1990s that it made its way into French dictionaries," is defined as an American tendency (known as identity politics) to privilege the "social function of community identities (ethnic, religious, sexual, etc.)" over the civic loyalty due to the state.[50] Fears of *communautarisme* have been growing with the influx of North African immigration into France over the past half-century and have reached crisis proportions of late with critics such as Alain Chevalérias prophesizing the dissolution of the Republic under the weight of rivalling bonds. The specter of *communautarisme* drove the French government to pass the 2004 law prohibiting Muslim girls from wearing head scarves to school, and the 2011 law forbidding Muslim women from wearing burqas in public, and it is prompting wider reaching legislation as well. Certain kinds of ethnic weddings are generating complaint at present; perhaps they will be the next specter of *communautarisme* to fall under the blade. After backing down from the ill-fated creation of a ministry of immigration, integration, and national identity in 2007, the Sarkozy government in 2010 took a number of measures aimed at bolstering citizens' loyalty to the state.[51] They now require schools to fly the French flag, to keep the

49. Loiserolles's story has, however, become a favorite among Evangelical Christians who interpret him as Christ-like figure; see Harold Vaughn, "Hell's Desperate Cry! A Prayer from Perdition," *Christ Life Ministries Report* 26.3 (2003), p. 3, http://christlifemin.org/publications/Newsletter/newsletter_2003-3.pdf.

50. Alain Chevalérias, "La Menace du communautarisme, Le Terrorisme depuis le 11 septembre 2001," http://www.recherches-sur-le-terrorisme.com/Analysesterrorisme/communautarisme-france.html.

51. Steven Erlanger, "French 'Identity' Debate Leaves Public Forum," *New York Times*, February 8, 2010, http://www.nytimes.com/2010/02/09/world/europe/09france.html.

1789 Declaration of the Rights of Man and of the Citizen in every class-room, to ensure that children learn "the values of the republic," and to take part in an as-yet-undefined ceremony of unity.

If these measures sound familiar, it is because they began in 1792. Ever since the First Republic was formed, the French state has been trying to forge a communal identity that would transcend the primordial ties of blood and kinship. Robespierre and Marat contributed to this mentality, each in his own peculiar way, by promoting a kind of public service that foreswore all other bonds, and by accepting death as a kind of republican witnessing. Their works and lives, and the stories that grew up in their wake, should remind us that heroism and sacrifice are slippery concepts and will always be subject to revision, as each generation will rewrite the past in search of a better present.

6

The Sentimental Construction of Martyrdom as Motivation in the Thought of Maximilien Robespierre, 1789–1792

David Andress

IN THE LATER eighteenth century, European culture grappled with the thorny question of how to understand the human psyche outside of older models that addressed the "soul." Enlightenment materialistic science offered new routes to explaining the impact of sensory stimulus, but although thinkers toyed with mechanistic accounts of conduct, these were widely deemed unsatisfactory. Ultimately, a broad field of romantic and post-romantic discussion of the "self" would carry such debates into the nineteenth century, but before these ideas solidified, a generation was taken up with exploration of the potential uniformity of healthy emotional response, and the question of whether "sensibility" ought to be a guiding principle of life was vigorously debated.[1] Jean-Jacques Rousseau in his *Discourse on the Origins of Inequality* (1754) presented empathetic "pity" for suffering others as the grounding of all social feeling, and Adam Smith's *Theory of Moral Sentiments* (1759) offered a similar conclusion from very different premises. His fellow-Scot David Hume argued at length that

---

1. On the emergence of "modern selfhood," see Jan Goldstein, *The Post-Revolutionary Self: Politics and Psyche in France, 1750–1850* (Cambridge, Mass.: Harvard University Press, 2005). A wider-ranging study is Jerrold Seigel, *The Idea of the Self: Thought and Experience in Western Europe since the Seventeenth Century* (Cambridge: Cambridge University Press, 2005).

"reason" was always a slave to "the passions."[2] The doctrine of sensibility in the late eighteenth century was underpinned by more than just the speculations of philosophy. It drew on an evidence-base that spanned a wide range of advances in the physical and human sciences to assert that the human "heart" or "soul" responded to complex emotional stimuli in much the same way, it was assumed, that sensory organs responded to simpler stimuli of contact, vision, sound, and so on.[3]

Like a fine palate or a well-attuned ear, the heart could effectively (and in some sense literally) vibrate in sympathy with the perception of suffering, joy, or other strong emotion.[4] This was a "natural" response, but as such, it required a great deal of work to remain so, at least for those fortunate or un-fortunate enough to be subjected to the "corrupting" influences of affluent society. Wealth and sophistication could dull the emotional palate, rend-ering one insensible unless regularly "refreshed" by exposure to appropriate stimuli. Art, literature, and drama could provide these, as too could travel to "uncorrupted" environments such as Rousseau's favorite Swiss moun-tains, where more "natural" country dwellers could remind jaded aesthetes of how they were supposed to feel. The capacity of all this to devolve into self-indulgent wallowing was evident at the time, both to skeptical critics who denounced it all as meaningless *sensiblerie*, and to the more serious-minded among the sentimentalists themselves, who treasured the possibility of re-generation of such corrupted elites through enforced exposure to real and represented virtues. Such individuals also feared that, for some at least, their corruption might have become irredeemable.[5]

---

2. See Jean-Jacques Rousseau's *Discourse on the Origins of Inequality*, http://www.constitu-tion.org/jjr/ineq_03.htm; David Hume's *Treatise of Human Nature*, http://ebooks.adelaide.edu.au/h/hume/david/h92t/; and Adam Smith's *Theory of Moral Sentiments*, http://www.econlib.org/library/Smith/smMS1.html.

3. Note that "sensibility" in this context is a specific historical-cultural formation, distinct from the use of "sensibilities" as a label for general sensory-emotional dispositions, as in, for example, Daniel Wickberg, "What is the History of Sensibilities? On Cultural Histories, Old and New," *American Historical Review* 112 (2007), pp. 661–84.

4. See notably Jessica Riskin, *Science in the Age of Sensibility: The Sentimental Empiricists of the French Enlightenment* (Chicago: Chicago University Press, 2002) and Anne C. Vila, *Enlightenment and Pathology: Sensibility in the Literature and Medicine of Eighteenth-Century France* (Baltimore: Johns Hopkins University Press, 1998). Sensibility is in this sense a subset of, and an elaboration on, the "sensationism" which had penetrated French ideas on physiology and philosophy since mid-century, see John C. O'Neal, *The Authority of Experience: Sensationist Theory in the French Enlightenment* (University Park: Pennsylvania University Press, 1996).

5. See Lynn Festa, *Sentimental Figures of Empire in Eighteenth-Century Britain and France* (Baltimore: Johns Hopkins University Press, 2006) and also Markman Ellis, *The Politics*

In the turbulent political atmosphere of the French Revolution, such questions assumed a new urgency. The sentimental construction of personal identity and rhetorical positions in the French Revolution has received sporadic attention over the past two decades, and has never achieved the same ubiquity as more cerebral accounts of the themes and tropes of revolutionary discourse.[6] In part this may be due to the inherent difficulty in assigning emotional significance to historical traces, and in part also to the ambiguity equally inherent in the wider discourse of sentimentality or sensibility about the real or confected nature of such feelings. However, as sentiment has received growing attention from a wide body of scholars, its salience to the discursive context of the 1790s, in realms from fiction to physiology, has been reinforced, to the point where the overspill of these notions into politics should no longer be sidelined—despite inevitable difficulties of interpretation.[7]

This is particularly the case as an address to the emotional dynamics of the period allows us to consider political discourse in wider frameworks of identification and relationship than is otherwise possible. It particularly permits the anchoring of some aspects of radical conceptualization within such frameworks, thus resolving issues that earlier scholars—as late as the 1990s—were content to leave as signs of ideological derangement or inexplicable contradictions.[8] In this chapter, I shall show how Maximilien

of Sensibility: Race, Gender and Commerce in the Sentimental Novel (Cambridge: Cambridge University Press, 1996), pp. 5–6, for a selection of competing contemporary descriptions. For a critical examination of the tendency to dramatic, but self-serving, depictions of violence and their emotional impact, see Ian Haywood, *Bloody Romanticism: Spectacular Violence and the Politics of Representation, 1776–1832* (Basingstoke: Palgrave Macmillan, 2006).

6. William M. Reddy, *The Navigation of Feeling: A Framework for the History of Emotions* (Cambridge: Cambridge University Press, 2001); see also David J. Denby, *Sentimental Narrative and the Social Order in France, 1760–1820* (Cambridge: Cambridge University Press, 1994); Anne Vincent-Buffault, *Histoire des larmes, XVIIIe–XIXe siècles* (Paris: Rivages, 1986); and Anne Coudreuse, *Le Goût des larmes au XVIIIe siècle* (Paris: Presses Universitaires de France, 1999).

7. For examples of "political" sensibility in the Anglophone world, see Siraj Ahmed, "The Theater of the Civilized Self: Edmund Burke and the East India Trials," *Representations* 78 (2002), pp. 28–55; and Sarah Knott, *Sensibility and the American Revolution* (Chapel Hill: University of North Carolina Press, 2009).

8. See Patrice Higonnet, *Goodness beyond Virtue; Jacobins during the French Revolution* (Cambridge, Mass.: Harvard University Press, 1998), whose chapter on the origins of Jacobinism ends, at p. 324, with expression of the "constant puzzlement" that the whole topic provides. Keith Michael Baker, "Transformations of Classical Republicanism in Eighteenth-Century France," *Journal of Modern History* 73 (2001), pp. 32–53, discusses how the political language of Jacobins first "metastasized into a discourse of terror" (p. 47) and

Robespierre (1758–1794) used an explicitly sentimentalist understanding of human capacities to construct a powerful rhetoric of popular and personal martyrdom, interlacing past and prospective episodes of victimization and sacrifice into a fully articulated program for the redemption of that suffering through militant triumph, and explicitly sentimentalist regenerative cultural reconstruction. Robespierre is commonly identified as the leading spokesman for the radical, republican "Jacobinism" that carried France into the period of war, civil war, mass mobilization, and purges that we label as "the Terror." Many explanations have been put forward for the attitudes and decisions that led toward that consummation. Here I shall show that the radical Jacobinism for which Robespierre spoke is linked intimately to an emotional engagement with, and commitment to, the ongoing martyrdom of the people, and the cause for which they suffer.

The conflict between purity and corruption, between what the people might become, and the forces holding them back, was at the heart of many revolutionary political interventions, but perhaps nowhere as strongly or consistently as in those of Robespierre.[9] Although as Julia Douthwaite shows in this volume, Robespierre as a youth experimented with writing in many genres, there remained a core commitment to virtue within even his more "frivolous" writings. From his pre-revolutionary writings, and his correspondence in 1789 and after, it is possible to see a figure entirely committed—at the rhetorical level, at least—to the sentimentalist diagnosis of revolutionary possibilities and perils.[10] During his first revolutionary career as a deputy in the National Assembly, he rose from provincial obscurity, against a tide of elite mockery, to become a figurehead for the popular voice in an institution that had dedicated itself since 1789 to building a new constitutional order. Many of his speeches, often delivered against a background of hostile interruptions, demonstrated emphatically sentimental reasoning. To take one example, a speech of early June

---

then continued to undergo "mutation" (p. 51) into a final state of "metaphysical exaltation" (p. 53).

9. On Robespierre's character and antecedents in general, see the penetrating biographical study by Peter McPhee, *Robespierre: A Revolutionary Life*, (New Haven: Yale University Press, 2012); the brief political biography by John Hardman, *Robespierre* (London: Longman, 1999), and two collective works around the Incorruptible: Colin Haydon and William Doyle, eds., *Robespierre* (Cambridge: Cambridge University Press, 1999) and Annie Jourdan, ed., *Robespierre: Figure-réputation* (Amsterdam: Rodopi, 1996).

10. See David Andress, "Living the Revolutionary Melodrama: Robespierre's Sensibility and the Construction of Political Commitment in the French Revolution," *Representations* 114 (2011), pp. 103–28.

1791 called for the dismissal of the entire army officer corps and their replacement by democratic means. Officers "gifted with too little sensibility and virtue to attach their individual happiness to the public happiness" by far outnumbered the minority "sincerely attached to the cause of the revolution, animated by the purest civic sentiments of liberty." The army as a whole had been engaged, he claimed, in driving out common soldiers who displayed any sign of patriotism by a host of illegal and nefarious means, so that now more than fifty thousand such men were left "without resources and without bread...expiating their services and their civic virtues in indigence and opprobrium."[11]

The memory of events at Nancy the previous year, where mutinous soldiers were shot down by militia led by aristocratic officers, drew from him an extended passage of rhetorical paralipsis, in which, while supposedly declining to relive the horrors, he vividly portrayed them:

> But my horrified imagination revolts from the retracing of these lugubrious ideas! I cannot consent to re-open all the wounds of my soul: I would have to speak of the crimes and catastrophes of Nancy: I would have to carry my gaze to those scenes of blood, where the friends of liberty plunged into the breast of its defenders the arms which should have been terrible only for tyrants, and deployed the courage of *civisme* and virtue only to prepare the most frightful of triumphs for despotism: I would have to see the victims escaped from the iron of the victors, falling in crowds to the blows of executioners; presenting for several days the sweetest of spectacles in the eyes of the enemies, who could at leisure gorge on their tortures, and the first days of liberty soiled by cruelties that have not branded the memory of the cruellest tyrants.[12]

Here Robespierre is using a sentimentalist construction of politics, with the invocation of identification with suffering and of the psychology of the senses, as a visual spectacle is invoked to make concrete that identification

---

11. Robespierre, *Oeuvres complètes* (Paris: Société des Études Robespierriste, 2000), vol. 7, pp. 470, 475. The real history of what was happening in the revolutionized military was, of course, much more complex: see Samuel F. Scott, *The Response of the Royal Army to the French Revolution: The Role and Development of the Line Army 1787–1793* (Oxford: Oxford University Press, 1978) and Rafe Blaufarb, *The French Army, 1750–1820: Careers, Talent, Merit* (Manchester: Manchester University Press, 2002).

12. Robespierre, *Oeuvres*, vol. 7, pp. 470–71.

through (imagined) sensory impact. The sense of identification with these suffering figures strengthened in later rhetoric, and was laid alongside an increasingly strongly expressed commitment to personal martyrdom, in the cause of redeeming a martyrdom that so many of "the people" had, in his interpretation, already suffered.

Some months after the speech above, when the National Assembly had completed its constitution-making and retired from the scene, Robespierre found himself confronting the faction in the newly elected Legislative Assembly that was steadily progressing toward the view that a war was necessary to cleanse the frontiers of a counterrevolutionary threat.[13] Seeing peril in a confrontation that the king, his ministers, and the *émigré* counterrevolutionary leadership all seemed to think would serve their purposes, he began to forge a lonely stance of suspicious pacifism—not opposing war as such, but dreading that martial ardor might be used to draw the people into a trap. Robespierre dwelt in detail in several speeches toward the end of 1791 on the perfidious coalition advocating war, declaring for example that "I do not hope that my words will have power at this moment," and that he wanted only to pay "the last debt" he owed the *patrie* and could but wish that his predictions did not come to pass: but if they did, "one consolation will remain to me, I will be able to attest to my country that I had not contributed to its ruin."[14]

On January 11, 1792, he returned to the fray at the Jacobin Club, which had developed over the past two years from a gathering of a few radicals into a major Parisian, and national, institution, bringing regular crowds to witness its debates. This was his main oratorical outlet since the National Assembly had concluded its business, and here he deployed the earnest tropes of popular victimhood to mock claims put forward by Jacques-Pierre Brissot, the leading pro-war advocate. Brissot and his associates were asserting the invincibility of the liberated French, but Robespierre apostrophizes the men who had stormed the Bastille in 1789 to join this fight, only to find that "indigence, persecution, the hatred of our new despots has dispersed you":

Come, at least, soldiers of all those immortal units that have deployed the most ardent love for the people's cause. What! The

13. See David Andress, *The Terror: Civil War in the French Revolution* (London: Little, Brown, 2004), pp. 66–70.

14. Robespierre, *Oeuvres*, vol. 8, p. 64.

despotism that you had vanquished has punished you for your *civisme* and your victory. What! Struck with a hundred thousand arbitrary and impious orders, a hundred thousand soldiers, the hope of liberty, without revenge, without occupation, and without bread, expiate the fault of having betrayed crime to serve virtue![15]

The victims of "sanguinary" martial law—as declared at Nancy—are no longer available to serve, let alone those killed in massacres even outside its bloody ambit: "Ah! What had these women, these massacred children done? Did the all-powerful criminals have such a fear of women and children?" Countless others were also gathered into the bosom of martyrdom, in a retrospective roll call of popular suffering through incidents of conflict and oppression since 1789:

You who perished beneath the blows of assassins encouraged by our tyrants; you who languish in irons where they have cast you, you will not come with us: no more will you come with us, you unfortunate and virtuous citizens, who in so many provinces have succumbed beneath the blows of fanaticism, aristocracy and perfidy! Ah! God! So many victims, and always amongst the people, always amongst the most generous patriots, when the powerful conspirators breathe and triumph![16]

Having here already placed martyred victimhood in a central role as witness to the perfidy of counterrevolution, Robespierre went on in his peroration to invoke the role of these martyrs as witnesses in another context. Using a dense emotive structure, he wove past, present, and future together, addressing the future generations of "nascent posterity," the "sweet and tender hope of humanity" that he hoped would be the beneficiaries of the current struggle. These generations were to learn the lessons of the revolutionary past by being exposed to its full horrors:

May lies and vice vanish at thy aspect; may the first lessons of maternal love prepare thee for the virtues of free men; instead of the

---

15. Ibid., vol. 8, pp. 97–110, citation at p. 107.

16. Ibid., vol. 8, pp. 107–8. Robespierre's "victimology" here can be contrasted with the account of Annie Jourdan, "Robespierre and Revolutionary Heroism," in Haydon and Doyle, *Robespierre*, pp. 54–74, esp. pp. 60–63, where many of the same tropes are noted, but without their sentimental resonances.

poisoned songs of voluptuousness, may the touching and terrible cries of the victims of despotism ring in thy ears; may the names of the martyrs of liberty occupy in thy memory the place usurped in ours by the heroes of imposture and aristocracy; may thy first spectacles be the Field of Federation inundated with the blood of the most virtuous citizens; may thy ardent and sensitive imagination roam amongst the corpses of the soldiers of Châteauvieux [the Nancy mutineers], upon those horrible galleys where obstinate despotism detains the unfortunates claimed by the people and by liberty; may thy first passion be the scorn of traitors and the hatred of tyrants; may thy motto be: protection, love, benevolence for the unfortunate, eternal war on oppressors! Nascent posterity, hasten to grow and to bring forth the days of equality, of justice, and of happiness![17]

Here Robespierre manages to blend the sentimental tropes that swirled around the concepts of parenthood, family, and children with a politicized sense of how the collision of certain vibrant—and horrific—spectacles of counterrevolutionary evil can cement, through a kind of sentimental imprinting, the patriotism of this next generation. The "martyrs of liberty" will stand as bloodstained witnesses in every classroom, and even nursery, to what is at stake in the education of good citizens.

Two weeks after this speech, Robespierre proved his consistency with yet another lengthy diatribe at the Jacobins on the risks of war, its empowerment of the executive, and the possibility of corruption that military power brings. He crowned this with a further elaborate metaphor:

I believe I see an immense people, dancing upon a vast terrain covered in greenery and flowers, playing with its weapons, making the air ring with its cries of joy and its martial songs; suddenly the ground collapses, the flowers, the men, the weapons disappear; I see nothing more but a gulf filled with victims. Ah! Flee, flee; there is still time, before the ground where you stand caves in beneath the flowers with which they cover it.[18]

---

17. Robespierre, *Oeuvres*, vol. 8, p. 110. The passage uses the intimate form *tu* throughout.

18. Ibid., vol. 8, pp. 132–52, citation at p. 151.

This invocation of a vision offered his listeners a *tableau* of afflicted innocence. The *tableau* was an absolutely central element of sentimentalist aesthetics, deriving from the innovative theatrical practice of immobilizing the action on a striking point of emotive resonance, with the explicit aim of eliciting appropriate sentimental response in an audience. Spreading into pictorial art, literature, and ultimately as here into political rhetoric, it directed attention very clearly toward the conscious effort at invocation of emotion, something deemed both essential and praiseworthy in a sentimentalist outlook.[19]

Over the following weeks, Robespierre added further building blocks to the edifice of martyred heroism he was erecting. On February 10, 1792, he delivered an epic address at the Jacobins on "the means to save the State and liberty," covering over twenty-five close-printed pages, in which he rehearsed a mass of arguments against Brissotin blind optimism, but framed them within what amounted to a vision of a new possible future. The speech drew on tropes of sentimentalist psychology to argue for the regenerative effects of environmental alteration. Foreshadowing what was to become explicit, if abortive, policy in the years of the Terror, Robespierre indicated that consciously working to remold communities' physical and cultural surroundings, enveloping them with messages about appropriate beliefs and practices, would make them better citizens and patriots.[20] Education, the theater, artistic exhibitions; Robespierre surveyed and invoked all these to the nation's aid, for the regeneration of a patriotic citizenry—and all of this, as he comes toward the end of the speech, is part of a titanic struggle, not with the innocent foreigners against whom the French Court wishes to direct the people's wrath, but with the internal enemies, the counterrevolutionaries themselves. Here Robespierre passed back from the prospect of sentimental regeneration to the melodramatic martyrdom that might bring it into being.

If, he suggested, such enemies have already won over the majority of the Legislative Assembly, and if "virtuous men despair" of making it see the light, "they can die at the tribune, defending the rights of humanity,"

---

19. See Denby, *Sentimental Narrative*, pp. 75–78 and p. 86; and Emma Barker, *Greuze and the Painting of Sentiment* (Cambridge: Cambridge University Press, 2005), esp. pp. 11–12.

20. Mona Ozouf noted this tendency, linking it to "a sensationism which privileged heteronomy over autonomy and tended to consider men primarily as sensitive and impressionable beings"; see "La Révolution française et l'idée de l'homme nouveau," in Colin Lucas, ed., *The French Revolution and the Creation of Modern Political Culture, vol. 2, The Political Culture of the French Revolution* (Oxford: Oxford University Press, 1988), p. 229.

denouncing the traitors to their constituents "and at least leaving a great example for posterity, and terrible lessons for tyrants":

> And to what more worthy use could one put one's life? It is not enough to obtain death at the hands of the tyrants; one must have deserved it.... If it is true that the first defenders of liberty must be its martyrs, they must die only while dragging tyranny into the tomb with them; the death of a great man must awaken the slumbering peoples, and the happiness of the world must be its prize.[21]

Robespierre reinforced the personal dimension of this conception still further on February 15, when his appointment as public prosecutor for the *département* of Paris brought him to the Jacobins to set out his principles for this new role. He disclaimed all political or factional motives: "I am solely the avenger of crime, and the support of innocence." This latter role, naturally, appealed to him greatly, and he made it a centerpiece of his self-definition: "the happiest day of my life" would be one when he would see in court before him "the most ardent of my enemies, the man the most opposed to the cause of humanity (the only man that I could regard as my enemy)"; and that man should be innocent and falsely accused. Then "spreading out upon his cause the light of severe and impartial truth, I could snatch him from death or infamy."[22] In his final peroration, Robespierre nonetheless managed to turn his thoughts back toward martyrdom. He would lay down his office, he said, if "my strength and my health" forced him to "sacrifice my place to my principles, and my personal advantages to the general interest"—if, in other words, he could not work both for the tribunal and the revolution. "In such moments, the post of a friend of humanity is in the place where he can defend it successfully.... No mortal can escape his destiny; and if mine is to perish for liberty, far from thinking of escaping it, I would hasten to fly to meet it."[23]

Despite Robespierre's stance, the political forces driving toward war proved irresistible, and it was declared on April 20, 1792. A week after the outbreak of war, and with events going badly wrong almost immediately, Robespierre moved again into the mode of martyrdom. Under the threat, he claimed, of Brissotin proscription, he asserted that one does not flee

---

21. Robespierre, *Oeuvres*, vol. 8, pp. 183–84.

22. Ibid., vol. 8, pp. 193–98, citation at p. 195.

23. Ibid., vol. 8, p. 198.

a *patrie* that is "menaced...torn...oppressed...One saves it, or one dies for it."

> Heaven that gave me a soul impassioned for Liberty and brought me to birth under the domination of tyrants, heaven which has prolonged my existence into the reign of factions and of crimes, calls me perhaps to trace with my blood the route which must lead my country to happiness and to Liberty; I accept with transports that sweet and glorious destiny.

He has one further, even greater sacrifice, if "you demand it from me." He will sacrifice not merely life but also the honor of his reputation: let his enemies come and defame him, "I only want a reputation for the good of my country; if to preserve [that reputation] I must betray, by a culpable silence, the cause of truth and of the people, I abandon it to you."[24]

Shortly after this, Robespierre took up a new outlet for his ideas, becoming like many of his political colleagues and rivals the editor and chief writer of a newspaper. His *Défenseur de la Constitution* adopted a variety of rhetorical and political strategies. In some respects, it was self-consciously moderate, particularly with regard to institutional change. As its title indicated, Robespierre argued that the inherent merits of the constitution that he and others had sweated over for two years were worth defending—against counterrevolution but also against calls for a republic that might open the door to chaos. In other respects, his prose was uncompromisingly, and sentimentally, combative.

In the first issue of this journal, on sale around May 19, 1792, Robespierre offered his thoughts on "means to make war usefully." He noted that combat had "begun with a setback; it must end with the triumph of liberty, or with the disappearance of the last Frenchman from the earth." Conventional complaints from the political and military leadership were scorned; charges of "indiscipline" were:

> An eternal accusation against the civic spirit of the citizen soldiers, who began the revolution. That word has already caused the slaughter of those who have given [the revolution] the most signal services; that word has already chased from the army, by arbitrary

---

24. Ibid., vol. 8, pp. 315–16. For a gentleman, of course, honor is worth more than life, so here Robespierre is really offering an ultimate sacrifice.

orders, by illegal and monstrous judgments of the patrician and military tyranny, more than sixty thousand soldiers whose wisdom and energy were the terror of despotism.[25]

This repeated trope of past martyrdom was used to argue for greater energy and emotional commitment to the struggle:

> Frenchmen, fight and be watchful at the same time; be watchful in your reverses; be watchful in your successes; fear your own penchant for enthusiasm; and put yourselves on guard against even the glory of your generals. Know how to uncover all the routes that ambition and intrigue may open, to reach their goals; be watchful, either that our internal enemies, in contact with those outside, meditate plans to deliver us to the blade of despots, or that they wish to make us purchase, through the loss of the most energetic citizens, a fatal victory, which would only be turned to the profit of aristocracy.[26]

The military situation continued to deteriorate as spring turned to summer, with growing tensions between radicals and the Brissotin leadership. The continuing war emergency brought forth yet more developed examples of Robespierre's juxtapositions of past sufferings, current evils, and future revenge. On July 29, he declaimed at the Jacobins in favor of the French people, "betrayed by the holders of its authority, delivered by the government itself to the insults and the iron of foreign despots, reviled, oppressed, despoiled in the name of the laws." An "eternal toy of the intriguers who have governed since the start of the revolution," the people was now "in the final period of the long crisis which torments it," and still foolishly prepared to trust its unfaithful mandatories.[27] Labeling current events unambiguously as a conspiracy by the majority of the political class against the people and the patriots, his call for action was equally clear:

> Proscribed by the new government, we must find all our resources in ourselves. We must rise to all the prodigies that the love of liberty

---

25. Robespierre, *Défenseur de la Constitution, published in Oeuvres complètes*, vol. 4, p. 22.

26. Ibid., vol. 4, p. 26.

27. Ibid., vol. 8, p. 408.

may give birth to. The fate of all nations is attached to ours; and we have a fight against all the powers, physical and moral, that have oppressed them until this moment; we have a fight against the numerous and redoubtable traitors who live amongst us and against ourselves. The French people must support the weight of the world, and must subdue at the same time all the monsters that desolate it. [The people] must be, amongst peoples, what Hercules was amongst heroes.

Yes, I have already said it at several occasions, and I repeat it again in this moment; there remain to us only two alternatives, either to perish and to bury with us the liberty of the human race, or to deploy great virtues and resolve ourselves to great sacrifices.[28]

What followed within two weeks was, of course, the fall of the French monarchy, an event already a *fait accompli*—the royal family surrendering itself into the custody of the Legislative Assembly—before open violence erupted between patriotic National Guards and loyalist Swiss troops at the Tuileries Palace.[29] The resultant several hundred casualties gave rise to a wide variety of justificatory and condemnatory comment. Robespierre's approach, in issue no. 12 of his newspaper, published in late August 1792, offered these reflections on the scene on August 10:

Who might paint the interesting pictures of that day? Who could express the sublime sentiment that filled all souls? The heaped victims of the Court's fury offered themselves on all sides to the eyes of the citizens, in the vast lair it had inhabited, in all the nearby places: the citizens had their fathers, their friends, their brothers to weep for; but the love of the *patrie*, the enthusiasm of liberty dominated over all affections; one regarded, without emotion, the cadavers of the satellites of tyranny; one shed sweet tears upon those of the defenders of liberty, swearing to avenge them.[30]

---

28. Ibid., vol. 8, p. 418.

29. See Munro Price, *The Fall of the French Monarchy: Louis XVI, Marie-Antoinette and the Baron de Breteuil* (London: Pan, 2002), pp. 298–300. This draws on the detailed account of Rodney Allen, *Threshold of Terror: The Last Hours of the Monarchy in the French Revolution* (Stroud: Sutton, 1999).

30. Robespierre, *Défenseur*, p. 364.

Sentiment, and particularly strong sentimental response to the visual spectacle of martyrdom, is again central to Robespierre's account and to the conclusions he draws. He noted earlier that the Swiss Guards at the château had initially "held their hands out to the citizens, several wore the bonnet of liberty," but this "sweet illusion" was broken by treacherous fire. As a result of this, he says, "The château was stormed, the Swiss put to flight, pursued; a great number of them were sacrificed to the shades of the defenders of liberty [*immolé aux mânes des defenseurs de la liberte*], who had perished under the blows of tyranny."[31] The connection between martyrdom and retaliation could not be clearer. His final peroration links past and future into one combative message:

> All must arise, all must arm themselves, the enemies of liberty must hide in the shadows. The alarm sounded in Paris must be repeated throughout the departments. Frenchmen, know how to reason and to fight. You are henceforth at war with all your oppressors; you will only have peace when you have punished them. Let pusillanimous weakness be far from you; or that cowardly indulgence that tyrants, thirsty for the blood of men, claim only for themselves. Impunity has given birth to all their crimes and all your ills. Let them all fall beneath the blade of the laws. The clemency that pardons them is barbaric; it is a crime against humanity.[32]

What direct influence rhetoric like this had on subsequent events is an open question, but it is clear that forces within the Parisian radical movement were in these same weeks gearing themselves up for ruthless purgative action. What followed in early September was a series of infamous massacres in the prisons of the capital that claimed over a thousand lives.[33] Tacitly accepted by the political class as they occurred, these would shortly become the touchstones of further factional rage, and Robespierre's conceptions of sacrifice and martyrdom were at the heart of this conflict. Elected to the new National Convention by a Parisian electoral assembly that he chaired, and which met during the very days of massacre, he was

---

31. Ibid., p. 354. See also Schechter, "Terror, Vengeance, and Martyrdom in the French Revolution: The Case of the Shades", in this volume.

32. Robespierre, *Défenseur*, p. 360.

33. See Andress, *Terror*, chap. 4, for a detailed discussion of the context and nature of the September Massacres, and pp. 119 ff., for a discussion of the ensuing political conflicts.

soon engaged in vicious declamatory struggle. At the end of October 1792 he addressed a long speech at the Jacobins to the "influence of calumny on the Revolution," placing the "faction" formerly called Brissotins, now increasingly labeled as the "Girondins," at the heart of its ills: "they are the respectable people, the ones who are *comme il faut* in the Republic; we are the sans-culottes and the rabble." In charge of the government, and with the agenda of the Convention and its committees in their hands, the Girondins are, he claims, all-powerful:

> Woe to the patriots who, unaided, will still dare to defend liberty! They will be crushed like vile insects. Woe to the people, if it dares show some energy or sign of existence! They know how to divide the people, to have it slaughtered by its own hand; and they are thirsty for its blood. When they fought against another faction and sought to make deals with the Court, they were forced to caress the people and to treat the patriots with a certain amount of care, to intimidate their adversaries, or to fight them. [But now] they want to get rid of the most intrepid friends of the *patrie* and crush them with the weight of their power.[34]

A few days later, responding in the Convention to charges of aspirant dictatorship and complicity in the September Massacres laid by the Girondin Jean-Baptiste Louvet, Robespierre noted the already prevalent sentiment of grief for the victims of those events, which he found hypocritical:

> Let us keep some tears for more touching calamities. Weep for the hundred thousand patriots immolated by tyranny; weep for our fellow-citizens dying on their burning roofs, and the sons of citizens massacred in the cradle, or in the arms of their mothers. Do you not have enough brothers, children, wives to avenge? ... Weep then, weep for humanity slain beneath [tyrants'] odious yoke; but recover if, imposing silence on all the vile passions, you wish to assure the happiness of this country and of the world; recover if you wish to recall exiled justice and equality back to the earth, and to block up, by just laws, the wellsprings of crimes and of the misfortunes of your fellows.

---

34. Robespierre, in *Oeuvres*, vol. 9, pp. 44–60, at p. 59.

> The sensibility that laments almost exclusively for the enemies of liberty is suspect to me. Cease to wave before my eyes the bloody robe of the tyrant, or I shall think that you wish to put Rome back in chains.[35]

Concluding his speech, as so often before, Robespierre invoked personal as well as collective martyrdom:

> I renounce the just vengeance that I would have the right to pursue against the calumniators; I demand only from them the return of peace and the triumph of liberty. Citizens, traverse with a firm and rapid step the superb course ahead of you; and may I, at the expense of my life and even my reputation, travel with you to the glory and happiness of our common *patrie*![36]

The sentiments and identifications here, the yoking together of past popular martyrs and redemptive mission, guaranteed by the offer of self-sacrifice, are what created the remarkable moral authority of Robespierre in the revolutionary context. His real influence on particular events waxed and waned: in the months surveyed here, he went from popular idol to neglected Cassandra, and back, after August 10, to serious political player, stepping up from a sudden election to the Paris Commune, to dominating the choice of representatives for the city to the National Convention, and there facing accusations of a master plan to rule as dictator. In the months to come, often his specific suggestions would be ignored or decried—his calls for Louis XVI to be executed without trial put him in a tiny minority—and other figures of more ardent aggression or diplomatic wiles frequently took center stage. The firebrand Parisian journalist (and also now Convention deputy) Jean-Paul Marat and the radicals of the Paris Commune, grouped around another journalistic mouthpiece, the *Père Duchesne* of Jacques-René Hébert, were the Girondins' chief antagonists until the latter were purged from the Convention by a Parisian uprising on June 2, 1793—an uprising which Robespierre shied away from supporting. Meanwhile the Parisian lawyer Georges-Jacques Danton, a seamless blend of rough-edged demagogue and backroom dealmaker,

---

35. Robespierre, *Oeuvres*, vol. 9, pp. 79–101, at p. 93.

36. Ibid., vol. 9, pp. 100–101.

appeared firmly in charge on the Committee of Public Safety managing the war. It took new dimensions of crisis, as external enemies pressed across the frontiers, and the Girondins' provincial supporters launched a "federalist rebellion" against their toppling, to bring Robespierre into the circles of power. Joining the Committee of Public Safety in late July 1793 a few weeks after Danton's resignation, it was not his political acumen, but essentially his moral authority that brought him there, offering the opportunity for an embattled government to frame itself in the sharp contours of right and wrong. Robespierre, ever-consistent, provided over the next year countless examples of his unchanging views on the relationship between a true, sentimentalist attachment to the martyred people, and the need for decisive and relentless action.

Taking one notable example in detail, we can see how, in his famous speech of February 4, 1794, in which he presented the course of the revolution as one toward "the reign of that eternal justice whose laws have been inscribed . . . in the hearts of all men," and also yoked together "virtue" and "terror" as inseparable components of that journey, Robespierre revisited once more his central identifications.[37] The "people" assumed again the mantle of martyrdom, infused also with that heroism that had made the Revolution, and the subsequent emergence of the Republic, possible. That people had broken "the chains of despotism" by "prodigious efforts of courage and reason," and thus "by force of its moral character" left "the arms of death in order to recapture the vigour of youth." Robespierre emphasized the emotional palette with which popular actions and virtues should be painted: "in turn sensitive and proud, intrepid and docile," this people was thus unstoppable by enemies that faced it openly, but lived in dread of those that would undermine its virtue from within, and especially from within its government. Keeping government sufficiently pure to merit the people's support was thus essential, and this was the core of his remarks.

Robespierre tore into the arguments of "indulgents," those associated with Danton who were calling for measures of Terror to be reined in. This was a view he called "mercy for the scoundrels" who opposed the people, and he retorted by making popular martyrdom an unanswerable claim on continued rigor: "No—mercy for innocence, mercy for the weak, mercy

---

37. Quotations from this speech are from the translation in Keith M. Baker, ed., *The Old Regime and the French Revolution*, University of Chicago Readings in Western Civilization 7 (Chicago: Chicago University Press, 1987), pp. 369–84.

for the unfortunate, mercy for humanity!" The indulgent do not weep for the "two hundred thousand heroes, the elite of the nation, cut down by the iron of liberty's enemies or by the daggers of royalist or federalist assassins," they save their tears for traitors. "Our women horribly mutilated, our children murdered at their mothers' breasts...the misery of generous citizens who have sacrificed their brothers, children, husbands to the finest of causes" are not enough to move such people, who "lavish their most generous consolations upon the wives of conspirators"—a nod to the widespread reports that many politicians were giving sympathetic hearings, if not more, to the more attractive supporters of imprisoned aristocrats.

Yet Robespierre, in pursuit of his narrow version of a political purity that could live up to the moral weight of the people's martyred heroism, also attacked "ultra-revolutionaries" on the other side (of a very narrow spectrum). These were those like Hébert and his Parisian associates (many of whom had taken leading positions in the War Ministry, run by a sympathizer) who insisted on their plebeian "sans-culotte" superiority to Robespierre and the Convention, and talked darkly of purging that group in the name of the people. For Robespierre, to oppose him in that name was to take it in vain. For him, these "ultras" were men who "don the mask of patriotism in order to disfigure, by insolent parodies, the sublime drama of the revolution." The people, "made the dupe of their intrigues," threaten the Republic with excesses, which true patriots in government must resist, even though "the destiny of men who seek only the public good is to be made the victims of those who seek to advance themselves." Thus, sanctified by the image of collective martyrdom, Robespierre once again cements his case by invocation of the willingness to be martyred in person.

In practice, the first outcome of the thinking behind this speech was an acceleration of the rising tensions between the Committee of Public Safety and the Hébertist and Dantonist "factions," leading by the late Spring of 1794 to their dramatic purging and execution. These purges were a turning point in the evolution of the Terror, leading to four months of ever-accelerating suspicion at the heart of republican politics, to the point whereby, in late July 1794, Robespierre and his band of closest associates appear to have decided that almost every other figure of note in the Republic was corrupt and counterrevolutionary, and also needed to be purged. The result was that Robespierre himself was purged. One of his personal enemies, Marc-Guillaume-Alexis Vadier, openly mocked him on the floor of the Convention as "the cunning individual who has been able to assume every mask," ridiculing his habitual rhetorical claims: "he is the only defender of liberty, he is giving it up for lost, he is going to quit everything; he is a man of rare modesty," and his persistent invocation of martyrdom.[38]

Men who had actually taken part in the bloody actions of "terrorist" repression in Lyon, Toulon, and the West were able to perform a remarkable inversion in these critical hours. Robespierre's version of the Terror, unlike theirs, was one in which argument and identification, rhetorical claims of authority and justification, mattered more than practical action. The persuasive claim of popular identification—which carried with it the authority to exclude particular persons from "the people"—had been cemented by Robespierre's earlier revolutionary career. It made the almost literally ludicrous travesty of Danton's trial possible, Robespierre in all apparent seriousness reinterpreting the life of a man he had defended as a revolutionary hero only months before, to paint it as a succession of deliberate plotted betrayals. But what this also created was the atmosphere in which Robespierre's own condemnation became possible. Victimhood—the state from which Robespierre had always striven to defend the people, the state which gave access to claims of virtue, of meriting martyrdom—became accessible against Robespierre. On 8 Thermidor (July 26, 1794), one representative spoke in the Convention, with apparently authentic dread, of the fear of repression that hung over him: he was "overwhelmed with slanders" that he was a profiteer, "a scoundrel...a plunderer...a man dripping with the blood of the prisons, I who have such a sensitive and tender soul," and who could not even, he said, afford new clothes for his children.[39] The following day, in the climactic session that saw Robespierre outlawed, one of the key accusations was that he had maintained the need for the repressive law of 22 Prairial (June 10, 1794), that accelerated executions by the Revolutionary Tribunal, when almost all agreed it had become dangerous; and that "in the impure hands he had chosen [it] could be so fatal for patriots."[40]

By seizing the mantle of victims and prospective martyrs, the "Thermidorians" (who, again, to reemphasize, were all complicit to

---

38. Richard Bienvenu, ed., *The Ninth of Thermidor: The Fall of Robespierre* (Oxford: Oxford University Press, 1968), p. 198.

39. Andress, *Terror*, p. 335. The speaker was Etienne Panis, a former member of the Committee of General Security.

40. Ibid., p. 338.

various degrees in the excesses of the Terror) were able nonetheless to end that Terror, and save their own lives, without resort to overt and illegitimate violence. "Thermidor" was not a *coup d'état*, still less a putsch. Everything was done by following the letter of the law. Echoing Robespierre's key tropes gave the new leaders of opinion in the National Convention the legitimacy to place the "Robespierrists" in custody, and when a rising seemed to be starting in Paris, publicly outlawing them as counterrevolutionaries snuffed out the capital's resistance with no more than isolated scuffles. The condemned men, after a few hours of tentative freedom, were taken into custody like a gang of surrounded bandits.

The process of containing "Terror" after Thermidor also proceeded rhetorically along lines established by Robespierre's sentimental identifications. The period of radical dominance was branded as a trail of martyrdom for innocent men, women, and children, reaching a peak (or nadir) with the exposure of massacres at Nantes—hundreds of actual deaths being reimagined as a genocide that killed tens of thousands—and framing the "terrorist" as a social and cultural outcast, a barbaric savage for whom no punishment was too severe. All those who now sought re-entry into the political world could use the mantle of victimhood to obscure any actual questions about why they might have been suspected, and those who used the uncertainties of the period to seek brutal revenge always claimed that this was an act of justice.[41]

One cannot say definitively how far Robespierre's particular brand of sentimental melodrama influenced these inverted reiterations of his favorite tropes: victimhood had become such a common experience under the Terror that it is unsurprising that some turned it into an emblematic and justificatory martyrdom. The fact that these terms echo back and forth through the politics of the 1790s is, perhaps, testimony to the fact that, even before the Terror, Robespierre had done a great deal to construct revolutionary politics as a constant battle between the prospect of sacrifice, sanctified by the memory of martyrdom, and the reckoning with evil. The blood of martyrs cries out for vengeance and demands the demonization

41. See Bronislaw Baczko, *Ending the Terror: The French Revolution after Robespierre* (Cambridge: Cambridge University Press, 1994), for a detailed exploration of these processes. Ronald Schechter, "Gothic Thermidor: The Bals des victimes, the Fantastic, and the Production of Historical Knowledge in Post-Terror France," *Representations* 61 (1998), pp. 78–94, discusses the aspects of fully fledged myth-making associated with "victimhood" in this period.

of those who martyred them. That is true in many eras, but almost certainly, the sentimentalist outlook of this particular time and place, with its focus on psychological impressionability, visual spectacle, and emotive identification with suffering, made the claims of such victims particularly intensely present in revolutionary politics.

7

Terror, Vengeance, and Martyrdom in the French Revolution

THE CASE OF THE SHADES

Ronald Schechter

HISTORIANS SPEND THEIR days reading, writing, and talking about the dead, but what typically interests historians about their human subjects is their lives. Historians tend to lose interest in the people they study after those people are dead. The eminent historian William Doyle writes that "when impatient crowds forced an entry to the inner courtyard [of the Bastille on July 14, 1789] the garrison panicked and opened fire, killing almost a hundred."[1] He never mentions these victims again. However, to the French revolutionaries those roughly one hundred martyrs who died in the assault on the Bastille went on to a new existence. They became "shades."

What were shades? They were ghosts, but ghosts of a particular kind. They were typically portrayed as corporeal, often "still bleeding." They therefore inhabited a liminal world between the dead and the living. As taboo and therefore dangerous beings, they represented a threat to the living.[2] They haunted the living but wanted to rest, so they resembled "undead" beings such as vampires. Also like vampires, they showed a predilection for blood. Yet unlike such monstrous revenants, they were sacred

---

1. William Doyle, *The Oxford History of the French Revolution*, 2nd ed. (Oxford: Oxford University Press, 2002), p. 110.

2. Mary Douglas, *Purity and Danger: An Analysis of Concepts of Pollution and Taboo* (London: Routledge and Kegan Paul, 1966).

and enjoyed moral authority. Victims of some counterrevolutionary force, they had sacrificed their lives for the Revolution, and they could therefore demand sacrifices from the living. Their principal demand was for vengeance. If they were not "satisfied," they threatened to turn their desire for vengeance upon the revolutionaries themselves.

In what follows I would like to take a closer look at the shades. I would like to argue that the shades enable us to see the French Revolution in a new light. They help us understand the motivation for revolutionary action, the willingness of political actors to kill and to risk their own lives for new and otherwise abstract causes: liberty, the fatherland, the Republic. Likewise, the shades help us understand the elusive Reign of Terror (or simply the Terror, as the French call it) and the role of martyrs and martyrdom in producing it. Finally, the shades reveal a profound spirituality in the revolutionaries, a religiosity that is usually discounted or dismissed in the historical scholarship.

The French had two words for shades: *ombres* and *mânes*. The revolutionaries much preferred the latter, especially when they were referring to shades of martyrs. The word *ombre* also had the ordinary meaning of "shadow," whereas the term *mânes* was unmistakable. It derived from the Latin *manes*, which literally meant "the good ones" but which the Romans used to refer specifically to departed souls.[3] As an appellation it had the patina of antiquity, and the revolutionaries were famously fond of Republican Rome and its tyrannicides. Strictly speaking, not all shades were martyrs, but all martyrs were shades. It is the shades of martyrs that I would like to focus on here, not merely because this volume is concerned with martyrdom, but because the shades of martyrs played such an important role in the French Revolution. Although it was possible to speak of "the shades of Rousseau" when paying homage to him, it was the shades of martyrs that really motivated the revolutionaries. Motivated them to do what? To kill. To risk their lives. To do things that do not come naturally and sometimes require supernatural intervention.

---

3. According to Jean Nicot's 1606 dictionary, the *Thresor de la langue francoyse*, the word indicated "the departed souls of human bodies" and derived from the Latin *manes*. According to the Dictionary of the Académie Française (of 1694), *manes* (without the circumflex accent) was the "[n]ame that the ancients gave to the shade (*à l'ombre*)." The editors noted that "one still makes use of it sometimes in Poetry, and in the sublime style." They gave an example from classical literature: "Polixena was sacrificed to the shades of Achilles." A similar definition appeared in the 1762 edition of the Academy dictionary; see "Dictionnaires d'autrefois" on ARTFL, http://artflx.uchicago.edu/cgi-bin/dicos/pubdico1look.pl?strippedhw=mânes.

In order to track the usage of *mânes* during the Revolution, I have con-
sulted digitized volumes of the *Archives parlementaires*, the massive record
of legislative debates, reports, and correspondence.[4] Comprising 101 volumes, roughly 60,000 folio pages and 70 million words, this corpus provides a unique lens onto revolutionary speech. A search of *mânes* in the
Archives parlementaires yields 433 hits for the period beginning in June 1789
and ending in July 1794. The term was particularly popular during the more
radical phase of the Revolution: during the period of the Constitutional
Monarchy (mid-June 1789 through early August 1792), when violence was
relatively sparse and emergency measures relatively limited, it only appears
42 times. By contrast, during the period beginning with the violent overthrow of the monarchy (August 10, 1792) and ending with the execution of
the revolutionary leader Robespierre (July 28, 1794) the word appears 391
times. Allowing for the difference in duration of these two periods (the
first lasting 37 months, the second lasting 23), and assuming that the volu-
minous *Archives parlementaires* are representative of the kind of language
revolutionaries used, we can say that *mânes* appeared in revolutionary
speech roughly fifteen times as frequently after the fall of the monarchy as
before. This discrepancy is easily explained. Shades in revolutionary discourse were almost always *martyred* shades who had died violently in acts
of sacrifice for their country. Insofar as the Revolution became more violent, insofar as it produced more martyrs, it had more shades to invoke.
The martyrs who died on August 10, 1792 had to be avenged, which led to
more violence, more martyrs, and more calls for vengeance.

Moving from a quantitative to a qualitative analysis of the shades, and
using quotations from the *Archives parlementaires*, I would like to describe
them in greater detail. In other words, I would like to attempt an anthropology (or spectrology) of an unjustifiably neglected group in French
revolutionary society. The 433 hits mentioned above, when carefully contextualized, afford a rich view onto the shades as well as their relationship
with the living and impact on the Revolution. Certain words, images, and

---

4. Thanks to such digital resources as ARTFL, Gallica, and Google books, it is possible to
track the usage of individual words in the first seventy-three volumes of the *Archives parlementaires*. These volumes, published between 1867 and 1914, are in the public domain: they
correspond to the period of the Revolution ending on September 17, 1793. In order to track
the usage of *mânes* through the period typically designated "the Terror" (September 1793
through late July 1794), I have scanned volumes 74 through 93 (which are not in the public
domain, but which cover the period through July 1794) and run them through an optical
character recognition (OCR) program, thereby making them similarly searchable.

ideas appear with notable regularity in proximity with *mânes*, and it is possible to say what the shades looked and sounded like, what their values and needs were, and how the living were expected to interact with them.

A eulogy by Pierre Duviquet on August 20, 1792, provides an entry point into the realm of the shades in revolutionary France. Duviquet was one of the directors of the Department of the Nièvre (in the former province of Burgundy); in other words, he was a provincial revolutionary official. He also happened to be a literary critic and was therefore highly sensitive to words and their meanings.[5] But as we will see, his language was not unusual for revolutionaries. Duviquet's eulogy was in honor of the martyrs of August 10, those insurgents who had stormed the Tuileries Palace in the overthrow of the monarchy and died in the ensuing combat (as with the storming of the Bastille roughly three years earlier, there were about 100 victims on the revolutionary side).[6] Duviquet gave his speech at a moment of crisis, even by the standards of the French Revolution. The three-year experiment in constitutional monarchy was over, but the Republic had not yet been constituted. It was not clear who was in power, and it was easy to imagine traitors taking advantage of the power vacuum. Moreover, France was at war with Austria (including the Austrian Netherlands, today Belgium) and facing what looked like imminent invasion and a violent end to the Revolution. In order for the Revolution to survive, political leaders, even minor ones such as Duviquet, had to motivate their fellow revolutionaries. The shades were part of this motivation.

Standing before his compatriots at a memorial service in honor of these victims, Duviquet invoked the "generous and patriotic shades" who had given their lives for "the land that was so dear to you, and which is still wet from your blood." He asked them to "inspire a trembling orator...penetrate me above all with that profound and generous indignation with which you were seized at the sight of the infamous and execrable treason of which you were the victims." He recalled the instant when the revolutionaries, gunned down by the King's Swiss Guard, called with their last breath for vengeance. "You shall obtain it, this vengeance, unfortunate victims," he promised, "and it will be terrible." He encouraged volunteers, "March bravely, fly to the borders that the tyrants want to cross; oppose

5. Michelle Cheyne, "L'Articulation d'une hiérarchie des rôles raciaux sur la scène française sous la Restauration," *French Colonial History* 6 (2005), p. 85.

6. Philippe Sagnac, *La Révolution du 10 août 1792; la chute de la royauté* (Paris: Hachette, 1909), p. 285 n.

the infernal magic of their plots with the shield of discipline and courage; then all the enemies of liberty and of France will be defeated, and our generous shades will rejoice and tremble with joy in the dust of their graves." Duviquet then addressed the victims of August 10, "August shades, we shall not betray your hopes or our oaths. Enlightened by your lessons; educated, enlarged by your examples, we swear to imitate you; we swear to uphold the liberty that you sealed with your blood, the equality that appeared to you more precious than life."[7]

Duviquet made it clear what role the shades played in the Revolution. By their "generous and patriotic" example they provided inspiration to the living, who might not otherwise be ready to kill and die for the Revolution. They provided "profound and generous indignation" to people (including Duviquet himself?) who risked being lukewarm toward the revolutionary cause or insufficiently angry about the presence of counterrevolutionaries in and near their country. They had "called with their last breath for vengeance," thereby bequeathing a heavy burden of guilt to anyone who denied this dying wish. One might consider negotiating with the counterrevolutionaries, or staying at home instead of volunteering to fight the Revolution's many enemies (both foreign and domestic), but that would mean denying the martyrs their last request. On behalf of his compatriots Duviquet promised to fulfill the shades' desire for vengeance: "You shall obtain it...and it will be terrible." Already the link between martyrdom and revolutionary terror is evident. The martyred shades were posthumous recruiters for the task of killing the Revolution's enemies. Thus Duviquet, with the moral authority of the shades behind him, impelled understandably apprehensive patriots to "march bravely, [to] fly" to the front. His communion with the shades, who after all had "penetrated" him, gave him the authority to promise that once the "enemies [are] defeated" the "generous shades will tremble with joy in the dust of their graves." Reinforcing the obligation the living had towards the "[a]ugust shades," Duviquet promised on behalf of his compatriots not to "betray your hopes or our oaths." These shades were not distant abstractions. The eulogist humanized them by endowing them with voices (they *called* for vengeance), a rich range of emotions, from anger and indignation to "trembl[ing]" joy, and, crucially, blood, from which France's soil was "still wet" (I will return to the importance of "wetness" later).

---

7. *Archives parlementaires*, vol. 50, pp. 668–70.

Although it is impossible to gauge the impact of Duviquet's eulogy, one can imagine it yielding at least some of the desired volunteers. Certainly revolutionaries continued to believe in the motivational power of the shades of August 10. In addition to invoking these martyrs for recruiting purposes, revolutionaries called on them when making a difficult decision: to kill the king. Let us take a closer look at this process. In late September 1792 France was officially declared a Republic and a new legislature known as the Convention replaced the previous parliament. This left the question of what to do with the king, who was still alive and in the custody of the revolutionaries. Should he be tried for treason? The king had tried to flee the country in June 1791 and join up with the forces of his brother-in-law, Emperor Joseph II of Austria to restore his (Louis's) power, but many revolutionaries believed that simply being a king made him a traitor: as Saint-Just said, "No man can reign innocently."[8] And if the king was tried and found guilty, should he be executed?

Judging and killing the person whom centuries of political theology had deemed sacred and divinely chosen took real nerve, and the shades could make it easier to do it. On December 3 Joseph Lakanal, a deputy in the Convention, apostrophized the "[m]agnanimous heroes of August 10," declaring, "[I]t is before your bleeding shades that I denounce the defender of your cowardly assassin [i.e., the king]."[9] Why could not Lakanal simply "denounce the defender" of the Swiss Guards? Why did he have to bring the shades into the room? Because the deputies might have disputed Lakanal, but it was harder to deny satisfaction to the "bleeding shades." Their blood made them human enough to inspire empathy, but their status as shades gave them authority over the living. The shades had sacrificed themselves; now it was time for them to receive a sacrifice: a blood sacrifice. Deputy Brice Gertoux made this bargain explicit: "Shades of the heroes of August 10, you shall be satisfied; the blood of the chief of your assassins shall flow to appease you."[10] It is surprising to see democratic deputies invoking the aristocratic value of "satisfaction" and the feudal ethos of personal obligation. It is also surprising to see modern, enlightened lawmakers claiming to be haunted by specters that require

---

8. Michael Walzer, *Regicide and Revolution: Speeches at the Trial of Louis XVI* (New York: Columbia University Press, 1992), p. 64.

9. *Archives parlementaires*, vol. 54, p. 226.

10. Ibid., vol. 54, p. 199.

appeasement. But the more one reads the *Archives parlementaires*, the less surprising such invocations become.

Other deputies called on the shades of August 10 when arguing for the king's punishment, thereby personalizing an otherwise abstract debate. For Deputy Joseph Lequinio the very question of whether the king ought to be tried was an "insult to the shades of the citizens immolated on the day of August 10".[11] As with the concept of "satisfaction," the idea of "insulted" shades harkens back to an aristocratic worldview based on personal honor. Lequinio was echoed by Pierre Baille of Marseille, who sang the praises of his native city and the capital, "Cities forever famous in the history of the world... Paris, and you Marseille, whose children first scaled the Tuileries castle and cemented with their blood the liberty of nations... men of August 10, we know our duties; the shades of our comrades in arms call for vengeance; Louis XVI shall be judged; and without a doubt his condemnation shall be prompt."[12] Again, the political has become personal, with vengeance taking precedence over procedure. Similarly, Pierre Bourbotte addressed his fellow lawmakers, "I hear the plaintive shades of the victims immolated on August 10... reproaching you for your cowardice [in delaying the king's trial] and calling for vengeance against you."[13] Here it is the deputies themselves who are subject to "vengeance," that is, if they do not avenge the "plaintive" shades. Someone has to die to satisfy the shades: either the counterrevolutionaries (chief among them the king) or the lukewarm revolutionaries. How the shades could revenge themselves against the revolutionaries is unclear, but evidently the former have the power to issue a deadly curse on the latter.

The shades of August 10 were not alone in the speeches surrounding the king's trial. Other ghostly personages joined them. Before granting the king immunity, as some deputies had recommended, Deputy François Robert suggested "question[ing] the shades of those generous citizens who had been enchained, abused, suffocated in the dungeons of the Bastille."[14] Deputy Audouin dismissed all talk of inviolability by observing that the "shades of victims immolated at Nîmes, at Montauban, in the colonies, at Avignon, at Nancy, on the Champ de Mars, on the plains of

---

11. Ibid., vol. 54, pp. 236–37.

12. Ibid., vol. 54, p. 100.

13. Ibid., vol. 54, p. 140.

14. Ibid., vol. 52, p. 395.

Longwy, at Verdun, at Lille, within the walls, outside the walls, of Paris, in the eighty-three departments, even in foreign countries, are not at all avenged!"[15] This litany of sites at which French patriots lost their lives is now obscure to most readers and I will not digress to fill in the details. What matters is that these place names resonated with contemporaries. Thus Deputy Louis Turreau referred to many of the same places when insisting, "It is for us to appease the shades of the unfortunate victims who perished in Nancy, Nîmes, Montauban, and on the Champ de Mars. They cry vengeance; we owe it to them."[16] Deputy Antoine Girard similarly conjured a host of different shades when justifying his regicide vote: "What do I hear, citizens? In the august portico of the Senate of the French Empire, I am persecuted, called, torn a thousand times by the lugubrious accents of the plaintive shades that traverse this sanctuary; I fly before you, sacred shades of the Deciuses of the Bastille." This was a reference to a family of martyrs to the ancient Roman Republic, updated to assimilate the fallen heroes of the Bastille. Girard continued, "I take you as a witness, immortal ashes of the heroes of the Champ-de-Mars, you shall soon be satisfied and avenged. Unfortunate victims of Lille, of Thionville; and you, French soldiers, at once worthy of the palm of triumph and civic crowns, you expired as martyrs of the *patrie* at the post of honor, at the famous epoch of August 10. The day of vengeance has arrived."[17] Deputy Joseph Antoine de Boisset was also ecumenical in his evocation of shades: "It is enough for me to remember the massacred [citizens] of the Tuileries garden, of Nancy, of the Champ-de-Mars, of Nîmes, of Montauban, of Jalès…it is enough for me to have seen the pavement of the place du Carrousel, the peristyle of the tyrant's palace, still stained with the blood of my brothers on the day of August 10; their shades pursue me and demand vengeance."[18] One is reminded of the Furies that pursued Orestes.

Other revolutionaries were less precise about the location or identity of the shades. An orator from one of the radical *sans culottes* wards of Paris conjured a gothic scene as he harangued the lawmakers: "Dare to bring your imagination to those fields inundated by a deluge of blood; see the cadavers whose still menacing look reproaches you for your slowness;

---

15. Ibid., vol. 56, p. 273.

16. Ibid., vol. 56, p. 575.

17. Ibid., vol. 57, p. 391.

18. Ibid., vol. 57, p. 403.

listen to those angry shades; you owe them the satisfaction that they ask for; they demand the blood of the crowned assassin."[19] Deputy Roger Ducos was similarly imprecise about the identity of the shades, though he was equally convinced of the king's guilt. "Could I doubt it," he asked rhetorically, "when I hear surrounding me the shades of so many victims of his treasons, of his conspiracies, crying vengeance against this illustrious scoundrel[?]."[20] According to Camille Desmoulins, also vague about the shades' identity but making up for this imprecision by augmenting their number, the immediate execution of the king (without a trial) was necessary "to appease the shades of one hundred thousand citizens whom he caused to perish."[21]

Of course, the blood of one man, even a king, could not appease the shades of a hundred thousand victims. On the contrary, the king's execution, which took place duly on January 21, 1793, immediately produced new shades who in turn demanded vengeance. Specifically, Deputy Louis-Michel Lepeletier (also spelt Le Peletier or Lepelletier) was assassinated after having cast his regicide vote, and revolutionaries would repeatedly appeal to his shades. Thus administrators of the department of Meurthe wrote to the Convention to congratulate it on the execution of the king and in consolation for the death of Lepeletier, concluding, "You shall be satisfied, illustrious shades of Lepeletier! The hymn of immortality that you sang in the French Pantheon has echoed in the soul of every citizen. The soldiers of the *patrie* shall avenge you in the blood of its enemies."[22] Implicitly, Lepeletier was demanding a blood sacrifice. Citizen Mignot Genety, a municipal officer in the commune of Thiers and Moutier, in the Puy-de-Dôme department, made the sacrificial blood exchange more explicit. Speaking at a memorial service for the fallen patriot, Genety proclaimed, "Yes, Lepeletier, I see them already, our generous cohorts, those soldier citizens who have promised their blood to the *patrie*; I see them animated with an indomitable ardour, running to avenge your shades in the very blood of the tyrants, and if they can penetrate all the way to their thrones and...immolate for you, oh Lepeletier, that horde...of cowardly agitators, infamous assassins."[23] Other revolutionaries used Lepeletier's

19. Ibid., vol. 54, p. 53.

20. Ibid., vol. 54, p. 180.

21. Ibid., vol. 54, p. 176.

22. Ibid., vol. 59, p. 540.

23. Ibid., vol. 59, p. 696.

shades to encourage revolutionary zeal. The Jacobin club of Saumur wrote to the Convention: "We swear by your sacred shades, Oh Lepeletier, virtuous citizen...we swear by your shades to devote all our moments to pursuing the infamous conspirators and not to stop until there is no longer a single enemy of the Republic."[24] The citizens of the commune of Montendre in the Charente department finished their service in honor of Lepeletier by pointing their pikes, bayonets, and sabers towards a "mausoleum" erected in his honor and swearing "to avenge the shades of Lepeletier by making liberty and equality triumph."[25]

Without a doubt the most famous French revolutionary martyr was the deputy and journalist Jean-Paul Marat. Marat is known to posterity thanks largely to the painting *Death of Marat* by Jacques-Louis David. But in the year of his death revolutionaries repeatedly communed with his shades. Like Lepeletier a victim of an assassin's blade, and therefore frequently paired with his predeceased fellow-martyr, Marat died at the hand of a fellow revolutionary, whereas Lepeletier had been killed by a royalist. Marat's assassin, Charlotte Corday, was a follower of the Girondins, those revolutionaries who had supported the establishment of a republic but opposed the efforts of their rivals (the "Montagnards") to let radical Parisians (*sans culottes*) determine revolutionary policy through periodic insurrections. Popular in the provinces, where "federalist" revolts had unseated pro-Montagnard municipalities in major cities (such as Bordeaux, Marseilles, Lyons, and Corday's native Caen in Normandy), the Girondins had made the fatal mistake of calling for a national referendum on the king's sentencing (they had all agreed on his guilt, but the Girondins suggested the possibility of allowing the king to go into exile). This made them look lukewarm at best and secretly royalist at worst. The Girondins also had the misfortune of counting among their number General Dumouriez, who conspired in early 1793 to overthrow the Montagnards in Paris and defected to the Austrian enemy when his troops refused to follow him. Thanks in large measure to Marat's philippics against them, the Girondin deputies were purged from the Convention on June 2, 1793. This event had added fuel to the federalist revolts, and it is in the context of that internecine conflict that Charlotte Corday struck on July 13.

---

24. Ibid., vol. 59, p. 585.

25. Ibid., vol. 60, p. 73.

Just four days later a deputation of Jacobins from Paris declared to the Convention, "We have promised, by the shades of Marat, to place the seal of opprobrium on the brow of the infidel legislator [i.e., the Girondins] who sold and betrayed his country." This language reflected a truly religious veneration of Marat's shades. The Jacobins added, "[W]e shall go further, legislators, we shall place it on the brow of his children...and we hope by this means to extirpate all the traitors of present and future races from the territory of liberty."[26] This was a new regression. The idea of inherited guilt, or infamy, was anathema to the Enlightenment, as was the aristocratic superstition of inherited honor, and indeed Robespierre himself had argued against the barbarous practice of punishing children for the crimes of their parents.[27] Moreover, the image of extirpation (in "present and future races") hinted at an endless process of weeding. This in turn was very much in keeping with Marat's tendency to demand larger and larger numbers of heads in exchange for France's freedom.[28] And if it was hard to argue with Marat, it was even harder to argue with his shades.

Other invocations of Marat's shades quickly followed. On July 17, the same day as the Jacobin deputation discussed above, the Republican Society of Tonnerre wrote to the Convention, "It is for you to avenge, citizen representatives,...may the sword of the law fall, may the assassins, their accomplices, finally all the conspirators perish, may their blood be poured to satisfy the shades of the martyr of liberty; we demand it in the name of the violated national dignity."[29] This language characterized Marat as a kind of god who demands blood sacrifices, but it also inadvertently made him into a vampire, an undead being that can only be "satisfied" by blood. In this respect he was simultaneously a martyr and a terrorist. The "republican sans-culottes" of Nogent-le-Rotrou (department

---

26. Ibid., vol. 69, p. 84.

27. *Discours couronné par la société royale des arts et sciences de Metz, sur les questions suivantes, proposées pour sujet du Prix de l'année 1784. 1° Quelle est l'origine de l'opinion qui étend sur tous les individus d'une même Famille, une partie de la honte attachée aux peines infamantes que subit un coupable? 2° Cette opinion est-elle plus nuisible qu'utile? 3° Dans le cas où l'on se décideroit pour l'affirmative, quels seroient les moyens de parer aux inconvéniens qui en résultent? Par M. de Robespierre, Avoc. en Parlement* (Amsterdam, 1785).

28. "Eleven months ago five hundred heads cut off would have sufficed; today fifty thousand would have sufficed: perhaps five hundred thousand will fall by the end of the year; France will have been inundated with blood, but it will not be any freer," *L'Ami du peuple*, May 27, 1791, p. 8.

29. *Archives parlementaires*, vol. 69, p. 350.

of Eure-et-Loire) also vowed to avenge Marat's death, swearing, "Shades of Marat, proud and terrible shades! Yes, you shall be avenged. All of us, your friends and brothers, we all swear it by your shades...they shall perish, your murderers."[30] The "montagnards of Autun" wrote to the Convention, imagining that "already the shades of Marat are embracing those of the immortal Lepeletier," and calling for both men to be avenged.[31]

The pairing of the two martyrs was typical in the year following Marat's death. In contemporary engravings a revolutionary allegory (such as Liberty, Equality, or Victory), represented as a woman, presents a large commemorative medal on which the two men are pictured. And the prints always accompany, either as a caption or an inscription on a monument, the words "to the shades of [Le]Pelletier and Marat" (or "Marat and [Le] Pelletier"). In one such engraving a winged victory holds a crown of laurel leaves over a medal of the two martyrs. They appear serene, reflective, and above all attached to one another (fig. 7.1). The two men gaze into each other's eyes. They look like a placid couple. This is a far cry from the angry, demanding shades of revolutionary speech, but it makes sense when one considers the presence of Victory. This goddess looks distractedly away from the martyred pair and from us, but significantly a Masonic Eye of Surveillance emanates from her breast. The shades are happy because Victory has come and remains ever vigilant. Yet this is a promise of future felicity. In 1793 and 1794 Marat and Lepeletier were decidedly unhappy and it was up to their compatriots to change that mood.

The execution of Charlotte Corday for the murder of Marat did not stop the conjuring of his shades. The Republican Society of Tonneins (department of Lot-et-Garonne) wrote to the Convention on August 4, "We mourn the death of the friend of the people, the incorruptible, immortal Marat. The sword of the law has struck his assassin, but that same sword must strike all those who impelled this fury. We demand this in the name of justice and of the bleeding shades of this famous man, this martyr of liberty."[32] On August 19, 1793, a speaker from Revel (department of Haute-Garonne) addressed the Convention. Mourning Marat's death, he nevertheless assured his audience that "his errant shades will sharpen our swords [and] direct our avenging arms toward that execrable horde

---

30. Ibid., vol. 69, p. 232.

31. Ibid., vol. 70, p. 154.

32. Ibid., vol. 72, p. 633.

LA VICTOIRE

Aux Mânes de Pelletier et Marat

A Paris, chez Basset, M.^d d'Estampes, rue Jacques, au coin de celle des Mathurins.

5342

FIGURE 7.1. A winged Victory crowns a medallion of the martyrs Lepeletier and Marat. The print reads, "Victory to the Shades of Lepeletier and Marat"

Bibliothèque Nationale de France (BNF), Paris, Département Estampes et Photographie, Collection de Vinck, 5342, reproduced courtesy of the BNF.

of aristocrats and federalists."[33] On October 11, 1793, the Popular Society of Fontainebleau erected a statue of Marat and held a ceremony to inaugurate it. A speaker explained, "To appease the shades of this virtuous republican, we have made a bonfire composed of all the effigies of the despots."[34] On October 16, 1793, a cortège inaugurating busts of Marat and Lepeletier burned the act of accusation against Marat (it was presumably a copy). They then brought it (partially burned?) to the Convention, "to make the shades of this courageous victim happy."[35] Marat was also cheered by the death of Marie-Antoinette, according to the Popular Society of Loche (department of Indre-et-Loire), which wrote to the Convention on November 4, "You have just paid a just tribute to the shades of [Le]Pelletier and Marat by giving to the national sword the head of that fury that Austria seemed to have vomited to the shame and misery of humanity," though it added that more executions were needed.[36] At a festival on January 25, 1794, revolutionaries in Uzès (department of Gard) repeatedly spoke of (or to) Marat's shades. One citizen proclaimed, "It is your shades, oh Marat, that I invoke: inspire me: may your beautiful soul penetrate mine! May your shades tell all of my compatriots that man lives, that he must live and die for the *Patrie!*"[37] Another urged his fellow citizens, "[L]et us avenge the shades of this popular legislator [Marat]. . . . Let us exterminate that impious race [of aristocrats]."[38] Yet another speaker explained that "to satisfy the shades of Marat it is necessary for the guilty ones, for the conspirators to be struck by the sword of the law."[39]

Another pair of revolutionary martyrs emerged when the British (having joined the war against France in February 1793) seized the Mediterranean port city of Toulon in September 1793. Pierre Bayle was a local official who was arrested during the siege and hanged himself in his prison cell, thus depriving the British of the power to execute him. His colleague Charles Beauvais de Préau survived imprisonment and was released following the French retaking of Toulon, but he died shortly thereafter (March 28, 1794),

---

33. Ibid., vol. 74, p. 88.

34. Ibid., vol. 77, p. 648.

35. Ibid., vol. 76, p. 488.

36. Ibid., vol. 78, p. 621.

37. Ibid., vol. 85, p. 482.

38. Ibid., vol. 85, p. 487.

39. Ibid., vol. 85, p. 491.

presumably of maltreatment under incarceration. Yet according to rumors Beauvais had already died at the time of Bayle, so as early as October the two men were depicted together as martyred shades of the siege of Toulon (Beauvais's shades alone were also invoked prior to Beauvais's death). The council of the district of Lauzun (Lot-et-Garonne) wrote to the Convention on October 15, 1793, "let us swear eternal hatred of the English government, let us swear to pursue it until the shades of Beauvais and Bayle are appeased and the Pitts, the Georges, all the former nobles and other cannibals... have expiated their crimes."[40] That same day the Jacobins of Saint-Dié wrote to the Convention, "Representatives, the shades of Beauvais-Préau are crying vengeance, appease them with victims." They reminded the lawmakers that "by immolating Englishmen you will not sully yourselves with human sacrifice," thereby confirming the suspicion that they were indeed engaged in human sacrifice. "[Y]ou will only snuff out monsters. Their perfidy places them outside the law of nations, their atrocious character puts them outside nature."[41] The Montagnard Society of Saint-Omer wrote to the Convention on October 23, 1793, "The arrest of a few Englishmen, representatives, is incapable of appeasing the shades of Beauvais. The voice of his blood can still be heard.... Take advantage of opportunities, it says to us, avenge me, avenge yourselves.... Who could not recognize in this voice a father of the *patrie?*"[42] On December 8, 1793, the Convention received a letter from "the sans-culottes of Digne" calling for the punishment of the traitors who delivered Toulon to the English. The letter demanded that British prisoners of war "be taken to the walls of Toulon... that their blood be a hecatomb of vengeance to the shades of Beauvais."[43]

The martyrs of Toulon continued to appear after the city was retaken by the revolutionaries. The "Popular and Montagnard Society of Libremont" (previously Remiremont) in the department of the Vosges held a civic festival featuring a song in which citizens responded to the cries of vengeance of Beauvais and Bayle.[44] Similarly, on December 27, 1793, the city of

40. Ibid., vol. 77, p. 643.

41. Ibid., vol. 78, p. 104. On the prevalent idea that enemies of the Revolution were "outside the law of nations" and subject to summary execution, see Dan Edelstein, *The Terror of Natural Right: Republicanism, the Cult of Nature, and the French Revolution* (Chicago: University of Chicago Press, 2009).

42. *Archives parlementaires*, vol. 78, p. 162.

43. Ibid., vol. 81, p. 106.

44. Ibid., vol. 83, p. 299.

Metz held a celebration for the retaking of Toulon. The mayor spoke of the "cadavers expiating by iron their revolt, their treason," and he added, "They perished, and their impure blood served as a holocaust to the bleeding shades of the representatives of the people eviscerated in Toulon by the ferocious English in league with the fanatical Spaniards."[45] On January 4, 1794, a citizen, Le Couturier of the Popular Society of Falaise, wrote a song in which he addressed the "infamous" city of Toulon, "You shall expiate your crimes," and he apostrophized the shades of the representatives killed there, "Rejoice in your tomb, / Shades of our representatives, / France is preparing for your bleeding shades an illustrious hecatomb."[46] Whereas at the end of 1792 it had appeared as if the death of a king might suffice to satisfy the shades, a year later revolutionaries were regularly calling for hecatombs and holocausts to slake the shades' thirst.

Beauvais and Bayle were sufficiently motivating martyrs to be included in the artist/revolutionary Jacques-Louis David's plan for the curtain of a new opera house and the festival that would have dedicated it. The end of the Terror and the arrest of David's faction—David had sided with Robespierre and barely escaped execution as a *terroriste*—left the project unfinished, but the artist's sketches and accompanying program notes tell us how David saw Beauvais and Bayle. They also tell us how he, as a member of the Committee on Public Instruction, intended the French to see the martyred pair. In the sketch Beauvais is holding the shackles, now broken, with which he had been imprisoned in Toulon, while Beauvais is pulling on the scarf that he used to hang himself in his cell (fig. 7.2).[47] Each man has an arm around the other's shoulder in a pose reminiscent of the brothers in David's painting *The Oath of the Horatii* (1784), and Bayle's outstretched arm (though grasping shackles) simulates the Roman oath. David drafted a report on the planned festival to the Committee of Public Instruction. In that report he wrote, "Sacred shades of our dead martyrs...appear, I evoke you! I see you!...You, Bayle, show the fatal scarf that covered your eyes with the shadows of the night. You, Beauvais, [show] the wounds that slowly opened the gates of your tomb."

---

45. Ibid., vol. 83, p. 112.

46. Ibid., vol. 83, p. 238. On March 28, 1794, a member of the Popular Society of Montpellier gave a eulogy for Beauvais. He addressed the "Soldiers of the Patrie," "Remember that you must avenge the martyrs of liberty; hear the shades of Beauvais demanding that you deliver the country from tyrants"; see *Archives parlementaires*, vol. 88, p. 257.

47. Agnes Mongan and Miriam Stewart, *David to Corot: French Drawings in the Fogg Art Museum* (Cambridge, Mass.: Harvard University Press, 1996), p. 56 (catalogue number 70).

FIGURE 7.2. A sketch by the artist Jacques-Louis David of the martyred pair Beauvais and Bayle, and dedicated to their "shades"

Harvard Art Museums/Fogg Museum. Reproduced courtesy of Imaging Department © President and Fellows of Harvard College.

As a visual artist, David was unsurprisingly inclined to *see* the shades, but this was unusual. The revolutionary speeches evoking the shades, as is evident by now, focused much more on the *sound* of the shades. One heard them more than saw them. If encounters with Catholic saints took the form of *apparitions*, encounters with revolutionary martyrs were mainly *auditions*. The shades cried, called, asked, demanded, and reproached. Yet if one could not (normally) see them, they could see what was happening in France. This made them the perfect vehicle of surveillance. Typically invisible to the living, they would make themselves heard when it was necessary to intervene in worldly affairs.

In some cases they could be remarkably loquacious. On August 10, 1793, the mayor of Ernée (previously Mayenne) Julien Quantin spoke at a festival commemorating the one-year anniversary of the overthrow of the monarchy. At one point he specifically addressed the lukewarm patriots who were willing to negotiate a shameful peace with France's enemies. He blamed "weak men" for having enlarged the armies of France's enemies and suggested that "if you had remained faithful to your initial oaths...your immolated sons...would still be among us...enjoy[ing] with us the fraternal pleasures that the Festival of the Unity of the Republic offer us." He then turned to the women, "sensitive mothers" who had suddenly become "[wicked] stepmothers, shameful victims of fanaticism." He asked, "Will you be able to resist the plaintive voices of your children?" and declared, "Outraged nature points your ferocious glances toward their shades, floating in blood and carnage." Although this image provided a visual impression of the shades, Quantin was more interested in what they would say. He imagined them reproaching their bad mothers: "Oh you who were once our hope; already you have forgotten us! Our blood flowed to make you happy and free, and you have repaid this generous death with ingratitude!...At least let yourselves be moved by the cries of your grandchildren; the tears that they shed at your breast are less the expression of childlike pains than impatience and the desire to see us again; we lived enough for ourselves, and for them the Constitution is going to revive."[48]

So much for what the shades were telling their contemporaries: what do the shades tell *us*? To begin with, they tell us that they were an important constituency in the French Revolution. How many shades were there? Camille Desmoulins referred to "the shades of one hundred thousand citizens" martyred by Louis XVI.[49] That number only increased after the execution of the king, the ensuing civil war, and the expansion of the European war to include more belligerent powers. On July 4, 1794, the Popular Society of Sens (department of the Yonne) wrote to the Convention:

Hurry to decree that the English people is the sworn enemy of nature, that the Republicans have risen *en masse* to destroy the Brigands...who are in horror of the sacred rights of man; that an island that only nourishes barbarians shall be erased from the list of nations, shall return to the ocean from which it never should have emerged: in that way you will appease the shades of so many

---

48. *Archives parlementaires*, vol. 73, p. 189.

49. Ibid., vol. 54, p. 176.

millions of men who died victims of their cowardly cupidity, of their odious perfidy: it is time for the blood of so many unfortunates to fall back onto these monsters.[50]

Whether we number the shades at 100,000 or "many millions" or assign some other figure, the fact is that revolutionaries considered them numerous. To be sure, some shades were more influential than others, and a ghost of Marat was certainly worth many anonymous specters, however much the revolutionaries insisted upon the principle of equality. Whatever the number of shades, collectively they made up a formidable lobby. Like (living) war veterans, they had moral credibility. They had made a sacrifice, and in turn they deserved sacrifices. It was hard to deny their wishes and demands. The fact that they were dead should not prevent us from considering their political influence. It is in the nature of a representative government that some people speak on behalf of others. The representatives in the Convention and in other political bodies were used to *representing* others, and in this respect speaking on behalf of the dead was no different from advocating for other absent, but living, constituents.

In addition to reconfiguring our picture of revolutionary politics, the shades tell us about the persistence of Old Regime habits, if not their atavistic return, in the midst of the Revolution. If the Revolution was the font of modernity, as is often supposed, then its citizens' loyalty should have been to an impersonal state, not the ghost of a specific person. Moreover, a rationalized system of laws should have replaced the practice of personal vendetta. Likewise, an aristocratic sensitivity to impugned honor should have gone the way of noble titles, inherited privilege, and coats of arms. Yet the shades call into question all of these developments. Even when they were imagined as a collective voice, they seemed to speak as a particular caste, a body privileged through its specific experience of self-sacrifice. They thereby repeated the nobles' prerevolutionary ideal.

Furthermore, the shades give us insight into the revolutionary origins of gothic literature. Julia Douthwaite has explored this connection very convincingly in her remarkable book, *The Frankenstein of 1790 and other Lost Chapters of Revolutionary France* (2012). She has shown that the literature of the revolutionary era, which drew on the lived experiences of the revolutionaries, laid the foundations of the Gothic, a style with an emphasis on blood and violent death and a proliferation of uncanny creatures

---

50. Ibid., vol. 93, p. 119.

such as ghosts and vampires, though in Britain the gothic literary mode pre-dated the French Revolution The many references to shades in revolutionary speech give us yet another glimpse of the creation of a gothic trope. Georges Bataille has identified the liminal state of decomposition, a realm in between wet and dry, as a site of taboo, and certainly the "still bleeding shades" occupied this space, much like the undead of gothic literature.[51] In this respect the shades, born (as it were) of revolutionary violence and trauma, began to haunt France in the 1790s and went on to haunt the world for more than two centuries.

The shades are also eloquent witnesses to the connection between martyrdom and terrorism, the dual subject of this volume. In the context of the French Revolution we should understand terrorism as *terrorisme*, that neologism coined in August 1794 to indicate (and repudiate) support for the (now defunct) Terror.[52] "The Terror" in turn usually refers to the period from September 5, 1793, when a Jacobin orator Claude Royer, supporting a popular insurrection urged the Convention, urged legislators to "[m]ake terror the order of the day," to July 28, 1794, when Robespierre went to the guillotine.[53] It also refers to the emergency laws passed during that period that essentially made it easy to be brought up on political charges and hard to defend oneself. More figuratively the term "Terror" stands for the political violence perpetrated by the revolutionary government on those deemed enemies of the *patrie*. The shades appear in both the more and less restricted understandings of this term. On August 12, 1793, Robespierre announced to his fellow lawmakers in the Convention, "At Toulon, every hour sees the head of a hero of patriotism fall under the axe of tyrants.... May these scoundrels, by falling under the sword of

---

51. Georges Bataille, *Erotism: Death and Sensuality*, trans. Mary Dalwood (San Francisco: City of Lights Books, 1986), pp. 40–48. I have discussed the production of Gothic literature as a phenomenon of *post*-revolutionary memory in "Gothic Thermidor: The *Bals des victimes*, the Fantastic, and the Production of Historical Knowledge in Post-Terror France," *Representations* 61 (1998), pp. 78–94. Douthwaite's findings and my own work on shades have convinced me that the Revolution itself, not merely its memory, provided material for the Gothic.

52. The first reference I have found to the word *terrorisme* in the *Archives parlementaires* comes from a speech by Jean-Lambert Tallien on August 28, 1794; see *Archives parlementaires*, vol. 96, p. 58.

53. On Royer, see Edelstein, *Terror of Natural Right*, 138 n. Jean-Clément Martin observes that the Convention never officially decreed terror to be "the order of the day," see *Violence et révolution: Essai sur la naissance d'un mythe national* (Paris: Seuil, 2006), pp. 186–93. Nevertheless, the repetition of this phrase in revolutionary speech indicates that revolutionaries thought of their policies in terms of terror.

the law, appease the shades of so many innocent victims! May these great examples annihilate sedition by the terror that they inspire in all the enemies of the patrie."[54] During the insurrection of September 5, 1793, Claude Royer, in the same speech in which he called for "terror" as "the order of the day," justified the new measures by declaring, "The shades of victims piled up by treason are asking you for a striking vengeance."[55] Later that month the Popular Society of Tour-du-Pin wrote to the Convention, "What hand other than yours can with greater justice cast the terrible thunderbolt that must strike down those guilty heads that spilled the blood of their fellow citizens? We ask you in the name of the shades of the heroes of liberty; let no guilty public functionary escape the avenging blade; it is in their punishment that the salvation of the *patrie* resides."[56] This meant the execution of the Girondins, which other revolutionaries justified by referring to martyred shades. Thus, on October 3, Jean-Baptiste Lacoste of the Cantal gave a speech to the Convention in which he called for the punishment of the Girondins: "The nation has been violated: it must be strikingly avenged. The blood of republicans was spilled in streams: the punishment of the conspirators, the accomplices of Capet, of Dumouriez, must appease their irritated shades."[57]

Martyred shades perpetuated a cycle of violence. They did so in two ways. First, by provoking terrorist violence, the shades assured their own proliferation, since violence was unlikely to go without retribution. Shades were most effective when fresh, that is to say when "still bleeding." The shelf-life on martyrdom meant that however powerful Lepeletier's shades were, they needed to be supplemented by Marat's more recent shades, while both martyrs receded to the background when Bayle and Beauvais took their place (in this respect they are unlike the more familiar "undead," who become all the more perilous the longer they remain in that liminal condition). These later shades incited yet more violence, which in turn produced more shades. Second, despite the repeated claim that the shades needed to be "appeased," there was real doubt about just how much blood would be needed to accomplish this goal. The many references to hecatombs and holocausts reveal the extreme extent of the

---

54. *Archives parlementaires*, vol. 72, p. 103.

55. Ibid., vol. 73, p. 420.

56. Ibid., vol. 74, p. 393.

57. Ibid., vol. 75, p. 679.

shades' apparent thirst for blood. Other indications suggest an insatiable need for sacrificial victims. For example, on October 20, 1793, the Jacobins of Sens wrote to the Convention congratulating it on the execution of Marie-Antoinette, "But this bloodthirsty tigress only suffered one death, whereas a thousand would not have been enough to expiate her crimes and to avenge the shades of the patriots eviscerated on August 10."[58] Of course, Marie-Antoinette could only die once, so how many others did the government need to kill before the shades would be happy? Similarly, the Jacobins of Hennebont (Morbihan) inadvertently suggested the futility of vengeance when they wrote the Convention on September 25, 1793: "If blood is needed, let the blood flow! All that of the federalists, poured onto the tomb of the victors of Jemmapes and of August 10, will not suffice to appease the shades of these heroes."[59]

One visual representation is particularly eloquent in showing the bloodthirsty nature of martyred shades. A print dedicated "To the Shades of Our Brothers Sacrificed by the Traitor" depicts the severed and bleeding head of General Custine, who had been executed for allegedly treasonous losses in southwestern Germany (fig. 7.3).

The head, which an arm (of the executioner?) is holding by the hair, is accompanied by the inscription, "Ecce Custine" (here is Custine) and the phrase, only slightly adapted from the Marseillaise, "His impure blood watered our fields" ("*Son sang impur abreuva nos sillons*").[60] The proximity of the term "sacrificed" to "impure blood" underscores the sacrificial nature of Custine's death. Although it is French "fields" that absorbed Custine's blood, the implication is that the shades somehow consumed the offering. Perhaps they have become part of the sacred body or soil of France, thereby embodying an idea with blood.

If the idea of pure shades demanding "impure" blood appears incongruous, it is worth remarking that similar language accompanies other accounts of the shades. In April 1794, the Popular Society of Saverdun (in the Ariège department of southwestern France) wrote to the Convention:

> May terror be constantly on the agenda! It produces salutary effects when the infected vapors of the swamp [a reference to the moderate party] try to obscure the pure light that gilds the summit of

---

58. Ibid., vol. 78, p. 116.

59. Ibid., vol. 77, p. 613.

60. The *Marseillaise* contains the line, "Qu'un sang impur abreuve nos sillons."

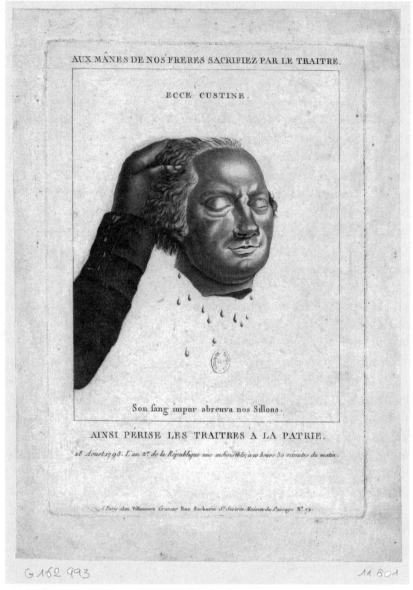

FIGURE 7.3. The guillotined head of Custine. The print is titled, "To the Shades of Our Brothers Sacrificed by the Traitor"

Bibliothèque Nationale de France (BNF), Paris, Département Estampes et Photographie, Collection Michel Hennin, 11601, reproduced courtesy of the BNF.

the mountain [a reference to the Montagnards]! Legislators, remain at your posts, for you must not leave them until all the enemies of the people have mounted the scaffold and their impure blood, mixed with the ashes of the last tyrant, have appeased the shades of Frenchmen who have died for the cause of liberty.[61]

Such accounts of the shades suggest that the shades were nearly insatiable. To be sure, the Terror in the French Revolution did end; it was not "the order of the day" forever. But it bequeathed a legacy of cyclical martyrdom and terrorism that is with us to this day.

The most obvious objection to my account of the shades is that I am taking the revolutionaries literally. The great historian François Furet cautioned us against reproducing the Revolution as portrayed by the revolutionaries themselves.[62] In other words, we should not be naïve. Did the revolutionaries really believe in the shades? Perhaps the repeated references to shades were nothing more than a rhetorical trope. After all, invocation of the shades was an ancient habit, going all the way back to the Greeks, whose *skia* are mentioned in the Odyssey, long before the Roman *manes*. One way of answering this objection is to refer to Keith Michael Baker's observation that there is no such thing as "mere rhetoric." Revolutions are constituted by language, after all.[63] Even if the revolutionaries did not literally believe in the shades, evoking the memory of martyred compatriots had an effect on listeners and readers, who in turn repeated the figure of speech until it became part of a powerful discourse that in turn helped to constitute the Revolution. It would be tempting to stop at that, but I would like to suggest that those who evoked the shades were doing more than giving figurative shape to their ideals. They were communing with the dead. In this respect they were little different from Christians who believed that their departed relatives and friends were "looking down" on them from Heaven. Their social world was not exclusively constituted by living beings.

Thus I am suggesting that the shades reveal a deep spirituality among the revolutionaries. But how do I know that the revolutionaries really

---

61. *Archives parlementaires*, vol. 89, p. 275.

62. François Furet, *Interpreting the French Revolution*, trans. Elborg Forster (Cambridge: Cambridge University Press, 1981), pp. 3 and 14.

63. Keith Michael Baker, *Inventing the French Revolution: Essays on French Political Culture in the Eighteenth Century* (Cambridge: Cambridge University Press, 1990), p. 18.

believed in the shades? I would answer this question with the question: how do we know that any member of a religious group believes what her religion teaches? If we second-guess revolutionary religion, we should do the same with all religions. Of course, it would be possible to posit a "false consciousness" to religious people. But revolutionary religion appears particularly vulnerable to historiographical skepticism simply because it never became established like Christianity. The readiness to doubt expressions of revolutionary spirituality stems from a teleological view of Christianity as triumphant, or a Romantic organicism à la Edmund Burke that insists on the failure or fraudulence of any "new" worldviews.[64]

To be sure, commentators have previously compared the French Revolution to a religion. The nineteenth-century political theorist and historian Alexis de Tocqueville observed in a much quoted passage that the Revolution, though "political," nevertheless "proceeded in the manner of religious revolutions."[65] In 1976 Mona Ozouf, in her ground-breaking book on revolutionary festivals, applied Émile Durkheim's notion of a "transfer of sacrality" to the revolutionaries, arguing that the nation acquired the sacred character formerly ascribed to God.[66] And in his monumental *Citizens: A Chronicle of the French Revolution* (1989) Simon Schama aptly titled a chapter on the Reign of Terror "Chiliasm," thereby underscoring the millennialism of Robespierre and his followers.[67] But historians, by and large, have been content to observe the similarities between revolutionaries and Christians, and in the end have confirmed the reputedly secular nature of the Revolution. Thus Tocqueville limits the Revolution's religiosity to its missionary zeal, its desire for converts beyond France's border; Ozouf sees the revolutionaries as fundamentally grounded in this world; Schama sees revolutionary ideology as stemming from a combination of neoclassical republicanism and eighteenth-century *sensibilité*, and locates revolutionary violence in a political dynamic by which leaders threaten or endorse violence and end up as its victims. The Revolution awaits its

---

64. Edmund Burke, "Reflections on the Revolution in France" [1790], in *The Works of the Right Honourable Edmund Burke, Collected in Three Volumes* (London: J. Dodsley, 1792), vol. 3, pp. 122–35.

65. Alexis de Tocqueville, *L'Ancien Régime et la Révolution* (Paris: Michel-Lévy Frères, 1856), pp. 15–20.

66. Mona Ozouf, *Festivals and the French Revolution*, trans. Alan Sheridan (Cambridge, Mass.: Harvard University Press, 1988), pp. 262–82.

67. Simon Schama, *Citizens: A Chronicle of the French Revolution* (New York: Knopf, 1989), pp. 822–47.

religious historian who studies the movement as religious studies scholars or anthropologists study Christianity, Hinduism, or the religion of the Iatmul people of New Guinea.[68] Perhaps the conviction that revolutionary utterances were nothing more than language, that they were "mere" rhetoric not corresponding to an actual spiritual life, is responsible for the absence of a religious historian of the Revolution.

I do not claim to be that historian, at least not yet. But I would like to question the assumption that the Revolution was a strictly secular phenomenon. In his brilliant book on eighteenth-century French nationalism, David Bell argued that the Revolution represented the triumph of a this-worldly ideology over a transcendent, other-worldly orientation.[69] But the many speeches that I have read invoking the shades point to a persistence of "Old Regime" otherworldliness. Again, other readers will be more skeptical and might accuse me of being overly literal in my reading, but I would like to call for an Occam's razor approach to spiritual claims by revolutionaries and offer the simplest interpretation: that is, they reflect spiritual feelings.

And why would they not? The revolutionaries were heirs to an ancient tradition of believing in the immortality of the soul. It must have been hard for them to repudiate this belief. Explicit attempts at resuscitating, as it were, the doctrine of immortality, reveal a real anxiety about its durability. Robespierre's Festival of the Supreme Being was a famous attempt at affirming Deism. A less well-known attempt, also sponsored by Robespierre, was a law that the Convention passed on 18 floréal Year II (May 7, 1794) confirming the existence of God and the immortality of the soul.[70] We might smile at an attempt to legislate God's existence and the soul's deathlessness; and indeed the need to make such a law reveals serious doubts about the very doctrine it was proclaiming. But there is evidence that even the most hardcore apostles of "Reason" were unsure that death was, to put it in Fouché's terms, only "an eternal sleep."[71] Thus on November 30, 1793, the Popular Society of Corbeil held a Festival of Reason at which the president addressed the "shades of Marat and Lepeletier" that

---

68. Clifford Geertz, "Religion as a Cultural System," in Michael Banton, ed., *Anthropological Approaches to the Study of Religion* (London: Tavistock Publications, 1966), pp. 1–46.

69. David Bell, *The Cult of the Nation in France: Inventing Nationalism, 1680–1800* (Cambridge, Mass.: Harvard University Press, 2001).

70. *Archives parlementaires*, vol. 90, pp. 140–41.

71. Doyle, *Oxford History*, p. 260.

they "bear witness to the triumph that Reason has won over the religious prejudices that had so long dazzled our eyes."[72] This paradox of apostles of reason expecting ghosts to "bear witness" reveals the persistence of the idea that the soul is immortal.

On the other hand, the evocations of shades that we have seen in this chapter suggest that not all souls were immortal: rather only virtuous citizens could achieve eternal life, and death in combat was one way to achieve this. Lest we believe that the martyred warrior entering paradise is a strictly "jihadist" promise, it is worth reflecting on the official description of the Festival of Unity, held on August 10, 1793, the date of the promulgation of the new Constitution and the first anniversary of the fall of the monarchy. This festival featured a chariot with an urn containing "the revered ashes" of martyrs to liberty (precisely whose ashes was not specified). But it was not a sad occasion, since "even pious grieving would have profaned this apotheosis." Rather the surviving relatives passed by with flowers on their brows, trumpets played a martial tune and "everything in this triumphal march removed from death everything funereal and reanimated…the sacred shades of the citizens who had become immortal in combat."[73] This restricted understanding of immortality as reserved for martyrs only reinforced the larger tendency of martyrdom to promote revolutionary violence or *terrorisme*.

72. *Archives parlementaires*, vol. 85, p. 183.

73. Ibid., vol. 74, p. 49.

8

John Foxe and British Attitudes to Martyrdom after the French Revolution

Dominic Janes

THE POWER OF the Roman Catholic Church was significantly undermined in the course of the French Revolution. Not only were many clerics killed, but so too were many aristocrats who varied from being nominally to profoundly devout.[1] These events were watched with horror by Christians in Britain despite that country's record of strident anti-Catholicism since the Reformation.[2] The reason why the Revolution in general, and its high points of violence during the "Terror" in particular, had such a powerful effect on British opinion was that the revolutionary attack on the Catholic Church was widely conflated with an atheistic drive to destroy Christianity.[3]

1. Useful introductions include Dale K. Van Kley, *The Religious Origins of the French Revolution: From Calvin to the Civil Constitution, 1650–1791* (New Haven: Yale University Press, 1996); and Michael Burleigh, *Earthly Powers: Religion and Politics in Europe from the Enlightenment to the Great War* (London: Harper Collins, 2005). See also Olwen Hufton, "The Reconstruction of a Church, 1796–1801," in Gwynne Lewis and Colin Lucas, eds., *Beyond the Terror: Essays in French Regional and Social History, 1789–1815* (Cambridge: Cambridge University Press, 1983), pp. 21–53.

2. David Rice, "Combine against the Devil: The Anglican Church and the French Refugee Clergy in the French Revolution," *Historical Magazine of the Protestant Episcopal Church* 50.3 (1981), pp. 271–81.

3. Colin Haydon, *Anti-Catholicism in Eighteenth-Century England, c.1714–80: A Political and Social Study* (Manchester: Manchester University Press, 1993), p. 264; and Maria Purves, *The Gothic and Catholicism: Religion, Cultural Exchange and the Popular Novel, 1785–1829* (Cardiff: University of Wales Press, 2009), p. 28.

Many Roman Catholic priests and monks fled to England and, since they were seen as victims of the godless Republic, British opinion regarded them much more favorably than might have been expected. Indeed, King George III visited French Trappists sheltering in Lulworth, Dorset.[4] The force of contemporary sentiment appears very clearly in the novelist Fanny Burney's *Brief Reflections Relative to the French Emigrant Clergy* (1793): "let us look at the Emigrant French Clergy.... Flourishing and happy ourselves, shall we see cast upon our coasts virtue we scarce thought mortal, sufferers whose story we could not read without tears, martyrs that remind us of other days, and let them perish?"[5] Perhaps the most influential Protestant voice raised in defense of the French clergy was Edmund Burke, who included some strikingly pro-Catholic passages in his *Reflections on the Revolution in France* (1790). In particular, he condemned the actions of the revolutionaries as being comparable to those of the "tyrant" Henry VIII whom he depicts as riding roughshod over the rights of private property.[6] David Beales has written in relation to these references that "Burke was virtually 'coming out' as a sympathizer with Catholicism.... He was soon to become active again in working to achieve relief for British and Irish Catholics, in a campaign which (for example) legalized the building of Catholic Churches in England and gave the county vote to Irish Catholics. Burke also helped to bring about the astonishingly friendly welcome that French priests and monks received in England when they fled from the Revolution."[7]

In this chapter I will be exploring the effect of the French Revolution on the history of Protestant anti-Catholicism during the first decades of the nineteenth century by focusing on one of the key texts of the English Reformation, John Foxe's (1517–87) *Acts and Monuments*, four editions of which appeared during the author's lifetime, the first of which was published in 1563.[8] It became established as a key anti-Catholic martyrology, and appeared in wide range of versions, bowdlerizations and abridgements

---

4. Peter F. Anson, *The Call of the Cloister: Religious Communities and Kindred Bodies in the Anglican Communion*, 2nd ed., ed. A. W. Campbell (London: S.P.C.K., 1964), pp. 24–25.

5. Burney, quoted in Purves, *The Gothic and Catholicism*, p. 34. Note that she wrote this in the same year that she married Alexandre D'Arblay who was a French Catholic émigré.

6. Derek Beales, "Edmund Burke and the Monasteries of France," *Historical Journal* 48.2 (2005), pp. 415–36, at p. 425.

7. Ibid., p. 434.

8. Available online at http://www.johnfoxe.org. John Fox and *Actes and Monuments* are variant spellings.

which were often referred to as the *Book of Martyrs*, as in the following passage from Charles Dickens's novel, *David Copperfield* (1849–50):

> a beautiful little home it was. Of all the moveables in it, I must have been impressed by a certain old bureau of some dark wood in the parlour (the tile-floored kitchen was the general sitting-room), with a retreating top which opened, let down, and became a desk, within which was a large quarto edition of Foxe's *Book of Martyrs*. This precious volume, of which I do not recollect one word, I immediately discovered and immediately applied myself to; and I never visited the house afterwards, but I kneeled on a chair, opened the casket where this gem was enshrined, spread my arms over the desk, and fell to devouring the book afresh. I was chiefly edified, I am afraid, by the pictures, which were numerous, and represented all kinds of dismal horrors.[9] (see fig. 8.1)

Clara Peggotty, whose house this was, would appear to have regarded her copy of this book as one of her most valuable possessions. Dickens, by contrast, appears to pour scorn on such attitudes through the vehicle of the young David Copperfield who finds the volume to be only a source of sensational horror. That we are not meant to see this merely as the immature response of a boy is made clear by the ironic references to the volume being "enshrined" in a casket, a phrase that invokes the preservation of a Roman Catholic relic. Dickens expressed a similar fascinated disgust on seeing the enshrined bodies of saints in Italy when, for instance, he viewed the remains of St. Carlo Borromeo in Milan.[10] The implication of such responses might appear to be a shared disdain toward the treasured values of both Catholicism and Protestantism, but Dickens was no radical atheist. In 1842 he left the Church of England to join the Unitarians in protest at Catholic revivalism within the Church of England, yet his attitudes to Roman Catholicism were complex and ambivalent. He was interested in Catholic theatricality in worship, but he despised intolerance

---

9. Charles Dickens, *David Copperfield*, ed. Nina Burgis (Oxford: Oxford University Press, 1981), pp. 127–28. Note also that the (mis)adventures of the young David Copperfield were modeled on those of the author himself; see Nina Auerbach, "Performing Suffering: From Dickens to David," *Browning Institute Studies* 19 (1990), pp. 15–22.

10. Dominic Janes, "Dickens and the Catholic Corpse," in Michael Hollington and Francesca Orestano, eds., *Dickens and Italy: "Little Dorrit" and "Pictures from Italy"* (Newcastle: Cambridge Scholars Press, 2009), pp. 170–85.

FIGURE 8.1. An example of the horrors that fascinated the young David Copperfield

John Foxe, *An Universal History of Christian Martyrdom*, ed. "John Milner" [pseud. of F. W. Blagdon] (London: B. Crosby, 1817), plate between pages 70 and 71, © British Library Board, all rights reserved, 1232 d 25.

and narrow-mindedness, whether they derived from individual prejudice or from the impositions of a regulating bureaucracy. What he looked for was emotional warmth and a sense of faith that was calming, healing, and soothing.[11] It is, therefore, best to see him as occupying a center ground between what he would have seen as forms of religious extremism. He preferred a rather undogmatic flavor of moderate Anglicanism of the kind that was then referred to as "Broad Church."[12] I have used this example of Charles Dickens to illustrate the way in which, by the mid-nineteenth century, a prominent and respectable Protestant writer could present the treasuring of Foxe's *Book of Martyrs* as the subject matter for a complex and ambivalent personal response. I will now move on to examine a series of specific ways in which this corpus of texts came to participate in an increasingly nuanced set of responses to martyrdom as evidence of witness to Christian faith. In particular, I will discuss the role of the "Terror" in the transformation of such acts of witness into scenes of horror.

One of the key aims of John Foxe was to present the witness of Protestant martyrs of recent times, notably during the persecutions under Queen Mary (reigned 1553–58) as being in direct and comparable relation to related acts of witness during the early Church. Kate Cooper, in chapter 1 of this volume, has outlined the ways in which those Christians who were executed by the Roman authorities were championed as victors in a battle against worldly power. The martyrs of the Reformation were indeed, more or less self-consciously, acting in imitation of the martyrs of the early Church and, indeed, of Christ himself. Moreover, Gretchen Minton has argued that Foxe styled himself after Eusebius (c.263–339), bishop of Caesarea and the founder of the genre of ecclesiastical history. Both writers wished to write a universal history of the Church, based on authoritative documents and centered on witnesses to the faith through martyrdom. In Eusebius, the background narrative of events explained the key difference between earlier Roman emperors as evil persecutors and their Christian successor, Constantine the Great (272–337), as the savior of the Church since he legalized the religion. Likewise, Foxe's narrative

---

11. Valentine Cunningham, "Dickens and Christianity," in David Paroissien, ed., *A Companion to Dickens* (Oxford: Blackwell, 2008), pp. 255–76, at pp. 257 and 262.

12. On the divisions within Anglicanism known at this time as "Church parties," of which the "Broad Church" was one, see W. J. Conybeare, *Church Parties*, 3rd ed., ed. Arthur Burns, in Stephen Taylor, ed., *From Cranmer to Davidson: A Miscellany, Church of England Record Society* 7 (Woodbridge: Boydell, 1999), pp. 215–385.

provided the basis for his comparison between the allegedly evil reign of Mary, and the virtues of her Protestant successor Elizabeth, who is compared to Constantine in the edition of 1563.[13] Eusebius's *Ecclesiastical History* was claimed by Roman Catholics as a key document in what was, from their point of view, an unbroken tradition of heroism from the death of Jesus Christ and his (as they would see it) appointed successor St. Peter, the first bishop of Rome. For Protestants such as Foxe, by contrast, the formation of Roman Catholicism only took place in association with the rise of Papal power during the Middle Ages.

In 1570 the Privy Council instructed that copies of Foxe should be publically available (chained up) next to a copy of the Bible in parish churches; and, although this never became a compulsory requirement, it was widely so displayed.[14] This official backing encouraged a lively market in cost-effective new editions of the work for people to read at home. The afterlife of Foxe's text was to center on abridgements which often stripped away much of the original narrative that had originally acted to contextualize the death scenes themselves. Thus, when the *Acts and Monuments* as an ecclesiastical history "became the 'Book of Martyrs' in popular usage, so it lost much of what originally made it such a Eusebian endeavor."[15] The key difference was that the former was an ecclesiastical history referring to the practice of the Church as an institution (albeit divided), while the latter was a set of martyr acts focused upon personal performance. Linda Colley has emphasized the continuing importance of the textual traditions of Foxe to the creation of Britain as a Protestant nation during the eighteenth century when she argued that, through reading a version of the *Acts and Monuments*, "Protestant Britons learnt that particular kinds of trials, at the hands of particular kinds of enemies, were the necessary fate and the eventual salvation of a chosen people. Suffering and recurrent exposure to danger were a sign of grace; and, if met with fortitude and faith, the indispensable prelude to victory under God."[16]

---

13. Gretchen E. Minton, "'The same cause and like quarell': Eusebius, John Foxe, and the Evolution of Ecclesiastical History," *Church History* 71.4 (2002), pp. 715–42, at p. 722.

14. John N. King, *Foxe's Book of Martyrs and Early Modern Print Culture* (Cambridge: Cambridge University Press, 2006), pp. 112–13.

15. Minton, "The same cause," p. 741.

16. Linda Colley, *Britons: Forging the Nation, 1707–1837*, 2nd ed. (New Haven: Yale University Press, 2005), pp. 28–29.

Foxe's massive collection of martyr-acts focused upon those done to death under Queen Mary (reigned 1553–58) and was widely deployed by those seeking to prevent Catholic emancipation. This was the process by which campaigners sought to end the comprehensive legal restrictions that had been imposed upon Roman Catholics since the Reformation. A major impetus behind this process derived from the imperative to reduce religious unrest both at home and in the British Empire, since Britain ruled over substantial populations of Catholics not only in Ireland but also in the territory of Quebec in Canada that had been acquired in 1763 at the end of the Seven Years' War. In 1778 the first Catholic Relief Act allowed Roman Catholics to own property and serve in the army and the second, in 1791, gave them freedom of worship. Finally, in 1829, the passing of the Roman Catholic Relief Act enabled Catholics to sit in the Westminster Parliament. Several new editions and refutations of Foxe made their way into print during this process.[17]

In the eighteenth century, Foxe's *Book of Martyrs* appears to have been widely important as a totem of Protestant self-assertion but was, it seems, read less often than in the previous century.[18] British anti-Catholicism had been both boosted and undermined by progressive ideas in the course of the Enlightenment, in the light of which religious enthusiasm of any kind could be viewed with skepticism, as with Edward Gibbon's (in)famous account of the rise of the early Church in chapters 15 and 16 of his *Decline and Fall of the Roman Empire* (1776) in which he argued for human agency (not excluding fanaticism) as well as divine causation as lying behind the spread of Christianity.

> The theologian may indulge the pleasing task of describing Religion as she descended from Heaven, arrayed in her native purity. A more melancholy duty is imposed on the historian. He must discover the inevitable mixture of error and corruption which she contracted in

---

17. Peter Nockles, "The Nineteenth-Century Reception," *Foxe's Book of Martyrs, Variorum Edition online*, 2nd ed., version 1.1 (Sheffield: Humanities Research Institute, University of Sheffield, 2006), http://www.johnfoxe.org/index.php?realm=more&gototype=modern&type=essay&book=essay9.

18. Devorah Greenberg, "Eighteenth-Century 'Foxe': History, Historiography, and Historical Consciousness," *Foxe's Book of Martyrs Variorum Edition Online*, 2nd ed., version 1.1 (Sheffield: Humanities Research Institute, University of Sheffield, 2006), http://www.johnfoxe.org/index.php?realm=more&gototype=modern&type=essay&book=essay8.

a long residence on earth, among a weak and degenerate race of beings.[19]

J. G. A. Pocock has argued, concerning the ensuing controversy, that "history [as a literary genre] was not yet autonomous enough...to treat belief simply as history."[20] The result was that Gibbon's image as an "unbelieving historian was fixed to all posterity."[21] However, Gibbon appears today not as an atheist, but as a skeptic of excessive enthusiasm in religion who was much in sympathy with undogmatic deism.[22] This helps to explain the seeming paradox that it was the lack of militant fervency on the part of some of the contemporary Catholic clergy that made them more acceptable to certain spheres of fashionable British opinion. Being a monk, for instance, for Horace Walpole, politician and connoisseur of the fine arts, had little to do with primitive fanaticism, but was almost something of a picturesque lifestyle choice. For instance, on August 31, 1777, Walpole wrote to his friend the antiquary Rev. William Cole saying:

In short as I have told you before I often wish myself a monk at Cambridge. Writers on government condemn very properly a recluse life as contrary to nature's interest who loves procreation. But as nature seems not very desirous that we should procreate to threescore years and ten[,] I think convents very suitable retreats for those whom our Alma Mater does not emphatically call to her Opus Magnum.[23]

Nevertheless, all this did not mean, in the decades after the Revolution, that toleration of religious diversity was universal or even widespread. There continued to be a significant market for partisan publications of Foxe and equally partial refutations such as William Eusebius Andrews, *A Critical and Historical Review of Fox's Book of Martyrs. Shewing the*

19. Edward Gibbon, *The History of the Decline and Fall of the Roman Empire*, ed. Antony Lentin and Brian Norman (London: BCA, 1999), p. 250.

20. J. G. A. Pocock, *Barbarism and Religion*, vol. 5, *Religion: The First Triumph* (Cambridge: Cambridge University Press, 2011), p. 367.

21. Ibid., p. 306.

22. B. W. Young, "'Scepticism in excess': Gibbon and Eighteenth-Century Christianity," *Historical Journal* 41.1 (1998), pp. 179–99.

23. Horace Walpole, *Correspondence*, vol. 3 [of 3], 1770–79 (London: Henry Colburn, 1837), p. 164.

Inaccuracies, Falsehoods, and Misrepresentations in that Work of Deception (1824), which "contrasted the pseudo-martyrs of Fox's Church with the Missionary Catholic Priests who suffered death under Protestant Laws."[24] Weighing in on the other side, Michael Hobart Seymour's abridgement of 1838 was explicitly intended to bolster the flagging anti-Romanist campaign in general and to resist the re-establishment of the Roman Catholic hierarchy of bishops in Britain in particular (which was, nevertheless, to take place in 1850). For example, he wrote of Queen Mary that "we do not know what feminine amiabilities she may have naturally possessed, but we do know that she surrendered herself into the hands of the Italian Priests, and they, to use the language of Our Redeemer, 'made her two-fold more a child of hell than themselves'."[25] Seymour denounces in his introduction the appearance of monasteries in Britain and asks whether the souls of the next generation of his countryman would be "the merchandize of Friars, and their morals become contaminated by the Priests of the confessional?"[26] His principles of abridgement are interesting. He notes that "owing to the state of society in the age in which this work was written, there was a coarseness of expression, and an absence of delicacy and propriety, in some of the narrations, which render it unfit for family perusal, in the present state of society, and which have aided much in consigning the work itself into oblivion."[27] It is notable, however, that being for family use did not mean toning down the violence. Extreme descriptions such as that of the death of John Hooper, bishop of Gloucester, who was burnt at the stake in 1555 during the reign of Queen Mary, were left in full.[28]

The successes of Catholic legal emancipation were swiftly followed by the rise of the Catholicizing Oxford (or Tractarian) Movement within the Church of England itself. Based at the University of Oxford, members of this circle, notably John Henry Newman and Edward Bouverie Pusey, oversaw

---

24. William Eusebius Andrews, *Just Published, a Critical and Historical Review of Fox's "Book of Martyrs"* (London: Andrews, c.1827), p. 1.

25. John Foxe, *The Acts and Monuments of the Church, Containing the History and Sufferings of the Martyrs*, ed. M. Hobart Seymour (London: Scott, Webster and Geary, 1838), p. ii.

26. Ibid., p. vii.

27. Ibid., p. ix.

28. As for instance passages such as: "his lippes went, till they were shrounke to the gommes: & he did knocke his brest with his hands until one of his armes fel of, and then knocked still with the other, what time the fat, water, and bloud dripped out at his fingers' ends," quoted in James C. W. Truman, "John Foxe and the Desires of Reformation Martyrology," *ELH* 70.1 (2003), pp. 35–66, at p. 37; and Foxe, *The Acts and Monuments*, ed. Seymour, p. 730.

the publication of a series of *Tracts for the Times* (published from 1833–41), the aim of which was to present a vision of the Reformation as an unfortunate schism within the body of the universal (i.e., Catholic) Church. The success of this movement led to a sharp polarizing of attitudes within the Church of England over the status of the Reformation. This left the great Anglican attempt at an authoritative version, in the ponderous, eight-volume form of *The Acts and Monuments of John Foxe: A New and Complete Edition* (1837), open to attacks from Tractarians, as well as from Samuel Roffey Maitland who was shortly to become librarian of Lambeth Palace Library and who loudly accused both Foxe and his latest editor of Puritan tendencies and slipshod scholarship.[29] George Townsend, who had written the preface to that huge edition, went back into press with his *Remarks on the Errors of Mr. Maitland* (1842) which concludes with the words: "I persevere in my humble exertions, till the plague be stayed; and till the apostasy and the treason, which have begun with the Tractarian at Oxford, and which has extended to the Librarian at Lambeth [Maitland], be not only resisted, but subdued."[30] Cattley, the editor, insisted that the fight would continue because "Foxe's memory is still sacred and Foxe's editor is still unharmed!"[31]

Disputes between Protestants and Catholics led to debates in which one person's "witness" (the original meaning of the word martyr) was transformed into another's persecutor, such as when James Richardson in *Popery Unmasked* (1825) accused Thomas Baddeley in his *A Sure way to Find out the True Religion* (1823) of "gibbeting poor John Fox."[32] But, in

29. John Foxe, *The Acts and Monuments of John Foxe: A New and Complete Edition*, ed. Stephen Reed Cattley, 8 vols. (London: Seeley and Burnside, 1837); Samuel Roffey Maitland, *Six Letters on Fox's "Acts and Monuments" Addressed to the Editor of the "British Magazine" and Reprinted from that Work with Notes and Additions* (London: J. G. and F. Rivington, 1837); D. Andrew Penny, "John Foxe's Victorian Reception," *Historical Journal* 40.1 (1997), pp. 111–42; and Peter Nockles, "The Changing Legacy and Reception of John Foxe's *Book of Martyrs* in the 'Long Eighteenth-Century': Varieties of Anglican, Protestant and Catholic Response, c.1760–c.1850," in Robert D. Cornwall and William Gibson, eds., *Religion, Politics and Dissent, 1660–1832: Essays in Honour of James E. Bradley* (Farnham: Ashgate, 2010), pp. 219–48, at p. 246.

30. George Townsend, *Remarks on the Errors of Mr. Maitland* (Durham: Andrews, 1842), p. 23. Distortions and problems in this edition, as in others of the period, are highlighted by Thomas Freeman, "Texts, Lies, and Microfilm: Reading and Misreading Foxe's 'Book of Martyrs'," *Sixteenth Century Journal* 30.1 (1999), pp. 23–46.

31. John Foxe, *The Acts and Monuments*, ed. Cattley, p. 491.

32. James Richardson, *Popery Unmasked: Being a Full Answer to the Rev. T. Baddeley's "Sure Way to Find out the True Religion"* (London: Baldwin, Cradock and Joy, 1825), pp. 67–68; and Thomas Baddeley, *A Sure Way to Find out the True Religion*, 3rd ed. (Manchester: Robinson, 1823).

addition, changing attitudes within the Church of England created ambiguity within Protestantism itself over the status of Foxe, and hence of his martyrs. Even as anti-Catholicism persisted in the aftermath of the Enlightenment and the French Revolution, it was, nevertheless, becoming more of a matter of choice within British Protestantism, rather than being a defining element of Protestant identity. Catholic sympathizers within the Church of England increasingly turned their metaphorical guns on Foxe. One of the most extreme such attacks came from the prominent Anglo-Catholic, Richard Littledale, who regarded Foxe as being a mendacious partisan who "so overlaid all the History of the Reformation with falsehood, that it has been well-nigh impossible for ordinary readers to get at the facts."[33] In a fascinating passage, Littledale compares the events of the Reformation with those of the French Revolution:

> A Church which could produce in its highest lay and clerical ranks such a set of miscreants as the leading English and Scottish Reformers, must have been in a perfectly rotten state, as rotten as France was when the righteous judgement of the Great Revolution fell upon it. But though we cannot help acknowledging that a great deal was then swept away which was intolerable, and that many a head fell deservedly beneath the guillotine, we do not make heroes and martyrs of Robespierre, Danton, Marat, St. Just, Couthon, and the like, nor do we pity them when the axe they whetted for their foedal [sic—i.e., feudal] tyrants fell on them in turn. Yet they merit quite as much admiration and respect as Cranmer, Ridley, Latimer, Hooper, and the others who happened to have the ill-luck to be worsted in a struggle wherein they meant to serve their adversaries as they were served themselves.[34]

In this passage, therefore, a priest of the Church of England was saying that the Protestant martyrs of the Reformation "merit quite as much [or as little] admiration and respect" as the Terrorists of the French Revolution because they were all involved in what was essentially a worldly power struggle.

---

33. Richard Frederick Littledale, *Innovations: A Lecture Delivered in the Assembly Rooms, Liverpool, April 23rd, 1868* (London: Simpkin Marshall, 1868), p. 16.

34. Ibid., pp. 15–16.

Littledale's sense of these martyrdoms was, therefore, based on an understanding of their acts as essentially political. A parallel for this reading of martyrdom appears in relation to the events surrounding the "Glorious Revolution" of 1688. In that year the pro-Catholic James II of England (James VII of Scotland) was, in effect, ousted in a coup instigated by those who wished to exclude him from the succession because of what they saw as his political and religious autocracy. Those of their political position who had been persecuted in the reigns of James II and his brother Charles II were memorialized as martyrs in publications modeled on Foxe such as John Tutchin's *A New Martyrology, or the Bloody Assizes* (1689).[35] Littledale's polemic can, therefore, be seen in the context of a Whig tradition that viewed martyrdom in worldly terms, but it was novel insofar as previous Protestant discourse had been favorable to the actions of such martyrs. The rising moral ambivalence toward martyrdom in the decades after the French Revolution was, thus, predicated not only on the development of a diversity of pro- and anti-Catholic opinion within British Protestantism but also on disputes over whether Foxe's martyrs were political or spiritual figures, or both.

Such British debates were being replicated across the English-speaking world. Even in the case of the United States, where that country's own revolutionary origins might have led to a different configuration of thought, Marjule Anne Drury, in a review of recent scholarship, has argued that "the similarities between British and American anti-Catholicism are striking."[36] When Amos Blanchard (c.1801–69), a Presbyterian minister from Cincinnati, wanted to provide evidences of recent salutary horror to drive home his message he found them in Walter Scott's *The Life of Napoleon Bonaparte, Emperor of the French* (1827). In preparing a postscript to his new abridgement of Foxe's *Acts and Monuments*, Blanchard filleted Scott's work for its most sensational aspects such as the comparison between modern "terrorists" and pagan Romans, such that Robespierre was spoken of as having governed the French Republic like a Nero or a

---

35. John Tutchin, *A New Martyrology, or the Bloody Assizes, now exactly Methodized in one Volume. A Compleat History of the Lives, Actions, Trials, Sufferings, Dying Speeches, Letters and Prayers of all those Eminent Martyrs* (London?: for John Dunton, 1689), discussed with several other examples by Melinda Zook, " 'The bloody assizes': Whig Martyrdom and Memory after the Glorious Revolution," *Albion* 27.3 (1995), pp. 373–96, at p. 376.

36. Marjule Anne Drury, "Anti-Catholicism in Germany, Britain and the United States: A Review and Critique of Recent Scholarship," *Church History* 70.1 (2001), pp. 98–131, at p. 105.

Caligula: "blood was his element, like that of the other terrorists, and he never fastened with so much pleasure as on a new victim."[37] Scott's entire account of the fall of the Jacobin leaders was repeated verbatim:

> Their chief, Robespierre, in an unsuccessful attempt to shoot himself, had only inflicted a terrible fracture to his under-jaw. In this situation they were found like wolves in their lair, foul with blood, mutilated, despairing and yet not able to die.... [When Robespierre was about to be executed, the cloth was torn away and] the shattered jaw dropped, and the wretch yelled aloud, to the horror of the spectators. A masque taken from that dreadful head was long exhibited in different nations of Europe, and appalled the spectator by its ugliness, and the mixture of fiendish expression with that of bodily agony.[38]

Blanchard worked as the editor of the *Christian Journal* (renamed the *Cincinnati Journal* in 1830) before being ordained in 1831 and installed two years later at a Congregational Church at Lyndon, Vermont, which was to be the first of a series of pastoral attachments.[39] He was involved in competing with Jesuits in the evangelization of the Mississippi valley, and he noted that a side-effect of the French Revolution was to send Catholic priests to America (as some had also fled to Britain) where many of them worked as missionaries on the western frontier.[40] Their numbers were small in comparison with the estimated 115,000 priests who were active in France before the Revolution, but their presence was important locally as presenting a new level of competition to Protestant ministers.[41] However,

---

37. Amos Blanchard, *Book of Martyrs, or, a History of the Lives, Sufferings and Triumphant Deaths of the Primitive and Protestant Martyrs, from the Introduction of Christianity, to the Latest Periods of Pagan, Popish, Protestant, and Infidel Persecutions*, 10th ed. (Kingston, Ontario: Blackstone, Ellis and Graves, 1835), pp. 537–38 [1st ed., Cincinnati: Robinson and Fairbank, 1831], directly copied from Walter Scott, *The Life of Napoleon Bonaparte, Emperor of the French, with a Preliminary View of the French Revolution* (Paris: A. and W. Galignani, 1828), p. 152 [first published 1827].

38. Scott, *The Life of Napoleon*, p. 152.

39. Bela Chapin, *The Poets of New Hampshire* (Claremont: Charles H. Adams, 1883), p. 100; and Margaret C. DePalma, *Dialogue on the Frontier: Catholic and Protestant Relations, 1793–1883* (Kent, Ohio: Kent State University Press, 2004), pp. 70–74.

40. Blanchard, *Book of Martyrs*, p. vii.

41. Michael Pasquier, *Fathers on the Frontier: French Missionaries and the Roman Catholic Priesthood in the United States, 1789–1870* (Oxford: Oxford University Press, 2010), p. 27.

Blanchard was also writing against infidels in America who were, he al-
leged, propagating the same ideas as those of the Jacobins.[42] Blanchard
was well aware that his edition of Foxe was a compilation. His version
includes, among others, sections on Ireland in the seventeenth century,
on the persecution of Quakers in seventeenth-century Boston, and of
Protestants in the south of France and in Switzerland in the early nineteenth century. It is quite clear that, by modern standards, Blanchard pla-
giarized substantial chunks of these additional contributions to his *Book
of Martyrs* (1831) from British source texts.[43]

Many of the seventeenth- and eighteenth-century British editions of
John Foxe's work had added chapters of material on subsequent events,
as was the case with Edward Bulkley, *The Book of Martyrs* (London, 1732),
Henry Southwell, *The New Book of Martyrs* (1765), and Matthew Taylor,
England's Bloody Tribunal (1769).[44] Since Foxe himself had produced four
editions, Blanchard was thus joining a long-standing publishing enterprise of re-presentation for contemporary audiences. His action in adding his "sketch of the French Revolution of 1789, as connected with the
history of persecution," had, however the remarkable result that Roman
Catholics were positioned as the victims of terror rather than the origi-
nators of it.[45] His expressed opinion on this question was that "as protestants, we cannot abstractedly approve of the doctrines which render
established clergy of one country dependent upon the sovereign pontiff,
the prince of an alien state. But these priests did not make the laws for
which they suffered; they only obeyed them; and as men and Christians
we must regard them as martyrs, who preferred death to what they considered apostasy."[46] This meant that for Blanchard the enemy was not only
Rome as the Whore of Babylon but also the Goddess of Reason who had

42. Blanchard, *Book of Martyrs*, p. viii. On American anti-Jacobinism and connections with
evangelical campaigning, see Marcus Wood, *Blind Memory: Visual Representations of Slavery
in England and America, 1780–1865* (Manchester: Manchester University Press, 2000), pp.
84–85; and Rachel Hope Cleves, *The Reign of Terror in America: Visions of Violence from
Anti-Jacobinism to Antislavery* (Cambridge: Cambridge University Press, 2009).

43. Amos Blanchard, *Book of Martyrs*, seems to have been very popular bearing in mind that
it appeared in several subsequent editions.

44. Penny, "John Foxe's Victorian Reception," p. 115, n. 21; and Nockles, "The Changing
Legacy," p. 223.

45. Blanchard, *Book of Martyrs*, pp. 511–40.

46. Ibid., p. 519.

been brought into the Revolutionary Convention in the comely form of a dancing girl "whose charms most of the persons present were acquainted with from her appearance on the stage, while the experience of individuals was further extended."[47]

Blanchard's main publication, other than his version of Foxe, was his *American Military Biography; Containing the Lives, Characters, and Anecdotes of the Officers of the Revolution who were most Distinguished in Achieving our National Independence* (1825). In this work it is the British who are tyrannical, and the martyrs are American patriots such as Nathan Hale (1755–1776), who, having been captured by the British when on an intelligence-gathering mission in New York City, was executed in a "most unfeeling manner, and by as great a savage as ever disgraced humanity."[48] Blanchard asks, "Where can be found so sublime and impressive a scene as that which the United States now presents? It is in vain to look to history for an example; the annals of the world afford none; it [the American Revolution] is an event that stands alone."[49] It is clear from his edition of Foxe, however, that this godly revolution was endangered by its unholy counterpart in France, which had seen anarchy "from whose boiling surge blood spouted up in living streams, and on whose troubled waves floated the headless bodies of the learned, the good, the beautiful and the brave."[50] Atheistic animality would, he feared, render man a "demon, which you must chain and fetter, if you would preserve the race from annihilation."[51] The horrors of Catholicism were relativized by comparison with atheistic nihilism. The martyrdoms of Protestants were also thereby inadvertently robbed of their unique quality by being placed in relation to the deaths of Catholics during the Revolution.[52]

There was another source of ambivalence toward martyrdom which was rooted in the thought of a group of Protestants who were among the most likely to identify the Pope with anti-Christ. Works such as Henry

---

47. Ibid., p. 520.

48. Sir William Howe was the Commander-in-Chief of the British forces during the American War of Independence.

49. Amos Blanchard, *American Military Biography; Containing the Lives, Characters, and Anecdotes of the Officers of the Revolution who were most Distinguished in Achieving our National Independence* (Cincinnati?: printed for subscribers, 1825), p. 267.

50. Blanchard, *Book of Martyrs*, p. viii.

51. Ibid., p. 5.

52. Ibid., p. 512.

More, *History of the Persecutions* (1810) and John Milner [pseudonym of Francis William Blagdon], *Universal History of Christian Martyrdom* (1807) (fig. 8.1), bolstered a "prophetical understanding of Church history (resurgent in the wake of the French Revolution)" in which the martyr acts of the early Church (presented as proto-Protestant) and of the sixteenth century were linked into an eschatological scheme in which the symbolic language of the Revelation of John was recreated in flesh and blood.[53] Belief in the Second Coming of Christ and the establishment of the Kingdom of God on Earth is a key element in Christian eschatology. According to the literal readings of the Apocalypse of St. John this Kingdom will last for a thousand years or more (a millennium). English millenarians, such as Joseph Priestley in 1794, identified the rise of the French infidels as one of the signs of the last things, since it was understood that the coming of the Kingdom would be heralded by war and destruction.[54] Millennial excitement rose steadily in Britain, such that debates duly arose as to whether it was Napoleon Bonaparte or Pius VI who was the true type of the anti-Christ.[55] In the United States, Blanchard's preoccupations can be directly compared to those of the prominent anti-Catholic campaigner— and Cincinnati resident—Lyman Beecher, whose most influential tract, *A Plea for the West* (1835) argued not only that the millennium would come but that the key battleground would be the western frontier. He thought that all the "existing signs of the times lend corroboration" to these ideas, including the sign that was "the march of revolution."[56]

On the one hand, the urge to find villains was as alive and well as ever, but on the other hand, the eschatological imperatives of evangelical Protestants meant that the actions of Satan and his minions were, albeit deplorable, necessary for the unfolding of the divine plan as outlined in Revelation. This has interesting implications when it comes to evangelical interpretations of the French Revolution. For instance, when we read of Voltaire in Blanchard that "he hated government; he hated morals; he hated man; he hated religion. He sometimes bursts out into exclamations of rages and insane fury against all that we honour as best and holiest, that sound less like human lips

---

53. Nockles, "The Changing Legacy," p. 244.

54. Clarke Garrett, *Respectable Folly: Millenarians and the French Revolution in France and England* (Baltimore: Johns Hopkins University Press, 1975), p. 158.

55. Nigel Aston, *Christianity and Revolutionary Europe, c.1750–1830* (Cambridge: Cambridge University Press, 2002), p. 235.

56. Lyman Beecher, *A Plea for the West* (Cincinnati: Leavitt, Lord, 1835), p. 10.

than the echoes of the final place of agony and despair," we are invited to imagine a fallen angel who has been given a Providential role to play by God.[57]
We are also, in this case, reading the words of George Croly (1780–1860),
rector of St. Stephen Walbrook in London, since Blanchard pinched them
from that author's *The Apocalypse of St. John* (1827).[58] This book claimed to
outline how Revelation had predicted the French Revolution "not narrowed
into a few conjectural verses, as is usual; but detailed in an entire and un-
suspected chapter, with its peculiar characters of Atheism, and Anarchy; its
subsequent despotism, and its final overthrow by the armies of Europe."[59]
The nation had been saved by those titans fighting in her defense, Horatio
Nelson, William Pitt—and Edmund Burke:

> BURKE arose; his whole life had been an unconscious preparation
> for this moment. His early political connexions had led him close
> enough to democracy, to see of what it was made, like Milton's Sin,
>> '...woman to the waist and fair,
>> But ending foul in many a scaly fold.'
> ...Armed in panoply, he took the field. He moved among the whole
> multitude of querulous and malignant authorship a giant among
> pigmies, he smote their Babel into dust. His eloquence...here found
> its true region, here might gather its strength like cloud on cloud,
> touched with every glorious colour of heaven, till it swelled into tem-
> pest, and poured down the torrents and the thunders.[60]

In this fascinating description, Burke himself is presented as a terrifying
figure of the sublime.[61] He was fighting, we may recall, against the attacks
of democrats and atheists, not just on behalf of Protestant Britons but also

---

57. Blanchard, *Book of Martyrs*, p. 513, copied directly from George Croly, *The Apocalypse of St. John, or the Prophecy of the Rise, Progress, and Fall of the Church of Rome; the Inquisition; the Revolution in France; the Universal War; and the Final Triumph of Christianity* (London: C. and J. Rivington, 1827), p. 418.

58. Ibid. See also David C. Hanson, "Croly, George (1780–1860)," *Oxford Dictionary of National Biography*, Oxford University Press, 2004, http://www.oxforddnb.com/view/article/6746.

59. Croly, *The Apocalypse*, pp. 3–4.

60. Ibid., pp. 441–42.

61. I am thinking here of the sublime as presented by Burke himself in *A Philosophical Enquiry into the Origin of our Ideas of the Sublime and Beautiful*, ed. Adam Phillips (Oxford: Oxford University Press, 1998) [first published 1757].

of French Catholics. And he was doing this, for Croly, in apparent fulfil-ment of the prophecies of the Last Judgment.

In the nineteenth century, therefore, the writings of John Foxe were still employed as denominational propaganda, but they were increas-ingly judged in relation to conceptualizations of martyrdom that were be-coming more complex. The hotly contested claims of political martyrdom during the French Revolution made it increasingly difficult to distinguish between secular and spiritual acts of heroism. The cult of the shades, as examined by Schechter in this volume, had a similar effect by blurring the roles of victim and aggressor through the development of a cycle of vengeance. The execution of Catholics at the behest of avowed or sup-posed atheists in the course of the French Revolution made it increasingly problematic for British clergy to continue to demonize their counterparts within the Church of Rome. While some Protestants, notably those with Millenarian expectations of the imminent Second Coming, continued to see the role of terror and violence in the past and present as indications of the workings of God's plan, others felt an increasing concern that many occasions of what had once been held to be sacred witness were in fact evi-dences of worldly as opposed to spiritual preoccupations. In the aftermath of the "Terror," it became an increasingly complex matter to fully appre-ciate the spiritually salutary value of books that appeared to be composed primarily of "dismal horrors," however detailed, or brilliantly illustrated, they might be.[62]

---

62. Charles Dickens, *David Copperfield*, p. 128.

PART THREE

*Martyrdom, Terrorism, and
the Modern West*

9

Fenianism and the Martyrdom-Terrorism Nexus in Ireland before Independence

Guy Beiner

IRISH REPUBLICANISM IS commonly associated with martyrdom and with terrorism. The historical roots of these joined connotations can be found in nineteenth-century Fenianism. However, Fenianism is a somewhat elusive term.[1] In its strictest form, it relates to the members and associates of the Irish Republican Brotherhood (IRB) and its American counterpart the Fenian Brotherhood, transatlantic organizations committed to subverting British rule in Ireland and establishing an independent Irish republic. But the label has been applied liberally in reference to various militant Irish nationalist activities.[2] Whereas cultivation of martyrs was central to the self-perception and popular politics of Fenianism, its engagement with terrorism was marginal and, as a rule, terrorists were not elevated to martyrdom. Nonetheless, external perceptions of Fenianism, as evident in the discourse of British policy and in the pages of the English and American press at the time, tied it inextricably with terror, an association that the

---

1. See R. V. Comerford, "Fenianism: The Scope and Limitations of a Concept," in James McConnell and Fearghal McGarry, eds., *The Black Hand of Republicanism: Fenianism in Modern Ireland* (Dublin: Irish Academic Press, 2009), pp. 179–89.

2. See Owen McGee, *The IRB: The Irish Republican Brotherhood, from the Land League to Sinn Féin* (Dublin: Four Courts Press, 2005); M. J. Kelly, *The Fenian Ideal and Irish Nationalism, 1882–1916* (Woodbridge: Boydell Press, 2006).

Fenians themselves could not simply ignore. A republican publication at the turn of the nineteenth century tellingly noted: "'Fenian' is a sort of generic term which embraces all species of Irish revolutionists, and incidentally it may be remembered that it is a term synonymous with terror of the paralysis producing sort so far as the English mind is concerned."[3] The genealogy of the Irish martyrdom-terrorism nexus is evidently complicated and needs to be disentangled.

Fenianism, which recognized the potential of street parades for mobilizing supporters and influencing onlookers, adopted public funerals as a vehicle for creating martyrs. The trial run was the re-internment in 1861 of Terence Bellew McManus, a veteran of the Young Ireland movement. McManus, whose death transpired in non-heroic circumstances, was not an obvious candidate for martyrdom. He had participated in the failed rebellion attempt of 1848 but had not died in action and his death sentence for high treason was commuted to transportation to Van Dieman's Land, from where he escaped to America after two years. Although his arrival in the United States was celebrated by Irish-American nationalists, he chose to remain politically inactive and died in poverty in California as a result of an accident. It was only after his burial in San Francisco (January 16, 1861) that local Fenians resolved to reclaim his remains, disregarding objections of family members and of his fellow Young Irelanders. His corpse was exhumed in August 1861 and shipped with much celebration via Panama to New York, where it was greeted with a "great concourse and procession."[4] It was then sent on to Ireland, travelling by train from Cobh to Dublin and hailed en route by crowds at Cork and Limerick Junction railway stations. Ultimately, a massively attended funerary procession in Dublin (November 10, 1861) followed a route carefully planned for its evocative symbolism, including stopovers at the execution site of the archetypical republican martyr Robert Emmet (organizer of the 1803 Rebellion) and at the place where the United Irish martyr Lord Edward Fitzgerald was shot (an organizer of the 1798 Rebellion). The terminus was the necropolis at Glasnevin, effectively a national pantheon, where the funeral

---

3. *Irish Republic*, May 31, 1896; cited in Kelly, *Fenian Ideal*, p. 108.

4. New York Times, October 19, 1861, p. 4; see also Mary C. Kelly, *The Shamrock and the Lily: The New York Irish and the Creation of a Transatlantic Identity, 1845–1921* (New York: Peter Lang, 2005), pp. 134–37.

featured a militant graveside oration penned by the IRB leader James Stephens and delivered by an American Fenian delegate, Captain Smith.[5]

The cultural capital gained by co-opting the memory of McManus and elevating his status to a national martyr was immediately evident. The prominent Fenian Thomas Clarke Luby observed that the funeral gave "us faith and stern resolve."[6] The nationalist writer A. M. Sullivan, who at the time opposed the Fenians, conceded: "Those who saw the gathering that followed his coffin to the grave, the thousands of stalwart men that marched in solemn order behind his bier, will never forget the sight."[7] The public procession and graveside oration at Glasnevin were to become defining features of what would develop into a popular tradition of republican funerals.[8] Due to financial problems and Church opposition, it would take thirty-four years till a monument was constructed (1895) and another thirty-eight years till it was finally placed over the grave and unveiled (1933).[9] Nonetheless, the burial spot of McManus inaugurated a republican plot, which would become a site of pilgrimage, subsequently maintained by the National Graves Association.[10]

The commemorative rituals were repeated in 1877 at the funeral of the Fenian co-founder John O'Mahony. Although he had been sidelined by the factiousness of Irish-American republican politics and had lived his last years in neglect, dying in poverty in a New York tenement, O'Mahony's death put him back in the limelight. In New York, a crowd of 20,000

---

5. See Richard J. O'Duffy, *Historic Graves in Glasnevin Cemetery* (Dublin: J. Duffy and Co., 1915) and L. R. Bisceglia, "The Fenian Funeral of Terence Bellew McManus," *Éire-Ireland* 14.3 (1979), pp. 45–64. As can be expected, claims of attendance vary, with Fenians putting the numbers of participants in the procession between 30,000 to 50,000 and the onlookers at 200,000, and the police estimating the crowd between 10,000 to 30,000 (ibid., pp. 61–62). See also Owen McGee, "McManus, Terence Bellew," in James McGuire and James Quinn, eds., *Dictionary of Irish Biography* (Cambridge: Cambridge University Press, 2009), http://dib.cambridge.org.

6. D. George Boyce, *Nationalism in Ireland*, 3rd ed. (London: Routledge, 1995), p. 183.

7. T. D. Sullivan, A. M. Sullivan, and D. R. Sullivan, *Speeches from the Dock; or, Protests of Irish Patriotism*, 1st American ed. (Providence: H. McElroy, Murphy and McCarthy, 1878 [orig. ed. 1867]), p. 151.

8. Pauric Travers, " 'Our Fenian dead': Glasnevin Cemetery and the Genesis of the Republican Funeral," in James Kelly and Uáitéar Mac Gearailt, eds., *Dublin and Dubliners: Essays in the History and Literature of Dublin City* (Dublin: Helicon, 1990), pp. 52–72.

9. *Irish Times*, November 27, 1933, p. 4.

10. Mary Donnelly, *The Last Post: Glasnevin Cemetery; Being a Record of Ireland's Heroic Dead in Dublin City and County; also Places of Historic Interest* (Dublin: National Graves Association, 1994 [orig. ed. 1932]).

rallied in his honor and in Dublin, according to police estimates, 70,000 sympathetic spectators observed the 4,000 participants in the funerary procession, which ended with his burial beside McManus in Glasnevin (March 4, 1877). Since a graveside oration was forbidden, the Fenian writer Charles Kickham delivered a defiant speech outside the cemetery gates.[11] Unlike the near contemporaneous public funerals in Third Republic France, which were civic ceremonies, Irish nationalist funerals were demonstrations of opposition and resistance.[12] The making of martyrs out of former rebels marked the rise of a nationalist counter-hegemony that challenged British hegemony by audaciously occupying a public sphere previously dominated by imperial iconography.

The imitation of religious rituals in the construction of political martyrs reflects the unconscious influence of the devotional resurgence that Ireland was undergoing at the time.[13] Unlike militantly secular democrats in other Catholic European countries (Spain, Italy, and France), Fenians were, by and large, devout Catholics.[14] Yet theirs was an unorthodox, if not quite anticlerical, Catholicism that defied proscription by the hierarchy. Church opposition was spearheaded by the archbishop of Dublin, Paul Cullen, who was convinced that Fenianism was an anti-Catholic Mazzinian conspiracy and denounced its members as "men without principle or religion." Yet Cullen's refusal to admit the corpses of McManus and O'Mahony into the pro-cathedral in Dublin did not prevent crowds from attending their funeral processions.[15] Denial of sacraments, alongside vehement denunciations— most famously that of the bishop of Kerry, David Moriarty, who proclaimed that "eternity is not long enough, nor hell hot enough, to punish such miscreants," and even an excommunication issued by pope Pius IX (1870) did not succeed in ostracizing the Fenians.[16] Repeated reissue of the prohibitions

---

11. *Irish American*, February 24, 1877 (front page); Desmond Ryan, "John O'Mahony," in T. W. Moody, ed., *The Fenian Movement* (Dublin: Mercer Press, 1978), pp. 64–65; Travers, "Our Fenian dead," pp. 59–60; Maureen Murphy and James Quinn, "O'Mahony, John," in McGuire and Quinn, *Dictionary of Irish Biography*.

12. See Avner Ben-Amos, *Funerals, Politics, and Memory in Modern France, 1789–1996* (Oxford: Oxford University Press, 2000), pp. 110–35 and passim.

13. See Emmet Larkin, "The Devotional Revolution in Ireland, 1850–75," *American Historical Review* 77.3 (1972), pp. 625–52.

14. Peter Hart, "The Fenians and the International Revolutionary Tradition," in McConnell and McGarry, *The Black Hand*, p. 197.

15. Timothy J. Brophy, "On Church Grounds: Political Funerals and the Contest to Lead Catholic Ireland," *Catholic Historical Review* 95.3 (2009), pp. 491–514.

16. For Bishop Moriarty's rebuke see *Irish Times*, February 19, 1867, p. 3.

bears testimony to their limited effect and the Church, concerned with losing its standing in society, would eventually have to acknowledge the popular success of the republican cult of martyrdom and seek discreet ways to accommodate Fenianism.[17]

Commemoration of elderly leaders who died unglamorous deaths in exile was clearly not sufficient for the revolutionary cause and it was expected that a Fenian insurrection in Ireland would produce a new canon of martyrs, similar to the heroic pantheon generated by the United Irish risings of 1798 and 1803. The failure of the attempted rebellion in 1867 did not inhibit its leadership. Responding to the crushing defeat, the Fenian's chief of staff, Colonel Thomas J. Kelly, wrote: "Did not Christianity commence by defeats? Did it not, like us, water the ground with the blood of its martyrs"?[18] But with only twelve fatalities, none of whom were considered senior, the inglorious battlefields of 1867 failed to produce the desired martyrs. By commuting death sentences to long-term imprisonment or transportation, the Crown shrewdly tried to prevent the creation of new republican martyrs.

However, the filling up of prisons with Fenian suspects and convicts, mostly arrested under emergency regulations, turned them into a *cause célèbre* with popular connotations of political martyrdom. Reports of brutal prisoner abuse enraged nationalists and liberals at large, as in the case of Jeremiah O'Donovan Rossa, whose ordeals at a series of Victorian prisons were first brought to public attention in 1867 through letters published in the *Irishman*, resulting in a commission of inquiry chaired by Lord Devon, which sensationally vindicated claims of ill-treatment of Fenians.[19] Increasingly vocal campaigns for amnesty hailed the prisoners as victims of state injustice and effectively turned them into symbols of national resistance.[20] Initiatives to challenge imperial law enforcement through daring prisoner rescue attempts would facilitate conditions for the convergence of martyrdom and terrorism.

---

17. Oliver P. Rafferty, "The Catholic Bishops and Revolutionary Violence in Ireland: Some 19th and 20th Century Comparisons," *Studies: An Irish Quarterly Review* 83.329 (1994), pp. 30–42. See also Oliver P. Rafferty, *The Church, the State, and the Fenian Threat, 1861–75* (Basingstoke: Palgrave, 1999).

18. John Savage, *Fenian Heroes and Martyrs* (Boston: P. Donahoe, 1868), p. 175.

19. See Jeremiah O'Donovan Rossa, *Irish Rebels in English Prisons: A Record of Prison Life* (New York: P. J. Kenedy, 1899 [orig. ed. 1874]).

20. Seán McConville, *Irish Political Prisoners, 1848–1922: Theatres of War* (London: Routledge, 2003), pp. 140–213.

A rescue operation in Manchester that freed two prominent Fenians—Colonel T. J. Kelly and Captain Timothy Deasy—from police custody gave a much-needed boost to the movement in their time of failure (September 18, 1867). As noted in a prominent Irish newspaper, it offered "a strange if not an alarming illustration of the extent of the organisation and of the capacity of those who direct it."[21] The affair, which was decried in England as "one of the most audacious outrages that have occurred in this country for many years," caused much concern, as it appeared to have been undertaken "by a party of Irish desperadoes, who had prepared themselves to carry out the object of their enterprise at any cost to themselves or others."[22] Particular shock was caused by the killing of a policeman (Sergeant Charles Brett) in broad daylight on English soil.[23] The Times led public opinion in demanding "stern and decisive repression," arguing that "there is but one way of meeting unlawful terrorism. It must be repelled by lawful terrorism."[24] Of the twenty-eight arrested suspects, five were found guilty of murder and, despite widespread calls for clemency, three of them were executed outside the New Bailey prison in Salford, Manchester (November 23, 1867). Frederick Engels (who was residing in Manchester at this time with a Fenian woman, Lizzie Burns, and had supported the call for clemency) perceptively noted in a letter to Karl Marx:

> The *only thing* that the Fenians still lacked were martyrs. They have been provided with these by [Prime Minister] Derby and [Home Secretary] G. Hardy. Only the execution of the three has made the liberation of Kelly and Deasy the heroic deed as which it will now be sung to every Irish babe in the cradle in Ireland, England and America.[25]

Indeed, the three—William O'Meara Allen, Michael Larkin, and Michael O'Brien—were instantly transformed into the "Manchester Martyrs."

---

21. *Freeman's Journal*, September 19, 1867.

22. *The Annual Register: A Review of Public Events at Home and Abroad for the Year 1867* (London, 1868), part 2, "Chronicle of Remarkable Occurrences," pp. 131–34.

23. Norman McCord, "The Fenians and Public Opinion in Great Britain," *University Review* 4.3 (1967), pp. 227–40, esp. pp. 232–33.

24. *The Times*, October 8, 1867, p. 6.

25. Engels to Marx, November 24, 1867, in R. Dixon, ed., *Ireland and the Irish Question: A Collection of Writings by Karl Marx and Frederick Engels* (New York: International Publishers, 1972), p. 145 (Engels's emphasis).

The British authorities were unable to contain the massive commemorative processions, staged as mock funerals, which were held throughout Ireland and Irish diaspora communities. The Manchester Martyrs were immortalized in public monuments across Ireland and through a variety of commemorative souvenirs cherished privately in homes (fig. 9.1).[26] The date of the execution, November 23, became a national day of remembrance, marked by annual anniversaries that continued into the early twentieth century (and is still observed in republican circles today).[27] Putting aside its dogmatic aversion to the Fenians, the Church found itself obliged to recognize the popularity of secular rituals of martyrdom and many priests partook in the commemorative vigils.[28] Moreover, the popularity of the commemorations was so sweeping that they gained support from all varieties of Irish nationalists, putting Fenianism on the center stage.

In particular, the editors of the influential newspaper *The Nation*, MPs Alexander Martin (A. M.) Sullivan and Timothy Daniel (T. D.) Sullivan—constitutional nationalists who had criticized the republican tactics of physical force—soon came to recognize the popularity of pro-Fenian sentiment and its marketing potential. A. M. Sullivan published a series of articles and cartoons strongly condemning the Manchester executions in the *Weekly News*, a cheap publication which became Ireland's most popular newspaper. Following his arrest for participation in a Manchester Martyrs' demonstration, he was prosecuted and jailed for seditious libel, having declared that the three were "no murderers, but political martyrs, whose memories are to be cherished through future ages, and whose death had taught their countrymen another solemn lesson of constancy and courage."[29]

---

26. Gary Owens, "Constructing the Martyrs: The Manchester Executions and the Nationalist Imagination," in Lawrence W. McBride, ed., *Images, Icons, and the Irish Nationalist Imagination* (Dublin: Four Courts Press, 1999), pp. 18–36.

27. Owen McGee, "'God Save Ireland': Manchester-Martyr Demonstrations in Dublin, 1867–1916," *Éire-Ireland*, 36.3–4 (2001), pp. 39–66.

28. Oliver MacDonagh, "Ambiguity in Nationalism—The Case of Ireland," in Ciaran Brady, ed., *Interpreting Irish History: The Debate on Historical Revisionism, 1938–1994* (Dublin: Irish Academic Press, 1994), pp. 117–18.

29. A. M. Sullivan, *The Wearing of the Green: The Trials of Messrs. A. M. Sullivan, John Martin, J. J. Lalor, & C. for Taking Part in the Funeral Procession, Held in Dublin on December 8, 1867* (Dublin: Alley & Co., 1868); "The Funeral Processions," *Weekly News*, December 14, 1867; and *Report of the Trials of Alexander M. Sullivan and Richard Pigott, for Seditious Libels on the Government, at the County of Dublin Commission, held at the Court-House, Green-Street, Dublin, commencing February 10, 1868* (Dublin: H.M. Stationery Office, 1868), pp. 33–36.

FIGURE 9.1. Lithograph of the Manchester Martyrs, *The Martyrs of Ireland* (New York: J. Walsh, c.1869)

Reproduced courtesy of the Library of Congress, Washington, D.C.

State persecution did not prevent the Sullivan brothers from publishing at the end of 1867 the quintessential nationalist martyrology *Speeches from the Dock*, which has been recognized as "one of the most influential books in nineteenth-century Irish nationalist literature."[30] A collection of

_____

30. D. George Boyce, "'A gallous story and a dirty deed': Political Martyrdom in Ireland since 1867," in Yonah Alexander and Alan O'Day, eds., *Ireland's Terrorist Dilemma* (Dordrecht: Martinus Nijhoff Publishers, 1986), p. 14.

courtroom orations of "the men who fill the foremost places in the ranks of Ireland's political martyrs," it was an instant bestseller, reissued in frequent editions and repeatedly updated with new entries.[31] Among several ballads dedicated to the martyrs, the song "God Save Ireland," composed by T. D. Sullivan and first published in the *Nation* on December 7, 1867, achieved lasting fame. Set to a popular American military air, it was reproduced in countless songbooks and broadsides (sometimes renamed "The Manchester patriot martyrs") and served for over fifty years as an unofficial national anthem, which brazenly trumpeted martyrdom in the cause of the nation:

> *Whether on the scaffold high*
> *Or the battlefield we die,*
> *Oh, what matter when for Erin dear we fall!*[32]

By skilfully manipulating the commemorative media of public funerals, parades and demonstrations, monuments, songs and ballads, speeches, and an enormous array of hagiographic popular print, the Fenians wrote themselves into the canon of Irish history, building on, and contributing to, a nationalist tradition of cultural memory that focused on martyrdom through reconstruction of failed rebellions as a series of tribulations which bear witness and lead toward ultimate triumph.[33]

The success of the Manchester Martyrs' model could not be simply replicated, as was made evident in another lethal attempt to release Fenian prisoners—among them the man responsible for the operation in Manchester, Ricard O'Sullivan Burke—from the Clerkenwell House of

---

31. Sullivan et al., *Speeches from the Dock*, p. 8. The first American edition, which corresponded to the twenty-third Dublin edition, includes forty references to the term "martyr," of which half relate to the Manchester Martyrs.

32. For the composition of "God Save Ireland" and its instant success, see T. D. Sullivan, *Recollections of Troubled Times in Irish Politics* (Dublin: Sealy, Bryers & Walker and M. H. Gill & Son, 1905), pp. 178–80. For other songs and their variations, see Bodleian Library Broadside Ballads collection, 2806 c. 8 (73); Paul Bernard Rose, *The Manchester Martyrs: The Story of a Fenian Tragedy* (London: Lawrence & Wishart, 1970), pp. 129–35; and Colm O Lochlainn, *Irish Street Ballads* (Dublin: Three Candles, 1946 [orig. ed. 1939]), pp. 28–29, *More Irish Street Ballads* (Dublin: Three Candles, 1965), pp. 150–51, and *Treoir* 17.2 (1985), p. 20d (inserted page).

33. See Guy Beiner, "Between Trauma and Triumphalism: The Easter Rising, the Somme, and the Crux of Deep Memory in Modern Ireland," *Journal of British Studies* 46.2 (2007), pp. 366–89. See also Ian McBride, "Memory and National Identity in Modern Ireland," in Ian McBride, ed., *History and Memory in Modern Ireland* (Cambridge: Cambridge University Press, 2001), pp. 31–33.

Detention in London (December 13, 1867). The igniting of a barrel of gunpowder outside the prison walls, though not deliberately planned as an
act of terrorism, wreaked havoc on the adjacent row of tenement houses
on Corporation Lane, leaving a death toll of twelve (not including six
subsequent stillbirths and miscarriages) and injuring 126, among them
many women and children. *The Times* declared that "a crime of unexam-
pled atrocity has been committed in the middle of London."[34] Over the
following weeks, the surge in anti-Irish xenophobia of an English public
treated to graphic reportage of the damages and casualties amounted to
mass panic.[35]

Scares of terrorist plots were ubiquitous and the British State invested
all available resources in an effort to demonstrate that it could master
the situation. Responding to rumors of imminent horrendous attacks of
"Fenian Fire" (a popular renaming of "Greek fire"—a phosphorous-based
liquid used as a crude incendiary weapon), sand was scattered on the
floors of government buildings and the Home Office recruited tens of
thousands of special constables to secure public buildings from expected
bombings.[36] In a demonstration of the might of the rule of law, numerous
pleas to remit the death sentence conferred on the man convicted for the
Clerkenwell atrocity, Michael Barrett, were turned down.[37] Niggling doubts
about the even-handedness of the authorities persisted. At his hanging on
May 26, 1868, which was to be the last public execution in England, protest cries were heard from the crowd outside Newgate prison and the *Daily
Mail* observed that "the law and its ministers seemed to them the real
murderers, and Barrett a martyred man."[38] Yet of several broadside ballads

---

34. *The Times*, December 14, 1867.

35. See Michael de Nie, *The Eternal Paddy: Irish Identity and the British Press, 1798–1882*
(Madison: University of Wisconsin Press, 2004), pp. 164–79; for Scotland see Elaine W.
McFarland, "A Reality and Yet Impalpable: The Fenian Panic in Mid-Victorian Scotland,"
Scottish Historical Review 77.2, no. 204 (1998), pp. 199–223.

36. By February 7, 1868, there were 53,113 such constables in London and another 70,561
throughout the rest of the country; see John Newsinger, *Fenianism in Mid-Victorian Britain*
(London: Pluto Press, 1994), p. 65. For an assessment of these measures as a policy of
counterterrorism, see Brian Jenkins, "1867 All Over Again? Insurgency and Terrorism in
a Liberal State," in Isaac Land, ed., *Enemies of Humanity: The Nineteenth-Century War on
Terrorism* (New York: Palgrave Macmillan, 2008), pp. 87–89.

37. Brian Jenkins, *The Fenian Problem: Insurgency and Terrorism in a Liberal State, 1858–1874*
(Montreal: McGill-Queen's University Press, 2008), pp. 179–208.

38. Vic Gatrell, *The Hanging Tree: Execution and the English People, 1770–1868* (Oxford: Oxford
University Press, 1994), pp. 24, 589, 599, and 609. Mention of unrest was omitted from

marking the execution, only one explicitly expressed sympathy and compared Barrett to the Manchester Martyrs, while others dwelt on the fatalities of the explosion.[39] The widespread outrage from what was perceived as an act of mindless terror could not be overcome and ultimately Barrett did not become a major Fenian martyr.

By the end of the 1860s, as fears of Irish terrorist attacks following the Clerkenwell explosion proved to be largely unfounded, "Fenian Fever" in Britain subsided for the moment.[40] But the association between Fenianism and terror did not disappear. The surge of agrarian violence in Ireland in the 1870s, which peaked during the Land War of 1879–82, was regularly referred to as Fenian terrorism. Although the outrages were not the product of an organized IRB campaign, anti-insurgency measures (including suspension of Habeas Corpus) were sanctioned by the Coercion Bill [Protection of Person and Property Act] of 1881.[41] In the early 1880s, when a small number of Fenians actually resorted to terrorism, this was an initiative of minority factions within the American wing and from its inception was subject to internal criticism.

The main figure behind this development was the former Fenian convict Jeremiah O'Donovan Rossa, who was released on amnesty and emigrated to the United States in 1871. Realizing the ineffectiveness of mounting large-scale military operations, O'Donovan Rossa set about readapting the concept of "skirmishing," a term borrowed from military parlance in reference to small-scale confrontations on the margins of battlefields.[42] His

---

other newspaper reports. *The Times* insisted that the "vast concourse of spectators" was "greater, perhaps, and better behaved" in comparison to "ordinary executions." *The Times*, May 27, 1868, p. 9.

39. Of three ballads in the Oxford University Bodleian Library Broadside Ballads collection, the sympathetic ballad is "The Lamentation of Michael Barrett," 2806 b. 10(124); cf. "Sentence of Death on Michael Barrett for the Clerkenwell Explosion," Harding B. 14(175) and "The Lamentation and Last Farewell to the World of Michael Barrett," Harding B 14(176). For another ballad, see "Execution of Michael Barrett," in Charles Hindley, *Curiosities of Street Literature* (London: Reeves and Turner, 1871), p. 228.

40. León Ó Broin, *Fenian Fever: An Anglo-American Dilemma* (London: Gill and Macmillan, 1971), pp. 227–50.

41. See Charles Townshend, *Political Violence in Ireland: Government and Resistance since 1848* (Oxford: Clarendon Press, 1983), pp. 131–43; and Jonathan Gantt, *Irish Terrorism in the Atlantic Community, 1865–1922* (New York: Palgrave Macmillan, 2010), pp. 66–127.

42. See Niall Whelehan, "Skirmishing, the *Irish World*, and Empire, 1876–86," *Éire-Ireland*, 42.1 (2007), pp. 180–200.

original intention was to deter punitive law enforcement, arguing that in the event that Fenians apprehended during attempts to rescue prisoners were sentenced to death, "I would feel warranted in hanging the ministers that ordered the murder, or in burning up on the previous evening, the town or the city they were to be hanged in, *to prevent it* so that the murder could not take place there."[43] With the cooperation of Patrick Ford, the editor of the *Irish World*, he proposed a radical change in Fenian revolutionary tactics:

> We are not now advising a general insurrection. On the contrary, we should oppose a general insurrection in Ireland as untimely and ill-advised. But we believe in action nevertheless. A few active, intrepid and intelligent men can do so much to annoy and hurt England. The Irish cause requires Skirmishers. It requires a little band of heroes who will initiate and keep up without intermission a guerrilla warfare—men who will fly over land and sea like invisible beings.[44]

His outrageous proposals played on the deepest fears of the "Fenian Fever":

> Language, skin-color, dress, general manners, are all in favor of the Irish. Then, tens of thousands of Irishmen, from long residence in the enemy's country, know England's cities well. Our Irish skirmishers would be well disguised. They would enter London unknown and unnoticed. When the night for action came; the night that the wind was blowing strong—this little band would deploy, each man setting about his own allotted task, and no man, save the captain of the band alone, knowing what any other man was to do, and *at the same instant strike with lightning the enemy of their land and race.... In two hours from the word of command London would be in flames, shooting up to the heavens in fifty different places.* Whilst this would be going on, the men could be still at work. The

---

43. *Irish World*, March 4, 1876; cited in Whelehan, "Skirmishing," p. 185 (emphasis in the original).

44. *Irish World*, December 4, 1875; K. R. M. Short, *The Dynamite War: Irish-American Bombers in Victorian Britain* (Dublin: Gill and Macmillan, 1979), p. 38.

blazing spectacle would attract all eyes, and leave the skirmishers to operate with impunity in the darkness.[45]

The allure of terrorism appealed to many Irish-Americans at the time, offering an outlet for venting frustrations that had accumulated after the failed insurrection in Ireland and the fiascos of the Fenian Canadian raids.[46] Contributions to a Skirmishing Fund, launched in 1876 in the midst of a prolonged economic recession, far exceeded the expected goal of $5,000 and by 1880 had almost reached $90,000.

The Fenian leadership (including prominent figures such as James Stephens, John Devoy, John O'Leary, Michael Davitt, and Thomas Clarke Luby) unequivocally denounced O'Donovan Rossa's terrorist schemes. The Skirmishing Fund was appropriated by Clan na Gael, the central organization of Irish-American Fenianism and renamed the Irish National Fund. Significantly, the initial outlay was committed in 1877 to support the transportation of the body of John O'Mahony to Dublin and finance his funeral procession, thus reaffirming the value of political martyrdom in the service of revolution. Yet, nationalist imagination had been ignited by fantasies of lashing out at the hitherto seemingly indomitable British Empire and there was a demand to explore possibilities for unconventional warfare. Funding was promised to the Irish-American submarine inventor John Holland to finance the research and development of an underwater torpedo-armed "wrecking boat," with the intention of using maritime terror to strike at Britain's naval might. With its secrecy compromised by newspaper reports, the "salt water enterprise"—the code name given to the construction of the so-called "Fenian Ram" at the Delamater Iron Works in New York—fell prey to squabbles between rival Fenian groups and was terminated in 1881, without being tried in action.[47]

---

45. *Irish World*, August 28, 1880; reproduced in Walter Laqueur and Yonah Alexander, eds., *The Terrorism Reader: A Historical Anthology*, rev. ed. (New York: NAL Penguin, 1987), pp. 112–14 (emphasis in the original).

46. For botched Fenian attempts to seize territories in British North America, supposedly as bargaining chips for negotiating Irish independence, see Hereward Senior, *The Last Invasion of Canada: The Fenian Raids, 1866–1870* (Toronto: Dundurn Press, 1991) and David A. Wilson, "Swapping Canada for Ireland: The Fenian Invasion of 1866," *History Ireland* 16.6 (2008), pp. 24–27.

47. R. K. Morris, "John P. Holland and the Fenians," *Journal of the Galway Archaeological and Historical Society* 31.1–2 (1964), pp. 25–38; and John P. Holland, *1841–1914: Inventor of the Modern Submarine*, new ed. (Columbia: University of South Carolina Press, 1998), pp. 21–48.

In practice, terror came to the fore in the early 1880s, when a string of Irish-American agents carrying "infernal machines" (to use contemporary terminology) crossed the Atlantic to plant bombs in England and Scotland.[48] Initially, O'Donovan Rossa's skirmishers opted for gunpowder as their preferred explosive. Their inaugural attack, on January 14, 1881, symbolically took place in the proximity of where the Manchester Martyrs were executed. While only minor damage was caused to the actual target—Salford Infantry Barracks, the explosion demolished a nearby butcher's shed killing a 7-year-old boy and severely injured his mother, as well as two other bystanders.[49] Two months later, an "atrocious attempt" to blow up the Mansion House, residence of London's Lord Mayor, was prevented by the dramatic discovery of a twenty-kilogram box of blasting gunpowder, with the fuse still burning (March 16, 1881).[50] A subsequent pipe bomb targeted a police barracks in Liverpool (May 16, 1881), causing only light damage.[51] The unreliability of old-fashioned gunpowder had already been demonstrated in the earlier debacle at Clerkenwell and Fenians soon recognized its ineffectiveness. A follow-up attack of the Liverpool team on the Town Hall (June 10, 1881) employed a newer explosive—dynamite, though casualties were prevented by swift police action.[52]

The invention of dynamite offered revolutionary militants the means for "scientific warfare." Notably, the American-German émigré Johann Most—an early advocate of propaganda by deed—published *The Science of Revolutionary Warfare* (*Revolutionäre Kriegswissenschaft*), in which he asserted that "modern explosives...are going to be the decisive factor in the next period of world history" and advised revolutionaries that they "should always have on hand adequate quantities of nitroglycerin, dynamite, hand grenades, and blasting charges—all easily concealed under

---

48. See Short, *Dynamite War*; Townshend, *Political Violence*, pp. 158–66; McConville, *Irish Political Prisoners*, pp. 326–60; Gantt, *Irish Terrorism*, pp. 128–86; Niall Whelehan, *The Dynamiters: Irish Nationalism and Political Violence in the Wider World, 1867–1900* (Cambridge: Cambridge University Press, 2012); and Shane Kenna, *War in the Shadows: The Irish-American Fenians who Bombed Victorian Britain* (Dublin: Irish Academic Press, 2014).

49. *Manchester Guardian*, January 17, 1881.

50. *The Times*, March 18, 1881, p. 8; see also *The Times*, March 19 and 21, 1881.

51. *The Times*, May 18, 1881.

52. *Liverpool Mercury*, June 20, 1881; see also John Belchem, *Irish, Catholic and Scouse: The History of the Liverpool-Irish, 1800–1939* (Liverpool: Liverpool University Press, 2007), pp. 178–79.

clothing."[53] In 1881, just as the Fenian bombings commenced, Most was accused of inciting international terrorism and prosecuted in England (where his defense counsel was A. M. Sullivan).[54] Provoking much intrigue, the enigmatic "Professor Mezzeroff"—a New York liquor salesman who went under the guise of a Russian émigré nihilist scientist and was nicknamed "the chemist of the Irish dynamite party"—regularly lectured American Fenians on the destructive possibilities of new explosives. His advocacy of terrorism was circulated in pamphlets titled *Dynamite against Gladstone's Resources of Civilisation or the Best Way to Make Ireland Free and Independent* (c. 1882) and *Scientific Warfare or the Resources of Civilization* (1888).[55] Irish-American extremists did not hide their enthusiasm for dynamite. Speaking at a Manchester Martyrs' anniversary in 1885, the pro-Fenian congressman William Erigena Robinson declared: "I thank God for the invention of dynamite.... We don't want to raise money now for molasses, nor for taffy, but for war, for slaughter."[56]

The main Fenian terror campaign, which raged between 1883 and 1885, was brief but remarkable for its audacity. Skirmishers, goaded by O'Donovan Rossa's fiery articles in the *United Irishman* and sponsored by his newly established Emergency Fund and Resources of Civilisation Fund, competed with parties of dynamiters from Clan na Gael, funded by the Irish National Fund. The fact that Clan na Gael bombing operations were headed by William Lomasney, who had previously objected to O'Donovan Rossa's terrorist proposals on moral grounds, would seem to suggest that the conflict between the factions was more personal than ideological. At a ground level, there was apparently a degree of cooperation

53. Walter Laqueur, *The Guerrilla Reader: A Historical Anthology* (New York: New American Library, 1977), pp. 165–69. Originally serialized in Most's newspaper, *Freiheit*, it was also published as a pamphlet (1885); for a full version, see Johann Joseph Most, *Revolutionäre Kriegswissenschaft, together with the Beast of Property*, ed. Frederic Trautmann (Millwood, N.Y.: Kraus, 1983). See also Walter Laqueur, *A History of Terrorism* (New Brunswick, N.J.: Transaction, 2001), pp. 56–62.

54. See Bernard Porter, "The *Freiheit* Prosecutions, 1881–1882," *Historical Journal* 23.4 (1980), pp. 833–56.

55. *New York Times*, September 27, 1882, April 27, 1883, and July 24, 1885. See also Niall Whelehan, "The Brooklyn Dynamite School," *History Ireland* 16 (2008), p. 43; "'Cheap as soap and common as sugar': The Fenians, Dynamite and Scientific Warfare," in McConnell and McGarry, *The Black Hand*, pp. 115–16; and *The Dynamiters*, pp. 160–62 and 168–72.

56. *United Ireland*, December 5, 1885; cited in Bridget Hourican, "Robinson, William Erigena," in McGuire and Quinn, *Dictionary of Irish Biography*.

between operatives of the two organizations as evident from a secret agreement between O'Donovan Rossa and Dr Thomas Gallaher, who led a Clan
na Gael team.[57] Attacks partly succeeded in causing havoc in major urban
centers. Glasgow, for example, was seriously disrupted after skirmishers
caused a massive fire by bombing a gasworks plant and set off two additional explosions at a railway station and canal bridge (January 20, 1883).[58]

Caught up in the zealousness of their acts and carried away by the inevitable compulsion of terrorism to justify harming of innocents, the Fenian
bombers overcame compunctions against hurting civilians. Several
attacks were deliberately aimed at public transport, including explosives
set off in the London underground (two attacks on October 30, 1883, and
another on January 2, 1885), as well as four attempts to bomb mainline
trains, three of which were disarmed by the police (February 26, 1884).[59]
Particular emphasis was put on targeting places of symbolic importance.
A failed attack on the offices of The Times was overshadowed on the same
day (March 15, 1883) by a massive explosion in Whitehall, the epicenter
of the Civil Service, causing damage to the Home Office, Foreign Office,
Colonial Office, and the Local Government Board (which, significantly,
was responsible for the administration of Ireland). The ultimate event of
the "Dynamite War" was particularly spectacular, setting off on a single
Saturday (January 24, 1885) near-simultaneous explosions in the Tower
of London, Westminster Hall, and the House of Commons, in what was
described by The Times as an attempt "to strike terror into the souls of
Englishmen; whether by the indiscriminate slaughter of holidaymakers
and working people, or by the destruction of precious monuments."[60]

The total of twenty-five major explosions, which occurred between
1881 and 1885, created an imperative for counterterrorist policing, insti-
gating what Bernard Porter has labeled the foundation of the "vigilant
state."[61] Although customs surveillance intercepted several consignments

---

57. Short, Dynamite War, p. 126.

58. Máirtín Ó Catháin, Irish Republicanism in Scotland, 1858–1916 (Dublin: Irish Academic
Press, 2007), p. 132. For the wider context of Fenian terrorism in Scotland, see Máirtín
Ó Catháin, "Fenian Dynamite: Dissident Irish Republicans in Late Nineteenth-Century
Scotland," in Oonagh Walsh, ed., Ireland Abroad: Politics and Profession in the Nineteenth
Century (Dublin: Four Courts Press, 2003), pp. 160–71.

59. Roland Quinault, "Underground Attacks," History Today 55.9 (2005), pp. 18–19.

60. The Times, January 26, 1885, p. 9. See also Kenna, War in the Shadows, pp. 205–18.

61. Bernard Porter, The Origins of the Vigilant State: The London Metropolitan Police Special
Branch before the First World War, new ed. (Woodbridge: Boydell, 1991), esp. pp. 50–79.

of explosives smuggled over from the United States, as in the infernal machines found in Liverpool on board the SS Malta (June 30, 1881) and SS Bavaria (July 2, 1881), routine procedures were clearly inadequate. After a police raid uncovered a large bomb factory in Birmingham (April 5, 1883), which had been set up by Gallaher, the Explosive Substances Act was rushed through Parliament (April 10, 1883), putting greater authority in the hands of the police. Arrests succeeded in preventing several attacks, as in the apprehension of John Daly at Birkenhead Station (April 11, 1884), during which the police discovered bombs and a large quantity of nitroglycerin, allegedly intended for an attack on the House of Commons. Some dynamite schemes were foiled by accidents, as in the premature explosion at London Bridge, which resulted in the death of Lomasney alongside two accomplices (December 13, 1884).

Yet, even when hunted down, Fenian dynamiters showed remarkable resilience in striking back. A bomb planted in the Rising Sun public house in Westminster (May 30, 1884) caused severe damage to the adjacent headquarters of the Scotland Yard, destroying the office of Chief Superintendent Adolphus ("Dolly") Williamson, the operational head of the recently created Metropolitan Police Service's Criminal Investigation Department (CID), which was charged with dealing with the threat of Fenian terror. Moreover, on the same day, an explosion went off at the Junior Carleton Club, a traditional haunt of Conservative politicians, and an attempt was also made to blow up Nelson's column in Trafalgar Square. With the terrorists appearing to be irrepressible, the public was once again struck by "Fenian Fever."[62]

Apart from bombing public places, Fenians also engaged in personal terrorism by assassination. On May 6, 1882, a breakaway group known as the Invincibles stabbed to death the newly appointed Chief-Secretary Lord Frederick Cavendish and his permanent undersecretary Thomas H. Burke in Dublin's Phoenix Park, near the Lord Lieutenant's residence.[63] Although mainstream Fenianism disassociated itself from this act by attributing it to the foreign influence of Russian nihilism, yet another Coercion Bill (May 11, 1882) further increased police and judicial powers, virtually allowing for the suppression of any nationalist demonstration in

62. See Kenna, *War in the Shadows*, pp. 95–6 and 162–66.

63. See Tom Corfe, *The Phoenix Park Murders: Conflict, Compromise and Tragedy in Ireland, 1879–1882* (London: Hodder & Stoughton, 1968) and Senan Molony, *The Phoenix Park Murders: Conspiracy, Betrayal and Retribution* (Cork: Mercier Press, 2006).

Ireland by defining "intimidation" as an offense.[64] The creation of a new Secret Service, which was placed under an Assistant Under-Secretary for Police and Crime in Dublin Castle, led to the formation of the Special Branch within the CID, which signified the genesis of a dedicated British counterterrorist organization.[65] Yet espionage was, by its very nature, a murky business. A Clan na Gael plot to assassinate Queen Victoria and members of her Conservative government by setting off a dynamite explosion in Westminster Abbey during the Golden Jubilee celebrations in July 1887 may have been instigated by an *agent provocateur* in the service of the Prime Minister, Lord Salisbury.[66] Similarly, a government agent may have been behind the plans of Patrick Tynan, a former member of the Invincibles, to disrupt the Diamond Jubilee in 1896 with renewed dynamite attacks.[67] Beset by astonishing conspiracies, both real and imagined, terror and counterterrorism played on each other.

Despite several humiliating setbacks, the British state effectively crushed Irish-American terror, either killing or incarcerating most of its adherents. Although, from a positivist point of view, terrorism could be dismissed as a tangential and mostly insignificant phenomenon, it was central to what can be labeled the "myth of Fenianism."[68] Terrorism played a key role in shaping English and international perceptions, which were instrumental in determining government policy to Ireland. If after the thorough routing of the rebellion in the spring of 1867 it seemed that Fenianism could be dismissed, the incidents in England in late 1867 put republicanism back at the center of attention and are even credited with convincing William Gladstone of the imperative to address the "Irish Question." As put by Paul Bew, "The Clerkenwell effect was not confined

---

64. See Kelly, *Fenian Ideal*, p. 16; Robert Kee, *The Laurel and the Ivy: The Story of Charles Stewart Parnell and Irish Nationalism* (London: Hamish Hamilton, 1993), p. 448; and Townshend, *Political Violence*, pp. 166–80.

65. Lindsay Clutterbuck, "Countering Irish Republican Terrorism in Britain: Its Origin as a Police Function," *Terrorism and Political Violence* 18.1 (2006), pp. 113–14; and Owen McGee, "Dublin Castle and the First Home Rule Bill: The Jenkinson–Spencer Correspondence," *History Ireland* 15.5 (2007), pp. 44–49.

66. Christopher Campbell, *Fenian Fire: The British Government Plot to Assassinate Queen Victoria* (London: Harper Collins, 2002).

67. McConville, *Irish Political Prisoners*, pp. 397–400.

68. For a critique of the limits of "terrorist studies" in discerning between the historical and mythic aspects of Fenianism and grasping its global dimensions, see Máirtín Ó Catháin, "'The black hand of Irish Republicanism'? Transcontinental Fenianism and Theories of Global Terror," in McConnell and McGarry, *The Black Hand*, pp. 135–46.

simply to one of widespread panic. Despite, or perhaps because of, all the moral outrage, there was a political dividend for the 'popular' cause in Ireland."[69]

However, political reforms were never presented as a concession to violence and Irish nationalism was badly tarnished by "Fenian Fever." From 1867 onward, the leading satirical weekly *Punch, or the London Charivari* led the comic press in publishing blatantly racist images of Fenians, with simian or monstrous features and explicitly implicated with terrorism (fig. 9.2). Such images, as Michael de Nie has pointed out, "resonated with their readers and the rest of the press" and "though not all readers shared the opinions behind every cartoon, the majority certainly understood them."[70] Impregnated with the discourse of social Darwinism, these depictions, alongside heated journalistic commentary on terrorism, constructed Irishmen as primitive and irrational exponents of anarchy who posed a threat to the civilization of the British Empire and who were inherently incapable of self-rule. At the same time, the repulsion from horrific violence was coupled with a near voyeuristic attraction to sensationalist accounts and graphic depictions, which bestowed upon the character of the Fenian terrorist an aura of mystery. This morbid fascination filtered into popular literature and can be found in such works as Tom Greer's *A Modern Daedalus* (1885), Robert Louis Stevenson and Fanny van de Grift's short story collection *The Dynamiter* (1885), and Arthur Conan Doyle's short story "That Little Square Box" (1881).[71] All-in-all, by attracting publicity, Fenian acts of terror contributed to sustaining Irish revolutionary republicanism through its setbacks.

Martyrdom was not a goal of Irish terrorism, which did not encourage suicide missions. Fenian "dynamitards" (a term coined, together with "dynamiter," by the contemporary press) did not share the same ideal of self-sacrifice upheld by the contemporary Russian revolutionaries of the People's Will (*Narodnya Volya*), who purposely designed the explosive packages for the assassination of Tsar Alexander II with a close destructive parameter so as to prevent the possibility of escape from the assailants.[72]

---

69. Paul Bew, *Ireland: The Politics of Enmity, 1789–2006* (Oxford: Oxford University Press, 2007), p. 266.

70. De Nie, *Eternal Paddy*, p. 172.

71. "That Little Square Box" was first published in *Land Society* (1881) and subsequently included in Arthur Conan Doyle, *Mysteries and Adventures* (London: W. Scott, 1889).

72. See James H. Billington, *Fire in the Minds of Men: Origins of the Revolutionary Faith* (New York: Basic Books, 1980), p. 408.

THE FENIAN GUY FAWKES.

FIGURE 9.2. John Tenniel, "The Fenian Guy Fawkes," *Punch, or the London Charivari*, December 28, 1867

Although constantly in need of new martyrs, Fenians showed reluctance to bestow this honor on terrorists directly responsible for indiscriminate death of noncombatants. Ultimately, it was O'Donovan Rossa, labeled by a biographer "the shadow of a dynamiter" for not actually partaking in the terror attacks he espoused,[73] who would be selected for recognition as a martyr, rather than his Clan na Gael rival Lomasney, who died in action while attempting an act of terror. After O'Donovan Rossa passed away debilitated from senility in a hospital on Staten Island (June 29, 1915), his body was shipped to Ireland by nationalists who planned a carefully choreographed burial in Glasnevin. The president of the funeral committee was Thomas Clarke, a former Clan na Gael dynamitard who had been arrested in 1883, before he even commenced activities, and had served fifteen years of particularly harsh imprisonment. Clarke, who was revered by a young generation of radicals as "the embodiment of Fenianism," applied himself to reviving the dilapidated IRB organization he found on his release.[74] He entrusted the delivery of the funeral oration to one of his most promising protégés, Patrick Pearse, instructing him to "make it as hot as hell, throw discretion to the winds."[75]

For Pearse, "O'Donovan Rossa was not the greatest man of the Fenian generation, but he was its most typical man."[76] Pearse's stirring graveside panegyric (fig. 9.3), became a founding text of Irish political martyrdom, capturing its umbilical dependence on state repression:

> Life springs from death; and from the graves of patriot men and women spring living nations. The Defenders of this Realm have worked well in secret and in the open. They think that they have pacified Ireland. They think that they have purchased half of us and intimidated the other half. They think that they have foreseen everything, think that they have provided against everything; but the fools, the fools, the fools!—they have left us our Fenian dead, and while Ireland holds these graves, Ireland unfree shall never be at peace.[77]

---

73. Owen Dudley Edwards, "Rossa, Jeremiah O'Donovan," *Oxford Dictionary of National Biography* (Oxford: Oxford University Press, 2004).

74. P. S. O'Hegarty, "Introduction," in Thomas James Clarke, *Glimpses of an Irish Felon's Prison Life* (Dublin: Maunsel and Roberts, 1922), p. xiii.

75. James Quinn, "Clarke, Thomas James ('Tom')," in McGuire and Quinn, *Dictionary of Irish Biography*; and Seán Farrell Moran, *Patrick Pearse and the Politics of Redemption: The Mind of the Easter Rising, 1916* (Washington, D.C.: Catholic University of America Press, 1994), p. 146.

76. Pádraic Pearse, "O'Donovan Rossa: A Character Study," in *Souvenir of Public Funeral to Glasnevin Cemetery, Dublin, August 1st, 1915* (Dublin, 1915); republished in *Collected Works of Pádraic H. Pearse*, 5 vols. (Dublin: The Phoenix Publishing Co., 1916), vol. 5, pp. 127–32.

77. Pearse, *Collected Works*, vol. 5, p. 137.

FIGURE 9.3. Funeral of O'Donovan Rossa, Glasnevin Cemetery, August 1, 1915

National Library of Ireland, Keogh Collection, Ke 234, reproduced courtesy of the National Library of Ireland, Dublin.

Within less than a year, Pearse and Clarke would be executed alongside the other main leaders of the Easter Rising. Although their takeover of the General Post Office in Dublin (April 24–29, 1916) was intended as an act of open insurrection rather than of terrorism, it could also be construed as a spectacular display of propaganda by deed.[78] Its brutal suppression and the claimed martyrdom of its executed leaders inspired thousands to commit themselves to "direct action," effectively sparking the Irish Revolution for which the Fenians had craved.

---

78. Neville Bolt, "Propaganda of the Deed and the Irish Republican Brotherhood: From the Politics of 'Shock and Awe' to the 'Imagined Political Community'," *RUSI Journal* 153.1 (2008), pp. 48–54.

IO

Spurning "This Worldly Life"

TERRORISM AND MARTYRDOM IN CONTEMPORARY BRITAIN

Akil N. Awan

RECENT YEARS HAVE witnessed a rapid proliferation of radical Islamist activity in Britain, best illustrated by both actual terrorist atrocities (such as those carried out on the London transport network in 2005), and MI5's sensational warning in 2006 of thirty incipient "terror plots" and 1,600 individuals then under surveillance.[1] Many of these cases have included individuals willing to countenance ending their own life in furtherance of their beliefs and cause, or in the perceived defense of their faith and community (*ummah*). These cases confound and perplex our modern sensibilities. How could they do such a thing? What could possibly compel ostensibly well-adjusted, educated, and indeed integrated young Britons (which virtually all are) to adopt such a bleak outlook on life; one in which they felt of greater worth dead than alive? Why were their familial ties, social networks, careers, aspirations, passions, interests, possessions and myriad other connections to reality, not sufficient to anchor them to "this worldly life."[2]

---

1. Akil N. Awan, "Antecedents of Islamic Political Radicalism among Muslim Communities in Europe," *PS: Political Science and Politics* 41.1 (2008), pp. 13–17, at p. 13.

2. This phrase is taken from a letter recovered soon after the 9/11 attacks and is thought to be the final instructions given to the lead hijacker, Mohammed Atta; it reads "purify your soul from all unclean things. Completely forget something called 'this worldly life,'" http://www.abc.net.au/4corners/atta/resources/documents/instructions1.htm.

Muhammad Siddique Khan, for example, the ringleader of the 7/7 London Transport Network bombings, epitomizes these tensions and contradictions. Khan's posthumously released farewell video message recorded with his infant daughter reveals his increasingly conflicted emotions over his impending suicide mission. The video highlights Khan's clear adoration and affection for his daughter, starkly juxtaposed against what appears to be a profound sense of duty and sacrifice. How do we reconcile Khan's tender paternal instincts and "rootedness" in this world with the seemingly incongruous acts of carnage later committed which, of course, took his own life too. Moreover, considering Khan's seemingly successful background (a university education, a well-regarded career, and a loving family)—by all accounts, not uncommon among radical Islamists—what lay behind the eventual recourse to "martyrdom"?

These "martyrdom" operations, as they are alluded to in the idiom of contemporary Jihadist discourse, may represent the apogee of Jihadist praxis to its adherents, but are only the most strikingly visible and shocking manifestation of the phenomenon. Indeed, it is more helpful to view the range of acts that fall under the rubric of radical Islam or Jihadism as constituting part of a much broader spectrum, in which terrorism and martyrdom are only one of a number of the possible outcomes. Other manifestations of this ideology or other forms of Jihadist "praxis" do exist and in fact are far more prevalent than martyrdom, but nevertheless, all stem from the same shared ideology and worldview. While this chapter is principally concerned with contemporary Jihadist articulations of martyrdom in Britain, we must acknowledge the commonalities that exist in the motivations, antecedents, processes, and trajectories of those drawn to radical Islam, irrespective of whether martyrdom is the desired, or unintended, outcome. This chapter attempts to engage with these complex issues by providing a fuller, more nuanced understanding of some of the motivations and causes of Jihadist martyrdom in Britain and by exploring the life narratives of a number of these individuals. In addition, the chapter seeks to explore the contemporary relevance of traditional and historical Islamic notions of martyrdom and *Jihad* and their seemingly profound resonance with these modern-day *shuhadā* (martyrs).

The word *shahīd* (martyr) in the Qur'an, stems from the Arabic verb "to see" or "to witness," closely mirroring its Latin equivalent in both etymology and usage.[3] Indeed, the Islamic conceptualization of martyrdom

---

3. For example, the Qur'an mentions bearing witness to righteousness and piety (2:143) or bearing witness to financial transactions (2:282). The use of word *martyr* as witness

also correlates closely with Western understandings. In the technical language of the Church, the martyr represents those who die in, or as a result of, *odium fidei* (hatred of the faith).[4] Weiner and Weiner expand on this theological understanding by suggesting that a historical examination of Judeo-Christian martyrs points to three principle types: (1) those that elect to suffer and die rather than reject their faith or principles; (2) those that suffer torture and death as a result of their convictions; and (3) those that endure great suffering for long periods of time.[5] It is this historical understanding of martyrdom that has strongest parallels within the Islamic tradition, which not only recognizes persecution on account of faith but also various forms of worldly suffering as worthy of *istishād* (martyrdom).[6]

The distinctly Islamic conception of *istishād* as death during *Jihad* has much more tenuous links to the Judeo-Christian tradition, but nevertheless remains the most popularly recognizable conceptualization of martyrdom within Islam, particularly in the West.[7] This peculiar category of martyrdom as death "whilst striving in the path of God" (the literal translation of *Jihad*), has generally been associated with death on the battlefield in God's cause.[8] However, crucially, it is not primarily the type of activity engaged in prior to death that confers martyrdom, but rather the intention (*niyyah*) upon which the activity was predicated. So, for example, a well-known tradition relates that "whoever leaves his house in the way of God then dies or is killed is a martyr, whether his horse or camel tramples him, or a venomous animal stings him, or he dies in his bed, or in any kind of death God wills, truly he is a martyr and shall have Paradise."[9]

---

was originally employed within both the secular and sacred spheres (as articulated in the New Testament); see Cooper, this volume, and Allison Trites, *The New Testament Concept of Witness* (Cambridge: Cambridge University Press, 2004).

4. Lawrence Cunningham, "Christian Martyrdom: A Theological Perspective," in Michael Budde and Karen Scott, eds., *Witness of the Body: The Past, Present, and Future of Christian Martyrdom* (Grand Rapids, Mich.: William B. Eerdmans Pub., 2011), p. 14.

5. Eugene Weiner and Anita Weiner, *The Martyr's Conviction: A Sociological Analysis* (Lanham, Md.: University Press of America, 2002).

6. Examples of worldly suffering worthy of martyrdom include death from drowning, plague, fire, and during childbirth; see, for example, Muhammad bin Ismail Bukhari, *Sahih al-Bukhari* (Beirut: Dar al-Fikr, 1991), vol. 3, nos. 2829–30.

7. Ibid., no. 2829.

8. See, for example, Qur'an 3:140, which refers to the martyrs from one of the earliest battles during Muhammad's life, the Battle of Uhud.

9. Abu Daud Sulayman ibn al-Ash`ath al-Sijistani and Ahmad Hasan, *Sunan Abu Dawud* (New Delhi: Kitab Bhavan, 1990), vol. 14, p. 2493.

Moreover, the Islamic canon also introduces the concept of martyrdom as death in any defensive context: "whoever is killed defending his wealth is a martyr; whoever is killed defending his religion is a martyr; whoever is killed in self-defence is a martyr."[10] The idea of defense here is broad enough to subsume a great number of activities and thus lends itself to a multiplicity of interpretations vis-à-vis achieving martyrdom. Indeed, it is this vagueness of definition that has largely engendered the proliferation of modern-day Jihadist martyrdom-seekers (istishādi). The conceptualization of martyrdom in Islam has not remained static, and as Cook's historical study of martyrdom shows, the legal and social basis of that which constitutes martyrdom has changed significantly throughout the Muslim world over time.[11] Our concerns here, however, are with contemporary articulations of martyrdom amongst Jihadists, such as those of al-Qaeda and their ilk, and despite the rhetoric of these modern-day Salafi-Jihadists, invoking the precedents of the first three generations in Islam as the basis for their praxis, theirs is, in fact, a very modern understanding of martyrdom that draws on eclectic sources of legitimacy and authority.[12]

In recent years there has been a general conflation of martyrdom in the Islamic tradition with terrorism to such an extent that the suicide bomber is now popularly perceived to be the archetypal Islamic martyr.[13] However, this characterization is highly problematic for a number of reasons. The "Muslim suicide bombing" or "martyrdom operation" is a relatively recent phenomenon borrowed largely from secular nationalist groups such as

10. Muhammad ibn `Isá Tirmidhi, Abu Khalil, and Abu Tahir Zubayr `Ali Zai, English Translation of Jami` at-Tirmidhi = Jami` al-Tirmidhi (Riyadh: Darussalam, 2007), p. 1421.

11. David Cook, Martyrdom in Islam (New York: Cambridge University Press, 2007). See also Afsaruddin, in this volume.

12. The term Salafi-Jihadism was first used by Giles Kepel to describe Salafists who began to develop an interest in Jihad in the early 1990s, in Jihad: The Trail of Political Islam, 4th ed. (London: I. B. Tauris, 2006). Salafism refers to a broad body of Muslims from those who are peaceful and apolitical to politically violent terrorists. They are generally characterized by a fundamentalist worldview, particularly their reverence for the sacred texts in their most literal form, and follow the practices and precedents of the pious predecessors (the as-Salaf as-Salih) who are usually understood to represent the historic first three generations of Muslims; see, for example, Akil N. Awan, Andrew Hoskins, and Ben O'Loughlin, Radicalisation and Media: Connectivity and Terrorism in the New Media Ecology (London: Routledge, 2011), pp. 25–47.

13. Indeed, the very title of this volume is testament to the amalgamation of these two terms in both popular and academic discourse.

the Liberation Tigers of Tamil Eelam.[14] Indeed, even the seminal *Jihadi* literature from the 1980s concerning Afghanistan, for example, does not mention "martyrdom operations."[15] Moreover, the development of suicide bombing as a tactic is almost entirely predicated upon technological advances in the manufacture of explosives in the late twentieth century, thus rendering it a highly modern innovation with no real historical precedents in Islamic praxis.[16] Perhaps most problematic is that the act of suicide is itself categorically prohibited in the canonical texts of Islam, and suicide bombings often violate other fundamental religious precepts, such as targeting noncombatants, thereby posing serious legitimation challenges to the Islamic appropriation and sanctification of the suicide bomber.[17]

However, one could argue that these are moot points, for whatever the theological and historical obstacles to locating suicide bombing within the realm of Islamic martyrdom, it remains an indelible statistical fact that Muslims have been responsible for the overwhelming majority of suicide bombing attacks in the last few decades. According to Robert Pape, 224 of the 300 suicide attacks between 1980 and 2003 were carried out by Islamist groups or occurred in predominantly Muslim countries.[18] If one examines the suicide attacks after 2003 (when Pape's survey ends), the bias is skewed even further toward Muslim perpetrators.[19] Moreover, these individuals not only considered themselves to be Muslims, but martyrdom in the name of Islam provided (at least in their minds) the raison d'être for their acts of self-sacrifice.

---

14. Suicide bombing was pioneered by others, particularly secular Lebanese groups, but it is the Tamil Tigers who ultimately "mastered" the tactic; Bruce Hoffman, *Inside Terrorism*, rev. and expanded ed. (New York: Columbia University Press, 2006).

15. David Cook, "Suicide Attacks or 'Martyrdom Operations' in Contemporary Jihad Literature," *Nova Religio* 6.1 (2002), pp. 7–44, at p. 8.

16. The closest parallel is found in historical accounts of individual Muslim fighters charging enemy lines during battle in displays of heroism and personal valor in the knowledge that they would probably not survive the encounter (*al-inghimas fi as-saf*); Cook, *Martyrdom in Islam*, p. 153.

17. See, for example, Qur'an 2:195 and 4:29; Al-Bukhari, *Sahih al-Bukhari*, vol. 4, p. 26 (nos. 3014–15); and Afsaruddin, in this volume.

18. Robert Pape, *Dying to Win: The Strategic Logic of Suicide Terrorism* (New York: Random House, 2005), p. 15.

19. See, for example, Scott Atran, "The Moral Logic and Growth of Suicide Terrorism," *Washington Quarterly* 29.2 (2006), pp. 127–47.

Nevertheless, these statistics do not necessarily exonerate the modern-day obfuscation and linkage between Islamic martyrdom and terrorism—which, it should be noted, is largely attributable to the modern mass media. While it may be correct to state that the vast majority of suicide bombers today are Muslim "martyrs," the obverse is not true. Indeed, the vast majority of modern-day "Islamic martyrdoms" have occurred not through suicide bombings or associated acts of terrorism, but instead as the outcome of more conventional warfare on the battlefields of Afghanistan, Bosnia, Chechnya, the Palestinian Territories, Iraq, and various other theaters of conflict raging in the Muslim world. For Muslim audiences, the martyrs created within these arenas include not only the dead combatants who were engaged in conventional and legitimate modes of warfare but also (and perhaps more importantly) the large numbers of civilians also killed as "collateral damage." Conversely, the suicide terrorists who are posthumously recast as martyrs by the Jihadists represent a much smaller, but nevertheless highly visible, minority within the faith. It is with these individuals that this chapter is principally concerned, and it is to their attraction to this peculiar form of "martyrdom" that we now turn.

Political and Socio-Cultural Motivations

In explaining the putative appeal of martyrdom among contemporary British Jihadists, it is now clear that motivations can often be amorphous and complex and with no simple cause and effect calculus appearing to be tenable.[20] Instead, individuals may be drawn to the prospect of becoming martyrs for a multitude of (sometimes conflicting) reasons. Here we are not concerned primarily with the reasons behind the adoption of suicide bombing as a tactic by modern terrorist organizations. Indeed, a number of studies have attempted to explain the underlying strategic reasons for the adoption of "martyrdom operations" by terrorist organizations, identifying factors such as tactical efficacy, symbolic value, out-bidding and intra-group competition, and societal support.[21] Instead, I am principally

---

20. Awan, "Antecedents of Islamic Political Radicalism," p. 16.

21. See, for example, Pape, *Dying to Win*; Assaf Moghadam, *The Globalization of Martyrdom: Al Qaeda, Salafi Jihad, and the Diffusion of Suicide Attacks* (Baltimore: Johns Hopkins University Press, 2008); and Mia Bloom, *Dying to Kill: The Allure of Suicide Terror* (New York: Columbia University Press, 2005).

concerned with the appeal of martyrdom among individuals recruited to the organization or cause, which has tended to receive far less rigorous academic focus. Moreover, those studies that have attempted to elucidate suicide bombers' individual motivations typically create taxonomies that demarcate personal motivations as being verifiably distinct from ideological motivations.[22] This approach is highly problematic, however, for it assumes an innate dichotomy in motivations which is clearly not borne out in reality. Instead, it is extremely difficult, if not almost impossible, to distinguish between the personal and the political, and, more crucially, it is therefore difficult to determine how the two spheres interact to manifest violence.

Following Max Weber's classic postulation of ideal types, one can tentatively identify three broad motivational motifs underlying martyrdom among British Jihadists, namely: (1) altruism and identity; (2) religion and salvation; and (3) impotence and ennui.[23] By motifs I mean the key defining experiences or themes which make each type of martyrdom substantially different and distinctive. While I do not wish to contest the uniqueness of each convert's individual experiences, or dispute the patently high degree of biographical specificity contained within each individual's life narrative, these motifs are considered to be broad enough to be able to accommodate the diversity of motivating factors from within our sample, under their respective overarching rubrics. In addition, if radicalization toward Jihadism entails a process, as has been convincingly argued by me and by others, then we must also acknowledge the existence of a range of potential motivations that may span the journey toward eventual martyrdom; the impulse for joining the cause may be very different from the incentive for remaining committed to the group or network, which in turn may be quite distinct from the eventual motivation for embarking on a suicide mission.[24] Moreover, these broad explanatory frameworks should not be considered to be in any way mutually exclusive. Rather, individuals may exhibit aspects of multiple motifs at any given time, particularly as different motifs may become more or less salient at different stages over the course of their trajectory to martyrdom. Finally, in some cases it may

---

22. See, for example, Ami Pedahzur, *Suicide Terrorism* (London: Polity Press, 2005).

23. Max Weber, *Methodology of Social Sciences* (New York: Free Press, 1949), p. 89.

24. Awan, "Antecedents of Islamic Political Radicalism"; Awan, Hoskins, and O'Loughlin, *Radicalisation and the Media*; and Clark R. McCauley, *Friction: How Radicalization Happens to Them and Us* (Oxford: Oxford University Press, 2011).

also prove problematic to discern definitively a hierarchy of motivational motifs from an individual's life narrative.

To Western audiences inured to depictions of Jihadist suicide bombers as either evil, bloodthirsty savages, or deranged, religious zealots, there must be something inherently incongruous and deeply unsettling about recognizing the essentially altruistic nature of suicide bombing.[25] As discomfiting as this revelation may be, it is nevertheless important to recognize that many individuals who undertake, or at least attempt, "martyrdom operations" tend to do so for largely selfless reasons, being sincerely compassionate to those they see themselves as helping.[26] Indeed, empathy for fellow Muslims inculcates many potential radical Islamists with a profound sense of duty and justice, which finds effective expression through the conduit of Jihadism. For example, Hussain Osman—one of the failed 7/7 bombers—told Italian investigators that during preparations for the attack the cell steeled its resolve by "watching films on the war in Iraq...especially those where women and children were being killed and exterminated by British and American soldiers...of widows, mothers and daughters that cry."[27] Similarly, Umar Farouk Abdulmutallab, a Nigerian graduate of University College London, who failed to detonate explosive-lined underwear on a trans-Atlantic flight in 2009, justified his actions to United States prosecutors by stating that

> I carried with me an explosive device onto Northwest 253, again, to avenge the killing of my innocent Muslim brothers and sisters by the U.S....and in retaliation for U.S. support of Israel and Israeli massacres of innocent Palestinians, [and] for the United States' tyranny and oppression of Muslims...I attempted to use an explosive device which in the U.S. law is a weapon of mass destruction,

---

25. A point corroborated by Durkheim's sociological taxonomy of suicide, through which "martyrdom operations" can also be considered to be altruistic in nature. See Émile Durkheim, *Suicide: A Study in Sociology*, trans. George Simpson (London: Routledge, 1897); Steven Stack, "Emile Durkheim and Altruistic Suicide," *Archives of Suicide Research* 8.1 (2004), pp. 9–22. For more on this general characterization, see Atran, "The Moral Logic" and "Soft Power and the Psychology of Suicide Bombing," *Global Terrorism Analysis* 2.11 (2004), pp. 1–3.

26. Atran, "The Moral Logic."

27. C. Fusani, "'Non volevamo colpire l'Italia': la lunga confessione nella notte," *La Repubblica*, July 30, 2005.

which I call a blessed weapon to save the lives of innocent Muslims, for U.S. use of weapons of mass destruction on Muslim populations in Afghanistan, Iraq, Yemen, and beyond.[28]

Robert Pape's comprehensive study of suicide terrorism corroborates this view by suggesting that suicide bombings are almost always conceived of as a liberation strategy in response to occupation that places the community over and above the self. This is the very reason why the occupied communities often perceive them as martyrs and consider their actions to be altruistic.[29]

We may dispute the notion that the suicide terrorists who carried out the 9/11 World Trade Center attacks, or the 7/7 London transport network bombings, hailed from "occupied" communities, however, to do so would be to ignore the communal and supra-national nature of radical Islamist discourse, and the widely held perceptions of Western domination and hegemony in the Muslim world more broadly.[30] Indeed, one of the cornerstones of Jihadist discourse has been the rejection of a more parochial conceptualization of community that is predicated upon the traditional ambits of ethnicity or nationalism, in favor of a global community of belief instead. As an example of the championing of this global community of belief and purpose—the *ummah*—the Global Islamic Media Front, a prominent media organ of al-Qaeda, stated in 2005 that "the [battle]front does not belong to anyone. It is the property of all zealous Muslims and knows no geographical boundaries."[31] This official endorsement of the *ummah* as the sole locus of identity and belonging is often echoed in the language of individual "martyrs" themselves. For example, Shahzad Tanweer, one of the 7/7 bombers, attempted to justify his actions by pointing to British

28. Detroit Free Press, "Transcript: Read Abdulmutallab's Statement on Guilty Plea," *Detroit Free Press*, October 12, 2011.

29. Pape, *Dying to Win*.

30. In the case of 9/11 at least, it is clear that the large number of US troops stationed in the Arabian Gulf, particularly in the hijaz during the First Gulf War, was seen as an occupation by al-Qaeda and their supporters, and indeed the removal of US troops constitutes the earliest articulated demand by Osama bin Laden; see "The Ladinese Epistle: Declaration of War (I)," *MSANEWS*, October 12, 1996, http://msanews.mynet.net//MSANEWS/199610/19961012.3.

31. Cited in Akil N. Awan, "Transitional Religiosity Experiences: Contextual Disjuncture and Islamic Political Radicalism," in Tahir Abbas, ed., *Islamic Political Radicalism: A European Comparative Perspective* (Edinburgh: Edinburgh University Press, 2007), p. 222.

tacit support for injustices perpetrated against what can be termed his "fictive kin":[32]

> To the non-Muslims of Britain you may wonder what you have done to deserve this. You have those who have voted in your government who in turn have and still continue to this day continue to oppress our mothers, children, brothers and sisters from the east to the west in Palestine...Iraq and Chechnya. Your government has openly supported the genocide of over 50,000 innocent Muslims. You will never experience peace until our children in Palestine, our mothers and sisters in Kashmir, our brothers in Afghanistan and Iraq live in peace. Our blood flows across the earth, Muslim blood has become cheap. Better those who will avenge the blood of our children in Palestine and the rapes and massacres of our sisters in Kashmir.[33]

Similarly, Mohammed Siddique Khan, in his posthumously released "martyrdom" testament, repeatedly invoked a communal identity in which he identified the subjugation of his community as being a key item among his grievances:

> Your democratically elected governments continuously perpetuate atrocities against my people all over the world. And your support of them makes you directly responsible, just as I am directly responsible for protecting and avenging my Muslim brothers and sisters. Until we feel security, you will be our targets. And until you stop the bombing, gassing, imprisonment and torture of my people we will not stop this fight.[34]

Khan and Tanweer exhibit a confusing and melodramatic sense of duty to this nebulous and disparate body of peoples ("my Muslim brothers and sisters," "our children in Palestine," "our mothers and sisters in Kashmir"), who ultimately become the object of their altruistic sacrifice, despite the fact that neither has little direct connection to, or identification

---

32. This term is borrowed from Scott Atran, "Genesis of Suicide Terrorism," *Science* 299.5612 (March 7, 2003), pp. 1534–39, at p. 1534.

33. Available at http://www.guardian.co.uk/uk/2006/oct/15/terrorism.alqaida1.

34. Available at http://news.bbc.co.uk/1/hi/uk/4206800.stm.

with, them (in terms of ethnicity, nationality, language, culture or customs to name but a few salient markers of identity). This attitude is all the more perplexing when juxtaposed against the feelings of indifference and open hostility displayed toward their British victims, with whom they did actually share many facets of identity.

This disconcertingly misplaced identification can be partially explained through a process I describe elsewhere as dual cultural alterity.[35] This phenomenon refers to a staunch repudiation of, or at least a distinct lack of identification with, both minority (ethnic or parental) culture, and majority (mainstream or host society) culture, as a result of being unable or unwilling to fulfil either group's normative expectations, and this is thus likely to inspire feelings of uprootedness and lack of belonging. Minority culture may be relegated to obsolescence for a number of reasons including, the imposition of conservative socio-sexual mores; a profound sense of alienation from one's family and the presence of cultural power structures (such as the South Asian *biraderi*), which can have the effect of divesting youth of any real tangible control over their own lives.[36] The authors of the Home Office Report *Preventing Extremism Together Working Groups* (hastily compiled in the wake of 7/7) concurred, arguing that "many young Muslims feel that they do not have a voice or a legitimate outlet for protest, political expression, or dissent. Leadership roles are traditionally held by the elders, and the young people can feel frustrated at their inability to actively engage in decision making structures."[37] Perhaps the most damning indictment of minority culture for many Jihadists, however, is that it holds little or no relevance in the diaspora. There is no "myth of return," no solace to be found in a nostalgic struggle for the homeland, and ethnic languages become defunct through neglect while

---

35. Awan, "Transitional Religiosity Experiences," p. 219.

36. Indeed, in the cases presented before us, none of the families appear to have been cognizant of the paths upon which their children were embarked: Hasib Hussain's distraught mother, unaware of her son's actions, reported him missing to the Police Casualty Bureau on the evening of July 7; see Jason Burke et al., "Three Cities, Four Killers," *Observer*, July 17, 2005. Similarly, Mukhtar Said Ibrahim, one of the failed bombers on July 21 was only identified after his bewildered family recognized their estranged son from CCTV images distributed throughout the media; Duncan Gardham and Philip Johnston, "Terror Suspect is a Convicted Mugger," *Telegraph*, July 27, 2005.

37. Home Office Working Groups, *Preventing Extremism Together* (London: Home Office, 2005), p. 15. A slew of earlier reports following the "race riots" of 2001 in Oldham, Burnley, and Bradford had all drawn attention to precisely this sort of cumulative marginalization of youth voices by decision-makers and community leaders, see, for example, Ted Cantle, *Community Cohesion: A Report of the Independent Review Team* (London: Home Office, 2001).

English assumes the role of *lingua franca*.[38] Moreover, ambient cultural racism serves to negate any intrinsic worth thought to reside in ethnic traditions and customs, while concomitantly those very same traditions and customs are exposed as adulterating a pristine Islamic orthodoxy.[39]

The disenchantment with majority culture, on the other hand, is less clear-cut, particularly as many Jihadists who, by virtue of being raised in a pervasively British environment and having imbibed many of its values and cultural norms, display a remarkably easy immersion into majority culture (particular popular, mainstream youth culture) prior to their radicalization. However, this comfortable embedment is clearly disrupted at some point and gradually superseded by disillusionment with majority culture, as a result of perceptions of hedonism, consumerism, racism, inequality, and the general imposition of conflicting core value systems from the "host" society, which may render the individual unwilling or unable to perpetuate assimilation into the predominant paradigm. One way to account for this cultural schizophrenia of sorts is by examining identity through the lens of self-categorization theory.[40] This contends that identity is not a static construction and that the self may be defined at different levels of abstraction depending upon differing circumstances; at times it may be in terms of individual uniqueness and at others in terms of specific group membership.

The salience of a communal identity, for example, may arise during periods of perceived group crisis or threat. For Jihadists these flashpoints may have been evoked by a range of contemporary events including, the Iraq war and the wider Global War on Terror; the Palestinian *Intifada* or the stagnation of the Middle East peace process; the banning of the veil and other European sartorial restrictions on Muslim women; the provocative publication of Danish cartoons of Muhammad deemed offensive to Muslims; and the resurgence of the Far Right and its convergence with the

---

38. Awan, "Transitional Religiosity Experiences," p. 217.

39. Modood argues that the familiar "biological racism" has gradually been displaced by a newer "cultural racism," which focuses on language, religion, family structures, dress, and cuisine—traits that define what it means to be Asian, see Tariq Modood, *Multicultural Politics: Racism, Ethnicity and Muslims in Britain* (Edinburgh: Edinburgh University Press, 2005). The growth of an austere Wahhabism or Salafism among diasporic Muslim youth, that condemns many ethnic customs and norms as *bidah* (reprehensive religious innovation) is testament to this fact.

40. John C. Turner, *Rediscovering the Social Group: A Self-Categorization Theory* (Oxford: Basil Blackwell, 1988) and Penelope J. Oakes, *Stereotyping and Social Reality* (Oxford: Blackwell, 1994).

rise in Islamophobia in the United States and Western Europe more generally.[41] It is in these instances, that individuals become much more prone to reassessing what religious identity means to them, either as reconstruction in part of the lost minority identity or as a response to pressing questions and challenges from a pervasively non-Muslim environment.[42]

Thus, in the absence of an appealing cultural paradigm from either minority or majority group, the individual simply resorts to a cultural entrenchment that assumes a religious hue by default, thus transforming religion from religion per se into the principal anchor of identity. Consequently, religion is seen to provide not only an emphatic rejoinder to Western identity but also is interpreted de novo, without the perceived cultural accretions of the Islam associated with the individual's parental or ethnic identity, thereby upholding a legitimate identity outside both minority and majority cultures. Take, for instance, the case of Umar Farouk Abdulmuttalab, who wrote in the final text messages to his father back in Nigeria, "I've found a new religion, the real Islam"; "You should just forget about me, I'm never coming back"; "Please forgive me. I will no longer be in touch with you"; and "Forgive me for any wrongdoing, I am no longer your child."[43] Olivier Roy argues that globalized radical Islam is particularly attractive to diasporic Muslims precisely because it legitimizes their sense of deculturation and uprootedness by refusing to identify Islam with the pristine cultures of their parents and so pointing to a strong correlation between deculturation and religious reformulation.[44] This dual cultural alterity and the attendant forging of an identity distinct to both that bequeathed by parents, or assimilated from the wider host society, may help to explain why a British Jihadist of Pakistani or Jamaican provenance (Muhammad Siddique Khan or Germaine Lindsey, respectively) who feels little or no identification with Britain (or their country of parental origin) but complete allegiance to the global community of believers or *ummah*, might undertake a martyrdom operation in Britain, ostensibly in response to occupation in Iraq, Palestine, or elsewhere.

---

41. Peter Gottschalk, *Islamophobia: Making Muslims the Enemy* (Lanham, Md.: Rowman and Littlefield Publishers, 2008).

42. Awan, "Transitional Religiosity Experiences," p. 218.

43. Adam Nossiter, "Lonely Trek to Radicalism for Terror Suspect," *New York Times*, January 16, 2010.

44. Olivier Roy, *Globalized Islam: The Search for a New Ummah* (New York: Columbia University Press, 2004).

However, it would be erroneous to assume that an altruistic identification with an imagined community deemed to be under attack, *ipso facto*, leads to a proclivity toward martyrdom. Many individuals experiencing identity dislocation through dual cultural alterity, and identifying instead with a beleaguered *ummah*, nevertheless eschew violence of any form and accept (either tacitly or apathetically) the status quo, or instead seek redress through conventional political channels. Instead, those few individuals who are genuinely willing to countenance martyrdom appear to do so for the two following reasons: political empowerment and/or diverted altruistic energies.

The eventual recourse to martyrdom can be understood in part as a desperate response to acutely felt feelings of political impotence. Political powerlessness, such as that witnessed in the wake of unprecedented anti-war marches and demonstrations in 2003 that nevertheless failed to avert the course of the Iraq war, can lead to disillusionment with, and alienation from, conventional political processes. Anwar al-Awlaki, perhaps the most important ideologue among English-speaking Jihadists until his killing in 2011, wrote a missive to the Somalian Jihadist group al-Shabaab in 2008 that lauded its employment of violence in the face of political impotence, saying that "al-Shabab [sic] [has given] us a living example of how we as Muslims should proceed to change our situation. The ballot has failed us but the bullet has not."[45] Hussain Osman, similarly alluding to political disenfranchisement of this nature, claimed that the bombs on July 21 were never meant to detonate or inflict death, but only to draw attention to the Iraq war: "I am against war...I've marched in peace rallies and nobody listened to me. I never thought of killing people."[46]

The inefficacy of conventional politics may be brought into sharper relief when starkly juxtaposed against the potent efficacy of illegitimate political interventions—take, for example, perceptions of the 2004 Madrid train bombings as having ostensibly precipitated the early withdrawal of Spanish troops from the conflict in Iraq. Moreover, the potency of suicide terrorism, in particular, as a force multiplier that helps equalize an otherwise asymmetric conflict has long been recognized by both terrorist

---

45. Available at: http://www.nefafoundation.org/miscellaneous/FeaturedDocs/awlakishe-bab1208.pdf.

46. CNN, "London Bomb Suspect Arrested," July 27, 2005, http://www.cnn.com/2005/WORLD/europe/07/27/london.tube.

groups and those they fight.[47] Ayman al-Zawahiri, for example, extols the merits of suicide bombings to his readers stating that "the method of martyrdom operations is the most successful way of inflicting damage against the opponent and the least costly to the mujahideen in casualties."[48] Pape suggests that, even with the exclusion of the 9/11 attacks, suicide bombings conducted between 1980 and 2004 accounted for 48 percent of all terrorism-related deaths even though they represented only 3 percent of all terrorist incidents.[49] Western Jihadists, often self-conscious of their own lack of training and general military competence, no doubt astutely recognize the lethal effectiveness of suicide terrorism and its ability to compensate for their own shortcomings as disempowered modern males.[50]

Muhammad Siddique Khan also expresses frustration with the apparent futility of conventional modes of political engagement, powerfully invoking a somewhat Fanonesque explanation for his eventual recourse to violence: "and our words have no impact upon you, therefore I'm going to talk to you in a language that you understand. Our words are dead until we give them life with our blood."[51] Perceiving a loss of personal agency and, in particular, feeling that he has been rendered powerless to prevent further violence against his community, Khan contends that he must now communicate instead in the language of violence. The predication of the recourse to violence upon this realization appears to be a familiar sentiment among many terrorists throughout history, who have claimed, often quite sincerely, that they only turned to violence when they felt they had no other choice.[52] The understanding of terrorism as "talking in the language

---

47. Pape, *Dying to Win*, pp. 62–76; Dipak K. Gupta and Kusum Mundra, "Suicide Bombing as a Strategic Weapon: An Empirical Investigation of Hamas and Islamic Jihad," *Terrorism and Political Violence* 17.4 (2005), pp. 573–98; and Jeffrey William Lewis, *The Business of Martyrdom: A History of Suicide Bombing* (Annapolis, Md.: Naval Institute Press, 2012).

48. Ayman al-Zawahiri, *Fursan Taht Rayah Al-Nabi (Knights under the Prophet's Banner)* 2001, http://www.scribd.com/doc/6759609/Knights-Under-the-Prophet-Banner.

49. Pape, *Dying to Win*, p. 3.

50. Awan, Hoskins, and O'Loughlin, *Radicalisation and the Media*, pp. 47–66.

51. Available at http://news.bbc.co.uk/1/hi/uk/4206800.stm. Frantz Fanon wrote that the colonialist society is violent by its very nature and therefore violence is the only language it understands: "Colonialism is not a machine capable of thinking, a body endowed with reason. It is naked violence and only gives in when confronted with greater violence." See Frantz Fanon, *The Wretched of the Earth* (New York: Grove Press, 2004), p. 23.

52. See, for example, Nelson Mandela's famous statement at the Rivonia trial in 1961, "[I] came to the conclusion that as violence in this country was inevitable...when all channels of peaceful protest had been barred to us, that the decision was made to embark on violent

of blood" is itself a largely uncontested concept; as Schmid and De Graaf suggest in their seminal text, *Violence as Communication: Insurgent Terrorism and the Western News Media*, terrorism is far better understood if it is viewed in the first instance as communication rather than as mere violence.[53]

It is alluringly simple to conflate all Jihadist actions under the overarching rubric of terrorism, but there has long existed a hierarchy of legitimacy for Jihadist acts.[54] Causes associated with national independence struggles against regimes perceived as repressive, such as those of Chechnya, Kashmir, and Palestine, enjoy widespread sympathy among Muslim publics and consequently have far greater legitimacy than, for example, obscure movements attempting to resurrect the Caliphate, or the global Jihadism of al-Qaeda. Similarly, conventional modes of warfare with combatants and military personnel are not granted the same taboo status as indiscriminate acts of terrorism against civilian populations. This then leads one to the second reason for the recourse to martyrdom; although individual Jihadists may ultimately undertake "martyrdom" operations as an altruistic response to perceived occupation, there is little evidence to suggest that those individuals who commit acts of suicide terrorism do so as a matter of choice (or at least first choice). Instead, it appears that in many cases, potential radicals with romanticized and earnest, if largely inchoate, notions of defending their community, can have their often laudable empathies diverted (due to a lack of accessibility to the principle cause), or manipulated to deadly effect.[55]

Western Muslim Jihadists are particularly amenable to deflectionary tactics for a variety of reasons, including their proficiency in European languages, their lack of restrictions on international travel, and their potential ability to evade suspicion within their host societies. Bearing in mind their very limited combat training experience, they possess much greater value as "smart bombs" than as conventional guerrillas or foot

---

forms of political struggle," http://law2.umkc.edu/faculty/projects/ftrials/mandela/mandelaspeech.html.

53. Alex Peter Schmid and Janny de Graaf, *Violence as Communication: Insurgent Terrorism and the Western News Media* (London: Sage, 1982).

54. For more on legitimacy of Jihadist actions, see Awan, Hoskins, and O'Loughlin, *Radicalisation and the Media*.

55. Awan, "Transitional Religiosity Experiences," p. 223.

soldiers.[56] Consequently, although volunteering for the Jihadist cause usually entails some degree of choice, recruits may quickly discover that individual agency is usurped by the group, through the *bay'ah* (oath of allegiance) and normative expectations on obedience and conformity, as this chilling warning from Omar Khyam, the ringleader of the Crevice plot, to Muhammad Siddique Khan on how to behave at the training camp demonstrates: "The only thing, one thing I will advise you yeah, is total obedience to whoever your emir is whether he is Sunni, Arab Chechen Saudi, British, total obedience, I don't know if heard about the [unclear] he disobeyed one order [unclear] lies cut out his throat, I'll tell you up there you can get your head cut off."[57]

Even in the case of the most infamous example of suicide terrorism to date, the attack on 9/11, it is patently clear that the key members of the Hamburg cell originally held aspirations to fight alongside separatist rebels in Chechnya, but were re-directed to Afghanistan for training, before later being told that "the Chechens do not need [fighters] anymore."[58] Similarly, there is strong evidence to suggest that at least two of the 7/7 bombers, Muhammad Siddique Khan and Shahzad Tanweer, initially spurred on by the prospect of fighting in the "Jihad" in Afghanistan against the "invading Crusaders," were later diverted to attack the London transport network in 2005. In a 2004 conversation with Omar Khyam, Khan appears to be relishing the prospect of fighting in Afghanistan, fully aware of the fact that he will not be allowed to return to the United Kingdom:

OMAR KHYAM: "Are these lot ready bruv?" [ready to go to Afghanistan]
Mohammed Siddique Khan: "Yeah."
OMAR KHYAM: "What I'll do is, I will talk to you tonight, inshallah. How quickly can these guys go?"
MOHAMMED SIDDIQUE KHAN: "Listen this can't come quick enough for them...."

---

56. This term is adapted from Mohammed M. Hafez, *Suicide Bombers in Iraq: The Strategy and Ideology of Martyrdom* (Washington, D.C: U.S. Institute of Peace Press, 2007), p. 9.

57. MI5 transcript of conversation between Muhammad Siddique Khan and Omar Khyam, March 23, 2004, http://7julyinquests.independent.gov.uk.

58. National Commission on Terrorist Attacks upon the United States, *The 9/11 Commission Report: Final Report of the National Commission on Terrorist Attacks upon the United States* (New York: Norton, 2004), p. 165; and Peter Finn, "Hijackers had Hoped to Fight in Chechnya, Court Told," *Washington Post*, October 23, 2002, http://www.washingtonpost.com/wp-dyn/articles/A2079-2002Oct22.html.

OMAR KHYAM: "The Big Emir of the brothers is saying they can come, but it is a one way ticket. That's it if you agree with that bruv, it's not a problem bruv. If it's a one way ticket. You understand that. You agree with that, inshallah."

MOHAMMED SIDDIQUE KHAN: "Inshallah."[59]

However, clearly illustrating the established hierarchy of legitimacy for Jihadist actions, Khan, eager to wage defensive *Jihad* in Afghanistan against NATO troops, displays uncertainty and discomfort over Omar Khyam's connections to terrorism later in the conversation:

MOHAMMED SIDDIQUE KHAN: "Are you really a terrorist eh?"

Omar Khyam: "They're working with us."

MOHAMMED SIDDIQUE KHAN: "You're serious, you are basically."

Omar Khyam: "No I'm not a terrorist but they are working through us."

MOHAMMED SIDDIQUE KHAN: "Who are, there's no one higher than you (unclear)."[60]

In some cases, a gradual progression to increasingly more egregious modes of violence that subvert the individual's initial largely humanistic aspirations may be witnessed. British Jihadists, having partaken in (and survived) "legitimate defensive Jihad" in theaters of conflict from Bosnia to Iraq, inevitably return to their host societies. These survivors, brutalized by the ravages of war and possibly suffering from post-traumatic stress disorder, may prove less capable of rehabilitation into mainstream society and, consequently, may more easily resort to more extreme or taboo modes of violence in the future. In all of the scenarios presented above, individuals may not have initially wished to participate in these highly "controversial" operations, but by that point they have long crossed the Rubicon. One of the patent successes of al-Qaeda has been its ability to co-opt diverse motivations, aspirations, grievances, and causes, and ultimately divert, channel, and redirect these energies for their own ends.

---

59. MI5 transcript of conversation between Muhammad Siddique Khan and Omar Khyam.

60. Ibid.

Religious and Personal Motivations

One of the enduring myths surrounding suicide bombers has been the ascendancy of religious motivations for "martyrdom" over other more "worldly" concerns, with many commentators pursuing a prurient focus on *hoor al-ayn* or heavenly maidens. This is not to contest the fact that the recourse to martyrdom may be shaped by substantive religious or spiritual desires, yearnings and experiences that cannot simply be summarily dismissed, as is often the wont of many reductive strains of literature on religious change within the social sciences.[61] Indeed, it is patently evident from the religious rhetoric of many Jihadists drawn to martyrdom that salvific motives do ostensibly appear to factor heavily in their decisions. Many of these individuals frequently allude to canonical traditions that explicitly reinforce the notion of "other-worldly" rewards as recompense for "this-worldly" sacrifice. These may include, *inter alia*, forgiveness for one's sins; evading the reckoning on the Day of Judgment; marriage to seventy-two heavenly maidens; intercession on behalf of seventy sinful family members; bestowal of dignity and glory; and ultimately, the guarantee of eternal Paradise.[62]

Shahzad Tanweer, who earlier claimed to be motivated by the West's injustices against his community, nevertheless invokes the "promise" of Paradise as being central to his rationale:

We are 100 per cent committed to the cause of Islam, we love death the way you love life.... As for you who have been affected by this reminder give your lives for Allah's cause. For in truth this is the best transaction.... Better that Allah has chosen to deliver their lives and their properties for the price that they should be the paradise; they fight Allah's cause so they kill and are killed is the promising truth that is binding.... And who is truer to his promise than Allah? Then rejoice in the life in which you have concluded that is the supreme success.[63]

---

61. Lewis R. Rambo, *Understanding Religious Conversion* (New Haven: Yale University Press, 1993).

62. Tirmidhi, Abu Khalil, and Zai, *English Translation of Jami` at-Tirmidhi = Jami` al-Tirmidhi*, 1663.

63. Available at http://www.guardian.co.uk/uk/2006/oct/15/terrorism.alqaida1.

Muhammad Siddique Khan also tempers his earlier altruistic, "secular" motives by introducing a sacred dimension to his rationale. This is accomplished through the invocation of familiar tropes from *istishādi* testaments such as obedience to God, the conscious spurning of worldly pleasures and a yearning for paradise:

> I and thousands like me are forsaking everything for what we believe. Our driving motivation doesn't come from tangible commodities that this world has to offer. Our religion is Islam—obedience to the one true God, Allah, and following the footsteps of the final prophet and messenger Muhammad....This is how our ethical stances are dictated...I myself, I make *dua* (pray) to Allah...to raise me amongst those whom I love like the prophets, the messengers, the martyrs and today's heroes like our beloved Sheikh Osama Bin Laden, Dr Ayman al-Zawahri and Abu Musab al-Zarqawi and all the other brothers and sisters that are fighting in the name...of this cause. With this I leave you to make up your own minds and I ask you to make *dua* to Allah almighty to accept the work from me and my brothers and enter us into gardens of paradise.[64]

Umar Farouk Abdulmutallab presents a similarly curious mix of secular and sacred motives, by first providing a very careful reasoning of his participation in *Jihad* as constituting not only a religious duty, but a virtuous deed:

> In late 2009, in fulfilment of a religious obligation, I decided to participate in Jihad against the United States. The Koran obliges every able Muslim to participate in Jihad and fight in the way of Allah, those who fight you.... Participation in Jihad against the United States [*sic*] is considered among the most virtuous of deeds in Islam and is highly encouraged in the Koran.... If you laugh at us now, we will laugh at you later in this life and on the day of judgment by God's will, and our final call is all praise to Allah, the lord of the universe, Allahu Akbar.[65]

---

64. Available at http://news.bbc.co.uk/1/hi/uk/4206800.stm.

65. Detroit Free Press, "Transcript."

However, the essential and underlying reasons for his recourse to martyrdom are, once again, highly political and secular:

> I had an agreement with at least one person to attack the United States in retaliation for U.S. support of Israel and in retaliation of the killing of innocent and civilian Muslim populations in Palestine, especially in the blockade of Gaza, and in retaliation for the killing of innocent and civilian Muslim populations in Yemen, Iraq, Somalia, Afghanistan and beyond, most of them women, children, and non-combatants.[66]

Consequently, it becomes extremely difficult, if not almost impossible, to delineate that which is genuinely "religious" from other more secular factors, particularly if all we have to base this on is the overtly sanctified and highly stylized discourse of the individuals themselves. Thus, while we must give credence to their stated sacred intentions, and their own attribution of meaning to their actions, we must also be cognizant of the *post hoc* attribution of meaning and validation to these acts. As Speckhard and Akhmedova, studying the motivations of Chechen female suicide terrorists, suggest: "[The] statements of the individuals involved in terrorism appear less of a driving force for their participation than as a means of justifying their actions."[67]

Martyrdom testaments belong to a highly stylized genre, and thus need to display certain religious tropes and conform to established archetypes for conferral of the status of martyr by the wider community. Indeed, if an individual is to be successfully accepted as a martyr, she or he not only needs to look and behave like a martyr, but also needs to adopt the language of the martyr. As Robert Pape suggests, "only a community can make a martyr...using elaborate ceremonies...to identify the death of a suicide attacker, [and] promote the idea that their members should be accorded martyr status."[68] This desire to fulfill the normative expectations of an imagined community of belief (the *ummah*), combined with the dual cultural alterity identified earlier, through which identity can assume a religious hue by default, may help explain the conspicuous religiosity

---

66. Ibid.

67. Anne Speckhard and Khapta Akhmedova, "The Making of a Martyr: Chechen Suicide Terrorism," *Studies in Conflict and Terrorism* 29.5 (2006), pp. 429–92, at p. 425.

68. Pape, *Dying to Win*, 82.

contained within many Jihadist narratives. This frequent invocation of "the sacred" by individuals is also likely to be symptomatic of the primacy of theological legitimation among Jihadist ideologues themselves, who have shrewdly, and indeed successfully, managed to yoke religion to profane political goals in order to manufacture constituencies, legitimize violence and eliminate dissent.[69] Indeed, Jihadist ideologues, who often display a glaringly conspicuous absence of personal religious credentials, having undergone modern secular educations, have long been astutely cognizant of the immense potency religion offers.[70] Thus, as I have argued elsewhere, the efforts of Jihadist leaders to adorn themselves in the regalia of religion, most recognizably in their impeccable white robes, pious beards and saintly turbans, alongside the employment of a superfluously religio-canonic rhetoric, should be understood first and foremost as a compensatory mechanism for theological illiteracy and a fervent desire to usurp this potent religious mantle from traditional religious authority figures.[71]

Conversely, however, many individuals display largely apathetic attitudes toward religion and so, in these cases, it may even be disingenuous to associate religious sentiments with martyrdom.[72] Hussain Osman, for example, informed Italian investigators in no uncertain terms that "religion had nothing to do with it. We were shown videos of the Iraq war and told we must do something big."[73] In fact, one of the most intriguing

---

69. For more on theological legitimation by Jihadists, see Awan, Hoskins, and O'Loughlin, *Radicalisation and the Media*, pp. 29–37, and, for a discussion of the manipulation of religion by terrorists, see Mark Juergensmeyer, *Terror in the Mind of God: The Global Rise of Religious Violence* (Berkeley: University of California Press, 2003).

70. For example, Osama bin Laden studied civil engineering; both al-Zawahiri and Sayyid Imam al-Sharif (one of the founding members of al-Qaeda) studied medicine; Abu Mus'ab al-Suri (the most important strategist of modern Jihadism) and Khalid Sheikh Mohammed (the principal architect of the 9/11 attacks) both studied mechanical engineering; Abd al-Salam Faraj (who wrote the highly influential Jihadist primer, *The Neglected Duty*) was an electrician; Abu Musab al-Zarqawi (the former head of al-Qaeda in Iraq) was a high school dropout and common criminal. Indeed, even Sayyid Qutb, often regarded as the ideological godfather of Jihadism, was a journalist and literary critic; on which, see Awan, Hoskins, and O'Loughlin, *Radicalisation and the Media*, p. 34.

71. Ibid., p. 35.

72. As Marc Sageman suggests, in many cases "[the motivation] is not religious, it is psychological and personal," in *Understanding Terror Networks* (Philadelphia: University of Pennsylvania Press, 2004), p. 108.

73. Duncan Campbell and John Hooper, "Second Bomb Suspect was Seen in Rome," *Guardian*, August 1, 2005.

findings vis-à-vis the religiosity of Jihadists has been the discovery that the vast majority of those drawn to Jihadism are not particularly religious prior to their radicalization. Most individuals were either raised in largely secular households, or possessed only a rudimentary grasp of their parental faith, which rarely extended to religious praxis of any sort.[74] It is only after experiencing a religious awakening or a "transitional religiosity experience," in conjunction with the dual cultural alterity (through which Islam becomes, by default, the principal anchor of identity), that religion becomes a potentially useful variable in the overall analysis.[75]

It is alluringly simple to posit that those drawn to Jihadist martyrdom are likely to be highly ideologically committed individuals, possessing coherent and well-developed worldviews, and harboring clear, cogent motives for their participation in acts that will ultimately claim their very lives. Bainbridge and Stark, writing on the *weltanschaung* or meaning system of religious adherents in general, suggest this is a highly contentious assumption to make, though surprisingly common among social scientists.[76] I would suggest this inference is all the more appealing to researchers studying suicide terrorism, as the projection of rationality, cogency, agency, and coherency onto subjects and their acts ostensibly helps us to make sense of the "senseless" and explain the "unexplainable." Nevertheless, it appears that an increasing number of individuals engaging in, or at least aspiring to suicide terrorism, are drawn to the phenomenon for reasons that may initially seem inexplicable. Indeed, for some of these aspiring Jihadists, the recourse to martyrdom is less about altruism, salvific yearnings, or political disenfranchisement, and more about an egotistical desire for meaning and purpose in one's life, often in order to overcome an unbearable ennui borne largely of underachievement. In these instances, the turn to Jihadism serves as an emphatic rejection of the banality and monotonous inanity of daily life, providing, perhaps for the first time, a sense of being part of an elite group that compensates

---

74. Sageman's detailed analysis of Jihadists arrived at a similar conclusion: of the 394 individuals he surveyed, only 13 percent had partaken in religious education or attended madrassas; see Marc Sageman, "Islam and Al Qaeda," in Ami Pedahzur, ed., *Root Causes of Suicide Terrorism: Globalization of Martyrdom* (New York: Routledge, 2006), pp. 122–36.

75. For more on the shifts in religiosity prior to incipient radicalism, see Awan, "Transitional Religiosity Experiences."

76. William Sims Bainbridge and Rodney Stark, "The 'Consciousness Reformation' Reconsidered," *Journal for the Scientific Study of Religion* 20.1 (1981), pp. 1–16, at p. 1.

for the shortcomings of one's own trivial existence or, as Sageman suggests, "martyrdom lifts them from their insignificance."[77]

Anthony Garcia, one of the failed 2004 "Bluewater bomb" plotters, appears to epitomize this motif. Garcia left school at the age of 16 with few qualifications and no discernible ambitions, instead peripatetically drifting from one menial job to another. Prior to his arrest, Garcia had been working nightshifts stacking shelves at a local supermarket, but spent much of his time daydreaming about becoming a *Jihadi* fighter, with the Jihadist fantasy clearly providing a form of escapism from the daily tedium and drudgery of his otherwise uneventful life.[78] Both Richard Reid, the "shoe bomber" who tried to detonate an Atlantic flight in mid-air in December 2001, and Mukhtar Said Ibrahim, one of the failed 7/7 bombers, also potentially fit this profile well. Reid was raised in a largely dysfunctional home, quickly descending into petty street crime, and spent much of his early life in prison.[79] Similarly, Ibrahim, a child asylum seeker from Eritrea, spent much of his youth in and around drugs, street gangs, violence, and youth-offender institutions.[80] While the ennui thesis certainly goes some way toward accounting for Reid's and Ibrahim's fascination with martyrdom, both individuals also appear to have been drawn to radical Islam while incarcerated, suggesting that the espousal of Jihadism may possibly also constitute a form of recidivism that supplants more conventional modes of criminality.[81]

These latent feelings of purposelessness can, in some cases, be triggered or compounded by a sense of personal impotence, particularly if the individual begins to feel that the debilitating effects of an emasculating, atomizing, anomic modernity have rendered him into a mere husk of a man.[82] It is only via the redemptive prism of the chivalrous *Jihadi*

---

77. Awan, "Transitional Religiosity Experiences," p. 220; Martha Crenshaw, "Explaining Suicide Terrorism: A Review Essay," *Security Studies* 16.1 (2007), pp. 133–62, at p. 153; and Marc Sageman, *Leaderless Jihad: Terror Networks in the Twenty-first Century* (Philadelphia: University of Pennsylvania Press, 2008), p. 152.

78. BBC News, "Profile: Anthony Garcia," April 30, 2007, http://news.bbc.co.uk/1/hi/uk/6149798.stm.

79. BBC News, "Who is Richard Reid?" December 28, 2001, http://news.bbc.co.uk/1/hi/uk/1731568.stm.

80. Gardham and Johnston, "Terror Suspect."

81. Awan, "Transitional Religiosity Experiences," p. 213.

82. For more on masculinities in crises, see John Beynon, *Masculinities and Culture* (Buckingham: Open University Press, 2002) and Sally Robinson, *Marked Men: White Masculinity in Crisis* (New York: Columbia University Press, 2005).

warrior, through which he is recast as the community's champion as a result of his heroic sacrifice, that the individual then discerns a mechanism to reclaim agency, purpose, self-esteem, and manhood.[83] Muhammad Siddique Khan's martyrdom video emphatically refers to his coterie of martyrs as "real men," pointedly distinguishing them from the emasculated individuals who "stay at home."[84] The appeal to the valiant holy warrior or chivalrous knight is a recurring trope in Jihadist literature, and indeed it is no accident that Ayman al-Zawahiri's most important work is entitled, *Knights under the Prophet's Banner (Fursan Taht Rayah Al-Nabi)*, shrewdly seeking to exploit traditional Muslim male sensitivities around chivalry, honor, shame, and sacrifice.[85] The astute framing of this loss of dignity as being somehow sinful, offers up the prospect of redemption, and absolution through sacrifice and martyrdom.[86] Muhammad Siddique Khan exemplifies the transformative power offered by the martyr's mask, by undergoing the ready metamorphosis from children's learning mentor to heroic avenging soldier:

> I am directly responsible for protecting and avenging my Muslim brothers and sisters....And until you stop the bombing, gassing, imprisonment and torture of my people we will not stop this fight. We are at war and I am a soldier. Now you too will taste the reality of this situation. I make *dua* (pray) to Allah...to raise me amongst those whom I love like the prophets, the messengers, the martyrs and today's heroes like our beloved Sheikh Osama Bin Laden.[87]

However, martyrdom provides not just the means through which the powerless individual can reclaim agency and manhood, but increasingly the ability to brazenly usurp traditional authority and power normally reserved for clerics, and religious or political leaders. These shifts in influence are in part due to the fact that the individuals act predominantly within the New Media environment, whose largely egalitarian and democratizing nature

---

83. In some cases, the lascivious proffering of seventy-two heavenly maidens, yearning for the heroic martyr's embrace, may conveniently intersect with this apparent loss of virility.

84. Available at http://news.bbc.co.uk/1/hi/uk/4206800.stm.

85. Al-Zawahiri, *Fursan Taht Rayah Al-Nabi (Knights under the Prophet's Banner)*.

86. Farhad Khosrokhavar, *Suicide Bombers: Allah's New Martyrs* (London: Pluto Press, 2005), p. 133.

87. Available at http://news.bbc.co.uk/1/hi/uk/4206800.stm.

is conducive to the "levelling" of hierarchies of knowledge and power.[88] Equally importantly, this reconfiguration of power and authority is also predicated in large part upon the ascendancy of deeds over words. As I have contended elsewhere, the Jihadists' tangible response to perceived attack against the *ummah* is uniquely placed in the Muslim world, particularly when starkly juxtaposed against the apathy, weakness, or inaction of Muslim rulers, clergy, and even other Islamists. No matter how odious or counterproductive this response has been, the Jihadists cannot be accused by opponents of procrastination or indolence. Consequently, their manifest deeds enable them to undermine the credibility of other dissenting voices that use words alone, thus arrogating to themselves the authority of "Islamic officialdom."[89] As evidence of this trend within the British context, we might point to the example of Muhammad Siddique Khan, who despite being "theologically illiterate" nevertheless felt emboldened enough to disparage traditional Muslim scholars in Britain, suggesting that "real men" like himself, whose deeds and sacrifices were self-evident, were far more worthy of the Prophet's legacy: "Our so-called scholars today are content with their Toyotas and their semi-detached houses....If they fear the British Government more than they fear Allah then they must desist in giving talks, lectures and passing fatwas and they need to stay at home—they're useless—and leave the job to the real men, the true inheritors of the prophet."[90]

Conclusions: Hyperreality and the Media of Martyrdom

As mentioned above, the Arabic word for martyr in the Qur'an, *shahīd*, stems from the Arabic verb "to see" or "to witness" and, therefore, if martyrdom is understood to mean bearing witness through sacrifice and the publicity that surrounds it, then the arena that has largely enabled the publicizing of martyrdom has been the Internet. Indeed, it is now well

---

88. Manuel Castells, *Communication Power* (Oxford: Oxford University Press, 2009); Gary R. Bunt, *Islam in the Digital Age: E-Jihad, Online Fatwas, and Cyber Islamic Environments* (London: Pluto Press, 2003); Akil N. Awan and Mina Al-Lami, "Al-Qa'ida's Virtual Crisis," *The RUSI Journal* 154.1 (2009), pp. 56–64; and Awan, Hoskins, and O'Loughlin, *Radicalisation and the Media*, p. 34.

89. Awan, Hoskins, and O'Loughlin, *Radicalisation and the Media*, p. 44.

90. Available at http://news.bbc.co.uk/1/hi/uk/4206800.stm.

recognized that within the last decade the Internet has become the principal platform for the dissemination and mediation of the culture and ideology of Jihadism.[91] Furthermore, the unique multimedia environment of the Internet lends itself to the construction of a hyper-reality; the paradoxical notion of a mediated phenomenon that appears more real than reality itself.[92] This hyper-reality can be thought of as an enhanced reality that "cocoons" the participant in a wholly mediated environment concocted from a plethora of images, texts, and videos (which may have been manipulated in a myriad disingenuous ways), all filtered through the Jihadist lens through which the individual unwittingly experiences reality by proxy.[93]

It is in this cloistered yet highly immersive environment, that relies on emotive imagery and other affective content to venerate the martyr above all else, that the true power of the medium in lionizing martyrdom becomes patently evident. The appeal to the emotions or senses, through polished Jihadist video montages, stirring devotional songs, and fawning hagiographies of martyrs, in lieu of appeals to reason, or theological and ideological considerations, appears tailored toward the newer generation of young, diasporic, non-Arabic-speaking "digital natives" who now contribute disproportionately to the Jihadist demographic.[94] The hyper-reality of the Internet has been so eminently successful in engendering martyrdom that those individuals who substantially contribute to this arena are lauded as "celebrities," in some cases even by traditional Jihadist figureheads. Take, for instance, the example of Younis Tsouli (aka Irhaabi 007 or Terrorist 007), a web-savvy student in London whose contributions to the global *Jihad* were confined to autonomously promulgating the visual culture of Jihadism from his bedroom PC, but who nevertheless

91. Akil N. Awan, "Virtual Jihadist Media: Function, Legitimacy and Radicalizing Efficacy," *European Journal of Cultural Studies* 10.3 (2007), pp. 389–408.

92. Jean Baudrillard, *Simulations* (New York: Semiotext(e), 1983) and Umberto Eco, *Travels in Hyper Reality: Essays* (San Diego, Calif.: Harcourt Brace Jovanovich, 1987).

93. Akil N. Awan, "Jihadi Ideology in the New Media Environment," in Jeevan Deol and Zaheer Kazmi, eds., *Contextualising Jihadi Thought* (London: Hurst and Co., 2012), pp. 99–119, at p. 110.

94. The term "digital natives" is adapted from Prensky, and by which I mean a generation of young people who, having been born and raised in an omnipresent digital world, are so comfortably immersed in this virtual environment that they no longer make significant distinctions between it and the "real" world; see also Marc Prensky, "Digital Natives, Digital Immigrants, Part 1," *On the Horizon* 9.5 (2001), pp. 1–6; Awan, "Jihadi Ideology," p. 114; and Awan and Al-Lami, "Al-Qa'ida's Virtual Crisis," p. 62.

received considerable acclaim from Jihadists around the world, including Jihadist "luminaries" like Abu Musab al-Zarqawi (the infamous head of al-Qaeda in Iraq). The important role played by these "media Jihadists" in encouraging martyrdom is evident from Tsouli's fawning exchange with a fellow forum member, "Abuthaabit":

> This media work, I am telling you, is very important. Very, very, very, very... Because a lot of the funds brothers are getting is because they are seeing stuff like this coming out. Imagine how many people have gone [to Iraq] after seeing the situation because of the videos. Imagine how many of them could have been shahid [martyrs] as well.[95]

As Durkheim's seminal thesis demonstrated more than a century ago, motivations for suicide can be extraordinarily complex even under "normal" circumstances, and thus discerning the motivations for an act as complicated as taking one's life in a violent manner that deliberately harms others too, is no simple feat.[96] As shown by the life narratives of a number of Jihadists in Britain, individuals can engage in suicide terrorism for many reasons. However, I have tentatively suggested that this plethora of motivations and biographical diversity can be fundamentally accommodated by the following three ideal types: (1) a diversion of altruistic empathies, positing martyrdom as a strategic liberation strategy that equalizes the asymmetry of an unjust conflict, conducted on behalf of an "imagined," besieged community; (2) a highly ritualized form of sacralized, performative violence, in fulfilment of deeply felt salvific yearnings, and as a path to paradise; and (3) a mythical or heroic sacrifice, conferring immortality through the prospect of living on in the memory of others, and motivated by ennui or impotence.

Considering the field internationally, one may be able to identify the existence of a number of other potential motifs that ostensibly do not appear to have any resonance within the British context. Take, for example, poverty as a motivator for suicide terrorism, as evidenced by the case of Ajmal Kasab, the lone surviving terrorist from the 2008 Mumbai attacks, whose impoverished family were promised Rs 150,000 by Lashkar e-Taiba

---

95. "Internet Jihad: A World Wide Web of Terror," *Economist*, July 12, 2007, http://www.economist.com/node/9472498.

96. Durkheim, *Suicide*.

upon successful completion of the operation.[97] Alternatively, we might draw attention to the numerous cases of suicide terrorism in actual theaters of conflict that have been motivated by direct personal loss and trauma, such as those of the "Black Widows" in Chechnya, who in many cases volunteer for operations after having witnessed the deaths of their husbands or other family members by Russian forces.[98] Finally, we might identify certain communities, such as Palestinians in the Occupied Territories, who, as a response to occupation and to feelings of humiliation and shame, appear to promulgate a celebratory "cult of martyrdom," thus providing a socio-cultural sanction for suicide bombings.[99] While these three examples may seem far removed from the experiences of Jihadist martyrs in Britain, one of the central arguments of this chapter has been that feelings such as loss, trauma, occupation, humiliation, or poverty can be experienced vicariously, particularly through the hyper-reality offered by the New Media environment whose simulacra of injustice may be perceived by the participant to be as "real" as any lived reality.

As these examples demonstrate, even the relatively simple task of establishing linkages between experiences and actions can be problematic, and thus discerning motivations for martyrdom is clearly fraught with difficulties. Indeed, even in our final analysis, we are left, rather curiously, with a potentially unhelpful set of mutually exclusive dichotomies:

(1) The suicide terrorist as the **altruist**, selflessly sacrificing his life in defense of his community, in stark contrast to the **egoist** who selfishly uses his death to escape from ennui and impotence in order to claim agency, purpose, manhood, or salvation.

---

97. It is now fairly well understood that there is no obvious correlation between poverty and terrorism, however, that is not to suggest that poverty does not contribute to the prevalence of terrorism in some contexts; see Alan B. Krueger, *What Makes a Terrorist: Economics and the Roots of Terrorism* (Princeton: Princeton University Press, 2008) and Richard Esposito, "Mumbai Terrorist Wanted to "Kill and Die" and Become Famous," *ABC News*, December 3, 2008, http://abcnews.go.com/Blotter/story?id=6385015&page=1#.UVWuoFd25jU.

98. Speckhard and Akhmedova, "The Making of a Martyr," p. 468.

99. Mohammed M. Hafez, *Manufacturing Human Bombs: The Making of Palestinian Suicide Bombers* (Washington, D.C.: United States Institute of Peace Press, 2006).

(2) The suicide terrorist as the **profane**, this-worldly martyr who seeks fame, adulation, agency and political power, in stark contrast to the **sacred**, other-worldly martyr who seeks religious salvation and Paradise.[100]

Having devoted this chapter to elucidating the motivations and causes of suicide martyrdom, it seems fitting to conclude by reviewing the consequences and results of these actions too. In the overwhelming majority of cases, Jihadist suicide terrorism has been shown to be not only ineffectual, but largely counter-intuitive. Indeed, al-Qaeda and its affiliates, having diverted the energies of hundreds of young Muslim men and women by sending them to their premature deaths, have failed to achieve any of the aims with which Muslim publics may have been deemed to initially share some sympathy.[101] Instead, their strategy has proven to be grossly counter-productive, resulting in the invasion and occupation of two Muslim majority countries by Western powers, and the demise of al-Qaeda and its affiliates through the so-called Global War on Terror.[102] Perhaps more importantly, the Jihadists' penchant for bloodshed and violent excess, allied with their frighteningly dystopic and intolerant vision of a post-Jihadist future, has also led to widespread alienation among Muslim audiences.[103] Consequently, Jihadism is now largely a spent force, having simultaneously been both undermined and side-lined by the Arab Spring sweeping through the Middle East and North Africa which has been inspired by similar grievances, such as the hatred of Western-backed autocratic rulers and the lack of employment and other opportunities for the rapidly growing "youth bulge" in the Arab world.[104] Indeed, one might conclude by contrasting the senseless futility of the hundreds of al-Qaeda affiliated suicide martyrdoms that have wrought death and destruction,

---

100. The terms "this-worldly" and "other-worldly" are adapted from Francis Robinson, "Other-Worldly and This-Worldly Islam and the Islamic Revival: A Memorial Lecture for Wilfred Cantwell Smith," *Journal of the Royal Asiatic Society* 14.1 (2004), pp. 47–58.

101. For a discussion of these aims and grievances that had tacit support in the Muslim world, see Michael Scheuer, *Imperial Hubris: Why the West is Losing the War on Terror* (Washington, D.C.: Potomac, 2008).

102. Although one could argue that terrorist strategies are often predicated upon the expectation that a terrorist act will provoke a vastly disproportionate response from the enemy, forcing it to reveal its true nature and thus forcing the otherwise apathetic masses into support for the group; on which, see Beiner, in this volume.

103. Awan, Hoskins, and O'Loughlin, *Radicalisation and the Media*, p. 45.

104. Fawaz A. Gerges, *The Rise and Fall of Al-Qaeda* (Oxford: Oxford University Press, 2011).

but little else, with the suicide martyrdom of a young *Jihad* Tunisian protestor, Mohamed Bouazizi, whose self-immolation proved to be the catalyst for not only the successful socio-political revolt in Tunisia but also provided the critical spark for the Arab Spring that has potentially transformed the Arab political landscape forever.

I I

Martyrdom and Hostage Executions in the Iraq War

THE CASES OF KENNETH BIGLEY AND MARGARET HASSAN

Alex Houen

OVER THE LAST four decades militant Islamic groups have executed their enemies on numerous occasions, and the increase in these killings over recent years has engendered a gruesome new genre: hostage-execution videos. In the 1980s and 1990s, recruitment videos made by Islamist groups were mostly comprised of footage from conflicts in Afghanistan, Bosnia, and Chechnya, accompanied by rousing speeches from militant leaders. In 2002, however, an Algerian organization, the Salafist Group for Preaching and Combat (GSPC), produced a recruitment video that included footage showing militants cutting the throats of three Algerian soldiers.[1] That year also saw the abduction and videoed decapitation of the American journalist Daniel Pearl by a group calling itself The National Movement for the Restoration of Pakistani Sovereignty. Filmed hostage executions—often involving beheading with a knife—subsequently burgeoned in number before peaking in the Iraq war between 2004 and 2005. By late 2005, 273 foreigners from thirty-seven countries had been taken hostage by Iraqi militants, and by May that year thirty-five of those

---

1. Jason Burke, "Terror Video Used to Lure UK Muslims," *Guardian*, January 27, 2002, http://www.guardian.co.uk/uk/2002/jan/27/september11.afghanistan.

foreigners had been executed, six of them by beheading.[2] It is important to note, however, that the number of foreign victims was far fewer than the number of Iraqi nationals who were abducted and executed as a result of conflict spreading between Shi'ite and Sunni communities in 2005. The political and religious motives behind the abductions and executions were therefore varied: some were carried out primarily for sectarian reasons; some were committed as part of holy war (*Jihad*) against foreign occupiers; some were for reasons of nationalism and political gain; some had ransom payments as their goal; and many of the instances involved a mixture of these motives. Indeed, even videoed executions by avowedly religious militants manifested degrees of ambivalence. On the one hand, as Farhad Khosrokhavar has pointed out, the killers' use of a knife or sword is intended "to recall the feats of arms of Islam's heroes" and to cast the victim as "an animal sacrificed in a holy action."[3] Such practice also bears allusion to the tradition of capital punishment meted out in accord with *Shari'a* law in Saudi Arabia, which executed ninety people by beheading in 2005 alone. On the other hand, the use of video technology disseminated via email, satellite television, and the Internet is evidence of how Islamists have embraced contemporary technology, even if they do so in part to strike at Western audiences through their own media networks. Writing about Iraqi militants' videos, Jason Burke commented that "the executions are now cascading onto the internet. They are half-shown by our own news organisations on the screens that are now in our pubs, in so many of our public spaces, in our kitchens and bedrooms, even on our mobile phones."[4] But the videos were not only meant for Western audiences; they were also intended to recruit sympathizers and so to establish networks of support through the Internet and media. For Khosrokhavar, this kind of networked Islamist activism is "a by-product of a plural modernity that no longer has any centre of gravity," and he associates this in particular with the innovations of al-Qaeda, whose martyrs, he claims, "experience [tragedy] through cables, television and digital media."[5] In

---

2. Pete Lentini and Muhammad Bakashmar, "Jihadist Beheading: A Convergence of Technology, Theology, and Teleology?" *Studies in Conflict and Terrorism* 30 (2007), p. 317.

3. Farhad Khosrokhavar, *Suicide Bombers: Allah's New Martyrs*, trans. David Macey (London: Pluto, 2005), pp. 68–69.

4. Jason Burke, "Theatre of Terror," *Observer*, November 21, 2004, http://www.guardian.co.uk/theobserver/2004/nov/21/features.review7.

5. Khosrokhavar, *Suicide Bombers*, pp. 151 and 233.

my view it is too reductive to argue that al-Qaeda's activities are simply a "by-product" of such modernity, but I do think that the martyrdom and militancy of contemporary Islamist groups need to be seen as involving exchanges between religion and secularization, as well as culture and media technology.

In previous work that I have done on suicide bombing I discussed how various Islamic militant groups view the practice as a "martyrdom operation"; a martyrdom (istishad or shahadat) that needs to be understood in terms of bearing witness to community and political cause as well as religious faith.[6] Looking back at the recent evolution of radical Islamic notions of martyrdom I argued that they also frequently evince cross-cultural and syncretistic exchanges. The writings of the Iranian theologian Ali Shariati are just one example, drawing as they do on European existential philosophy while revising a notion of Shi'ite militant martyrdom for the Iran-Iraq war.[7] In the last two decades, suicide bombings have also frequently been complex affairs in mixing theology, politics, and culture, for the bearing witness to faith performed by the martyr (shahid) is usually done in part by video testimony, martyr cards, posters, or other forms of cultural production.[8] All of this led me to argue that the contemporary shahid does not simply bear witness to religious faith; more modern concepts of revolution (thawra) and sacrifice (fida') are also frequently at stake, such that "martyrdom operations" manifest wider exchanges among matters of politics, culture, religion, and the mass media.

In this chapter I shall consider how such matters of exchange were evident in the kidnapping, videoing, and execution of hostages by militants in the Iraq war. I will focus on two cases: those of Kenneth Bigley and of Margaret Hassan, both of whom were kidnapped and executed within weeks of each other in 2004. The case of Bigley is important partly because it shows his kidnappers casting him as an abject secular subject that is intended to contrast with the faithful agency of a Jihadi martyr. With

---

6. Alex Houen, "Sacrificial Militancy and the Wars around Terror," in Elleke Boehmer and Stephen Morton, eds., Terror and the Postcolonial (Oxford: Wiley-Blackwell, 2009), pp. 113–40.

7. See, for example, Ali Shariati, "A Discussion of Shahid," in Mehdi Abedi and Gary Legenhausen, eds., Jihad and Shahadat: Struggle and Martyrdom in Islam (Houston: The Institute for Research and Islamic Studies, 1986), pp. 230–43.

8. On this point, see, for example, Anne Marie Oliver and Paul F. Steinberg, The Road to Martyrs' Square: A Journey into the World of the Suicide Bomber (Oxford: Oxford University Press, 2005), part 2.

Hassan, what comes to light more through the responses to her death in the British and Irish media is the issue of modern Christian martyrdom. In both cases, the matter of testifying to religious and political beliefs pertains to the militants' dissemination of the hostage's statements via videos that were usually broadcast on *Al Jazeera* and radical websites before being reported by other national presses, television stations, and Internet media. As I shall show, once the press and media are involved in such cases testimony turns ambivalent, for it becomes unclear as to what the hostages and kidnappers are seen to stand for. The equivocation around media representation also bears on crises of political representation, particularly regarding liberal democracy and secularization. Before I turn to discussion of Bigley and Hassan, though, I shall first briefly outline the importance of bearing witness in Islamic and Christian conceptions of martyrdom, and offer consideration of how those conceptions have been affected by pressures of politics and secularization.

Like the Greek word *marturos*, the Qu'ranic Arabic word *shahid* (plural *shuhada*) denotes both "witness" and "martyr." The Qu'ranic teachings on martyrdom are diverse. When the word *shahid* is used, it is primarily in the sense of bearing witness. *Shahid* bears the same root as the word for the Muslim profession of faith, the *shahada*—"There is no God but God, and Muhammad is his prophet"—and there are numerous instances in the Qu'ran that discuss the importance of being a *shahid* simply in the sense of attesting to the good of the Muslim community, or the evils of those opposing it (see, for example, 2:143). There are very few passages in the Qu'ran that do use *shahid* more in the sense of a martyr prepared to give up his life in fighting for the Islamic faith (see 3:138–42, and 3:169–70). In general, then, the Qu'ranic passages on martyrdom do not incline it toward militant sacrifice, and neither do early *hadith* writings (records of the Prophet Muhammad's sayings and doings), which served more to widen the conception of a *shahid* as a person who bore testament to Islam simply by living a virtuous life and dying a death worthy of paradise. For this reason, scholars such as Talal Asad have been right to take issue with claims that suicide bombing is a form of sacrificial militancy that incarnates classical Islamic notions of martyrdom and sacrifice.[9] Asad does, however, concede that sacrificial militancy has come to play a part in the development of radical ideologies that posit suicide bombing as a "martyrdom operation," but he goes on to argue that "the suicide bomber

---

9. Talal Asad, *On Suicide Bombing* (New York: Columbia University Press, 2007), pp. 43–45.

belongs . . . to a modern Western tradition of armed conflict for the defense of a free political community."[10]

My view is that while Asad is right to associate suicide bombing with modern Western conflict he understates the role of Islamic revisions of martyrdom that have cast it in terms of sacrificial militancy and holy war. Those revisions largely occurred through the long tradition of *Jihad* literature that dates back to the eighth century. Theological developments in Shi'ism have also played a part in linking martyrdom to militancy.[11] Since the seventeenth century, it has been the spread of European colonialism in Muslim countries that has led to repeated debates about martyrdom in relation to *Jihad*.[12] As those debates were largely inspired by nationalism, they also introduced a broadening in the character of martyrdom such that it bore testament to exchanges between the religious, political, and cultural. As David Cook has stated: "Calls for *Jihad* were consequently muted and often seen as subsidiary to a general pan-Arab or nationalist call to unity against the foreign invader. Many nationalist movements have lists of *shuhada*, even though the cause in which they died was not Muslim, strictly speaking."[13] Nationalist revisions of martyrdom arose from political exigency, just as subsequent revisions indicate pressures of modernization and Western secularization which different Muslim countries have embraced and resisted to varying degrees. These revisions need to be seen as exchanges in the sense of interfusions, for while religious militant groups have cast martyrdom politically, the sacrificial militancy of secular groups has also been inspired by religious conceptions of martyrdom. Palestine is an interesting case in point. As Asad points out, Palestinians have not seen martyrdom in the conflict with Israel as being limited to militants; the term can be applied to any Palestinian killed as a result of Israeli military operations.[14] Regarding militant organizations, though, the interfusions around martyrdom that I have mentioned are evident in the use of strikingly similar imagery by both nationalist and religious groups. For example, in the second intifada a martyr card from the nationalist

---

10. Ibid., p. 63.

11. See Khosrokhavar, *Suicide Bombers*, chap. 1.

12. See David Cook, *Understanding Jihad* (Berkeley and Los Angeles: University of California Press, 2005), chaps. 4 and 5.

13. David Cook, *Martyrdom in Islam* (Cambridge: Cambridge University Press, 2007), p. 136.

14. Asad, *On Suicide Bombing*, p. 49.

organization Fatah typically stated "My country is my bride, and her *mahr* [bride-price] is my martyrdom," while a card for an Islamic group would state "Blood is the [bride-price] of the precious gifts"[15]—a reference to the delights awaiting the *shahid* in paradise.

While it is problematic to discount the influence of Islamic revisions of martyrdom on suicide bombings and other militant operations, it is also true that recent developments show that what is often in evidence with such operations is the jettisoning of traditional Islamic notions of martyrdom in favor of practices that are expedient. For Khosrokhavar, the influence of the mass media and modern secularization in Muslim countries has been fundamental in promulgating values of individualism, worldliness, and celebrity—values which are difficult to attain, he points out, if you are a Muslim living in Palestine, Chechnya, or Algeria. One consequence of this, he suggests, is a novel form of martyrdom in which "the sacred is not so much a theologically defined Islamic ideal as a desire to be part of the world, to be recognised as having a right to one's identity."[16] Again, such a view becomes reductive if it is used to support a claim that al-Qaeda is a "by-product" of "plural modernity" and thus working for secular and not religious beliefs. It is true, though, that key members of al-Qaeda have been influential in individualizing martyrdom, not only by virtue of the notoriety and media interest garnered by some of them (particularly bin Laden) but also by asserting that waging *Jihad* is an individual responsibility for Muslims around the world. On that score the 1998 fatwa "Jihad against Jews and Crusaders" issued by the World Islamic Front (WIF) with signatures by Osama bin Laden and other al-Qaeda members was an important development. After denouncing occupations and invasions of Muslim holy lands by America, the fatwa announced that "the ruling to kill the Americans and their allies—civilians and military—is an individual duty for every Muslim who can do it in any country in which it is possible to do it...in order for their armies to move out of all the lands of Islam, defeated and unable to threaten any Muslim."[17] With classical Islam, *Jihad* was undertaken by a Muslim community led by the Caliph (chief civil and religious leader) or an *imam*; in the absence of a Caliph the WIF fatwa encouraged individuals to see *Jihad*

---

15. Both statements quoted in Oliver and Steinberg, *The Road to Martyrs' Square*, p. 76.

16. Khosrokhavar, *Suicide Bombers*, p. 46.

17. World Islamic Front, "Jihad against Jews and Crusaders" (1998), http://www.library.cornell.edu/colldev/mideast/wif.htm.

as their own responsibility. And with militant groups taking holy war into their own hands there has been a disturbing consequence with radical conceptions of martyrdom: militants have been deemed to be martyrs by virtue of killing enemy civilians. As Ivan Strenski has noted, this conception of martyrdom (which is particularly relevant to suicide bombings) can be seen as an "entirely modern innovation."[18] That clearly bears on the execution of hostages I will be discussing, and the extent to which this innovation in martyrdom implicates interfusions among aspects of religion, politics, and the media is something that I shall go on to explore in relation to the cases of Bigley and Hassan.

What about Christian martyrdom? Are there similar arguments to be made about it fusing with politics and secularization in modern times? As in Islam, dying for one's faith and bearing witness to it have certainly been intimately connected in Christianity. As Andrew Chandler and Anthony Harvey have pointed out, there have also been various attempts over the centuries to organize Christian witnesses and martyrs into categories, though there has been little uniformity to that endeavor.[19] Originally, living a life of Christian *martyria* meant witnessing to faith in Jesus Christ as Son of God. Over the course of the first three centuries of Christianity, martyrdom became dogmatically associated with religious persecution and being killed in hatred of one's faith (*in odium fidei*). Writings such as Tertullian's *To the Martyrs*, Origen's *On Martyrs*, and Eusebius's martyrology document the growth of "red martyrdom," but by the third century c.e. there was also a shift to the "white martyrdom" associated with living an ascetic life of piety.[20] With the waning of Rome's persecution of Christians, such white martyrdom was encapsulated by Saint Athanasius's description of Saint Anthony as a man who was a martyr every day of his life.

As with Islam, then, the early conceptions of martyrdom in Christianity are in no way limited to bearing witness to faith in holy war or through sacrificial militancy. "Red martyrdom" was, however, repeatedly reprised in the Crusades and in later wars between Catholics and Protestants in

18. Ivan Strenski, "Sacrifice, Gift and the Social Logic of Muslim 'human bombers'," *Terrorism and Political Violence* 15.3 (2003), pp. 1–34.

19. Andrew Chandler and Anthony Harvey, "Introduction," in *The Terrible Alternative: Christian Martyrdom in the Twentieth Century* (London: Cassell, 1998), p. 1.

20. See Josef Lössl, "An Early Christian Identity Crisis Triggered by Changes in the Discourse of Martyrdom," in Johan Leemans, ed., *More than a Memory: The Discourse of Martyrdom and the Construction of Christian Identity in the History of Christianity* (Leuven: Peeters, 2005), pp. 97–98.

Europe.[21] While it has persisted into the twentieth century and beyond, so too have conceptions of white martyrdom which have also been inflected with matters of politics and secularization, in line with ecclesiastical engagement with them. For example, the Second Vatican Council (1962–65) was instrumental in affirming a role of political responsibility for the Catholic Church—the Council's document *Gaudium et Spes* (1965) asserting, among other things, the right to economic justice and political equality for poor individuals and nations. Not only has the Church's political turn aided the development of Catholic "liberation theology," it has also been implicated in linking Christian martyrs to political conflicts.[22] More canonizations and beatifications of martyrs were made by the Catholic Church in the twentieth century than ever before, and these have included figures who died in numerous conflicts of previous centuries, including the French Revolution, the Spanish Civil War, and World War II. For Chandler and Harvey such developments are indicative of how Christian conceptions of martyrdom have changed:

> [I]n the twentieth century certain Christian cultures have progressively identified the churches with the Enlightenment values of freedom, democracy, and human rights.... This shift in theological priorities has produced a different set of conditions for possible martyrdom. Christians are now threatened and attacked, not because they profess the Christian religion, but because they show solidarity with those whose rights, dignity and livelihood are diminished by an uncaring or dictatorial regime.... If the self-sacrifice of a [Dietrich] Bonhoeffer, a Martin Luther King, a [Janani] Luwum, or a [Oscar] Romero appears to share with that of many others the motivation of a this-worldly commitment to human freedom and dignity in the face of tyranny, it has also been nourished and strengthened by an authentically twentieth-century Christian spirituality.[23]

In identifying a motivation of "this-worldly commitment to human freedom," Chandler and Harvey are alluding to the Latin sense of *saeculum*

---

21. See, for example, Jonathan Ebel, "Christianity and Violence," in Andrew R. Murphy, ed., *The Blackwell Companion to Religion and Violence* (Oxford: Wiley-Blackwell, 2011), pp. 149–62.

22. See Anna Peterson, "Martyrdom and Christian Identity in Latin America (1970–1990)," in Leemans, *More than a Memory*, pp. 435–50.

23. Chandler and Harvey, "Introduction," pp. 7–8.

as "world," thereby implying that the change in Christian martyrdom has arisen from involvement in secular affairs and institutions. I have stated that I will examine interfusions among aspects of religion, politics, and the media to analyze whether innovations in Islamic martyrdom are evident in the executions of Kenneth Bigley and Margaret Hassan. I shall also examine whether the exchanges of religion and secular politics that inhere in a "this-worldly" concept of Christian martyrdom are implicated in the two cases. In turning to discussion of them I should first emphasize that much of the material I had to consult in researching them was harrowing, particularly the photographs and videos, and for that reason I have chosen not to reproduce relevant images. I am also acutely aware of the sensitive nature of these cases, and I hope that by discussing them I can contribute to a better critical understanding of the religious, political, and cultural factors that are at stake in them.

Abduction and Execution of Kenneth Bigley

Kenneth Bigley was working with a Kuwaiti construction firm in Baghdad when he was kidnapped on September 16, 2004, along with two American colleagues, Jack Hensley and Eugene Armstrong. Responsibility for the abductions was swiftly taken by Abu-Musab al-Zarqawi's group, *Tawhid wal-Jihad* (Monotheism and Holy War), which, four months earlier, had kidnapped and beheaded Nick Berg, a freelance American contractor.[24] On kidnapping Bigley and his colleagues, the militants swiftly issued an ultimatum stating that they would kill the men in 48 hours unless the Coalition forces freed all Iraqi female prisoners. In response the UK and US governments stated that there were only two Iraqi women incarcerated, and it was swiftly arranged for both women to be released because no charges had been brought against them. Armstrong was nevertheless videoed being beheaded on September 20. Hensley suffered the same fate the following day, leaving the 62-year-old Bigley to beg the UK Prime Minister Tony Blair to help him in a video aired by the television station *Al Jazeera* on September 22:

> Please, please release the female prisoners who are held in Iraqi prisons. Please help them, I need you to help, Mr Blair. You are now

24. See Ariana Eunjung Cha, "Tape Shows U.S. Hostage Being Beheaded in Iraq," *Washington Post*, May 11, 2004, http://www.washingtonpost.com/wp-dyn/articles/A17639-2004May11.html.

the only person on God's earth that I can speak to. Please, please help me to see my wife who cannot go on without me.... Mr Blair, I am nothing to you, it's just one person in the whole of the United Kingdom, that's all. With a family like you've got.... I'm nothing, am only a small man. I'm nothing, I have no political gains. I have no ambitions of grandeur.[25]

One thing that has not been picked up by commentators is that al-Zarqawi's group forced Bigley to perform as an abject *antithesis* to the portrayal of Islamic militants immortalized on al-Qaeda's online martyrologies. As Mohammed Hafez has noted of the organization's online "Biographies of Eminent Martyrs": "Almost every clip of suicide bombers in Iraq shows the bombers as happy, eager to do the will of God. They usually wave goodbye with smiles on their faces, running toward their explosive-laden vehicles, reflecting the theme of joy in sacrifice in the path of God."[26] Such footage stands in stark contrast to the video imagery showing Bigley (and other hostages) anxious, breaking down, and pleading for their lives. Bigley's September 22 statement does not appear to be scripted, but he has clearly been forced into making it and directed in terms of what to say. Addressing Blair as "the only person on God's earth I can speak to" suggested that if there was any faith at stake for Bigley, it was not religious. As his statement had been directed under duress the extent to which it amounts to a testament of faith in Blair is also questionable. And if the matter of Iraqi female prisoners was largely a fiction, it served to show that Bigley was so fearful of dying he would even make a plea for what he did not know to be true. He certainly did not state a preparedness to die for Blair, or democracy, or some other ideal. Instead, Bigley was presented as *not* making a stand, which fed into his assertion that he stood for nothing but his familial ordinariness: "Mr Blair, I am nothing to you. It's just one person in the whole of the United Kingdom. With a family like you've got." Contrary to Khosrokhavar's view that the media martyrdom of contemporary Islamists like al-Qaeda is partly a bid for recognition of identity, al-Zarqawi's video of Bigley evidenced something else: masked militants using video to portray Western liberal individualism as a nullity.

---

25. Anon., "Ken Bigley's Transcript in Full," *Mail Online*, September 23, 2004, http://www.dailymail.co.uk/news/article-318867/Ken-Bigleys-statement-full.html.

26. Mohammed M. Hafez, "Martyrdom Mythology in Iraq: How Jihadists Frame Suicide Terrorism in Videos and Biographies," *Terrorism and Political Violence* 19 (2007), p. 106.

Presenting Bigley's citizenship as inconsequential also bears on the very system of political representation to which he was forced to appeal. That Blair and his government could not be seen to negotiate or bargain with al-Zarqawi's group showed that UK democracy could only go so far in representing individual members of the body politic. As the UK Foreign Secretary Jack Straw made clear, "I'm afraid to say [Bigley's appeal] cannot alter the position of the British government."[27] If the video made it questionable as to whether Bigley represented anything, it also raised questions about whether British democracy was capable of representing its citizens adequately. Those questions were raised explicitly at the end of the video with three frames of parallel Arabic and English text: "Does a British worth anything [sic] to Blair?"; "Will he try to save the hostage or will he not care?"; "Do leaders really care about their people?"[28] Effectively, then, al-Zarqawi's group was showing Bigley's life to be at risk for being the citizen of a democratic government that could not respond to his plight; a government that was nevertheless intent on keeping troops in Iraq mostly to help install democracy in it.

Bigley's captors may have been intent on making him a figure of liberal abjection, but the attention his video provoked swiftly turned him into a local, national, and international figure. The global exposure enabled one of his brothers, Paul Bigley, to campaign on his behalf and gain the support of various political figures around the world, including Colonel Muammar Gaddafi in Libya, the Palestinian leader Yasser Arafat, the Irish *taoiseach* Bertie Ahern, and the Sinn Fein leader Gerry Adams.[29] The support offered by the Irish government included issuing Bigley with an Irish passport (*in absentia*) on the grounds that his mother was Irish, then airing scanned images of it on *Al Jazeera*. As Bigley's brother Paul explained, the hope was that this could counteract the militants' desire to make an example of him as a British citizen: "The fact that Ken is Irish and that we have now proven that he is

27. Quoted in Rory McCarthy, "Mr Blair, I Don't Want to Die. Help Me See My Wife and Son Again," *The Guardian*, September 23, 2004, http://www.guardian.co.uk/world/2004/sep/23/iraq.iraq2.

28. Quoted in Anon., "Ken Bigley's Transcript in Full."

29. See, for example, "Adams Pleas for Bigley Release," *BBC News* online, September 30, 2004, http://news.bbc.co.uk/1/hi/northern_ireland/3704394.stm; and "Gaddafi Asks for Bigley Release," *BBC News* online, October 6, 2004, http://news.bbc.co.uk/1/hi/uk/3721090.stm.

Irish...I do not think there is any way that even the baddest people would harm an Irish person."[30] That sentiment turned out to be tragically jejune. On September 29 another video of Bigley was released of him in a cage wearing an orange jumpsuit like those worn by inmates of the US military camps of Guantánamo Bay—the abduction was thus partly presented by the militants as a macabre parodic response to indefinite detention in the camps. In his statement, Bigley followed his captors' direction in denouncing Blair as liar. His cooperation with them, along with his newly established Irish nationality, were not sufficient to dissuade Bigley's captors from beheading him.

The gruesome execution video of Bigley was not broadcast by *Al Jazeera* but was posted on Islamist websites and shows al-Zarqawi decapitating Bigley with a knife while his fellow militants inspire him with cries of "*Allahu Akbar*" (God is great). The use of a blade is relevant to Khosrokhavar's assertion: such beheadings present the victim like "an animal sacrificed in a holy action" and also hark back to the traditional association of sword and *Jihad*.[31] The attendant cries of *Allahu Akbar* are relevant to Strenski's point that radical Islamic revisions of martyrdom extend to bearing witness to one's faith by taking someone else's life. Suicide bombers do both simultaneously, and as Oliver and Steinberg have noted regarding the Israel-Palestine conflict, it has not been uncommon for these Palestinian bombers to be "certificated" for martyrdom as a "self-sacrificer" (*fida'i*) only after they have killed an Israeli or a Palestinian collaborator.[32] As for the tragic figure of Bigley, he was clearly in no position to bear witness to faith in religion or politics. Yet the perceived hopelessness of his situation is what prompted various political and religious leaders to make a public show of supporting and representing him. The Muslim Council of Britain (MCB), for example, sent a delegation to Iraq to plead for his life, the MCB's secretary Iqbal Sacranie stating "this is an action that is supported by communities around the world and a very clear message, as far as our faith is concerned, which has to be conveyed."[33] In Liverpool, Bigley's home town, his death was marked with

---

30. Quoted in Ewen MacAskill, Jamie Wilson, Brian Whitaker, and Rory McCarthy, "Bigley Given Irish Passport in Move to Sway Captors," *Guardian*, October 6, 2004, http://www.guardian.co.uk/world/2004/oct/06/iraq.iraq.

31. Khosrokhavar, *Suicide Bombers*, p. 69.

32. Oliver and Steinberg, *The Road to Martyrs' Square*, p. 73.

33. Quoted in Helen Carter, "Bigley's Brother Says Blair Has to Go," *Guardian*, September 28, 2004, http://www.guardian.co.uk/world/2004/sep/28/iraq.iraq.

a two-minute silence in churches, cathedrals, mosques, businesses, and homes across the city. A memorial service for Bigley on November 13 in the city's Anglican cathedral was even attended by Blair who read from St Paul's letter to the Corinthians, including the passage "Love does not delight in evil but rejoices with truth. It always protects, always trusts, always hopes, always perseveres."[34]

I cite such developments to relate them to the point I made earlier about contemporary martyrdom involving complex interfusions of politics, culture, religion, and the mass media. To sum up here: what we see in the case of Bigley's suffering and execution is a case of Islamic militants presenting him as a form of secular anti-martyr in order to contrast with their own political conviction and religious faith, and to reflect badly on citizens of liberal democracy. In response, numerous political and religious leaders took up the plight of Bigley to bear testament to their own desire to represent and support him, and thereby show him to stand for *something*; namely, their belief in the rights, dignity, and sanctity of human lives, a belief that in turn was based on their faith in the institutions of religion and government to safeguard those things. On the face of it, that sounds as though the responses bore hallmarks of the kind of "this-worldly" martyrdom that Chandler and Harvey see as being engaged with secularized values of freedom, democracy, and human rights. Yet the militants' dramatization of Bigley's anti-martyrdom can also be seen as resulting in a bifurcation of bearing witness and professing faith that does not accord with the kind of martyrdom that Chandler and Harvey describe. The bifurcation splits along the following lines: the political and religious leaders publicly bore witness to Bigley's persecution and suffering, while professing faith in various things (religious and secular) that he himself was not able to stand for. I shall offer more consideration of relations between martyrdom and secularization in my conclusion. For now, let us bear those bifurcations in mind while considering the case of Margaret Hassan who, after her execution, was declared to be a Christian martyr by the Archbishop of Westminster Cathedral, Cardinal Cormac Murphy-O'Connor.

---

34. See "Memorial Service for Ken Bigley," *BBC News* online, November 13, 2004, http://news.bbc.co.uk/1/hi/england/merseyside/4008389.stm.

Abduction and Execution of Margaret Hassan

Margaret Hassan was born in Ireland to a Catholic family, married an Iraqi national Tahseen ali Hassan when she was 27, and moved to Iraq in 1972 where she initially worked with the British Council. She had British, Irish, and Iraqi citizenship. She became fluent in Arabic and remained in Baghdad during the 1991 Gulf War, after which the British Council suspended operations in Iraq. She then took up a post with CARE International, a secular nongovernmental organization (NGO) specializing in fighting poverty and assisting in humanitarian operations. By the time Hassan was kidnapped on October 19, 2004, just twelve days after Bigley's execution, she was head of CARE's Iraqi operations.[35] An outspoken critic of the UN sanctions against Iraq, Hassan was also one of several aid workers who in the lead-up to the Iraq war voiced concerns to the UN and the UK parliament about the consequences of military action for the Iraqi people.[36] Unfortunately, none of those aspects of her career seemed to have made a difference to her kidnappers. With the release of their first video of her there were evident similarities to Bigley's predicament. She was made to address Tony Blair directly and ask for British troops not to be deployed to the north of Iraq. In the second video aired on *Al Jazeera* one of her captors prompted her to stick to the text of a forced confession in which she said that "we [CARE] worked with the occupation forces."[37] Hassan's directed speech thus echoed statements Bigley was forced to make, and she pleaded with Blair to accede to the demands she was relaying so that she could escape Bigley's fate. Like him, she was eventually executed wearing a blindfold and an orange jumpsuit.

There were, however, significant contrasts to Bigley's situation. Whereas al-Zarqawi's group made a show of publicizing itself with banners and uniforms in its videos of him, Hassan's captors remained anonymous and stayed off-screen apart from in the final video when one of them killed her not with a knife but by shooting her. And whereas al-Zarqawi

---

35. See Jason Burke, "Obituary: Margaret Hassan," *Guardian*, November 17, 2004, http://www.guardian.co.uk/society/2004/nov/17/internationalaidanddevelopment. guardianobituaries.

36. Denis J. Halliday, "Margaret Hassan" [obituary], *Independent*, December 11, 2004, http://www.independent.co.uk/news/obituaries/margaret-hassan-6156161.html.

37. Quoted in Robert Fisk, "The Tragic Last Moments of Margaret Hassan," *Independent*, August 7, 2008, http://www.independent.co.uk/opinion/commentators/fisk/the-tragic-last-moments-of-margaret-hassan-887135.html.

and his followers seemed intent on contrasting Bigley's abject pleas with their own religious zeal, Hassan's captors used her more as a political and financial bargaining chip. While Hassan, too, was made to ask for the release of Iraqi female prisoners, her captors appeared to be more politically astute than Bigley's when they filmed her relaying their demands about the deployment of Coalition troops the day after the UK government announced it would move 850 soldiers from the Black Watch regiment to a region near Baghdad.[38] The militants' videos were thus seemingly made not for individual or group publicity so much as for political strategy. Subsequent reports detailing the group's demand for a ransom of $10 million, however, suggest that its motives were also largely criminal.[39]

Having already been burned by the publicized disaster of the Bigley affair, Blair and Jack Straw were reportedly asked to "take a back seat in appeals" for Hassan's release, leaving it to CARE International to take the lead.[40] While Bigley's employment for the Kuwaiti construction firm was seen by al-Zarqawi's group as a form of collaboration in the war effort, Hassan's aid work was a very different matter. Indeed, al-Zarqawi's group itself posted a statement on the Internet calling on her captors to release her unless there was proof of her collaboration.[41] Her work for CARE also led to a different tenor of appeal from the Irish government. While for Bigley the Irish Prime Minister Bertie Ahern had hoped that an Irish passport would successfully testify to his not being an enemy of Iraq, in Hassan's case Ahern appealed to her kidnappers by stating: "Margaret has no political associations. She represents nobody but the vulnerable and the poor. Your quarrel is not with Margaret. Nor is it with the Irish people, who have been a firm friend of the Arab nations."[42] In Bigley's

---

38. Lee Glendinning, "Tearful Hassan Begs for Release of All Female Prisoners in Iraq in New Video," *Guardian*, October 28, 2004, http://www.guardian.co.uk/society/2004/oct/28/internationalaidanddevelopment.politicsandiraq.

39. See, for example, Richard Owen, "Margaret Hassan's Kidnappers Looked for €8m to Spare Her Life," *Irish Independent News*, January 31, 2006, http://www.independent.ie/world-news/margaret-hassans-kidnappers-looked-for-8m-to-spare-her-life-120271.html.

40. Peter Beaumont and Jason Burke, "Plea for Iraqi Kidnap Clues," *Observer*, October 24, 2004, http://www.guardian.co.uk/society/2004/oct/24/internationalaidanddevelopment.politicsandiraq.

41. Kim Sengupta, "Al-Zarqawi Group Calls for Irish Hostage to be Set Free," *Irish Independent News*, November 6, 2004, http://www.independent.ie/national-news/alzarqawi-group-calls-for-irish-hostage-to-be-set-free-142013.html.

42. Quoted in Richard Norton-Taylor and Michael Howard, "Kidnappers Threaten to Hand Aid Worker over to Zarqawi," *Guardian*, November 3, 2004, http://www.guardian.co.uk/world/2004/nov/03/iraq.internationalaidanddevelopment.

case the militants' presentation of him as someone who stood for nothing was countered by depictions of him in the British press and media as an unassuming, ordinary family man. In contrast, Hassan's aid work was emphasized by journalists, politicians, and religious leaders to portray her as someone who stood not for family but for the suffering of countless others. And if the militants who executed her did not care about that, the Catholic Church certainly did.

Although it was reported that Hassan had converted to Islam, this was not in fact the case; she had retained her Catholic faith throughout her life. Reflecting on that life in the homily he delivered at the requiem service for her in Westminster Cathedral, Cardinal Murphy-O'Connor linked Hassan's faith, care work, suffering, and execution to declare her a modern martyr:

> She was a peacemaker in a time of seemingly endless wars; she hungered and thirsted for justice for the Iraqi people; she was persecuted—brutally slain—because she was working in the cause of right....I have called her a "martyr." I use the word advisedly; the word "martyr" means "witness." Margaret witnessed, in both her life and her death, to the act of loving. Because Margaret's love was of the kind that is obviously nourished by the faith that was so important to her, her life, her death, and her way of loving have reminded people of her Master, of whom it was said, Greater love than this hath no one that a man lay down his life for his friends [John 5:13]. That is why I do not hesitate to describe Margaret as a martyr, here, in a Christian place.[43]

We can relate these statements back to the argument of Chandler and Harvey that I cited in my introduction; is Hassan's declared martyrdom exemplary of a "shift" whereby Christians are attacked not for professing their religious faith but because they "show solidarity with those whose rights, dignity, and livelihood are diminished by an uncaring or dictatorial regime"? That does seem to pertain to Murphy-O'Connor's statement that she was "persecuted—brutally slain—because she was working in the cause of right." This statement also has overtones of the more traditional

43. Cardinal Cormac Murphy-O'Connor, "Homily at Requiem Mass for Murdered Aid Worker Margaret Hassan," *Roman Catholic Diocese of Westminster Website*, December 11, 2004, http://www.rcdow.org.uk/archbishop/default.asp?content_ref=300.

"red martyrdom" associated with being killed in hatred of one's faith. It is, of course, possible that Hassan's kidnappers viewed her Catholicism as an evil that outweighed her secular humanitarian work, but if that was the case they did not make a point of it in the videos they made of her. It is also notable that while Murphy-O'Connor's reference to Hassan being "persecuted" and "brutally slain" appears to hark back to earlier periods of Christian persecution, when he subsequently justifies his description of Hassan as a martyr he is careful to allude more to white martyrdom in emphasizing the "love" (*caritas*) of her charitable humanitarian work.

Conclusion

Murphy-O'Connor's homily brings us back to relations of martyrdom and the secular. I have already suggested that Chandler's and Harvey's concept of "this-worldly" martyrdom implicitly draws on the Christian Latin sense of *saeculum* as "world." We also need to bear in mind that a concept of the secular emerged *from* the Christian Church, even though in modern times secularity is attributed to worldly affairs and institutions that are seen as being distinct from religion. As Charles Taylor has argued, the political process of secularization is attributable to the rise of the modern nation-state which has entailed advancing a universality of democratic citizenship over individual differences of identity.[44] As Talal Asad points out, the role of the media for Taylor also plays a key role in identifying citizenship with nationalism:

> When Taylor says that a modern democracy must acquire a healthy dose of nationalist sentiment he refers to the national media—including national education—that is charged with cultivating it. For the media are not simply the means through which individuals simultaneously imagine their national community; they *mediate* that imagination, construct the sensibilities that underpin it. When Taylor says that the modern state has to make citizenship the primary principle of identity, he refers to the way it must transcend the different identities built on class, gender, and religion, replacing

---

44. Charles Taylor, "Modes of secularism," in Rajeev Bhargava, ed., *Secularism and Its Critics* (Delhi: Oxford University Press, 1998), pp. 31–53.

conflicting perspectives by unifying experience. In an important sense, this transcendent mediation *is* secularism.[45]

Whether the press and media can so readily be described as "national" or associated with "national" sentiment is debatable nowadays. The spread of satellite television and the Internet has given media organizations and broadcasts an international reach such that the audience is not necessarily limited by nation-state. Indeed, the fact that one of *Tawhid wal-Jihad*'s videos of Bigley finished with frames of Arabic and English text is an indication that the group was targeting both "home" and enemy audiences. Such a video can thus "*mediate*" support from sympathizers internationally at the same time as repelling others. In that way, media productions are able to traverse national borders while consolidating political and religious differences. They may also inflame those differences while dislimning the distinction between the secular and the religious. A disturbing case in point is the "reality" television program "Terrorism in the Hands of Justice" that was broadcast on the Iraqi state television station *al-Iraqiya* after the contract for running the station was given to a US-based multinational company, the Science Applications International Corp (SAIC). The program featured suspected Iraqi insurgents, the majority of whom were Sunni, who were filmed being interrogated and making confessions. Many of the prisoners were already bruised, and one of them was found dead shortly after appearing on the show.[46] As Solomon Hughes has written, anxious captives gave what often appeared to be forced confessions in front of a banner of the "Wolf Brigade," the anti-insurgent commando group.[47] Like the militants' videos that presented grim parodic mimicry of Guantánamo detention, "Terrorism in the Hands of Justice" (with input from the US company SAIC) effectively presented a mimetic response to the videos made by precisely the kind of militants it was set up to interrogate. Such mimetic responses, I want to suggest, play a significant part in fostering interfusions of religion, secularization, and the media that in turn have altered conceptions of martyrdom and *Jihad*.

---

45. Talal Asad, *Formations of the Secular: Christianity, Islam, Modernity* (Stanford, Calif.: Stanford University Press, 1999), p. 5.

46. See Carlyle Murphy and Khalid Saffar, "Actors in the Insurgency Are Reluctant TV Stars," *Washington Post*, April 5, 2005, http://www.washingtonpost.com/wp-dyn/articles/A26402-2005Apr4.html.

47. Solomon Hughes, *War on Terror, Inc.: Corporate Profiteering from the Politics of Fear* (London: Verso, 2007), p. 129.

Despite the divisive intentions of the militants who filmed Bigley and Hassan, it is true that various religious and political institutions made a point of trying to "transcend" differences in showing unified support for the two hostages. In the case of Bigley that support engendered various professions of faith in British values of multiculturalism and liberal democracy. An editorial in *The Sunday Times*, for example, responded to Bigley's murder by suggesting that "The only good that can now come from the terrible death of Mr Bigley is that the coalition powers redouble their efforts to bring peace and democracy to Iraq."[48] Unfortunately, by that point many Iraqis were deeply unhappy with how the Coalition Provisional Authority (CPA) had been running the country. That was partly because the CPA had legislated for thousands of public sector workers with links to the ousted Saddam Hussein's Ba'ath party to be removed from their posts; it was partly because it had legislated for Iraqi companies to be privatized and opened up to foreign ownership and it was partly because the general management of the infrastructure was in disarray.[49] Such matters of state sovereignty and secularization involved in the Coalition of forces' occupation of the country clearly played a part in increasing the spread of *Jihad* and militant martyrdom in Iraq. And while groups such as *Tawhid wal-Jihad* mixed religion, politics, and media strategy in their militancy, rather than simply seeing that militancy as a "by-product" of secularized modernity, we need to understand that it has been more a matter of *contesting* the legitimacy of liberal secularization and democracy as ultimate guarantors of communal rights and well-being. In identifying motives behind the militants' cause, I am not suggesting that their methods are justified. Unfortunately, recent wars waged for regime change and the installation of democracy have not helped to diminish the number of Muslims prepared to martyr themselves for that cause.

---

48. Quoted in "It Was a Horror Beyond Belief," *Guardian*, October 11, 2004, http://www.guardian.co.uk/world/2004/oct/11/iraq.iraq.

49. See Alex Jeffrey, "Containers of Fate: Problematic States and Paradoxical Sovereignty," in Alan Ingram and Klaus Dodds, eds., *Spaces of Security and Insecurity: Geographies of the War on Terror* (London: Ashgate, 2008), pp. 43–63; and also I. Warde, "Iraq: A License to Loot the Land," *Le Monde Diplomatique*, May 2, 2004, http://mondediplo.com/2004/05/02iraq.

Filming the Ends of Martyrdom

Jolyon Mitchell

WHAT LIGHT CAN films shed upon martyrdom? Filmmakers have regularly attempted to re-present many different kinds of martyrdom. Cinematic depictions of what some have described as founding or proto-martyrdoms in the ancient world include the "noble death" of the "Father of Philosophy" in *Socrates* (dir. Robert Rossellini, 1970), "voluntary and heroic suicides" in the television mini-series *Masada* (dir. Boris Sagal, 1981), and several melodramatic executions in the Roman arena in *The Sign of the Cross* (dir. Cecil B. DeMille, 1932). Arguably the most magnetic martyrdom from the medieval period for filmmakers is the execution of Joan of Arc (1431), with well over two dozen films portraying her trial and burning at the stake.[1] There is another notable cinematic medieval martyrdom: the murder in Canterbury cathedral in the film *Becket* (dir. Peter Glenville, 1964). Starring Richard Burton (as Becket) and Peter O'Toole (as Henry II), the scene in *Becket* where four helmeted knights brutally stab the Archbishop with their long swords provides a dramatic climax to a 148 minute drama (fig. 12.1).

Martyrdom stories from outside Europe have also found their way onto the silver and digital screen.[2] While some screen martyrdoms are preserved, adapted, and circulated online, in this chapter I focus primarily upon stories initially portrayed on the silver screen. Cinematic

---

1. See the detailed list in Robin Blaetz, *Visions of the Maid: Joan of Arc in American Film and Culture* (Charlottesville: University Press of Virginia, 2001), pp. 249–61.

2. For more on the digitization of martyrdom, especially in Syria, see Jolyon Mitchell, *Martyrdom: A Very Short Introduction* (Oxford: Oxford University Press, 2012), pp. 42–46.

FIGURE 12.1. Four knights, intent on murder, move towards Archbishop Thomas Becket (played by Richard Burton)

Film still from Peter Glenville's *Becket* (1964), reproduced courtesy of Paramount and the Kobal Collection, ref. BEC004BR.

martyrdoms can help to make less well-known narratives more publically visible, though filmmakers commonly resort to oft-repeated and therefore well-known tales, particularly in the country of their origin. Several examples stand out. First, various Filipino films depict the execution in Manila of the Philippines' founding martyr Jose Rizal (e.g., *Rizal*, dir. Marilou Diaz-Abaya, 1998). Extracts of such films including Rizal's martyrdom are now also easily available online. Second, both *Salvador* (dir. Oliver Stone, 1986) and the biopic *Romero* (dir. John Duigan, 1989) portray the assassination on March 24, 1980, of the Archbishop of San Salvador Óscar Romero (1917–1980) while he was celebrating mass.[3] Third, there are numerous

---

3. Romero is one of ten modern martyrs commemorated by stone sculptures above the West Door in Westminster Abbey in London. For more on Romero, and other films about martyrs, see Theresa Sanders, *Celluloid Saints: Images of Sanctity in Film* (Macon: Mercer University Press, 2002), especially pp. 50–54.

online amateur films, of varying lengths, that capture the local Iranian plays which re-enact the founding martyrdoms within Shiʻa Islam.

Finally, more controversial "martyrdom operations" are explored in *Paradise Now* (dir. Hanu Abu-Assad, 2005) and the September 11 plane hijacking in *United 93* (dir. Paul Greengrass, 2006). For some viewers, self-inflicted deaths that have the intention of killing many others are not martyrdoms but little more than terrorism and murder. For other critical viewers, terrorists have become highly skilled in appropriating a wide range of screen media to promote their political or religious ends.[4] As we shall see several films re-create the ways in which those embracing terrorist or martyrdom operations make use of video testimonies, online dissemination, and news coverage. Nevertheless, these and other films bring to life not only stories of martyrdom but also ethical questions such as whether lives are wasted through what are known as passive, predatory, or dramatic martyrdoms.

The process of re-creating these deaths for the cinema raises several sets of related questions. What happens to a death, believed by many to be a martyrdom, when it is re-presented on the screen? And to what extent does screening a martyrdom from the past demystify its origins, bringing distant deaths close? The screening of an execution allows contemporary viewers to watch a historic martyrdom as if for the first time. The portrayal of a suicide bomber or "martyrdom operation" leads viewers, inhabiting comparatively safe spaces, into worlds where such bombings are regularly common. How far does dramatically screening a death contribute to the making of a martyr and does it add to rather than reduce the aura of such a death? Through this chapter, I consider these questions and how screen martyrdoms can shed light on different ways of ending a life.

---

4. There is an extensive scholarly literature on the relation between terrorism and media communications. This research is beyond the scope of this chapter but many texts on this topic include discussions of the interaction between different media and "martyrdom operations": see, for example, Anat Berko, *The Path to Paradise: The Inner World of Suicide Bombers and Their Dispatchers* (Washington, D.C.: Potomac Books, 2009); Mordecai Dzikansky, Gil Kleiman, and Robert Slater, *Terrorist Suicide Bombings: Attack Interdiction, Mitigation, and Response* (Boca Raton, Fla.: CRC Press, 2011); Boaz Ganor et al., eds., *Hypermedia Seduction for Terrorist Recruiting* (Amsterdam: IOS Press, 2007); Bruce Hoffman, *Inside Terrorism*, 2nd ed. (New York: Columbia University Press, 2006); Gus Martin, *Essentials of Terrorism: Concepts and Controversies*, 2nd ed. (Los Angeles: SAGE, 2011); Brigitte L. Nacos, *Terrorism and Counterterrorism*, 4th ed. (Boston: Longman, 2011); Pippa Norris, Montague Kern, and Marion Just, eds., *Framing Terrorism: The News Media, the Government, and the Public* (London: Routledge, 2003); and Philip Seib and Dana M. Janbek, *Global Terrorism and New Media: The Post-al Qaeda Generation* (New York: Routledge, 2011).

First, I consider passive cinematic martyrdoms. Second, I analyze predatory screen martyrdoms, and I observe how martyrdoms on screen can not only be spiritualized, militarized, and celebrated but also interrogated. Third, I consider dramatic film martyrdoms. Finally, I investigate how film can illuminate and interrogate the motives and purposes of martyrdoms.

This discussion raises another set of questions about both the end and the ends of martyrdom. To what extent can films contribute to ending certain communities' promotion of predatory martyrdoms? In other words by depicting cinematically the human impact of actually "dying to kill other people," can certain kinds of more violent martyrdom be halted? While it is highly unlikely that martyrdom will ever entirely come to an end, it is possible that the prevalence of certain kinds of intentionally violent martyrdoms may be reduced. Films also have the potential to highlight how the ends or goals of intentional martyrdoms are rarely achieved in the way that is expected. Few films explicitly explore how an individual's death can be put to many different ends. More often such questions are embedded within the film's narrative.

Passive Martyrdoms

It is possible to make a distinction between active and passive martyrdoms. At its simplest level "passive martyrs" accept their deaths without resistance or violence, while "active martyrs" precipitate their own deaths and sometimes even bring about the deaths of others. The ends or purposes of their martyrdoms are often very different. Obviously, these categories can blur, with some martyrs actively embracing a passive form of death, and some violent martyrs passively going toward their end. In the paragraphs that immediately follow I analyze how "passive martyrdom" is represented cinematically in two films, produced in two very different historical settings: *Gladiator* (dir. Ridley Scott, 2000) and *The Sign of the Cross* (dir. Cecil B. DeMille, 1932).

Some passive martyrdoms are hard to capture on screen. Even after they are filmed, they can find themselves on the editing floor. In *Gladiator* the single explicit reference to martyrdom was edited out of the final version. It can be found buried among the "bonus" material on the DVD version of the film, along with the director's commentary. It shows the protagonist Maximus (played by Russell Crowe) underground at the Coliseum. Not a word is spoken as he sees several lions going out into the arena. Through a barred window, he then catches a glimpse of a group of twelve people mostly kneeling in the sand. Many appear to be praying, either with their heads bowed or looking imploringly up to the heavens. The scene is reminiscent of several nineteenth-century paintings of martyrdom in the arena.[5] A small boy holds tightly onto a man whom we could presume to be his father. The lion goes to eat them both. Maximus turns away sadly. No words are discernible, only actions and gestures and facial expressions are shown.

This may be Hollywood-style storytelling, but the short sequence does capture the highly public nature of many early martyrdoms, common contemporary beliefs about ancient martyrdoms, as well as the apparent passivity of some early Christians in the face of death. According to director Ridley Scott, this incident, entitled "Fed to the Lions," was left out of the final version of the film because the lion did not "eat the child very well. It was too passive."[6] This is a very revealing statement. As with many other creators of Hollywood blockbusters Scott understands that the camera, and indeed the eye, are naturally drawn to violent action, and passive resistance is often hard to portray dramatically on screen. Scott was helping to create a cinematic spectacle, which would earn over 450 million dollars in box office takings. *Gladiator* was produced for a mass market, and unlike many art house films, rarely attempts to portray internal subjective mental states. Costing over 100 million dollars to create, *Gladiator* stands in the Hollywood tradition of sword-and-sandal action-packed historical epics, such as *Ben Hur* (dir. William Wyler, 1959), *Spartacus* (dir. Stanley Kubrick, 1960), and *The Fall of the Roman Empire* (dir. Anthony Mann, 1964). Given the kind of film that *Gladiator* was, it is not surprising that a "passive" martyrdom was left out of the final cut.

Likewise, Cecil B. DeMille was forced to edit out several scenes from his black and white film produced in the early 1930s *The Sign of the Cross*. This included not only seductive dancing and a rather revealing bath in milk by Nero's wife Poppea (famously played by Claudette Colbert) but also two deaths in the arena. In this controversial sequence from the Coliseum the camera acts like a predatory eye, relishing the demise of two female, and largely passive, victims. One scantily dressed simpering victim (played by Sally Rand) is stretched out horizontally between posts while several crocodiles crawl hungrily toward her. The viewer is shown

---

5. See, for example, Jean-Léon Gérôme's painting *The Christian Martyrs' Last Prayer* (1883), discussed in chap. 3 of Mitchell, *Martyrdom*.

6. See *Gladiator* (dir. Ridley Scott, 2000).

a crocodile open its jaws revealing sharp teeth, the victim screams and the crowd cheers. The reaction shots depict one woman in the crowd sadistically savoring the killing, which is not actually shown. The original film cut from baying crowd back to the arena and a close up of two faces. One is made of wood: a carved bearded face looking as if it is whispering into the ear of a live blond woman. This fades to the following shot which reveals that she is chained, semi-naked to this statue as a large silverback gorilla approaches. The reaction shots speak volumes. Another woman in the crowd turns her head away and covers her eyes with a scarf of feathers. She is clearly unable to watch the horror of what is likely to ensue.

Under the Motion Picture Production Code (also known as the Hays Code), this sequence had to be removed when the film was re-released in 1938. The scene, along with several others, was reinstated in the 1993 DVD version of the film. DeMille was trying to ensure that there was plenty of "worthy sinning" to give the film mass appeal, while other contemporaries saw it as "sex perversion" belittling the heroic stories of the early Christian martyrs.[7] Even though these are not entirely overlooked, with several "martyrdoms" portrayed through the movie (fig. 12.2), it was one of the films that led to the creation of the Legion of Decency: "To many Catholics, *The Sign of the Cross* symbolized an industry out of control."[8] It reflects both a fascination with and an appropriation of Nero's spectacles of death. Its mixed reception highlights how films can fail to meet some viewers' expectations about how martyrdom should be represented.

These two executions in the arena are sometimes seen as martyrdoms, though there is a gratuitous quality to the screen violence here. This is amplified by the following scene, which shows numerous gladiators fighting each other in the arena. A cartload of bodies is trundled away. These scenes are more like *hors d'oeuvres*, whetting the appetite of the audience for the "main course," which is the execution of one hundred Christians in the arena. The final sequence of *The Sign of the Cross*, based on the 1895 play of the same title by Wilson Barrett, is reticent in portraying how Christians embraced martyrdom in the arena. Viewers are simply shown women, men, and children ascending the steps toward the arena. They sing a hymn as they head up toward the light. Some walk confidently, some carry or lend an arm, while others hesitate and even turn to retreat.

---

7. Frank Walsh, *Sin and Censorship: The Catholic Church and the Motion Picture Industry* (New Haven: Yale University Press, 1996), pp. 78–80.

8. Ibid., p. 80.

FIGURE 12.2. An aged Christian leader lies dead, having been killed by a Roman arrow during an act of worship. Meanwhile, the lead female protagonist, Mercia (played by Elissa Landi), looks on in horror

Film still from Cecil B. DeMille's *The Sign of the Cross* (1932), reproduced courtesy of Paramount and the Kobal Collection, ref. SIG001CC.

One or two are whipped back upward. There are some screams. Perhaps most poignantly an older bearded man carries a smiling child. He covers her head with a cloak. Nevertheless, viewers are not taken back into the arena. Instead, all that is shown are a pack of growling and roaring lions leaping up another staircase. It is clear they are riled, hungry, and heading up to enter the arena through another entry point to meet the Christians whose ascent is juxtaposed with the lions' fierce ascent.

The denouement of the film's love story and of the entire movie brings the two protagonists together. The Roman Prefect Marcus (played by Fredric March) begs Mercia (played by Elissa Landi) to renounce her faith so that she can escape death and they can marry. She refuses. In response he declares his undying love, his tentative faith, and his hope that they will be together even after death, perhaps married in heaven. *The Sign of the Cross* ends as these two ascend the staircase, where all the other Christians have gone to meet their deaths. The film is once again visually reticent about their actual demise. Viewers are simply shown the arena doors closing behind them as the film concludes with an image of a bright cross superimposed on the wood.

The film raises questions as to why and how some early Christians embraced death both in and outside the arena. It also raises the question of whether a skillful director (such as DeMille) or a powerful film are able to create or at least reinforce devotion toward particular individuals as they faced death. For all its cinematic limitations, *The Sign of the Cross* also reveals how, behind a passive death, can be an active choice to embrace martyrdom. As with several other films portraying martyrdom, the choices, decisions or actions of the central protagonists becomes the determining factor in their deaths. Passivity in the face of death does not always translate well onto the screen. The result is that supposedly passive martyrdoms can be translated into something far more dynamic.

As we have seen in the earlier chapters of this book, martyrdom has a complex and contested history. By contrast, films such as *Sign of the Cross* and *Gladiator* almost inevitably simplify, romanticize, or even overlook stories concerning martyrdom. One of *Gladiator*'s most powerful scenes follows a set-piece fight in a North African arena, after which Maximus, who has just brutally dispatched about half a dozen other gladiators, turns to the crowd and twice shouts: "Are you not entertained?" There is an element of inverted dramatic irony in this question. While it is addressed directly to the crowd in the amphitheater, it is also to be witnessed by the film's actual audience, raising questions about who is watching the spectacle, why they are watching, and how are they being entertained. Cinematic martyrdoms are primarily intended to entertain, rather than to educate. Films rarely show how later communities helped to create martyrs, investing significance in the lives and, more significantly, the public deaths of earlier individuals within the Roman Empire.[9] Films, whether from the 1930s or from the last decade, tend to gravitate toward re-creating and even satirizing spectacular and violent entertainments, as for example in *The Hunger Games* (dir. Gary Ross, 2012). Carefully reflected upon and critically viewed, a cinematic martyrdom set under Roman rule could even raise questions about how the *pax Romana* could cast a shadow over the lives of slaves, peasants, soldiers, the environment, and anyone who would not fall into line with the unifying state religion and political rulers. A film showing the violence in and beyond the arena can illustrate some

---

9. See Elizabeth Castelli, *Martyrdom and Memory: Early Christian Culture Making* (New York: Columbia University Press, 2004).

of the fault lines that would regularly emerge from beneath the apparent peace of the Roman Empire.

Predatory Martyrdoms

"Predatory martyrdom" is a term used by some scholars to describe a person who aims to kill others through their own death.[10] It is not surprising that some filmmakers, in search of poignant stories, are drawn toward these more aggressive forms of death. The Palestinian film *Paradise Now* (dir. Hany Abu-Assad, 2005) explores the mixed motives of two Palestinian suicide bombers, childhood friends Khaled (played by Ali Suliman) and Said (played by Kais Nashef). The movie chronicles the two days before their mission's climax. These young men are depicted as neither particularly politically motivated nor particularly religious, but they become more determined once they are singled out to become *shaheeds* (martyrs). Their martyrdom videos simply begin with: "In the name of God the merciful" and recitations from the Qu'ran, but then go on to declare that "we have no other way to fight" and "we must continue our struggle until the end of the occupation." Like several other films *Paradise Now* highlights how those intending to participate in a martyrdom operation themselves attempt to embrace video-recording to bear witness to their beliefs, their motivations, and even their frustrations (fig. 12.3). There is an element of dark comedy in this process in *Paradise Now* as it takes several retakes to record Khaled's speech. He becomes increasingly annoyed and in the final take he even includes a recommendation of where his mother can find cheaper water-filters. The video recordings are followed by ritual shaving, careful dressing, arming, and a last supper.[11]

As these two young men are both driven toward Tel Aviv, the site of their planned attacks, they are offered final advice which includes: if searched detonate and "leave it to God" to do "the checking at the Gates of Paradise," and "when the first one of you carries out the operation . . . don't watch him

---

10. See Hugh Barlow, *Dead for Good: Martyrdom and the Rise of the Suicide Bomber* (Boulder, Colo.: Paradigm Publishers, 2007), especially part IV, "The new predatory martyrs." Barlow details a number of examples that illustrate how the "new predatory martyr" can be motivated by religious ideology or nationalism, or a combination of both, and dies for their cause while at the same time killing indiscriminately.

11. For a more detailed reading of *Paradise Now* and this sequence, see Phoebe Bronstein, "Reproducible Bodies: A Close Reading," *Jump Cut: A Review of Contemporary Media* 52 summer (2010), http://www.ejumpcut.org/archive/jc52.2010/bronsteinParadiseNow/2.html.

FIGURE 12.3. One of two "suicide bombers" prepares for his "martyrdom operation" by making a video recording for those he leaves behind

Film still from Hany Abu-Assad's *Paradise Now* (2005), reproduced courtesy of Lumen Films, Lama Prods, and the Kobal Collection, ref. PAR166AU.

do it." Following these instructions the two friends glance at each other and one asks: "And what happens next?" In the front seat their older guide pauses momentarily, looks away, and then replies: "Two angels will pick you up." This response leads to another question: "Are you sure?" Without hesitation they are answered: "Absolutely. You'll see." After this reply the camera reveals how their bearded middle-aged minder distractedly drums his fingers on the dashboard, keeping his eyes facing forwards. What is the impact of this close up and tight editing? His response appears to lack complete conviction. One is left wondering whether he believes his own affirmation that there will be paradise for these two soon-to-be-martyrs.

This underplayed and subtle questioning of the validity of their venture generates a tension that is heightened through the passionately asserted views of a young Palestinian woman Suha (played by Lubna Azabal). The fact that her very own father was a respected martyr does not prevent her from forcefully arguing that suicide bombing is both against Islam and ineffective. The night before his "operation" Said unexpectedly visits Suha. In a conversation, full of eye contact and repressed emotion, he suggests that Suha must be extremely proud of her Father. She simply replies: "I'd rather he were still alive than be proud of him.... There are always other ways to keep the cause alive." For her: "Resistance can take on many forms." Her views act as a balance to the film's central narrative, which is the movement of two surprisingly ordinary bombers toward an understated ending that simply fills the screen with bright white light. This film raises important questions about both the motives behind and values of suicide bombing, and, by extension, predatory martyrdom. While they are not directly attempting to deconstruct the celebration of martyrs, this movie does illustrate how filmmakers can provoke questions about how predatory martyrs are created, as well as how martyrdom can be both spiritualized and militarized.

This can clearly be seen and heard in *United 93* (dir. Paul Greengrass, 2006). Throughout this film the hijackers of United 93, the plane that crashed in a field near Shanksville, Pennsylvania, on September 11, 2001, are depicted reciting verses from the Qu'ran or praying to Allah. Once in control of the flight they exclaim: "Thanks be to God," and just before they crash the plane they repeatedly exclaim: "Allah Akbar" ("God is great"). In one sequence the prayers of the hijackers are contrasted with those of two passengers on board the hijacked plane who are independently reciting the Lord's Prayer. This begs the question as to who in the midst of this "martyrdom operation" were the martyrs and whose martyrdom in this controversial film is being remembered, celebrated, or interrogated?

This film begins in an understated fashion: a quietly spoken male voice intoning Arabic verses. The screen is entirely black. The first thing that we are shown is an extreme close-up of fingers cradling a small, open Qu'ran. The next shot is of a Middle-Eastern man. He is dressed simply, wearing a white t-shirt, legs crossed, swaying forward as he prays. This peaceful moment is interrupted first by the noise of an airplane, flying overhead and then by another Middle-Eastern male, who declares in Arabic: "It's time." There then follow aerial shots of yellow taxis made tiny by the height of the camera, tracking shots through skyscrapers and other establishing shots of a bright early morning cityscape. These are replaced by interior shots of a bathroom where one of the men shaves off his abdominal body hair, while in a neighboring room two others kneel, prostrate themselves, pray, and embrace. One tucks a small knife inside his trousers as the other kisses the Qu'ran. John Powell's melancholy music is combined with Arabic prayers, which holds this three-minute montage together. As they depart the music becomes louder. The viewer is taken out from the dingy claustrophobic space of the motel rooms onto the highway to Newark Airport. The next shot is of a large painted American flag in a container park and the words: "God Bless America." In the distance the camera offers a view of the World Trade Center. These images are loaded with dramatic irony. Viewers who have seen pictures or films of what happened on 9/11 understand the implications of these preparatory prayers, rituals, and actions. This opening sets the stage for what is to come.

The director, Paul Greengrass, in his own words, aimed to contrast the "modernity of the New York skyline" with the "depths of the religious pieties" inspiring the "certainties" of these four young men caught in "medieval rapture." His intention was to juxtapose cinematically the "forces in play that day."[12] As I have suggested elsewhere, for Greengrass, there were two hijacks that day: first, the hijack of all four planes by nineteen men leading to so much death and destruction, and second, the "hijack of a religion," the selection of pieces of the Qu'ran to create a "closed system" that "wilfully ignored" traditions of teaching and tolerance within Islam, and instead drew selectively upon texts to justify murderous violence.[13] *United 93* stands in sharp contrast to Oliver Stone's *World Trade Center* (2006), which even includes two visions of Christ. In *United 93* Greengrass eschews such images of spiritual transcendence. Instead viewers are offered a series of scenes that feature background chatter, multiple screens, information overloads, and rapid juxtapositions between scenes. The result is to underline how difficult it was to understand on the day what was happening. Only later after many images, stories, and films were replayed, reconsidered, and reinterpreted would some individuals be described as martyrs.

United 93 and *Paradise Now* raise profound questions about the ends of martyrdom. Like the vast majority of films they do this not through argument, but rather through cinematic storytelling. They leave it for the viewer to decide the value of the choices and actions that are being depicted. Nevertheless, both films are crafted in such a way as to interrogate the actions of those who embrace predatory martyrdom. Unlike the film *Four Lions* (dir. Chris Morris, 2010), which satirizes the attempt of four suicide bombers attempting to operate in the United Kingdom, *United 93* and *Paradise Now* approach the topic more sanguinely.[14] These

---

12. Paul Greengrass, "Feature Length Audio Commentary," *United 93*, Universal Studios, DVD, 2006.

13. See Jolyon Mitchell, "Mediating Religious Violence," in Andrew R. Murphy, ed., *The Blackwell Companion to Religion and Violence* (Oxford: Wiley-Blackwell, 2011), pp. 112–24.

14. A series of mishaps ensure that their attempts to bring terror to Britain largely result in a series of "unfortunate events" and their own apparently pointless or comic deaths.

films attempt to shed some light into the world of those who would use their own deaths to kill others. While both films reveal a little of the humanity of such killers, neither comes close to condoning predatory martyrdom.

Dramatic Martyrdoms

Some filmmakers are drawn to dramatic martyrdoms like moths are drawn to a flame. Consider, for instance, *Lady Jane* (dir. Trevor Nunn, 1986), staring Helena Bonham-Carter who plays the eponymous teenager (1537–1554) who ostensibly was Queen of England for nine days in 1553 before being ousted in favor of Queen Mary. This is the third film based on her life and death.[15] In the final moments of *Lady Jane* she is shown calmly walking to the scaffold, taking off her coat, forgiving her executioner, kneeling, and putting on her blindfold. Unlike in the earlier *Tudor Rose* (dir. Robert Stevenson, 1936), viewers are given a glimpse of the axe cutting down toward her neck. While obviously dramatized for film, some of the telling details resonate with a probable eyewitness account, in particular, as she reaches for the block and asks plaintively what she should do.[16] Lady Jane may not protest or fight, but this remains a dramatic and understandably climactic moment in the film. Artists too have been attracted to portraying her execution.[17] Soon after her actual beheading in 1554 she was portrayed in several texts not merely as an innocent victim used by powerful Protestant leaders but also as a martyr for Protestantism.[18] Thomas Chaloner goes further in his Latin *Elegy* (1579), celebrating her beauty,

15. See the silent film *Lady Jane Grey; or, The Court of Intrigue* (dir. Edwin Greenwood, 1923) and *Tudor Rose* (known in the United States as *Nine Days a Queen*) (dir. Robert Stevenson, 1936).

16. She was executed on February 12, 1554, at the Tower of London; see the anonymous account, possibly by an eyewitness of the scene, in *Chronicle of Queen Jane and of Two Years of Queen Mary*, ed. John Gough Nicols (London: J. B. Nichols for the Camden Society, 1850).

17. See, for example, Paul Delaroche's oil painting, *The Execution of Lady Jane Grey* (1833), which is set inside rather than where the execution actually took place on Tower Green within the grounds of the Tower of London in 1544.

18. See Foxe's *Acts and Monuments* (popularly known as the "Book of Martyrs"). A description of Jane Grey's execution and her final words are to be found in each of the four editions published during Foxe's life; the 1563 edition, p. 919; 1570, p. 1584; 1576, p. 1352; and 1583, p. 1422: these can all be conveniently referenced online at John Foxe's *The Acts and Monuments* (Sheffield: HRI Online Publications, 2011), http://www.johnfoxe.org/.

her learning, and her ability to face death steadfastly like Socrates.[19] At least one other contemporary, Roger Ascham, made a similar connection, recalling Jane reading Phaedo's account of Socrates' stoical death.[20]

Socrates' journey toward death has also attracted several filmmakers.[21] For example, in Hillary Anderson's play *Barefoot in Athens* (1951), which was adapted for television by George Schaefer (1966), Socrates wanders through Athens, criticizing the ruling elite. They in turn plot to bring about his downfall. Unsurprisingly, Socrates, played by Peter Ustinov in the film, is the pivotal figure in the film. He appears to be a lone voice promoting democracy and the freedom of speech. His life, teaching, and self-inflicted death are used indirectly to challenge those such as Joseph McCarthy (1908–1957) who believed that, in 1950s America, free speech was divisive to national unity and even a danger to the very foundations of the state. The point here is that Socrates' "noble death," which in this film is portrayed almost like a martyrdom for free speech, is being put to use over two thousand years later to make a social and political point.

As this cinematic adaptation of Socrates' dignified death illustrates, a dramatic historical narrative not only reflects contemporary concerns, but it can also provoke questions about the nature of martyrdom. For some his death is to be interpreted as a state-encouraged suicide, while for others it is the martyrdom of the "Father of Philosophy."[22] Nevertheless, films tend to portray dramatic action more effectively than rigorous philosophical discussion, as it is hard to re-create cinematically a sustained metaphysical or theological debate. Likewise it is difficult to adapt lengthy historical or polemical texts into short two-hour films. Filmmakers tend to be drawn toward a single dramatic moment or a series of dramatic instances that help to build a narrative. In this context a martyrdom becomes a starting or an ending point of a plot, or a pivotal moment to drive the story forward.

---

19. See the Latin elegy by Sir Thomas Chaloner the Elder on Lady Jane Grey published by William Malim, master of St. Paul's school, in *De rep. Anglorum instauranda decem libri* (London: William Malim, 1579).

20. Leande de Lisle, *The Sisters Who Would be Queen* (London: Harper Collins, 2008), p. 308.

21. For another screen portrayal of Socrates' martyrdom, see Roberto Rossellini's *Socrates* (1970). For a discussion of this film and other screen portrayals of Socrates, see Jolyon Mitchell, "Ethics," in John Lyden, ed., *Routledge Companion Volume on Religion and Film* (London: Routledge, 2009), pp. 482–500, especially pp. 484–85.

22. For a more detailed discussion of Socrates' death and later interpretations, see Mitchell, *Martyrdom*, especially chap. 2.

While no one has yet produced a film attempting to detail comprehensively the extensive early modern martyrdom texts, such as John Foxe's "Book of Martyrs" (first edition 1563)[23] or Thieleman J. van Braght's *Martyr's Mirror* (1660), the film *Elizabeth* (dir. Shekhar Kapur, 1998) begins with a graphic depiction of the burning at the stake of three "Protestant heretics" in post-Reformation England. A woman and two men are roughly shaved, bound, and then led toward the stake. Several overhead shots give viewers a sense of looking down on the violent proceedings. The crowd surges forward, though soldiers keep them back. The flames begin to lick up towards the victims. A darkly robed, bearded, official reads out the following in gruff tones: "By order of their gracious majesties Queen Mary and Prince Philip we have come to witness the burning of these Protestant heretics who have denied the authority of the one true Catholic Church and His Holiness the Pope. Let them burn for all eternity in the flames of Hell." At the same time there is crying, coughing, and shouting. A member of the crowd cries out "God Bless you master Ridley." A few moments later Bishop Ridley cries out: "For the love of God I burn too slowly." Another member of the crowd shouts: "For God's sake help them." More bundles of wood are brought through the surging crowd and thrown onto the fire, only for the spectators to be dispersed by cavalry who are attempting to bring some order.

It is revealing to compare this sequence with the accounts of the burning of Nicholas Ridley (1500–1555) and Hugh Latimer (1487–1555), in Oxford on October 16, 1555 in John Foxe's "Book of Martyrs."[24] It is clear from such a comparison that the filmmakers have played with historical details to create a more dramatic scenario, introducing a third victim who is a woman, and a cavalry charge.[25] The film does not linger on their deaths and provides little follow-up. For some Catholic writers these were "pseudo-martyrdoms," while for some Protestant authors these were like founding martyrdoms, standing in the footsteps of Saint Stephen or other

---

23. The full title of the first edition, published in 1563, is *Actes and Monuments of these latter and perilous Dayes, touching matters of the Church, wherein are comprehended and described the great Persecution and horrible Troubles that have been wrought and practised by the Romishe Prelates*.

24. Foxe describes the martyrdom of Nicholas Ridley and Hugh Latimer in some detail in each of the four editions of the *Acts and Monuments*; see the 1563 edition, pp. 1376–79; 1570, pp. 1937–39; 1576, pp. 1661–62; and 1583, p. 1769.

25. Nonetheless, the woodcut found in Foxe's book, illustrating the moments before the fire is lit, does something similar by compressing the narrative although, obviously, the compression is into a single scene.

early Church martyrs. In the film *Elizabeth* their deaths serve more as a visual piece of historical contextualization which is used to draw the audience into the story and help the viewer understand about the world in which Queen Elizabeth would reign.

The dramatizing of martyrdom is to be found in several different artistic forms and religious traditions. Some filmmakers draw on earlier dramatic forms. For example, the Iranian film director Abbas Kiarostami filmed audience responses to "passion plays" in Iran. These plays re-enact the founding martyrdoms within Shi'a Islam. In particular, the death of Husayn and his followers at Karbala in 680 C.E. Kiarostami used these audience reaction shots in a memorable film art installation entitled *A Look to Ta'ziyeh* (first performed in 2002).[26] This production sheds light on Iran's passion plays.[27] The tenth day of *Muharram* (*Ashura*), when Husayn was killed at Karbala, tends to be the final focal point of these dramatic enactments.[28] By re-enacting the drama of his last days through annual passion plays, as well as inflicting minor wounds to their foreheads, many Shi'ites attempt to atone for the failure to assist Husayn. After ten days of mourning which builds up to the crescendo of *Ashura*, audiences seeing or hearing these stories often weep or cry out, particularly when they are shown the sufferings, the thirst and the killing of Husayn, his family, and his followers.

For his installation, *A Look to Ta'ziyeh*, Kiarostami captured the powerful emotional impact of these plays upon rural audiences by filming them as they watched these traditional dramas.[29] Edited together, these shots of male and female spectators were then projected onto two large screens, along with the actual scenes of a traditional *Ta'ziyeh* performance, which was shown at the same time on a smaller television set positioned

---

26. *Ta'ziyeh* is sometimes interpreted as "condolence theater" or "theater of mourning"; see also Peter J. Chelkowski, ed., *Ta'ziyeh: Ritual and Drama in Iran* (New York: New York University Press, 1979) and Hamīd Dabaši, *Islamic Liberation Theology: Resisting the Empire* (Abingdon: Routledge, 2008), especially chap. 5 on "The Shi'i Passion Play," pp. 171–96.

27. These plays appear to have originated in earlier cathartic processions of mourning. They are commonly now complemented by retelling of the stories (*Rowzehs*) or by meditations (*Zekrs*) upon these martyrdoms.

28. In this tradition *Muharram*, after *Ramadan*, is the holiest month of the Islamic year, and fighting is forbidden. During the month of *Muharram* the events of thirteen centuries ago on the plains of Karbala are brought back to life.

29. See Nacim Pak-Shiraz, *Shi'i Islam in Iranian Cinema: Religion and Spirituality in Film* (London: I. B. Tauris, 2011), pp. 159–63.

between these two larger screens. This dramatic installation illustrates the powerful connection developed between audiences and performers who, as this tale of martyrdom unfolds, are increasingly drawn into the dramatic world created by the *Ta'ziyeh*.

Conclusion

Cinematic martyrdoms have the power to draw audiences into the film's central story, while also adding to the visibility, the memories, and even the heroic myths which can cluster around certain deaths. We have considered some of the many different ways of depicting various kinds of martyrdom on screen. First, there are passive screen martyrdoms, where the victim becomes little more than an object to be pushed toward death. Some filmmakers, such as Cecil B. DeMille, play with this passivity to highlight the action that swirls around a martyr's death. Second, there are predatory screen martyrdoms, where the victim becomes an active agent who in some cases is determined to destroy others through their deaths. Some filmmakers use these stories to question the value of such violent killing. This can be seen not only in feature films such as *United 93* but also in documentary films such as *The Cult of the Suicide Bomber* (dir. David Batty, 2005). Third, and commonly closely related to the first two groups, there are dramatic screen martyrdoms, where a death can be used not only as a magnet to attract viewers but also as a pivotal moment in the film's overall plot.

These are, of course, not watertight categorizations. Most martyrdoms, whether passive or predatory, are inherently dramatic. In film, distinctions between violent and nonviolent martyrs or active and passive martyrdoms are not always made clear. In some film narratives it is the courage, bravery, and sacrifice of the martyrs that is highlighted. In this way films can help to make martyrs or at least amplify or elaborate upon their stories. This can be seen in both a documentary *Beyond the Gates of Splendor* (dir. Jim Hanon, 2004) and the docudrama the *End of the Spear* (dir. Jim Hanon, 2005), which tells the story of five American missionaries who were killed as they attempted to proselytize the Huaorani (Waodani) people in the Ecuadorian jungle, as well as the responses of the families who lost their loved ones. Such films can be and are often used as evangelistic tools or didactic memorials.

A number of other recurring themes, practices, and questions raise their heads when looking over the multifaceted phenomenon of cinematic martyrdom. These cinematic memorials can function both as a reminder of those who have died, and as a provocative visual question. Films may claim to be apolitical, but these faces brought back from the dead present a challenge to the living. Even if it is not the intention of the filmmakers, these screen martyrdoms can be used to try and awaken viewers to perceived injustices or to model ways of embodying faith. Charged with pathos, the emotional weight of these screenings of martyrdom can be used to demand change or to encourage emulation. For this reason, those who are in power or are determined to preserve the status quo commonly contest the claims of those who use film martyrdoms to promote change or to encourage mimesis. Those creating cinematic martyrdoms have a number of different intended ends. These include participation in creating memorable and sellable genre movies, ideological transformation, or even attempting to encourage others to follow in the footsteps of earlier martyrs. There is a need for further research into precisely how or whether such representations can add to the "aura" of martyrdom, or contribute to perceptions of who is a martyr. This leads onto causal questions, which are difficult to answer conclusively, such as: To what extent can screen depictions lead to the creation of more martyrs? While some portrayals may celebrate earlier deaths, other may contribute to the critique of such deaths, raising questions as to whether certain kinds of martyrdom are valid expressions of faith.[30]

Inevitably, the way these screen portrayals of martyrdom are interpreted will depend on where they are viewed. The interpretation of a film such as *Paradise Now* by a Palestinian Muslim living in Gaza City, a Jewish settler in Jerusalem, or an Arab Christian in Damascus will be partly informed by their own experiences and living circumstances. Even films made primarily to entertain mass markets will be viewed and interpreted differently at contrasting points of reception. Some audiences override the original intentions of filmmakers, and transform cinematic entertainment into a resource for adding to the mythos surrounding an individual death or martyrdom. In the age before moving images, with the exception of martyrological dramas the vast majority of martyrs were portrayed statically, on frescoes, paintings, or manuscripts. Martyrs can now be brought back to life more easily. While there is no specific genre of martyr films, the digitization of martyrdom can bring new life to old stories.

---

30. For wider critical discourses within Islam, see Charles Kurzman, *The Missing Martyrs: Why There Are So Few Muslim Terrorists* (Oxford: Oxford University Press, 2011).

These observations raise additional questions, beyond the scope of this chapter, but worthy of further investigation. For example, what are the implications of the differences between epic Hollywood representations of martyrdom and the many different portrayals of martyrdom now to be found online? These include single images, short homemade films, longer documentaries and extracts from Hollywood features. How far do the digitization and the multiplication of images create new visions of martyrdom? What does the abundance of online images of both martyrdom and terrorism, combined with their unpredictable dissemination, imply when they are promoted as exemplary acts to be emulated? What are the implications for building peace in the face of this deluge of representation of what are commonly violent deaths? The exponential growth of easily accessible online imagery also sharpens questions about spectacular representations of martyrdom and terrorism that were raised at the beginning of the new Millennium.

Several scholars observed then that spectacular pictures can now all too easily be hijacked and put to violent or consumerist ends. Jean Baudrillard, for example, suggested in 2002 that the terrorists behind the attacks on 9/11 "exploited the 'real time' of images, their instantaneous worldwide transmission, just as they exploited stock-market speculation, electronic information and air traffic." In doing this they turned around the powerful communicative tools of Western societies and used them to shake these societies' very foundations. They made a movie in real time without the direct help of Hollywood that unsettled many audiences. For Baudrillard the "role of images is highly ambiguous. For at the same time as they exalt the event, they also take it hostage. They serve to multiply it to infinity and, at the same time, they are a diversion and a neutralization."[31] This process has evolved over the last twelve years. In an increasingly digital age films on the big screen can be reduced, imitated, and reproduced on countless smaller screens. They can be edited, merged, and made into something new. This endless re-creation and repetition of images of terrorism and martyrdom can blur specificities, entrenching heightened idealization of individuals who are willing to give away their lives, while also contributing to an environment in which their original meaning can become progressively lost in repetitive spectacles.

---

31. Jean Baudrillard, *The Spirit of Terrorism and Requiem for the Twin Towers*, trans. Chris Turner (London: Verso, 2002), p. 27.

These are not the only ends of the heightened and fragmented visualization of martyrdom. When a death, believed by many to be a martyrdom, is re-presented on the screen it can also demystify its origins, bringing a distant death close. It may even become simpler to imagine what it would be like to face such a death oneself. The screening of an execution, an assassination, or another kind of death, later described as a martyrdom, can enable contemporary audiences to step back in time or to travel imaginatively across vast distances of space. These representations, therefore, do not mark the end of martyrdom, even if these movies and screen portrayals are put to different ends. They point rather to the many different roles that a film, whether online or offline, can perform in relation to martyrdom. A moving image of martyrdom can move audiences in many ways. It may contribute to the making, remaking, or memorialization of a martyr, it may heighten or add to a death's aura but it may also raise many profound questions about the values of such a death.

Select Bibliography

Afsaruddin, Asma, *Striving in the Path of God: Jihad and Martyrdom in Islamic Thought* (Oxford: Oxford University Press, 2013).

Ahmed, Siraj, "The Theater of the Civilized Self: Edmund Burke and the East India Trials," *Representations* 78 (2002), pp. 28–55.

Andress, David, *The Terror: Civil War in the French Revolution* (London: Little, Brown, 2004).

Asad, Talal, *On Suicide Bombing* (New York: Columbia University Press, 2007).

Awan, Akil N., Andrew Hoskins, and Ben O'Loughlin, *Radicalisation and Media: Connectivity and Terrorism in the New Media Ecology* (London: Routledge, 2011).

Baczko, Bronislaw, *Comment sortir de la Terreur: Thermidor et la Révolution* (Paris: Gallimard, 1989).

Baczko, Bronislaw, *Ending the Terror: The French Revolution after Robespierre* (Cambridge: Cambridge University Press, 1994).

Barker, Emma, *Greuze and the Painting of Sentiment* (Cambridge: Cambridge University Press, 2005).

Barlow, Hugh, *Dead for Good: Martyrdom and the Rise of the Suicide Bomber* (Boulder, Colo.: Paradigm Publishers, 2007).

Baudrillard, Jean, *The Spirit of Terrorism and Requiem for the Twin Towers*, trans. Chris Turner (London: Verso, 2002).

Berko, Anat, *The Path to Paradise: The Inner World of Suicide Bombers and their Dispatchers* (Washington, D.C.: Potomac Books, 2009).

Blaetz, Robin, *Visions of the Maid: Joan of Arc in American Film and Culture* (Charlottesville: University Press of Virginia, 2001).

Bloom, Mia, *Dying to Kill: The Allure of Suicide Terror* (New York: Columbia University Press, 2005).

Bonner, Michael, *Jihad in Islam: Doctrines and Practice* (Princeton: Princeton University Press, 2006).

Borradori, Giovanna, *Philosophy in a Time of Terror: Interviews with Jurgen Habermas and Jacques Derrida* (Chicago: University of Chicago Press, 2003).

Bowersock, G. W., *Martyrdom and Rome* (Cambridge: Cambridge University Press, 1995).

Boyarin, Daniel, *Dying for God: Martyrdom and the Making of Christianity and Judaism* (Stanford, Calif.: Stanford University Press, 1999).

Boyce, D. George, " 'A gallous story and a dirty deed': Political Martyrdom in Ireland since 1867," in Yonah Alexander and Alan O'Day, eds., *Ireland's Terrorist Dilemma* (Dordrecht: Martinus Nijhoff Publishers, 1986), pp. 7–27.

Buruma, Ian, and Avishai Margalit, *Occidentalism: The West in the Eyes of its Enemies* (New York: Penguin, 2004).

Castelli, Elizabeth A., *Martyrdom and Memory: Early Christian Culture Making* (New York: Columbia University Press, 2004).

Chelkowski, Peter J., ed., *Ta'ziyeh: Ritual and Drama in Iran* (New York: New York University Press, 1979).

Cook, David, *Martyrdom in Islam* (Cambridge: Cambridge University Press, 2007).

Cook, Malcolm C., "Politics in the Fiction of the French Revolution, 1789–1794," *Studies on Voltaire and the Eighteenth Century 201* (1982), pp. 233–340.

Cormack, Margaret, *Sacrificing the Self: Perspectives on Martyrdom and Religion* (Oxford: Oxford University Press, 2009).

Coudreuse, Anne, *Le Goût des larmes au XVIIIe siècle* (Paris: Presses Universitaires de France, 1999).

Dabaši, Hamīd, *Islamic Liberation Theology: Resisting the Empire* (Abingdon: Routledge, 2008).

Darnton, Robert, *The Kiss of Lamourette: Reflections in Cultural History* (New York: W. W. Norton, 1990).

De Lisle, Leande, *The Sisters Who Would be Queen* (London: Harper Collins, 2008).

Denby, David J., *Sentimental Narrative and the Social Order in France 1760–1820* (Cambridge: Cambridge University Press, 1994).

Dillon, Anne, *The Construction of Martyrdom in the English Catholic Community, 1535–1603* (Aldershot: Ashgate, 2001).

Doyle William, *The Oxford History of the French Revolution*, 2nd ed. (Oxford: Oxford University Press, 2002).

Durkheim, Émile, *Suicide: A Study in Sociology*, trans. George Simpson (London: Routledge, 1897).

Dzikansky, Mordecai, Gil Kleiman, and Robert Slater, *Terrorist Suicide Bombings: Attack Interdiction, Mitigation, and Response* (Boca Raton, Fla.: CRC Press, 2011).

Eagleton, Terry, *Holy Terror* (Oxford: Oxford University Press, 2005).

Edelstein, Dan, *The Terror of Natural Right: Republicanism, the Cult of Nature and the French Revolution* (Chicago: University of Chicago Press, 2009).

Ellis, Markman, *The Politics of Sensibility: Race, Gender and Commerce in the Sentimental Novel* (Cambridge: Cambridge University Press, 1996).

Frank Walsh, *Sin and Censorship: The Catholic Church and the Motion Picture Industry* (New Haven: Yale University Press, 1996).

Freeman, Thomas S., and Thomas F. Mayer, eds., *Martyrs and Martyrdom in England, c.1400–1700* (Woodbridge: Boydell Press, 2007).

Ganor, Boaz, et al., eds., *Hypermedia Seduction for Terrorist Recruiting* (Amsterdam: IOS Press, 2007).

Gantt, Jonathan, *Irish Terrorism in the Atlantic Community, 1865–1922* (New York: Palgrave Macmillan, 2010).

Gerges, Fawaz A., *The Rise and Fall of Al-Qaeda* (Oxford: Oxford University Press, 2011).

Girard, René, *Violence and the Sacred*, trans. Patrick Gregory (Baltimore: Johns Hopkins University Press, 1977).

Goldstein, Jan, *The Post-Revolutionary Self: Politics and Psyche in France, 1750–1850* (Cambridge, Mass.: Harvard University Press, 2005).

Gottschalk, Peter, *Islamophobia: Making Muslims the Enemy* (Lanham, Md.: Rowman and Littlefield, 2008).

Gregory, Brad S., *Salvation at Stake: Christian Martyrdom in Early Modern Europe* (Cambridge, Mass.: Harvard University Press, 1999).

Hafez, Mohammed M., *Suicide Bombers in Iraq: The Strategy and Ideology of Martyrdom* (Washington, D.C: U.S. Institute of Peace Press, 2007).

Haydon, Colin, and William Doyle, eds., *Robespierre* (Cambridge: Cambridge University Press, 1999).

Haywood, Ian, *Bloody Romanticism: Spectacular Violence and the Politics of Representation, 1776–1832* (Basingstoke: Palgrave Macmillan, 2006).

Higonnet, Patrice, *Goodness beyond Virtue: Jacobins during the French Revolution* (Cambridge, Mass.: Harvard University Press, 1998).

Hoffman, Bruce, *Inside Terrorism*, 2nd ed. (New York: Columbia University Press, 2006).

Jackson, Richard, Jeroen Gunning, and Marie Breen Smyth, *Terrorism: A Critical Introduction* (Basingstoke: Palgrave Macmillan, 2011).

Jenkins, Brian, *The Fenian Problem: Insurgency and Terrorism in a Liberal State, 1858–1874* (Montreal: McGill-Queen's University Press, 2008).

Jourdan, Annie, ed., *Robespierre: Figure-réputation* (Amsterdam: Rodopi, 1996).

Juergensmeyer, Mark, *Terror in the Mind of God: The Global Rise of Religious Violence* (Berkeley: University of California Press, 2003).

Kelly, M. J., *The Fenian Ideal and Irish Nationalism, 1882–1916* (Woodbridge: Boydell Press, 2006).

Kepel, Gilles, *Jihad : The Trail of Political Islam*, 4th ed. (London: I. B. Tauris, 2006).

Khosrokhavar, Farhad, *Suicide Bombers: Allah's New Martyrs* (London: Pluto Press, 2005).

Knott, Sarah, *Sensibility and the American Revolution* (Chapel Hill: University of North Carolina Press, 2009).

Krueger, Alan B., *What Makes a Terrorist: Economics and the Roots of Terrorism* (Princeton: Princeton University Press, 2008).

Kurzman, Charles, *The Missing Martyrs: Why There Are so Few Muslim Terrorists* (Oxford: Oxford University Press, 2011).

Laqueur, Walter, *Terrorism* (Aldershot: Dartmouth, 1996).

Lewis, Jeffrey William, *The Business of Martyrdom: A History of Suicide Bombing* (Annapolis, Md.: Naval Institute Press, 2012).

Martin, Gus, *Essentials of Terrorism: Concepts and Controversies*, 2nd ed. (Los Angeles: Sage, 2011).

McConnell, James, and Fearghal McGarry, eds., *The Black Hand of Republicanism: Fenianism in Modern Ireland* (Dublin: Irish Academic Press, 2009).

McConville, Seán, *Irish Political Prisoners, 1848–1922: Theatres of War* (London: Routledge, 2003).

McGee, Owen, *The IRB: The Irish Republican Brotherhood, from the Land League to Sinn Féin* (Dublin: Four Courts Press, 2005).

McPhee, Peter, *Robespierre: A Revolutionary Life* (New Haven: Yale University Press, 2012).

Middleton, Paul, *Martyrdom: A Guide for the Perplexed* (London: Continuum, 2011).

Mitchell, Jolyon, *Martyrdom: A Very Short Introduction* (Oxford: Oxford University Press, 2012).

Monta, Susannah, *Martyrdom and Literature in Early Modern England* (Cambridge: Cambridge University Press, 2005).

Moss, Donald, ed., *Hating in the First Person Plural: Psychoanalytic Essays on Racism, Homophobia, Misogyny, and Terror* (New York: Other Press, 2003).

Nacos, Brigitte L., *Terrorism and Counterterrorism*, 4th ed. (Boston: Longman, 2011).

National Commission on Terrorist Attacks upon the United States, *The 9/11 Commission Report: Final Report of the National Commission on Terrorist Attacks upon the United States* (New York: Norton, 2004).

Norris, Pippa, Montague Kern, and Marion Just, eds., *Framing Terrorism: The News Media, the Government, and the Public* (New York: Routledge, 2003).

Ó Broin, León, *Fenian Fever: An Anglo-American Dilemma* (London: Gill and Macmillan, 1971).

O'Neal, John C., *The Authority of Experience: Sensationist Theory in the French Enlightenment* (University Park: Pennsylvania State University Press, 1996).

Owens, Gary, "Constructing the Martyrs: The Manchester Executions and the Nationalist Imagination," in Lawrence W. McBride, ed., *Images, Icons, and the Irish Nationalist Imagination* (Dublin: Four Courts Press, 1999), pp. 18–36.

Pak-Shiraz, Nacim, *Shi'i Islam in Iranian Cinema: Religion and Spirituality in Film* (London: I. B. Tauris, 2011).

Pape, Robert, *Dying to Win: The Strategic Logic of Suicide Terrorism* (New York: Random House, 2005).

Pasco, Allan H., *Sick Heroes: French Society and Literature in the Romantic Age, 1750–1850* (Exeter: University of Exeter Press, 1997).

Pedahzur, Ami, *Suicide Terrorism* (London: Polity Press, 2005).

Perdue, William, *Terrorism and the State: A Critique of Domination through Fear* (Westport, Conn.: Praeger, 1989).

Rapoport, David C., and Yonah Alexander, eds., *The Morality of Terrorism: Religious and Secular Justifications* (New York: Pergamon Press, 1982).

Reddy, William M., *The Navigation of Feeling: A Framework for the History of Emotions* (Cambridge: Cambridge University Press, 2001).

Riskin, Jessica, *Science in the Age of Sensibility: The Sentimental Empiricists of the French Enlightenment* (Chicago: University of Chicago Press, 2002).

Sagan, Eli, *Citizens and Cannibals: The French Revolution, the Struggle for Modernity, and the Origins of Ideological Terror* (New York: Rowman and Littlefield, 2001).

Sanders, Theresa, *Celluloid Saints: Images of Sanctity in Film* (Macon, Ga.: Mercer University Press, 2002).

Schama, Simon, *Citizens: A Chronicle of the French Revolution* (New York: Knopf, 1989).

Scheuer, Michael, *Imperial Hubris: Why the West is Losing the War on Terror* (Washington, D.C.: Brasseys, 2004).

Schmid, Alex Peter, and Janny de Graaf, *Violence as Communication: Insurgent Terrorism and the Western News Media* (London: Sage, 1982).

Seib, Philip, and Dana M. Janbek, *Global Terrorism and New Media: The Post-Al Qaeda Generation* (New York: Routledge, 2011).

Seigel, Jerrold, *The Idea of the Self: Thought and Experience in Western Europe since the Seventeenth Century* (Cambridge: Cambridge University Press, 2005).

Short, K. R. M., *The Dynamite War: Irish-American Bombers in Victorian Britain* (Dublin: Gill and Macmillan, 1979).

Sinclair, Andrew, *An Anatomy of Terror: A History of Terrorism* (London: Macmillan, 2003).

Sizgorich, Thomas, *Violence and Belief in Late Antiquity: Militant Devotion in Christianity and Islam* (Philadelphia: University of Pennsylvania Press, 2009).

Taliqani, Mahmud, Murtada Mutahhari, and Ali Shari'ati, *Jihad and Shahadat: Struggle and Martyrdom in Islam*, ed. Mehdi Abdi and Gary Legenhausen (Houston, Tex.: Institute for Research and Islamic Studies, 1986).

Theweleit, Klaus, *Male Fantasies*, 2 vols., trans. Stephen Conway, Chris Turner, and Erica Carter (Minneapolis: Minnesota University Press, 1987).

Townshend, Charles, *Political Violence in Ireland: Government and Resistance since 1848* (Oxford: Oxford University Press, 1983).

Townshend, Charles, *Terrorism: A Very Short Introduction* (Oxford: Oxford University Press, 2002).

Trites, Allison, *The New Testament Concept of Witness* (Cambridge: Cambridge University Press, 1977).

Turner, Johnson James, *The Holy War Idea in Western and Islamic Traditions* (University Park: Pennsylvania State University Press, 1997).

Vila, Anne C., *Enlightenment and Pathology: Sensibility in the Literature and Medicine of Eighteenth-Century France* (Baltimore: Johns Hopkins University Press, 1998).

Weiner, Eugene, and Anita Weiner, *The Martyr's Conviction: A Sociological Analysis* (Lanham, Md.: University Press of America, 2002).

Whelehan, Niall, *The Dynamiters: Irish Nationalism and Political Violence in the Wider World, 1867–1900* (Cambridge: Cambridge University Press, 2012).

Wicker, Brian, ed., *Witnesses to Faith? Martyrdom in Christianity and Islam* (Ashgate: Aldershot, 2006).

Žižek, Slavoj, *Living in the End Times* (London: Verso, 2010).

Index